MW00446330

John L. Olsen, CLU®, ChFC®, AEP®
Michael E. Kitces, MSFS, MTAX, CFP®, CLU®, ChFC®, RHU, REBC, CASL, CWPP™

In the period immediately preceding the publication of this book, annuity sales have increased by double-digit percentages. Not surprisingly, the number of rules governing the annuity arena has been steadily increasing as well. There are more rules affecting annuities now than ever before. This latest edition of *The Advisor's Guide to Annuities* is fully updated, revised, and expanded to deliver exclusive, expert insight into every key topic.

The stakes are high. Today, in certain circumstances, fixed annuity agents may get in serious trouble just for selling fixed annuities. "Source of funds" issues have raised many complicated questions about whether, or when, annuity agents are directly or indirectly providing investment advice. Anyone and everyone working in the annuities area must be fully informed of these issues in order to avoid the potentially serious consequences that can arise.

This comprehensive, single-volume guide to annuities enables you to:

- Make the best use of all types of annuities

- Handle both the investment and risk management goals of annuities

- Increase your understanding of not only how to sell annuities but how they work, when they should be used, and which sales techniques are best suited to which circumstances.

In these pages you'll find full coverage of:

- The threats posed by "source of funds" issues—**New Chapter**

- The value of annuitization, including analysis of recent and controversial studies on this subject—**New Chapter**

- Valuable new information on structured product-based variable annuities—**New Section**

- Updated and expanded discussion of Deferred Income Annuities (DIAs)

- Current coverage of annuity-related tax developments, including the rules on post-death 1035 exchanges

- A complete update on the new QLAC regulations

- Added material to the index annuity section

- Full update on the *Neasham* case and its implications for insurance agents and financial advisors

Written by two of the foremost experts in this field, ***The Advisor's Guide to Annuities, 4ᵗʰ Edition***, is designed specifically to help you make the most of all the opportunities—and avoid the pitfalls—in this active and ever-changing area.

To place additional orders for ***The Advisor's Guide to Annuities, 4ᵗʰ Edition***, or any of our products, or for additional information, contact Customer Service at **1-800-543-0874**.

The Advisor's Guide to Annuities

John L. Olsen, CLU®, ChFC®, AEP®
Michael E. Kitces, MSFS, MTAX, CFP®, CLU®

ISBN 978-1-939829-77-1

Library of Congress Control Number: 2014937761

THE NATIONAL UNDERWRITER COMPANY

Copyright © 2014

Fourth Edition

The National Underwriter Company
5081 Olympic Blvd.
Erlanger, KY 41018

Printed in the United States of America

About Summit Professional Networks

Summit Professional Networks supports the growth and vitality of the insurance, financial services and legal communities by providing professionals with the knowledge and education they need to succeed at every stage of their careers. We provide face-to-face and digital events, websites, mobile sites and apps, online information services, and magazines giving professionals multi-platform access to our critical resources, including Professional Development; Education & Certification; Prospecting & Data Tools; Industry News & Analysis; Reference Tools and Services; and Community Networking Opportunities.

Using all of our resources across each community we serve, we deliver measurable ROI for our sponsors through a range of turnkey services, including Research, Content Development, Integrated Media, Creative & Design, and Lead Generation.

For more information, go to http://www.SummitProfessionalNetworks.com.

About The National Underwriter Company

For over 110 years, The National Underwriter Company has been the first in line with the targeted tax, insurance, and financial planning information you need to make critical business decisions. Boasting nearly a century of expert experience, our reputable Editors are dedicated to putting accurate and relevant information right at your fingertips. With *Tax Facts, Tools & Techniques, National Underwriter Advanced Markets, Field Guide, FC&S®*, and other resources available in print, eBook, CD, and online, you can be assured that as the industry evolves National Underwriter will be at the forefront with the thorough and easy-to-use resources you rely on for success.

The National Underwriter Company Update Service Notification

This National Underwriter Company publication is regularly updated to include coverage of developments and changes that affect the content. If you did not purchase this publication directly from The National Underwriter Company and you want to receive these important updates sent on a thirty day review basis and billed separately, please contact us at (800) 543-0874. Or you can mail your request with your name, company, address, and the title of the book to:

The National Underwriter Company
5081 Olympic Boulevard
Erlanger, KY 41018

If you purchased this publication from The National Underwriter Company directly, you have already been registered for the update service.

National Underwriter Company Contact Information

To order any National Underwriter Company title, please

- call 1-800-543-0874, 8-6 ET Monday – Thursday and 8 to 5 ET Friday

- online bookstore at www.nationalunderwriter.com, or

- mail to The National Underwriter Company, Orders Department, 5081 Olympic Blvd, Erlanger, KY 41018

Dedications

John L. Olsen, CLU®, ChFC®, AEP®

To Katherine, who continues, even after 38 years, to put up with more than she should.

Michael E. Kitces, MSFS, MTAX, CFP®, CLU®, ChFC®, RHU, REBC, CASL, CWPP™

To my friends and family, and especially my wife Ellie, for their understanding, patience, and support while I pursue my passion for financial planning.

Acknowledgments

Any book, even one by a single author, is invariably the product of many minds. The authors have been blessed by the willingness of friends and colleagues to share their insights with us and our readers. We wish to thank Jack Marrion, Bruce Tannahill, Jack Underwood, Garth Bernard, Stephanie Curry, Terry Altman, Moshe Milevsky, Peng Chen, Curtis Cloke, Kyle Bossard, Jay Adkisson, Mary Ann Mancini, Mel Warshaw, Steve Leimberg, April Caudill, Tom Hegna, Mike McGlothlin, Dick Weber, and Ben Baldwin. We'd also like to thank Kelly Maheu of National Underwriter Company for her willingness to support another edition of this book.

John L. Olsen, CLU®, ChFC®, AEP®

Michael J. Kitces, MSFS, MTAX, CFP®, CLU®, ChFC®, RHU, REBC, CASL, CWPP™

Preface to the Fourth Edition

This book is the child of frustration. The authors have both been dealing with annuities for many years, and we had each been despairing over the lack of understanding of these instruments and of the absurdly partisan way in which annuities are regarded by many who write about them. Most articles we read about annuities were either "for" or "against" them, as if an annuity could be inherently either "good" or "bad." Articles appearing in insurance industry magazines routinely touted annuities as the greatest thing since sliced bread, while many financial journalists appeared to regard them as little better than satanic devices. Sadly, both conditions persist, with no sign of change, as we write this.

As practicing advisors working with annuities on a regular basis and frequent speakers at industry events, we were painfully aware that even those involved in recommending or evaluating annuities—professional financial advisors—often demonstrate little understanding of how these tools work (and when they do not).

Something, we both felt, ought to be done. What was needed, we thought, was a source of information about annuities that would be both accurate and balanced. So, when we were approached by The National Underwriter Company in 2005 for suggestions about potential book topics, the need for a book about annuities seemed clear, and we decided that we would take a stab at it.

The result is the book you are about to read. It was written, not for the consumer, but for the professional advisor—and that does not mean just those who sell annuities. It includes attorneys, accountants, financial planners, trust officers, and compliance officers. Anyone who may be called upon to render professional advice regarding an annuity—will, we hope—find this book worth reading.

The authors have tried to present the facts and to be as objective as possible in our conclusions. We have included a large amount of material about the taxation of annuities (including content we have never seen available in a product of this kind) and much about suitability and appropriateness. There is not a single sentence in here about how to sell annuities. There are many other books out there on that topic.

This book is entitled *The Advisor's Guide to Annuities, 4th edition* because it is a revision and update of our previous book of this name, which itself was an update of the first and second editions of *The Annuity Advisor*. The title change reflects the fact that this book is part of a new series of Advisor's Guides, offered by Summit Professional Networks and The National Underwriter Co. We have added totally new chapters on the "source of funds" issue and the latest research on the value of annuitization, updated the chapters on taxation of annuities to reflect new rules and rulings, provided guidance on the latest regulatory issues (including the resolution of the "infamous" Neasham case), and explored the emerging landscape of so-called "longevity annuities" as well.

We hope that you will find this book, not only instructive, but also genuinely useful.

John L. Olsen, CLU®, ChFC®, AEP®

Michael J. Kitces, MSFS, MTAX, CFP®, CLU®, ChFC®, RHU, REBC, CASL, CWPP™

April 1, 2014

About the Authors

John L. Olsen, CLU®, ChFC®, AEP®, is a financial and estate planner practicing in St. Louis County, MO. John has been involved in the financial services industry since 1973. In addition to providing insurance, financial and estate planning services to his own clients, John works with other advisors on advanced cases and product selection and offers expert witness services in litigation involving annuities, insurance, and securities.

John is a past president of the St. Louis chapter of the National Association of Insurance and Financial Advisors, a former Board member of the St. Louis chapter of the Society of Financial Services Professionals, a current Board member of the St. Louis Estate Planning Council, and a member of the Editorial Advisory Board of Tax Facts. He is a highly sought-after speaker, having given presentations on financial, insurance, retirement, and estate planning and other topics to many industry groups. John can be reached at:

Olsen Financial Group
131 Hollywood Lane
Kirkwood, MO 63122
(314) 909-8818 (voice)
(314) 909-7912 (fax)
jolsen02@earthlink.net

Michael E. Kitces, MSFS, MTAX, CFP®, CLU®, ChFC®, RHU, REBC, CASL, CWPP™, is Director of Research for Pinnacle Advisory Group, a private wealth management firm located in Columbia, Maryland. In addition he is the practitioner editor of the *Journal of Financial Planning*, and the publisher of the e-newsletter *The Kitces Report* and the blog *Nerd's Eye View* through his website Kitces.com, dedicated to advancing knowledge in financial planning.

Michael is extremely active at both the local and national level in the financial planning profession, serving on numerous boards and task forces. He is also a member of the Editorial Review Board for the *Journal of Financial Planning*, a commentator on retirement distribution and retirement planning issues for Leimberg Information Services Inc., and a co-founder of NexGen, a community of the next generation of financial planners that aims to ensure the transference of wisdom, tradition, and integrity, from the pioneers of financial planning to the next generation of the profession. For his active work in the profession, Michael was one of the 2010 recipients of the Financial Planning Association's "Heart of Financial Planning" awards for his dedication to advancing the financial planning profession. In addition, he has variously been recognized as financial planning's "Deep Thinker," a "Legacy Builder," an "Influencer," a "Mover & Shaker," and a "Rising Star in Wealth Management" by industry publications.

Michael welcomes your questions, comments, or inquiries at:

Pinnacle Advisory Group
Attn: Michael Kitces
6345 Woodside Court, Suite 100
Columbia, Maryland 21046
(410) 995-6630
michael@kitces.com

About the Publisher

Richard H. Kravitz is Vice President and Managing Director of the Professional Publishing Division of The National Underwriter Company. He is a CPA, MBA, and Fellow of the American College of Forensic Examiners and a member of the AICPA, the New York State Society of CPAs, and the American Society of Pension Professionals and Actuaries.

Prior to joining The National Underwriter he was Senior Vice President and Group Publisher of International Law and Business at Aspen/Wolters Kluwer and former Accounting and Tax Publisher at Thomson Reuters.

About the Developmental Editor

Deborah A. Miner, J.D., CLU®, ChFC®, has been writing and communicating about estate planning, business planning, and retirement planning for over twenty-five years. As Editorial Director of the Tax & Financial Planning Group at The National Underwriter Company from 1991 to 2010, Debbie worked with all the industry greats, writing many sections of *Tax Facts* and editing Steve Leimberg's *Tools & Techniques* series and Don Cady's *Field Guides*. She also spent several years as a Senior Advanced Sales Consultant at a Midwestern life insurance company. She holds a law degree from the Ohio State University College of Law and CLU and ChFC designations from the American College.

Recently, she started her own advanced sales consulting business, designing, writing, and updating advanced markets client and advisor materials and presenting educational seminars for life insurance companies and producer groups. Her company also provides consultative legal, tax, and life sales expertise and analysis on issues concerning large case planning and development and complex insurance strategies, as well as advanced markets phone support.

About the Editor

Jason Gilbert, J.D., M.A., is an assistant editor with the Professional Publishing Division of the National Underwriter Company, Summit Professional Networks. He edits and develops publications related to life and health insurance products, including titles in the *Advisor's Guide* and the *Tools & Techniques* series of investment and planning products. He also develops content for

Summit's other financial services publications and online products. He has worked on insurance and tax publications for more than nine years.

Jason has been a practicing attorney for more than a dozen years in the areas of criminal defense, products liability, and regulatory enforcement actions. Prior to joining Summit Professional Networks, his experience in the insurance and tax fields has included work as a freelance Westlaw contributor for Thomson Reuters and a tax advisor and social media contributor for Intuit. He is an honors graduate from Wright State University and holds a J.D. from the University of Cincinnati College of Law as well as a master's degree in Economics from Miami University in Ohio.

About the Editorial Director

Diana B. Reitz, CPCU®, AAI, is the editorial director of the Professional Publishing Division of The National Underwriter Company. As such she is responsible for the overall integrity of all division publications. She previously was the Director of the Property & Casualty Publishing Department of the Reference Division.

Ms. Reitz has been with The National Underwriter Company since 1998, when she was named editor of the *Risk Financing and Self-Insurance* manuals and associate editor of the *FC&S Bulletins®*. She also is coauthor of the National Underwriter publication, *Workers Compensation Coverage Guide, 1st Edition*, and has edited and contributed to numerous other books and publications, including *The Tools & Techniques of Risk Management and Insurance, Claims* magazine, and *National Underwriter Property & Casualty* magazine.

Prior to joining The National Underwriter she was with a regional insurance broker, concentrating on commercial insurance. She is a graduate of the University of Maryland and St. Francis College.

Editorial Services

Connie L. Jump, Supervisor, Editorial Services

Emily Brunner, Editorial Assistant

About the Director of Product Development

Kelly B. Maheu, J.D., is the director of product development and content acquisition for the Professional Publishing Division of Summit Business Media. She is responsible for acquiring expert authored content and working closely with Summit's editorial, sales, marketing, and technology teams to develop professional online and print reference libraries.

Kelly began work at Summit in 2006 as an editor for Fire, Casualty and Surety Service (FC&S). A graduate of the University of Cincinnati College Of Law, Kelly worked in the legal and insurance fields for LexisNexis®, Progressive Insurance, and a Cincinnati insurance defense litigation firm prior to joining Summit. Kelly holds a BA from Miami University, with a double major in English/Journalism and Psychology.

Kelly has edited and contributed to numerous books and publications including the Personal Auto Insurance Policy Coverage Guide, Cyberliability and Insurance, The Tools and Techniques of Risk Management for Financial Planners, Claims Magazine, and ProducersWEB.

Table of Contents

Chapter 1

Basics of Annuities

What is an Annuity?

The term annuity simply means a series of regular payments over time. In popular usage, however, annuity generally refers to a contract or policy, issued by an insurance company, providing for payment of a regular income by the annuity issuer to the owner, over a specified period or for the life of an annuitant (see the section entitled "Parties to the Annuity Contract"). These contracts, called commercial annuities, are what we will be talking about throughout this book.

Types of Annuities

There are different types of annuities, which are generally classified according to three different parameters:

1. how the annuity is purchased;

2. when annuity payments are to begin; and

3. how the cash value in the annuity is invested.

How the Annuity is Purchased

There are generally two different ways an annuity is purchased. A **Single Premium** annuity is a contract purchased with a single payment, or premium. No further premiums are required, or even allowable. A **Flexible Premium** annuity is purchased with an initial payment (to establish the contract) and typically contains a series of premiums that may be paid whenever, and in whatever amount, the purchaser wishes, subject to policy minimums and maximums. While deferred annuities may be purchased on either a single premium or a flexible premium basis, immediate annuities are always purchased with a single premium.

There is very little difference, if any, in the important policy provisions, guarantees, and payout options of the two types, and their tax treatment is identical. The significant distinction is simply that in some instances, contracts offered as single premium cannot receive additional subsequent payments, and therefore do not allow additional contributions under the original contract's terms—instead, additional money must be deposited to a new annuity contract.

When Annuity Payments Are to Begin

An **immediate annuity** is one in which regular income—or annuity—payments begin to be made to the owner[1] within one year of purchase. Another label sometimes used to describe an immediate annuity is **payout annuity**.

A **deferred annuity** is one in which annuity payments are deferred until later than one year after purchase—perhaps much later. The life of a deferred annuity is divided into two phases:

1.   The **accumulation phase**. This is the period from purchase of the contract until annuitization, during which the annuity contract may grow in value for the crediting of interest (in the case of a fixed annuity) or the change in value of the subaccounts (with a variable annuity). Annuitization is the exercise, by the owner, of a contractual option to begin receiving regular annuity payments, in accordance with an annuity payout option (see the section entitled "Types of Annuity Payouts"). Deferred annuity contracts typically require annuitization by some specified date or age by specifying a maximum annuity starting date or maturity date (e.g., policy anniversary following annuitant's age eighty-five, or annuitant's age eighty-five). Newer contracts may permit further deferral of annuitization provided the request is received within a specified period of time prior to the maturity date.[2]

2.   The **distribution phase**. This is the period from annuitization until the annuity payments cease, which may be at the end of the annuitant's life or after a specified number of years (see the section entitled "Types of Annuity Payouts").

Note: It is essential that the advisor understand the difference between an annuity contract's required annuity starting date (i.e., the date by which annuity payments must commence, absent an election to defer annuitization) and when annuitization is permitted under that contract. In January, 2005, a class-action lawsuit was filed alleging unsuitability, asserting that the deferred annuity purchased by a senior citizen allegedly did not permit annuity payments to begin until the annuitant's age was 115. However, it appears that age 115 was the contract maturity date, and annuity payments under the contract could start at any time the owner wished to annuitize. In fact, in some contracts a late maturity date is a benefit, allowing an owner to keep the contract in the accumulation phase as long as possible, if that is his/her wish.

There is no accumulation phase in the life of an immediate annuity, as annuity payments typically commence shortly after purchase, and must, by definition, commence within one year. Annuities that are in distribution phase (i.e., deferred annuities that have been annuitized and all immediate annuities) are said to be in payout status.

A third type of annuity, often called a **longevity annuity**, first appeared in the marketplace in 2007. It is similar to an immediate annuity in that it provides only for income (usually for life); there is no accumulation period. Unlike an immediate annuity, the longevity annuity income does not commence within one year of purchase; rather, it is deferred until a future date, which may be for many years after purchase. Currently, there are two types of longevity annuities: (a) "pure longevity annuities," which provide no death benefit if the buyer does not live to the annuity starting age and often specify a set starting age and (b) "Deferred Income Annuities," which often provide both a death benefit and a choice as to annuity starting ages. See Chapter 8 for a detailed discussion of longevity annuities.

How the Cash Value in the Annuity is Invested

A fixed annuity is an annuity in which the contract value is measured in dollars. A variable annuity is one in which the contract value is measured in terms of units—either accumulation units or annuity units, depending upon whether the contract is in the accumulation phase or the distribution phase. In both cases, the value of each unit can—and probably will—vary each business day, according to the investment performance of the separate accounts[3] chosen by the contract owner. We will look at how accumulation units and annuity units work shortly. First, however, let's understand the basic investment difference between fixed and variable annuities.

Fixed Annuities

A fixed annuity may be either immediate or deferred.

Fixed Immediate Annuities

All single premium immediate annuities (fixed or variable) provide an income (annual, semi-annual, quarterly, or monthly), either for a specified period or for life. These payout options are described later in this chapter.

Fixed Deferred Annuities

In a fixed deferred annuity, the contract values are guaranteed by the issuing insurance company. These values (discussed below) are all measured, as we've noted, in dollars. There is a common misconception that fixed, in the term "fixed annuity," refers to the rate of interest credited to the contract. This is not correct. While some fixed deferred annuities provide guarantees as to the period during which the current interest rate will be credited, and all deferred annuities provide a guaranteed minimum interest rate that will be credited during the entire accumulation period, the term fixed, when used in reference to fixed annuities, properly refers, not to the interest rate, but to the fact that the contract values are measured in fixed units—namely, dollars.

What are these contract values? In a fixed immediate annuity, or a fixed deferred annuity that has been annuitized, the contract value guaranteed by the issuing insurer is the dollar amount of the periodic annuity payment (which may be payable monthly, quarterly, semi-annually, or annually). In a fixed deferred annuity, there are several contract values:

1. **Cash Value.** The cash value, or accumulation value, of a fixed deferred annuity is the value on which interest is computed and to which interest is credited. It is generally the sum of all premium payments received, plus all prior interest credited, less any withdrawals (and, in the case of certain qualified annuities, unpaid loan interest). The cash value of fixed deferred annuities is always guaranteed. The cash value of variable annuities is not, except for monies deposited into the fixed account option of such contracts.

2. **Annuity Value.** The annuity value is the value to which an annuity payout factor will be applied if—and only if—the contract owner annuitizes the contract. In some deferred annuities, this value is identical to the cash value. In so-called tiered annuities (of the type where a higher interest rate is credited to the annuity value than is credited to the cash value) and in contracts providing for an annuitization bonus, the annuity value is higher than the cash value.

3. **Surrender Value.** The surrender value of a deferred annuity is the cash value, less any applicable surrender charge and market value adjustment (see Chapter 5: Basic Costs of Annuities) that will be paid to the contract owner upon surrender of the contract.

The basic investment difference between fixed and variable annuities is that in a fixed annuity, either immediate or deferred, the contract owner is offered no investment choices within the contract and assumes no investment risk. In a fixed deferred annuity, the cash value, which includes all premium payments and prior interest credited, is guaranteed against loss, as is a minimum interest rate. All fixed deferred annuities also offer a current—nonguaranteed—interest rate. Some, but not all, contracts guarantee the current declared rate for a certain period of time. By contrast, the contract owner of a variable annuity retains an investment risk. (See further discussion below regarding variable annuities.) In a variable immediate annuity, the amount of each year's annuity payment will vary with the performance of the investment accounts chosen. In a deferred variable annuity, it is essential for the advisor to understand that the guarantees in fixed annuities are only as good as the ability of the issuing insurer to pay them.

Variable Annuities

A variable annuity may be either immediate or deferred.

Variable Immediate Annuities

Like fixed immediate annuities, variable immediate annuities provide regular annuity payments, commencing within one year of purchase. The annuity payout options are typically the same as with immediate fixed annuities. The chief difference is that the annual income in a variable annuity will vary with the performance of the investment accounts chosen. A second difference is that, unlike fixed immediate annuities, variable immediate annuities typically impose an asset management charge that is taken into account by the insurer in declaring the current year's annuity payment.

Variable deferred annuities work very differently from fixed annuities, in both the accumulation phase and in the distribution phase.

Variable Deferred Annuities

The Accumulation Phase

In the accumulation phase of a variable deferred annuity,[4] each premium payment purchases, after applicable contract charges are deducted, a number of accumulation units for each investment subaccount chosen by the contract holder. The cash value will vary with the performance of those investment subaccounts; there is no guarantee either of principal or of minimum interest, except for cash values placed in the so-called "fixed account."

Example: Mr. Jones has chosen five investment subaccounts from among those available in his variable deferred annuity. He has directed that each premium payment[5] be allocated to these accounts as follows:

- Large Cap Growth Account A   20%

- Midcap Value Account M   20%

- Small Cap Value Account S   20%

- International Stock Acct I   15%

- Bond Account B   25%

The accumulation unit values of these accounts on the day his premium is received are as follows:

- Large Cap Growth Account A $21,435

- Midcap Value Account M $16,567

- Small Cap Value Account S $34,123

- International Stock Acct I $9,567

- Bond Account B $15,003

If Mr. Jones makes a premium payment of $1,000, and the contract charges applicable are $14, the net premium ($986) will purchase:

- Large Cap Growth Account A   9.1999 units

- Midcap Value Account M   11.9032 units

- Small Cap Value Account S   5.7791 units

- International Stock Acct I   15.4594 units

- Bond Account B   16.4300 units[6]

Accumulation unit values can, and often will, change each day according to the investment performance of the subaccounts, just as the net asset value of a mutual fund share does. However, there is a significant difference between the pricing of annuity accumulation units and that of mutual fund shares. When a mutual fund declares a dividend or capital gains distribution—through the realization of dividends or capital gains income by the fund—and the shareholder has elected to reinvest such distributions, additional shares are purchased for his account, and the price of all shares of the fund is reduced to reflect the distribution. If the shareholder has elected not to reinvest such distributions, he receives cash, and the share price is reduced. When a dividend or capital gain is realized by a variable annuity subaccount, the value of the accumulation unit is increased reflecting the dividend or gain received, but the number of units remains the same.

Investment Sub-Accounts

One of the main advantages of investing in a variable annuity is the access it provides to diversified investment types. The first variable annuities offered relatively few investment choices, and, often, the choices were limited to proprietary accounts; that is, accounts managed by the insurance company that issued the annuity, or a subsidiary. Many newer contracts offer subaccounts representing a wide variety of asset classes,[7] managed by a variety of money management firms. Typically, the contract owner is permitted to choose several subaccounts,[8] and to make exchanges among them—re-allocating existing contract values—and to reallocate ongoing contributions without charge.[9] Moreover, exchanges among subaccounts in a single contract are not taxable events for income tax purposes. These investment management features, together with features such as automatic portfolio rebalancing and dollar cost averaging from the annuity contract's fixed account[10] to the variable subaccounts, make the modern variable annuity a robust and powerful investment management tool.

Notably, the cash values in the investment accounts chosen by the buyer of a variable deferred annuity are not invested directly in the issuing insurance company's general account (and therefore are not subject to the credit risk of the insurer), but are held separately (which is why they are often called "investment accounts"). On the other hand, funds that are invested in the general account (often also known as the "fixed account") of a variable annuity *are* invested directly with the insurer, receiving the interest rate and potential income/growth guarantees of the fixed account, but also subject to the general credit risk of the insurer.

The Distribution Phase

In the distribution phase, fixed annuities—either immediate contracts or deferred contracts that have been annuitized—provide a regular income by application of a chosen annuity payout factor to the amount that is converted to an income stream. For example, if Mr. Smith purchases a fixed immediate annuity for $100,000 or annuitizes a fixed deferred annuity having an annuity value of that same amount, and if he elects a Life and Ten Year Certain payout arrangement, and if the annual annuity payout factor for that option, for his age and sex, is 5.67, his annuity payments will be $5,670 per year from that point until the later of his death or the expiration of ten years. Similarly, if he elects to annuitize a variable deferred annuity on a fixed annuity payout arrangement, and if the total value of the accumulation units in his contract, at the time of annuitization, is $100,000, he will receive that same income, assuming the same annuity payout factor.

If the annuity payout in a variable annuity is to be on a variable basis, however, the amount annuitized (either a lump sum, in the case of an immediate variable annuity, or, in a deferred variable annuity, the current value of the accumulation units the owner wishes to annuitize[11]) is not converted to a fixed income stream by applying an annuity payout factor. Instead, the purchase payment or amount annuitized is used to buy a certain number of annuity units.[12] The process works as follows:

- First, the payment, or annuitization amount, is reduced by any contract fee applicable and by any state premium tax due, and allocated to the investment subaccounts chosen by the contract owner.

- Next, the insurance company computes an initial income payment amount for that portion of the purchase payment or annuitization amount allocated to each subaccount, using (a) the age and sex[13] of the annuitant and (b) an assumed investment rate (AIR). Many variable annuity contracts allow the purchaser to choose among several AIRs (e.g., three percent, four percent, five percent, and six percent). The higher the initial AIR chosen, the higher the initial variable income payment will be.

- Finally, the initial income payment is divided by the value of the annuity unit for each subaccount chosen. The result is the number of annuity units of that subaccount which will be purchased by that payment. Subsequent annuity payments will increase or decrease in proportion to the extent to which the net investment performance, after application of the separate account charges, of the chosen variable subaccounts exceeds or lags the AIR.

Parties to the Annuity Contract

There are four parties to a commercial annuity contract.

1.   The **annuity company** is the party that issues the policy, and is obligated to keep all the promises made in it.

2.   The **annuitant** is the individual—and it must be an individual, a human being—who may or may not also be the owner of the policy. The age and sex of the annuitant determine—for life annuities—the amount of each annuity payment. The annuitant is merely the measuring life for purposes of annuity payment calculations. He or she has NO rights in the annuity contract as annuitant.

3.   The **beneficiary** is the party who will receive any death benefit payable under the annuity, whether as a lump sum or a continuation of annuity payments. However, not all annuities will have a beneficiary because if payments cease at the annuitant's death, there is nothing for a beneficiary to receive. In most cases, the beneficiary has no other rights, except if the beneficiary is named irrevocably.

4.   The **owner** is the individual or entity—it need not be a human—that has all ownership rights in the contract, including the right to name the annuitant and beneficiary, to elect commencement of annuity payments, and to surrender the contract. Occasionally, advisors will suggest that a nonqualified annuity[14] be owned jointly; usually when the owners are a married couple. As will be discussed in Chapter 3, this arrangement can produce unexpected problems and should be avoided unless the client and advisors are aware of the implications of such ownership.

Types of Annuity Payouts

An immediate annuity, or a deferred annuity that has been annuitized—where the contract owner has elected to begin receiving annuity payments—produces an income stream. The nature of this income stream can vary, according to the type of payout arrangement chosen.

The first arrangement, and the simplest, is **Life Only, No Refund**. When the contract owner elects this option, he or she will, upon annuitization, receive an income guaranteed to last for the annuitant's entire lifetime—no matter how long that annuitant lives. At the annuitant's death, no further payments will be due. Life Only, No Refund provides the highest payout of any of the annuity arrangements because if the annuitant dies prematurely—even if after receiving only one payment—the insurance company's obligation ceases. The insurance company, in making a Life Only, No Refund annuity payment guarantee, incurs no cost for guaranteeing a survivor benefit or, in the jargon of the insurance industry, a refund feature. It is the cost of these refund features that necessitates that annuity payments calculated using such a benefit be lower than the amount of a Life Only, No Refund annuity.

A second payout type is **Life Annuity, With Refund**. As with all life payout options, the main guarantee is that payments will continue for the annuitant's lifetime. But should the annuitant die during the refund period, the insurance company must pay the refund amount to the designated beneficiary.

Refund arrangements come in various flavors. The **Period Certain** refund type says that if the annuitant dies before the end of a certain period of time, payments will continue to the beneficiary for the remainder of that period. For example, the most common payout arrangement is **Life and Ten-Year Certain**. This arrangement provides for payments that are guaranteed to continue for the annuitant's life, however long. If that annuitant should not live to receive ten years' payments—if payments are monthly, that is 120 monthly payments—the remaining payments will continue to the beneficiary named in the policy until the ten-year term is complete.

The **Cash Refund** or **Installment Refund** payout option says that if the annuitant dies before receiving a specified amount—which may or may not be less than the amount originally annuitized—the balance will be paid to the beneficiary, either in a lump sum or in installments.

Not all annuities are payable for life. A third payout type, the so-called **Period Certain** option, pays an income for a certain period. A twenty-year period certain payout option will pay for exactly twenty years and no more or fewer. If the annuitant dies during that period, payments continue to the beneficiary (or to a contingent annuitant if one is named). If the annuitant is still living at the end of twenty years, payments cease.

The terminology almost begs for misunderstanding. Life and 10-Year Certain sounds a lot like Ten-Year Certain. But they are very different payout options. The first one will pay for the longer of ten years or the annuitant's lifetime. The second will pay, in any and all events, for exactly and only ten years. No more, no less. Many prospective annuity buyers will miss this distinction. No matter how careful the advisor is in explaining how that arrangement works, some people hear just the Ten Years part and focus on it. Many years ago, in talking with an elderly prospective client, one of the authors thought he had explained the Life and Ten Year Certain annuity he was recommending adequately. But, after he had finished, she expressed concern. "I like having that amount every month," she said, "and I especially like knowing that amount won't change, but I'm a bit worried. You see, I may live longer than ten years, and then what?"

One way of avoiding this confusion, when structuring life annuities, is to consider using either Cash Refund or Installment Refund arrangements to address the risk of the annuitant's dying prematurely. It is far more easily explained and understood, and does not let the duration of the certain element distract attention from the lifetime guarantee, which is, the main purpose of the arrangement.

The fourth type of payout includes arrangements that cover more than one annuitant. The most common type is that of the various **Joint and Survivor** payout options and normally allows only two annuitants. These are life annuity payouts—they persist until both annuitants have died. The amount of the annuity payment may remain unchanged at the first death (this is called Joint and 100 percent Survivor) or may be reduced by some percentage or fraction. For example, Joint and two-thirds means that the surviving annuitant will receive, commencing at the death of the first annuitant, an income equal to two-thirds of the original annuity amount. Some contracts allow Joint and Survivor payouts with a refund feature. A much less common option than the Joint and Survivor arrangement is called **Joint Life**. It, too, covers two annuitants, but pays a benefit only until the first annuitant dies.

Now that we have the basics and terminology of annuities out of the way—and the authors thank you, dear reader, for your patience—let's get to what annuities are used for.

The Annuity as a Tool

Annuities are tools. They are acquired because the purchaser has a particular job to be done and is willing to exchange his money for a tool to do that job. In many ways, this exchange transaction is like the purchase of a hammer. The hammer has certain specifications—type and strength of the metal, length of the handle, size of the hammer head—and when purchased from a quality company, often comes with a guarantee that the product will perform as specified.

The important key to understand about this metaphor is that we generally do not buy a hammer simply because it happens to be cheaper, or lighter, or shinier than any other hand tool in the hardware store. We purchase it because we have a need, for example, to pound a nail into a piece of wood, or anticipate having a need in the future that we want to be prepared for, and we believe that a hammer is the best tool to fulfill that need.

In addition, there are many different situations where we might need a hammer, and each of those situations may call for a different one. Clearly, using a sledgehammer to drive a small nail into your drywall to hang a picture is the wrong tool for the job. Thus, the key in purchasing the right hammer is understanding the need and the job you're hoping to accomplish with it. Only once you understand the right situation for any particular hammer can you determine whether a hammer is the right tool for the job, and which type you need.

To complete the analogy, the key to decision-making when it comes to annuities is first to understand the problems for which the annuity can represent a solution. Only then can one actually determine whether an annuity is the right tool to solve the problem, and which sort of annuity will best accomplish the task.

Overview: The Annuity as a Problem-Solving Tool

We are all familiar with the kinds of problems that hammers solve, such as driving a small nail, pounding a large nail, or forcing a wedge between two pieces of wood to separate them. The problems that the annuity-as-a-tool are meant to solve are quite varied because of the broad number and types of annuity-tools available. That said, the problems that annuities solve—the needs that they meet—can be identified and separated into several general categories:

1. **The need for a known income stream.** This is what annuities do best, because annuities—whether deferred or immediate—are really designed to generate income. The known part may be the amount of the income stream, the duration, or both. The amount might be fixed or determined by a formula. The duration might be for a specified period, for the lifetime of the annuitant, or the longer of the two. The amount of each annuity payment may be greater than one could obtain, with absolute certainty, from other savings or investment vehicles. However, it must be noted that annuity income (meaning regular annuity payments, not partial withdrawals) are part principal. An annuitant is not living on her income, but on income and principal.

2. **The need for a guaranteed rate of return.** As we've noted, the current interest crediting rate in most deferred annuities may potentially be changed every quarter, year, or at the discretion of the insurance company. A notable exception is the so-called CD annuity—a fixed deferred annuity with multi-year current rate guarantees. Often, the rate guarantee extends to the end of the surrender charge period, which is usually six years or less. Depending upon contractual provisions, especially the surrender charge schedule, and whether interest rates are rising or falling, longer rate guarantee periods may offer lower or higher rates than shorter periods. In any event, the rate of return is contractually guaranteed.

3. **The need for a better nonguaranteed rate of return.** Although their current crediting rate is usually not guaranteed beyond an initial period, deferred annuities

have, historically, paid somewhat higher current returns as a class, than some other fixed-dollar investments, such as passbook savings and certificates of deposit.

4. **The need or desire for tax advantages.** One of the main appeals of a deferred annuity is tax-deferred growth. Although the gain will ultimately be taxed (tax-deferred does not mean tax-free), tax deferral maximizes the benefit of compounding. Moreover, annual growth not distributed is not recognized as income for any tax purpose, including the taxability of Social Security benefits. Immediate annuities, too, receive favorable income tax treatment. A portion of each annuity payment is considered return of principal and is not taxable.

5. **A guaranteed payment in the event of death.** Although annuities are not life insurance policies, and are not taxed as such, they can provide guaranteed death benefits. A fixed deferred annuity offers a guarantee of principal (and previously credited interest), and most such contracts waive surrender charges upon death. Variable deferred annuities typically offer a guaranteed minimum death benefit. Immediate annuities, while designed to amortize both principal and earnings over the annuity payout period, may be structured with a refund feature to guarantee a minimum payout, whether to the living annuitant or her beneficiary (if the annuitant should die early). That said, annuities are designed primarily to provide living benefits. If a guaranteed death benefit is a client's main concern, life insurance is often a better tool (provided the client is insurable). Just as a hammer can be used to pry apart two-by-fours, a pry bar is probably a better choice (so long as the job does not involve driving nails).

Is an Annuity the Right Tool, and, If So, Which Kind Will Do the Best Job?

Now that we've defined some of the needs that annuities can solve, we will begin to focus on how to match particular kinds of annuities to manage the risks inherent in those needs, and understand the annuity as a **risk management** tool.

When the Client Needs a Known Income Stream

For the client who requires a certain income stream commencing within one year, an immediate annuity is an almost intuitive choice. Providing income—certain as to amount, duration, or both—is what an immediate annuity does. But first we need to ask a key question: For how long will the income stream be required?

If the need is for an income for life, an immediate life annuity makes good sense. It is the only financial instrument that can guarantee a specific amount of income for as long as the recipient lives. It allows the purchaser to manage the risk that the asset base that is used to create the payments may not earn an adequate rate of return, or may not be large enough to provide enough payments for life (i.e., the risk of outliving one's assets). Some immediate annuities can be structured so that annuity payments will increase each year by a specified percentage. This is sometimes known as the COLA (cost-of-living-adjustment) option. Unfortunately, many insurance companies do not offer such an option in their immediate annuity portfolios.

Similarly, if the need is for an income specified for a period of years, an immediate period certain annuity may be an appropriate choice. It, too, manages the risk of an unknown future rate of return over the time period, and the risk that the asset base, or the dollars used to create the income stream, may not be sufficient to produce the income required.

One risk often cited by critics of immediate annuities is that the buyer has locked in current interest rates. This criticism is generally voiced during periods when prevailing interest rates are unusually low. How valid is this criticism? In the authors' opinion, it has merit, from an investment perspective. The interest rate used in the calculation of the annuity payout factor—the number of dollars, per thousand dollars of purchase payment that the annuitant will receive each period—is, indeed, locked in. Should prevailing interest rates rise over the period of time during which annuity payments are made, those annuity payments will not reflect that rise. However, the authors feel that from a risk management perspective, this criticism is misdirected. If the goal is to ensure an income level, the relevant risk is whether the dollars invested to produce that income can do so with certainty. A rise in prevailing rates would not present that risk, but a decline would. To transfer that risk from the annuity buyer to the insurance company, the buyer must incur a cost. Locking in the annuity interest rate is part of that cost.

It should be noted, though, that the changes in interest rates used in immediate annuity calculations over the past two decades have been far less dramatic than the changes in interest rates for short-term instruments such as savings accounts and certificates of deposit. While it is true that the purchaser of an immediate annuity in June, 2014 is locking in an interest rate lower than would have been used for someone the same age and sex in, say, June, 2004, the difference is not as great as one might think. By the same token, if interest rates should trend sharply upward in the next ten years, the locked in rates ten years hence will probably not be substantially greater than the current ones.

When the Client Needs a Guaranteed Rate of Return

When a specific minimum return on investment and preservation of principal is required to accomplish a particular goal, an immediate annuity makes no sense because it does not preserve principal. The income payments from an immediate annuity, while they may be larger than might be achievable from alternatives, are not just a return on investment, but a combination of return on and return of investment. However, a deferred annuity offering a multi-year interest rate guarantee may well provide a solution. The risk of getting an inadequate rate of return is managed by transferring it to the insurance company issuing the annuity. This provides a total or minimum rate of return guaranteed to equal or exceed the return required. However, it is important to note that there is a lack of liquidity cost associated with these annuities. This is because the insurance company makes its guarantees assuming it will have use of the money used to purchase the annuity. Typically, a deferred annuity contract does not become profitable for an insurer until after it has been in force for several years due to commissions, other issuing charges, administrative costs, deferred acquisition costs, taxes, and reserve requirements. If the annuity owner elects to surrender or take withdrawals from the annuity in the early contract years, he will usually be required to pay a surrender charge. The amount and terms of this vary considerably from contract to contract.

Recently, many variable deferred annuities have been marketed with guaranteed living benefits. The structure and provisions of these policies vary greatly, but it should be noted that the guarantees provided may not be equivalent to the guaranteed minimum rate of return of fixed annuities, and usually require annuitization, minimum holding periods, or other conditions for the guarantees to be effective. For an extensive discussion of the various living benefits available with variable annuities, see Chapter 5.

When the Client Needs a Better Non-Guaranteed Rate of Return

With the exception of fixed annuities with multi-year current rate guarantees, or so-called CD annuities, no deferred annuity guarantees the current rate of return for more than a year at most. Although, all fixed annuities offer a guaranteed minimum rate of return. Variable deferred annuities generally do not offer any guarantees of return or of principal, except where the fixed investment account is used or as provided by optional riders. That said, we should bear in mind that most other long-term investments do not offer such guarantees either. For clients who require a guarantee of principal and are willing to accept a current rate that may change, deferred fixed annuities may offer better returns than certificates of deposit or individual bonds. The interest rate history of many fixed annuities has exceeded that of CDs, although there can be no assurance that this will hold true in the future.

When comparing the interest crediting rate of a deferred annuity with that of an alternative, the diligent advisor will point out not only any applicable surrender charges, but also the early distribution penalty that applies to withdrawals taken prior to age fifty-nine and a half, unless an exception is available. See Chapter 2 for an in-depth discussion of the income taxation of annuities. Those are essential elements in any sound risk management decision. So, too, is the fact that earnings in deferred annuities are not taxed until distributed.

When the Client Wants and Needs Income Tax Deferral

Tax deferral is perhaps the most advertised and promoted advantage of deferred annuities. Earnings are not taxed until distributed, either to living contract owners or beneficiaries. The advantages of such deferral are well recognized. However, the cost of such tax deferral, granted by Section 72 of the Internal Revenue Code, is a requirement in the same section that all distributions from annuities be taxed at ordinary income rates. No capital gains treatment is ever available under current law. Whether this trade-off is favorable, or appropriate, is a matter of considerable controversy. In the authors' view, it is always a matter of individual facts and circumstances, for reasons that will be discussed in later chapters.

When the Client Needs a Guaranteed Payment in the Event of Death

An often-overlooked feature of deferred annuities is the right of the beneficiary to receive a guaranteed payment, or a payment determined by a guaranteed formula, in the event of death. This payment may not occur until the distant future, but upon purchase of the contract the owner knows exactly what the minimum payment will be or how it will be determined.

When is this important? When the client requires that a certain amount be available upon death, regardless of investment performance in the meantime. This guarantee allows a variable deferred annuity owner to manage the risk that inadequate investment performance will cause a smaller amount to pass to her beneficiaries than desired, regardless of actual investment performance over the time period until death. The authors strongly believe, however, that, when the need for such guaranteed death benefit is a primary concern, life insurance generally represents a far more efficient solution, if available.

Summary: The Annuity as a Tool

The guarantees that the annuity-tool provides allow clients and their advisors to solve certain problems and to meet certain needs. Specifically, it allows us to meet those needs despite risks that might cause us to fail. Thus, at its most fundamental level, annuities serve as tools that allow us to manage risks—specifically, the risks that:

- **distributions** from an investment will be inadequate to meet specified goals;

- **earnings** on an investment will be inadequate to meet specified goals; and

- the **amount available to heirs**, from the investment, will be inadequate to meet specified goals.

Our discussion of annuities, and potential applications for them, throughout the remainder of this book will proceed with the understanding that annuities are nothing more than risk management tools that allow us to accomplish certain needs and goals with certainty—or at least increased likelihood—because of the underlying guarantees that they hold.

Determining When a Risk Management Tool (Annuity) is Appropriate

In all cases, the annuity tool solution will have a cost associated with it—the cost of the annuity and the guarantees that it provides. Because of these costs, the solution provided often will not be the solution with the highest expected value or projected return on investment. However, the decision to accept a lower fully guaranteed value in exchange for a higher, but unguaranteed, expected value is a risk-return tradeoff that can, and should, be examined and made on a case-by-case basis. In many instances, when presented with both options, the client will choose the option most likely to succeed, not the one with the highest expected return.

It is also important to remember that, in the search to maximize the probability of success, it is entirely possible that the client will not actually need to utilize the guarantees provided by an annuity. Annuities manage risks of loss; there is no guarantee that such losses will occur in the first place. Annuities offer purchasers options to utilize certain guarantees; they do not require the exercise of those options. Thus, it may be that a guarantee within a client's annuity is never actually put to use. Nonetheless, owning the annuity may very well have still been the right choice. That the guarantees may never be put to use does not mean the cost of those guarantees was a waste. Your house may never burn down, but it is still prudent to maintain your homeowner's insurance and pay premiums for years. Doing so buys you a guarantee that you will not lose the entire value of your house, and may produce ancillary benefits such as allowing you to obtain a mortgage. In any event, it can provide you with invaluable peace of mind, and the ability to enjoy your life knowing that a particular risk had been transferred—insured—away.

Endnotes

1. Some insurance companies will issue annuity checks to a nonowner annuitant if requested to do so by the owner.

2. Such deferral may require the insurance company's approval.

3. These are also referred to as investment subaccounts.

4. As we have noted, there is no accumulation phase in a variable immediate annuity.

5. After deduction for contract charges.

6. We have illustrated four decimal places precision for units purchased and three decimal places for unit values in this example. Some insurers use greater precision and some use less.

7. Asset classes are investment types having distinct risk/return characteristics, such as U.S. Large Cap Growth Stocks, Foreign Stocks, U.S. Real Estate, U.S. Long Term Gov't Bonds, etc.

8. Some contracts require a minimum initial and/or ongoing contribution per subaccount.

9. Most contracts impose a maximum on the number of exchanges permitted per month and may levy a charge for additional excess exchanges. These restrictions are generally in place to prevent active trading using the investment subaccounts, but are not intended to restrict normal occasional trading and re-balancing.

10. The fixed account in a deferred variable annuity typically guarantees a minimum interest rate and may offer a guaranteed duration for the current declared interest rate. In addition, the principal—including all prior credited interest—is typically guaranteed against loss.

11. Some variable deferred annuities permit partial annuitization. Others require that the entire value of the contractholder's accumulation units be annuitized.

12. Some variable annuity literature describes this process as a conversion of the existing accumulation units to annuity units.

13. If the annuity uses unisex annuity factors, the sex of the annuitant is not considered. Most commercial annuities use sex-distinct factors. Unisex factors are most often seen in contracts used to fund qualified retirement plans, where sex-distinct factors in such an employment context are considered to impose potentially unlawful discrimination.

14. An annuity purchased with after-tax dollars that will not fund an IRA or tax-qualified plan.

Chapter 2

Taxation of Annuity Benefits during Owner's Lifetime

The rules regarding taxation of annuities are complicated and, in many instances, not entirely clear. Unfortunately, it is very easy for an advisor to make mistakes in advising clients as to ownership, beneficiary designations, or distribution requirements. It is even easier to misinterpret or misapply the many complex rules governing lifetime withdrawals from annuities. Mistakes in these areas can have serious consequences both for the client and the advisor. For these reasons, we will devote considerable attention in this chapter not only to the rules themselves—including some that may be unfamiliar to the reader—but also to the practical, every day applications and implications of those rules.

The rules governing taxation of annuities are contained in Internal Revenue Code Section 72 (the Code) and the applicable Treasury regulations. However, it is extremely important for the reader to understand that most of Section 72 deals only with so-called nonqualified annuities, or annuities purchased with after-tax dollars, and not to fund tax-qualified Individual Retirement Accounts (IRAs) or tax-qualified retirement plans. The tax rules regarding the deferral of tax on annual earnings within annuities and the methods for determining how much of each annuity payment is taxable refer only to nonqualified annuity contracts. On the other hand, qualified annuities[1] are governed by parts of the Code dealing with the specific type of plan the annuity is funding (e.g., Section 408 for traditional IRAs, Section 408A for Roth IRAs, and Section 401 for pension plans). The rules that govern an annuity that is not purchased to fund an IRA or qualified plan (i.e., the rules for nonqualified annuities) are totally inapplicable to an annuity that is purchased to fund such a plan (a qualified annuity). This distinction is often not understood, and one of the most common mistakes made by advisors in the area of retirement planning is an attempt to apply regular annuity rules to a qualified annuity. The rules discussed in this chapter apply only to nonqualified annuities, except where indicated.

While Section 72 also deals with policy dividends and forms of premium returns, we will focus solely in our discussion on just two types of payments:

1.   amounts received as an annuity (i.e., annuity payments); and

2.   amounts not received as an annuity (i.e., withdrawals, surrenders, and other nonannuity payouts).

All distributions from an annuity, whether made to a living owner or to a beneficiary, are either one or the other of these two types.

Before we examine these two types of distributions, however, one very important point bears repeating: distributions made from an annuity while the owner of the annuity contract is living are taxable to that owner—even if made to an annuitant who is a different individual. For example, if A owns an annuity of which B is the annuitant, payments are generally made to A. Some annuity issuers will issue checks directly to a nonowner annuitant if the owner directs, but, even so, the tax liability is that of the owner.

Amounts Received as an Annuity

"The term *annuity* includes all periodic payments resulting from the systematic liquidation of a principal sum."[2] It "refers not only [to] payments made for the life or lives, but also to installment payments that do not involve a life contingency; for example, payments under a fixed period or fixed amount settlement option."[3] Amounts received as an annuity are taxed under Section 72 (discussed below), which considers each payment to be part principal and part gain. The part representing principal is excluded from tax (as a return of principal); the part representing gain is taxable as ordinary income.[4] The formula for allocating the amount of principal and gain of each payment for fixed annuities is different from that used with variable annuities.

In the case of a fixed annuity, this calculation is done by applying an exclusion ratio that is the total investment in the contract—adjusted for the value of any refund feature elected—divided by the expected return, which, for life annuities, takes into account life expectancies.

$$\text{Exclusion Ratio} = \frac{\text{Total Investment Contract}}{\text{Expected Return}}$$

In the case of a variable annuity, the expected return is unknown and is considered, for purposes of the exclusion calculation, to be equal to the investment in the contract. The ratio used to determine the portion of each variable annuity payment includible in income is the investment in the contract, adjusted for the value of any refund feature elected, divided by the number of years over which it is anticipated that the annuity will be paid.[5] For a detailed description of each method, see Appendix C. Once all principal has been received tax-free, the entire annuity payment is taxable as ordinary income.[6] It is important to note that, where the annuity starting date was prior to January 1, 1987, the exclusion ratio continues to apply, even after all the principal has been recovered. Consequently, when addressing the taxation of an existing annuity payment stream, it is absolutely critical to know when payments began.

Annuity payments, or amounts received as an annuity, include payments from an immediate annuity, or from a deferred annuity, or a Deferred Income Annuity (DIA)—also known as a "longevity annuity"[7] that has been annuitized, where the owner of a deferred annuity has elected to commence regular annuity payments under an annuity option offered by that contract.

Notably, amounts that are annuitized within a qualified plan are not subject to the exclusion ratio rules; instead, the amounts are taxable based solely on the tax treatment associated with distributions from the qualified plan itself. However, in the case of annuities held inside of retirement accounts that have been annuitized, they must comply with the Treasury Regulation requirements that both ensure Required Minimum Distributions (RMD) are satisfied, and that the benefits remain primarily for the retirement account holder and not others under the Minimum Distribution Incidental Benefit (MDIB) rules.[8] As a result of these rules, the choices for amount of survivor payments (especially for nonspouse beneficiaries), extent of period certain guarantees, and breadth of cost-of-living adjustments, may be limited (compared to their nonqualified immediate annuity counterparts) to ensure that the contract complies with the regulations.

Amounts Not Received as an Annuity

The tax treatment of annuity distributions other than regular annuity payments, including partial withdrawals, surrenders, and other nonannuitized payouts, depends upon when the annuity contract was issued.

Contracts Entered Into After August 13, 1982

For contracts entered into after August 13, 1982, nonannuity distributions are taxed according to the interest first rule, sometimes referred to as Last In, First Out (LIFO). All distributions that are amounts not received as an annuity are considered income until all gain in the contract has been received.

Amounts not received as an annuity are any amounts received from an annuity that do not qualify as amounts received as an annuity. This distinction may appear obvious, but it is not quite that straightforward because of how Section 72 treats the word received. Amounts not received as an annuity include not only outright distributions such as partial withdrawals and death benefits not taken under an annuity option, but also policy dividends unless retained by the insurer as premiums or other consideration,[9] amounts received as loans, "the value of any part of an annuity contract pledged or assigned,"[10] and amounts received on partial surrender. Such amounts "are taxable as income to the extent that the cash value of the contract immediately before the payment exceeds the investment in the contract."[11]

The preceding two sentences merit closer attention, however, because many advisors are unaware of these provisions. First, amounts taken from annuity contracts as loans are taxable,[12] although nonqualified annuity contracts generally do not contain loan provisions. Second, merely pledging an annuity as collateral for a loan causes recognition of income to the extent of the lesser of any gain or the portion of the annuity thus pledged.

Multiple Deferred Annuities: The Anti-Abuse Rule

One method of reducing the impact of the LIFO treatment of deferred annuities, for purchasers who contemplate using partial withdrawals, is to use multiple contracts.

> *Example*: Individual A purchases a single deferred annuity for $100,000. Five years later, it is worth $120,000. If A then withdraws $15,000, the entire $15,000 is taxable as ordinary income. Moreover, if A is under age fifty-nine and a half, he must pay the ten percent penalty tax for premature distributions unless an exception to the penalty applies. If, however, A purchases ten annuities for $10,000 each, and each annuity is worth $12,000 five years later, a surrender of one contract (for $12,000) and a withdrawal from a second, for $3,000, would produce a taxable amount of only $4,000 (the gain in the two annuities) for the same $15,000 withdrawal. Moreover, the penalty tax would be $400, instead of $1,500, as the penalty applies only to the taxable portion of early distributions.

Congress recognized this technique as abusive and enacted a provision that treats all annuities issued during a single calendar year and issued by the same insurance company as one annuity, for purposes of taxing withdrawals.[13] This provision does not apply to partial withdrawals or surrenders of deferred annuity contracts issued in the same calendar year by different insurance companies, or to deferred annuity contracts issued by the same insurance company in different calendar years.

Contracts Entered Into Before August 14, 1982

Amounts not received as an annuity from contracts entered into before August 14, 1982 and allocated to investments made before August 14, 1982 are taxed under the cost recovery rule, a treatment sometimes referred to as First In, First Out (FIFO). Under this rule, "the taxpayer may receive all such amounts tax-free until he has received tax-free amounts equal to his [total] pre-August 14, 1982 investment in the contract; [subsequent withdrawal] amounts are taxable only after such basis has been fully recovered."[14] It should be noted that this does not mean that all amounts not received as an annuity from an annuity contract entered into before August 14, 1982 are treated thus. Only amounts allocable to investments made before August 14, 1982 receive this treatment.

> *Example*: If a taxpayer had an annuity purchased in 1981 (thus, before August 14, 1982) for $25,000, and currently worth $125,000, the first $25,000 of withdrawals are received tax-free, and subsequent withdrawals are taxable as gain. If the taxpayer had made a total of

$50,000 of deposits by adding another $25,000 in 1984, the taxpayer would still only be able to receive the first $25,000 tax-free because the second deposit—although attributable to a pre-August 14, 1982 annuity—would not be allocable to a pre-August 14, 1982 investment in the contract. Note that if the taxpayer's two deposits had occurred in 1983 and 1984 thus, after August 14, 1982, the post-August 14, 1982 rules would apply and the contract with a $50,000 investment and a $125,000 current value would be taxed as gains first, to the extent of the $75,000 of gain inherent in the contract. Only then would withdrawals be a tax-free recovery of basis. Alternatively, if the $125,000 contract were annuitized, a portion of each payment would be a tax-free recovery of basis. This illustrates the three different ways that basis may be allocated to withdrawals from a contract: (1) all basis first and then gains for pre-August 14, 1982 contracts; (2) all gains first and then basis for post-August 14, 1982 contracts; and (3) pro-rata basis and gains on each payment for annuitized contracts.

Partial Versus Full Surrenders

Amounts withdrawn from an annuity, not allocable to pre-August 14, 1982 contributions, are treated as being taxable to the extent of gain in the contract. However, the method used to determine the amount of gain will vary depending on whether the withdrawal represents a partial or full surrender.

In the event of a partial surrender (i.e., a withdrawal for any amount less than the full value of the contract), the amount of gain is determined as the excess of the contract value over the investment in the contract (cost basis), without regard to any surrender charges. As a result, the amount of gain is calculated based on the gross cash value of the annuity to determine whether any of a withdrawal will be attributable to gain and subject to income taxation.[15]

On the other hand, if the withdrawal represents a full surrender of the contract, the preceding normal rule for withdrawals does not apply.[16] Instead, in the case of a full surrender, the tax code explicitly indicates that the amount of gain shall simply be the excess of the amount received (i.e., the actual net surrender value received) over the investment in the contract (cost basis).[17]

Example: Taxpayer holds an annuity that was purchased for $100,000, the investment in the contract. The current cash value of the annuity is $105,000, and the annuity has a $10,000 surrender charge. Thus, the net surrender value of the annuity would be $95,000. If the taxpayer takes a partial withdrawal, the amount of gain in the contract would be $5,000, based on the current cash value of $105,000, without regard to any surrender charges. Thus, any partial withdrawal will be taxable up to the first $5,000 of gain, and only the remainder will be treated as a return of principal. However, if the entire annuity is surrendered, the total amount received will be $95,000, with an original investment in the contract of $100,000; consequently, in the case of a full surrender, the taxpayer will report no gain, and will be eligible for a $5,000 loss. (See below for further discussion of the tax treatment of annuity losses.)

In the second edition of this book, it was noted that, "in conversations with the authors, representatives of two major insurers said that their company's policy is to apply Section 72(e) (3)(A) both to partial withdrawals and total surrenders and, where the cash value of the contract before a total surrender, reckoned without regard to surrender charges, exceeds the holder's investment in the contract, they will issue a 1099 reporting such excess as gain—even if the net amount (after surrender charges) received by the holder on such surrender does not exceed the investment in the contract. The policies of those companies, in this regard, may have changed. When we attempted to learn the current policy of the two companies referred to, we were unsuccessful. One company simply did not respond to our inquiry; a representative of the other company told one of the authors that it was against their policy to make a public statement of their policy on this issue. To say the least, this highlights the tax uncertainty in the area, at least with respect to how it will be reported on a Form 1099-R to the IRS.

Nonetheless, the authors do not believe there should be any ambiguity, and that the rules are clear in stating that a partial surrender should ignore surrender charges when calculating gain under 72(e)(3)(A), while a total surrender under 72(e)(5)(E) should simply measure gains by comparing final net proceeds to investment in the contract/cost basis, which implicitly adjusts for surrender charges paid. Evidently, the IRS author of Private Letter Ruling 200030013 agrees with the latter statement, as the PLR includes the following text:

> "Section 72(e)(5)(E) provides a statutory exception to section 72(e)(2)(A). The rule of section 72(e)(2)(A) is not applicable if the amount received is "under a contract on its complete surrender, redemption, or maturity." Section 72(e)(5)(A) provides that in situations in which paragraph (e)(5) applies, then paragraphs (2)(B) and (4)(A) shall not apply and if paragraph (2)(A) does not apply, then the amount distributed shall be included in gross income, but only to the extent that it exceeds the investment in the contract (basis-first rule). The basis-first rule provides that the taxpayer does not have to include any amounts into income to the extent that it does not exceed the taxpayer's investment in the contract."

Thus, readers considering a deferred annuity contract should be aware of how the insurance company issuing the policy intends to interpret this issue.

Deferral of Tax on Undistributed Gain

One of the most often-cited advantages of deferred annuities is that the annual increase in the cash value of these contracts is not subject to tax until the gain is withdrawn. Indeed, this tax-deferred growth is often touted as the most important benefit offered by deferred annuities.[18] The authors believe that this is both an oversimplification and a mischaracterization. A deferred annuity is not merely a tax-management instrument. It is also a platform for various investment strategies, and a mechanism for ensuring a known or determinable stream of income for a definite period or for the whole of one or two lifetimes. But above all, in the authors' judgment, a deferred annuity—or an immediate annuity, for that matter—is a potent risk management tool. We will explore this last functionality in detail in Chapter 12. For the moment, however, it should be recognized that there is much more to a deferred annuity than tax deferral!

Advisors sometimes ask what specific section in the Internal Revenue Code states that growth in the cash value of a deferred annuity is not taxable until distributed. As we have noted, the tax treatment of nonqualified annuities is governed by Section 72, but there is no specific line or paragraph in that section granting such tax deferral. Rather, the various subsections of Section 72(e) define what distributions, including imputed distributions, such as policy gain in an annuity pledged as collateral for a loan, will be taxed as amounts not received as an annuity. Growth in the cash value, or annuity value or surrender value, is not among the items defined as such. It is, therefore, not taxable, currently, by implication.

When Does a Deferred Annuity NOT Enjoy Tax-Deferred Treatment?

Not all deferred annuities enjoy the benefit of tax-deferred growth. As Code section 72(u) states, contributions made after February 28, 1986, to annuity contracts held by a corporation or other entity that is not a natural person will not be treated as an annuity contract for tax purposes[19] and will not enjoy tax deferral. "Income on the contract"[20] will be treated, each year, "as ordinary income received or accrued by the owner during such taxable year."[21]

There are five exceptions to this rule.[22] It does not apply to a contract that:

1. is acquired by the estate of a decedent by reason of the death of the decedent;

2. is held under a qualified pension, profit sharing, or stock bonus plan, as a Code section 403(b) tax sheltered annuity, or under an individual retirement plan;

3. is a qualified funding asset,[23] as defined in Code section 130(d) but without regard to whether there is a qualified assignment;

4. is purchased by an employer upon the termination of a qualified pension, profit sharing, or stock bonus plan or tax sheltered annuity program and held by the employer until all amounts under the contract are distributed to the employee for whom the contract was purchased or to his beneficiary; or

5. is an immediate annuity (i.e., an annuity that is purchased with a single premium or annuity consideration, the annuity starting date of which is no later than one year from the date of purchase, and which provides for a series of substantially equal periodic payments to be made no less frequently than annually during the annuity period).

Another very important exception to this general rule is granted by a sentence at the end of Section 72(u)(1), which states that "for purposes of this paragraph, holding by a trust or other entity as an agent for a natural person shall not be taken into account." In other words, if the nominal owner of the annuity is not a natural person but the beneficial owner is, the annuity will be treated as held by a natural person and treated as an annuity for tax purposes.

In what circumstances does this exception to an exception apply? In other words, when may a deferred annuity, held by a nonnatural person entity, be treated as an annuity and enjoy tax deferral? See Appendix C for a discussion of various letter rulings in which a trust has been held to be such an agent of a natural person. However, we would like to draw attention to one specific observation from that discussion, which we believe is worthy of the reader's attention:

> "It is clear that if all contributions to the contract are made after February 28, 1986 the requirements apply to the contract. It seems clear enough that if no contributions are made after February 28, 1986 to an annuity contract, a contract held by a nonnatural person is treated for tax purposes as an annuity contract and is taxed under the annuity rules... However, if contributions have been made both before March 1, 1986 and after February 28, 1986 to contracts held by nonnatural persons, it is not clear whether the income on the contract is allocated to different portions of the contract and whether the portion of the contract allocable to contributions before March 1, 1986 may continue to be treated as an annuity contract for income tax purposes. The Code makes no specific provision for separate treatment of contributions to the same contract made before March 1, 1986 and those made after February 28, 1986."[24]

What about a deferred annuity owned by a family limited partnership? Here, the applicability of the agent of a natural person exception is particularly unclear. The authors have not been able to locate any private letter rulings in which the IRS has held that such a partnership would qualify as such an agent, but Private Letter Ruling 199944020 is worthy of note. In this ruling, the IRS provides notice of a taxpayer withdrawal of a letter ruling request:

> "Two rulings were requested on the transaction described below. The first was whether the transfer of annuity contracts to a partnership in exchange for limited partnership interests qualified for nonrecognition under Section 72 (nonrecognition of gain or loss on contribution). The second is whether the annuity contracts after the transfer to the partnership will be considered as held by a natural person under Section 72(u)."[25]

Although the taxpayer requesting the letter ruling withdrew the request, Private Letter Ruling 199944020 states that:

> "We reached a tentatively adverse conclusion only with regard to the second requested ruling dealing with Section 72(u) (treatment of annuity contracts not held by natural persons)...

> Under the present facts, Partnership is not a mere agent holding the deferred annuities for natural persons, rather it is proposed that Partnership actually receive and possess the

deferred annuities as property of Partnership, thus, subjecting this property to any possible claims of creditors against Partnership. By way of contrast, the example set forth in the drafting history of Section 72(u) clearly demonstrates that the agency exception was limited to a situation where a pure agency was created as the nonnatural person holding the property had no interest other than as agent. S. Rept. No. 99-313, 99th Cong., 2d Sess. 567 (Group annuity held by a corporation as agent for natural persons who are the beneficial owners, the contract is treated as an annuity). See also Joint Committee on Taxation Staff, *General Explanation of the Tax Reform Act of 1986*, 99th Cong., 2d Sess. 658 (1987) (If an employer holds a group policy to satisfy state group policy requirements, but has no right to any amounts contributed to the contract and all amounts are employee contributions, the employer is merely the nominal holder of the contract and the contract is not treated as held by a nonnatural person)."[26]

What is the significance of this letter ruling? First, it is only a private letter ruling. Moreover, its tentatively adverse conclusion was reached based on specific facts and circumstances. However, the authors believe that the conclusion reached was both logical and valid, and that the mere agency required for an entity to qualify as the "agent of a natural person" under Section 72(u)(1) is fundamentally incompatible with the nature of a valid business partnership in general, and, specifically, with the business purpose requirement the Service has applied to family limited partnerships in an estate planning context. Thus, in practice, the more successfully the taxpayer argues that the family limited partnership is a separate entity with a discrete business purpose to validate its discounts for estate planning purposes, the more it undermines the argument that the annuity should be tax-deferred under Section 72(u)(1). At the very least, a private letter ruling approving the claiming of the Section 72(u)(1) exception should be obtained before recommending that an annuity be owned by a family limited partnership.

3.8 Percent Medicare Surtax on Net Investment Income

The Patient Protection and Affordable Care Act of 2010 enacted numerous changes to the health insurance and health care delivery system. As a part of the revenue-raising section of the legislation, a new 3.8 percent Medicare surtax[27] on net investment income was enacted under Code Section 1411.

The new 3.8 percent surtax applies to any "net investment income" to the extent it exceeds specified thresholds (of $200,000 of modified Adjusted Gross Income for individuals, and $250,000 for married couples). For the purposes of the rule, investment income is interest, dividends, royalties, rents, passive income, net capital gains, and also income from annuities. This investment income is subsequently reduced by any deductions properly allocable to the associated income to arrive at "net" investment income subject to the 3.8 percent surtax.

As a result, to the extent that annuity income is included in income for tax purposes, and is part of the income that exceeds the thresholds, a 3.8 percent surtax will apply to the annuity income, in addition to any other ordinary income taxes that apply. Notably, though, this surtax only applies to annuity proceeds that are actually included *in income* for tax purposes; thus, only gains from the annuity will apply, whether distribution as amounts not received as an annuity, or as the taxable portion of annuitized income payments. Return of principal payments from the annuity are not included in investment income for the purposes of the 3.8 percent surtax.

Penalty for Early Distributions from a Deferred Annuity

In granting the benefit of tax-deferral to deferred annuities, Congress intended that they should be retirement plans. To discourage the use of annuities as short-term financial instruments by young people, it enacted Section 72(q), which imposes a ten percent penalty tax on certain premature payments or distributions from annuity contracts. The penalty applies only to payments to the extent that they are includable in taxable income. There are certain distributions to which the penalty does not apply:[28]

(A)   made on or after the date on which the taxpayer attains age fifty-nine and a half;

(B)   made on or after the death of the holder or, where the holder is not an individual, the death of the primary annuitant;

(C)   attributable to the taxpayer becoming disabled;[29]

(D)   which are a part of a series of substantially equal periodic payments, not less frequently than annually, made for the life (or life expectancy) of the taxpayer or the joint lives (or joint life expectancies) of the taxpayer and his designated beneficiary;[30]

(E)   from a qualified pension, profit sharing, or stock bonus plan, Section 403(b) annuity plan, or IRA;

(F)   allocable to investment in the contract before August 14, 1982;[31]

(G)   under a qualified funding asset;

(H)   subject to the ten percent penalty for withdrawals from a qualified retirement plan;[32]

(I)   under an immediate annuity contract;

(J)   which are purchased by an employer upon the termination of a qualified plan and which is held by the employer until such time as the employee separates from service.

It is important to note that, under the exemption for an immediate annuity, Revenue Ruling 92-95 states that "where a deferred annuity contract was exchanged for an immediate annuity contract, the purchase date of the new contract for purposes of the ten percent penalty tax was considered to be the date upon which the deferred annuity was purchased. Thus, payments from the replacement contract did not fall within the immediate annuity exception to the penalty tax."[33] This illustrates a significant common pitfall: where an immediate annuity is purchased directly, its payments will always be penalty-free; however, where an immediate annuity is acquired as part of an exchange from a deferred annuity contract, annuitization is not penalty-free unless the payments happen to meet another exception.

> *Example.* Assume individual A (under age fifty-nine and a half) purchases an immediate annuity for a five-year period certain payout, and individual B (also under age fifty-nine and a half) acquires an immediate annuity via an exchange from an existing deferred annuity for a five-year period certain payout. Individual A's payments will be penalty-free. Individual B's payments, however, will not, because a contract that was initially a deferred annuity and is converted to an immediate annuity later does not meet the immediate annuity requirements.[34]

> On the other hand, let's assume that both individuals A and B selected lifetime annuitization options. In this case, individual A's payments will again be penalty free. Individual B's payments will also be tax-free in this case, but not because the exchanged-for contract was an immediate annuity. Instead, individual B's payments should be tax-free, because they will also satisfy the requirements of subparagraph D, substantially equal periodic payments.

Where an annuity is held by a grantor trust, the application of the exceptions for the ten percent premature withdrawal penalty appear to be more ambiguous. With respect to the age fifty-nine and a half exception, the IRS has confirmed that the grantor's life will be the measuring life to determine whether the age fifty-nine and a half exception has been met.[35] However, the guidance from the IRS on this issue addresses only the opportunity for a grantor trust-owned annuity to be eligible for the age fifty-nine and a half based on the age of the grantor. It is not clear whether such an annuity ownership structure would also be eligible for exceptions based on the disability of the grantor, or to be made based on substantially equal periodic payments over the life of the grantor. Alternatively, it is notable that based on a clear application of the tax code itself, the opportunity to receive penalty-free distributions in the event of death will be triggered based on the life and death of the primary annuitant, not the grantor of the trust.[36]

In the case of an annuity held by a nongrantor trust, where the trust taxpayer has no age or life expectancy, it does not appear that the trust would be eligible for a premature withdrawal exception on account on age fifty-nine and a half, disability, or for substantially equal periodic payments. Instead, the annuity proceeds could only be accessed penalty tax-free as a withdrawal due to the death of the primary annuitant, or by distributing the annuity itself to a trust beneficiary for subsequent withdrawal.[37] However, some commentators have suggested that if the trust is simply the beneficial holder of the annuity on behalf of a trust beneficiary, then the benenficiary's age should be available for at least the age fifty-nine and a half exception, especially in the case of a simple trust.[38] Other commentators have suggested that, per the rules under Code Section 72(s)(6), the company might look to the primary annuitant to evaluate whether early withdrawal penalty exceptions may apply where the holder of the annuity is not a natural person. Although technically, 72(s)(6) explicitly states its annuitant-in-lieu-of-holder rule applies only for the purposes of subsection (s). Suffice it to say, in the case of a non-grantor trust, the determination of whose age/health is used to determine the exceptions to the early withdrawal penalty remains uncertain, and reporting in certain situations may vary from one insurer to another.

On the other hand, in the case where the nongrantor trust is also not eligible to be treated as an agent for a natural person, the contract itself will not be treated as an annuity for tax purposes; although this makes all gains in the contract taxable annually, it would also mean indirectly that the annuity would not be subject to the ten percent early withdrawal penalty.[39]

Tax Deduction for Annuity Losses

An income tax deduction for a loss may be taken by a taxpayer only when the loss is incurred in connection with the taxpayer's trade or business or in a transaction entered into for profit.[40]

"Generally, the purchase of a personal annuity contract is considered a transaction entered into for profit. Consequently, if a taxpayer sustains a loss upon surrender of a refund annuity contract, he may claim a deduction for the loss, regardless of whether he purchased the contract in connection with his trade or business or as a personal investment. The amount of the loss is determined by subtracting the cash surrender value from the taxpayer's basis for the contract. His basis is gross premium cost less all amounts previously received tax-free under the contract (e.g., any excludable dividends and the excludable portion of any prior annuity payments). The loss is ordinary loss, not capital loss. Rev. Rul. 61-201, 1961-2 CB 46; *Cohan v. Comm.*, 39 F.2d 540 (2nd Cir. 1930), *aff'g*, 11 BTA 743. But if the taxpayer purchased the contract for purely personal reasons, and not for profit, no loss deduction will be allowed. For example, in one case, the taxpayer purchased annuities on the lives of relatives, giving the relatives ownership of the contracts. Later he acquired the contracts by gift and surrendered them at a loss. The court disallowed a loss deduction on the ground that the contracts were not bought for profit but to provide financial security for the relatives. *Early v. Atkinson*, 175 F.2d 118 (4th Cir. 1949)."[41]

How is this loss claimed on taxpayer's income tax return? There is some dispute as to the correct method for claiming the loss. "Some say that the loss should be treated as a miscellaneous itemized deduction that is not subject to the two percent floor on miscellaneous itemized deductions. Others, including some at the Internal Revenue Service in unofficial comments, say it is a miscellaneous itemized deduction subject to the two percent floor. And finally, others take a more aggressive approach and say that the loss can be taken on the front of the Form 1040 on the line labeled 'Other gains or (losses).'"[42]

The authors believe that the proper place to take this deduction is as a miscellaneous itemized deduction subject to the two percent floor in light of Section 67(b), which states that all deductions are miscellaneous itemized deductions unless specifically listed in Section 67(b)(1) through Section 67(b)(12)—and deferred annuities surrendered at a loss are not so enumerated. Section 67(b) was designed as a catch-all category for, quite literally, any miscellaneous itemized deductions not specified by the tax code to be taken elsewhere, and accordingly it appears appropriate to claim annuity losses there. Notably, as of 2013, the IRS updated Publication 575 (page twenty-two) to indicate that nonqualified annuity losses should be taken in this manner; regrettably, though, the Service has not yet provided any binding guidance on the issue.

Unfortunately, this is clearly not the most favorable treatment, due to the application of the two percent of AGI floor on itemized deductions, the requirement for itemized deductions to exceed the threshold of the standard deduction, the phaseout of itemized deductions for high-income taxpayersand, most significantly, the adjustment (loss) of miscellaneous itemized deductions for the purposes of Alternative Minimum Tax under Section 55(b)(1)(A)(i). Nonetheless, at this point a more favorable treatment of annuity losses would require an Act of Congress to change or adopt a more favorable provision in the tax code.

Tax Treatment of Hybrid Annuity/Long-Term Care Policies

Under the Pension Protection Act of 2006, Congress established provisions for the favorable tax treatment of a hybrid annuity/long-term care insurance policy (and also hybrid life insurance/long-term care policies).[43]

Effective on January 1, 2010, the new rules stipulated that when an annuity policy also provides long-term care insurance benefits, the long-term care policy will be treated as a separate contract for tax purposes; accordingly, any benefits payments from the long-term care portion of the policy will be received tax-free, not as a taxable distribution from the annuity.[44] In addition, any premiums extracted from the annuity policy for long-term care coverage will not be treated as a taxable distribution from the annuity; instead, the cost basis of the annuity will be adjusted downwards (but not below zero dollars) for any long-term care premiums.[45] However, no medical expense deduction will be allowed for long-term care premiums extracted directly from the cash value of the hybrid annuity.

Notably, this treatment—which effectively treats all long-term care insurance premiums as being paid with after-tax dollars (the cost basis of the annuity)—can actually be less favorable on an ongoing basis than simply paying premiums with outside dollars and claiming any available Federal or state long-term care insurance premium deductions or credits. Although, for some taxpayers ineligible for such deductions or credits due to income, this aspect of tax treatment is a moot point. On the other hand, hybrid annuity/long-term care policies may still be preferred for their underwriting flexibility and partial-self-insurance benefits features, regardless of tax treatment.

The new rules apply only to nonqualified annuities[46] (i.e., not annuities held inside of a retirement account.

Exchanges of and for Annuities

Under Code Section 1035, "no gain or loss shall be recognized on the exchange of" a life insurance policy for an annuity[47] or an annuity contract for another annuity contract,[48] under the so-called like-kind exchange rules. Instead, the acquired annuity receives a carryover basis from the surrendered insurance or annuity policy.[49] It is notable that an exchange of an annuity policy for a life insurance policy is not eligible for 1035 exchange treatment,[50] although the reverse transaction is.

Where a policy is exchanged not solely in kind, and is instead exchanged for another policy of lesser value, and the owner also receives cash or other property to boot, this causes recognition of taxable gain for the lesser of the amount of boot received or unrecognized gain.[51] However, if the owner has exchanged an annuity at a loss, the receipt of boot does not cause the loss to be recognized.[52] If an annuity meets the provisions of Section 1035, then no loss will be recognized, and the receipt of boot cannot change this. In addition, it is notable that application of Section 1035 is mandatory when its provisions are met—it is not an election, but is instead an automatic provision that applies when its stipulations are satisfied.

When a life insurance policy with a loan is exchanged for an annuity, the extinguishing of the loan with the proceeds of the insurance policy is considered to be the receipt of boot to the extent of the loan. Consequently, gain recognition will occur for the lesser of boot received (loan extinguished) or gain in the contract. Unfortunately, while transfer of the loan to an acquired life insurance contract will allow the insurance policy owner to avoid boot treatment,[53] this option is not available for an annuity, because a loan against an annuity is considered a withdrawal.[54]

Over the years, the IRS has clarified its views on what does and does not constitute a 1035 exchange through a series of revenue rulings, and to some extent through private letter rulings. Thus, the IRS has declared that a surrender and immediate subsequent purchase of an annuity does not qualify as a 1035 exchange if the taxpayer ever has control of the proceeds of the initial annuity.[55] However, a taxpayer can exchange an annuity into an existing annuity,[56] can combine multiple policies into a single annuity,[57] or can exchange a policy plus cash to a receiving annuity.[58] The receipt of cash in an exchange can be taxable boot, but the addition of cash to the exchange is not boot.

Under the new rules for hybrid annuity/long-term care insurance policies, Congress expanded Section 1035 to explicitly allow the exchange of a traditional annuity for a hybrid annuity/long-term care policy on a tax-deferred basis.[59] In addition, the new rules also allow for the direct tax-free exchange of an annuity policy for a qualified long-term care insurance policy.[60]

For many years, there was question about whether a taxpayer could complete a partial 1035 exchange, where a partial surrender from an annuity is exchanged for a new annuity contract while the remaining cash value stays in the existing, original policy. The IRS fought transactions of this nature for fear that taxpayers would use it as a tax avoidance scheme, where a partial exchange is completed and the new annuity is subsequently surrendered for a smaller recognized taxable gain than would have occurred if the original annuity contract had been partially surrendered. However, after losing a partial 1035 exchange case in court,[61] the IRS finally acquiesced to allow partial 1035 exchanges.[62]

Under current final rules issued in 2008, as updated by Revenue Procedure 2011-38, partial 1035 exchanges are allowed as long as the taxpayer does not take any withdrawals from either contract (the old or the new one) within 180 days of the partial exchange.[63] When a partial 1035 exchange is completed, the basis is divided pro rata between the old contract and the new one based on the relative value of the contracts when the split occurred. If a withdrawal does occur from either contract within the 180-day period, it will be taxed "in a manner consistent with its substance, based on general tax principles and all the facts and circumstances," generally as either boot received (from the original contract) and/or as a distribution.[64] A partial exchange of an existing deferred annuity into an immediate annuity is guaranteed to be treated as a tax-deferred 1035 exchange, as long as the immediate annuity is payable for a period of at least 10 years or for the lifetime(s) of the annuitant.[65] Notably, a prior rule in the temporary guidance issued in 2003, requiring that the taxpayer should not have contemplated inappropriate withdrawals at the time of the partial exchange, is not present in the final rules, nor is the rule from the 2008 guidance that stipulated an early withdrawal, within the 180-day period, can be excused if made for certain specified reasons (e.g., due to death, disability, divorce, or loss of employment).

Annuity contributions generally retain their original character after a Section 1035 exchange. Consequently, a contract with pre-August 13, 1982 contributions will retain treatment of those contributions even if the contract is subsequently exchanged via Section 1035[66] (see prior discussion of contracts entered into before August 13, 1982). Note, however, that a contract with pre-October 21, 1979 contributions will not retain the step-up in basis treatment at the death of the owner.[67] However, this tracing of the original contract contributions has its drawbacks: when a deferred annuity is exchanged for an immediate annuity, the original contribution date holds as the purchase date for the immediate annuity, and if not within one year of original purchase, the immediate annuity will not qualify for Section 72(q)(2)(I) provisions for the avoidance of the early withdrawal penalty.

A planning technique sometimes recommended by aggressive planners involves the harvesting of an otherwise nondeductible loss in a life insurance policy by using a tax-free exchange of that policy, under Code Section035, for a deferred annuity having no surrender charges, and subsequent surrender of that annuity, which will have acquired the substituted cost basis of the exchanged life policy, for an allegedly deductible loss. In the authors' opinion, the success of this strategy is questionable if the annuity is surrendered shortly after the exchange.

The IRS may well regard this as a step transaction and disallow the loss deduction, holding that the substance of the transaction—the surrender of the original life insurance policy—holds over the form of the transaction, the apparent surrender of an annuity policy. In addition, there is some risk that the IRS will adjust the cost basis of life insurance in such situations by reducing it for prior cost of insurance charges, dramatically diminishing or eliminating any losses, as applies when a life insurance policy is sold to an unrelated person or otherwise disposed of, especially for a loss.[68]

Gift or Sale of an Annuity

If the owner of an annuity transfers that annuity, by sale, to another taxpayer, there may be both gift tax and income tax consequences. Annuities may also be transferred by gift. Although gifts are not subject to income tax, they may be subject to federal and/or state gift tax.

Gift of a Deferred Annuity

An individual who transfers an annuity contract issued after April 22, 1987, for less than full and adequate consideration, is treated as having received as an amount not received as an annuity an amount equal to the excess of the cash surrender value of the contract at the time of transfer over the investment in the contract at that time.[69] Thus, the transferor realizes, in the year of the transfer, any gain on the contract. The transferee's cost basis will be the donor's adjusted cost in light of the tax recognition event, plus the donee's cost (if any), adjusted for, or increased by any gift tax actually paid.

An exception regarding the timing of income recognition applies if the contract was entered into prior to April 23rd, 1987; in such cases, the gain is not recognized by the donor until it is surrendered by the donee, although it is still the donor that recognizes the gain.[70] In this case, the subsequent gain after the transfer date would be taxable to the donee; only the embedded gain as of the transfer date is taxable back to the original donor. If there is a partial surrender by the donee of a pre-April 23rd, 1987 contract, there is no current guidance about how to apportion the gain recognition between the pre-transfer amount allocable to the donor and the post-transfer amount allocable to the donee. Nonetheless, the normal rules to determine the taxable gain for amounts not received as an annuity still apply, including the gains-first standard rule, and also the opportunity to harvest pre-August 13, 1982, cost basis first.

If the receiving donee is a charity, then a charitable deduction will also be available. For a post-April 22nd, 1987 annuity, the full value of the contract will be eligible for a charitable deduction,[71] but only because the full amount of the gain is recognized on the transfer. Thus, the value of the charitable deduction has been effectively reduced by the amount of gain that was also recognized on the transfer. In the case of a pre-April 23rd, 1987 annuity, where the donation is for ordinary income property and there is no income recognition at the time of transfer—because the gain is delayed until the donee surrenders the contract—the charitable deduction allowed will be limited to the cost basis of the contract as a donation of ordinary income property.[72] Notably, if the charity surrenders the gifted contract in the year received, the net result is equivalent under either treatment. In addition, when property is donated with a fair market value which is less than the cost basis (i.e., property at a loss) the amount of the gift is restricted to the fair market value of the property.[73]

So the bottom line is that the taxation of any gain in an annuity contract cannot be avoided or shifted to another party via a gift. The gain will still be fully recognized by the donor. At best, the timing of that gain recognition may be delayed, depending on when the contract was issued, and when the donee ultimately surrenders the contract. Consequently, it will virtually always be best to surrender an annuity first and then donate it, allowing the donor to recognize the annuity loss, or recognize the gain but ensure that the charitable deduction will be for the fair market value of the contract. In most cases, though, this usually means that it's in the client's best interests to donate some other kind of appreciated property instead for various estate or charitable planning purposes in the first place!

There are some exceptions to the gratuitous transfer rules, though. This rule does not apply to transfers between spouses or between former spouses incident to a divorce and pursuant to an instrument executed or modified after July 18, 1984.[74] In addition, "the IRS has ruled privately that the distribution of an annuity contract by a trust to a trust beneficiary will not be treated as an assignment for less than full and adequate consideration (i.e., a gift) since, for purposes of this rule, the trust is not considered to be an individual."[75]

Sale of a Deferred Annuity

The naming of a new owner of an annuity in exchange for full and adequate consideration is a sale of the annuity. The seller must recognize any gain as ordinary income.[76] However, there is no clear case law, statute, or regulations regarding the tax treatment of an annuity sale where the sale price exceeds the surrender value of the contract.[77]

In the case of a deferred annuity, the best analogous treatment may be the taxation of life insurance to a third party, which is currently treated as ordinary income to the extent of existing gain in the contract, and capital gains for any excess amount realized above the cash surrender value of the annuity.[78]

The treatment of the sale of a deferred annuity for a loss remains unclear. Some have theorized that it is still subject to the existing treatment for a loss when an annuity is surrendered (i.e., miscellaneous itemized deduction subject to the two percent-of-AGI floor), while others suggest that perhaps ordinary loss or even capital loss treatment would be more appropriate; the IRS has thus far remained silent on the issue.

In the case of an immediate annuity (i.e., where the contract is sold after maturity), "the cost basis of the contract, for purposes of computing the seller's gain, must be reduced by the aggregate excludable portions of the annuity payments that have been received. But the adjusted cost basis cannot be reduced below zero, for example, where the annuitant has outlived his life expectancy and was able to exclude amounts in excess of his net premium cost on a contract that was annuitized prior to January 1, 1987.[79] The taxable gain can never be greater than the sale price. Where an [immediate] annuity contract is sold for less than its cost basis, apparently the seller realizes an ordinary loss."[80]

Transfers of Annuities to Trusts

Generally speaking, the transfer of ownership of an annuity is a taxable event for both income tax and gift tax purposes, as discussed above. When ownership of an annuity is transferred to a trust, though, the tax consequences depend upon the nature of the trust.

1. The transfer of an annuity from an owner to the owner's revocable trust is not a taxable event for income or gift tax purposes, assuming that the trust is fully revocable and, thus, does not represent a completed gift or a change in ownership.[81]

2. The transfer of an annuity from an owner to the owner's irrevocable grantor trust is a problematic situation under the existing guidance on annuities. Although some would assert that the transfer should not be a taxable event for income tax purposes, because the trust is a grantor trust, the contribution of an annuity may be a taxable gift, since the gift is irrevocably completed. To the extent that the recognition of gain for an annuity transfer occurs anytime there is a "transfer without full and adequate consideration,"[82] and a contribution to an irrevocable grantor trust as a taxable gift without consideration, it thus appears to constitute a transfer without consideration. The authors believe that there is a risk that a transfer to an irrevocable grantor trust may still result in the recognition of gain when the transfer occurs, notwithstanding the trust's grantor status. In addition, to the extent that gain is triggered by any annuity not for full and adequate consideration, even a partial transfer with retained rights that represents an incomplete gift may still trigger income tax recognition as a transfer. As of the publication of the fourth edition of this book, the IRS has still not issued definitive guidance on this issue. See treatment of this issue in Chapter 10, Annuities and Trusts.

3. The transfer of an annuity from an owner to the owner's irrevocable nongrantor trust will trigger recognition of policy gain, because the transfer is without adequate consideration and the owner of the trust for income tax purposes is unambiguously someone other than the grantor, by virtue of the trust not being a grantor trust.[83] In addition, such transfers should be conducted cautiously, because if the transferee trust does not qualify as the agent of a natural person, the contract will no longer qualify as an annuity for income tax purposes,[84] and any income on the contract will be treated as taxable ordinary income to the trust owner,[85] in addition to the income tax gain recognition upon the transfer itself to the original owner. Moreover, the full value of the annuity will be considered a taxable gift for gift tax purposes, less the annual exclusion amount, if applicable.

Annuities Held within IRAs

An annuity held in an Individual Retirement Account (IRA)—a so-called qualified annuity—is taxed first and foremost under the rules applicable to retirement accounts; the general rules applicable to annuities under Section 72 do not apply. In this context, the annuity held within an IRA is simply an asset the IRA owns in a manner not unlike the IRA's ownership of a stock or bond.

However, due to perceived abuses where annuities have been held inside of IRAs as a method to avoid income taxation, the IRS and Treasury have altered the method by which annuities are valued for certain IRA taxable events in an effort to crack down on inappropriate tax avoidance strategies. As a result, special rules apply to the valuation of annuities held inside of IRAs for the purpose of both the calculation of required minimum distributions from annuities, and also when an IRA Roth conversion includes an annuity.

Required Minimum Distributions for IRA Annuities

Deferred Annuities

When a deferred annuity is held by an IRA, the annuity continues to be taxed under the rules applicable to IRAs; as a result, the IRA annuity will be subject to required minimum distributions under the normally applicable rules for IRA owners.

In calculating a required minimum distribution, the general rule requires IRA owners to divide the value of the entire interest of the IRA by the applicable distribution period. However, in the case of an IRA owned annuity, the value of the entire interest must include both the actual dollar value of the contract and the actuarial present value of any additional benefits, measured without regard to the individual's actual health.[86]

This requirement to include the actuarial present value of additional benefits is directed primarily towards the death and living benefit riders associated with today's variable annuity contracts. The concern of the Treasury was that in some situations, the fair market value of the annuity recognizing the value of additional benefits could be significantly higher than the actual dollar value of the annuity, producing a disparity that would result in an artificially reduced withdrawal for required minimum distribution purposes. For example, an annuity having a cash value of $300,000, but a current death benefit of $500,000, would arguably be worth something more than just $300,000 for an eighty-eight-year-old annuity owner. Under the new rules, the actuarial value of the excess $200,000 of pending death benefit would increase the total value of the account to something more than $300,000, and that higher value must be used to calculate the year's required minimum distribution.

To simplify the application of this rule slightly, the Treasury regulations do provide that if the value of any additional benefits are reduced on a pro-rata basis in the event of withdrawals, and the actuarial present value would add less than twenty percent to the value of the annuity, then the value of the additional benefits may be disregarded, and the entire interest will simply be treated as the actual dollar value of the contract.[87] In addition, if the only additional benefit is a return of premium death benefit guarantee, then the additional death benefit can be ignored for valuation purposes, regardless of the actuarial present value of that guarantee.[88]

Many contracts will be able to ignore the application of these new rules, because the value of additional benefits is not likely to add more than twenty percent to the value of the contract for relatively new contracts; but this exception still only applies to contracts where withdrawals will reduce the benefits on a pro-rata basis. Readers should be cautious on this issue, because many of today's additional benefit riders, particularly living benefit riders, do not exclusively offer pro-rata withdrawals. Many of these provide dollar-for-dollar withdrawals instead, or a hybrid treatment of partial dollar-for-dollar up to a specified amount followed by pro-rata withdrawals. In such cases, the entire amount of the actuarial present value must be included for required minimum distribution purposes. In most cases, annuity owners will need to contact the annuity company to obtain a valuation—incorporating the actuarial present value of rider benefits—for required minimum distribution purposes. On the other hand, it's important to note that the valuation of the annuity should only be its cash value plus the actuarial present value of its other benefits. Thus, an annuity with a cash value of $300,000 and a death benefit of $500,000 would have a value of $300,000 plus the cost of one-year term insurance for the remaining $200,000 death benefit based on the annuity owner's current age; it would not be appropriate to simply calculate the RMD based on the $500,000 gross death benefit amount.

In extreme cases, the requirement to incorporate the actuarial value of riders can actually cause a cash shortage for the annuity itself. In contracts where withdrawals reduce the death benefit on a dollar-for-dollar basis, some annuity owners have chosen to nearly exhaust the cash value of the contract, retaining only a death benefit. For example, if the owner of the aforementioned annuity with a $300,000 cash value and a $500,000 death benefit took a $299,000 withdrawal, the remaining annuity would have a $1,000 cash value and a $201,000 death benefit, anticipating that a required minimum distribution would only withdraw a fraction of the $1,000 death benefit. However, if the age of the annuity owner is high enough, such that the actuarial present value of the annuity increases significantly, it may even be possible that the required minimum distribution based on the actuarial value would be higher than the entire $1,000 cash value! In this case, the IRA owner may wish to take a withdrawal from another IRA to satisfy the required minimum distribution, since ultimately, all required minimum distributions and their tax consequences may be aggregated amongst IRAs.[89] However, if no other IRAs remain, the annuity owner may be forced to liquidate the entire annuity contract simply to extract the required minimum distribution, forfeiting the entire death benefit in the process.

Immediate Annuities

In the case of annuity contracts that are annuitized within an IRA or other retirement account, the Treasury Regulations evaluate annuitized contracts on a standalone basis to determine whether they meet the Required Minimum Distribution (RMD) rules. Generally, any annuitized payments within a retirement account will satisfy the associated RMD obligations for those dollar amounts by definition; the rules actually do not permit an annuitized contract within a retirement account unless the annuitization will satisfy the rules in the first place. This is done by ensuring that payments will begin in a timely manner (unless meeting the Qualified Longevity Annuity Contract rules discussed below), that the payments do not disproportionately shift benefits to later years (e.g., with uneven payments or significant cost-of-living adjustments), and that any incidental benefits to joint annuitants or beneficiaries are limited (to again avoid disproportionately shifting payments beyond the lifetime of the owner).[90]

Notably, because the rules for annuitized amounts inside a retirement account are treated entirely separately, it is *not* permissible to use the dollar payments from an annuitized contract to satisfy the RMD obligations for the remainder of the account, even if the annuitized payments are larger than what may have otherwise been due.

> *Example.* Harold has a $500,000 account that has a $20,000 RMD due this year. Harold chooses to split the account and annuitize half (Part A) while continuing to keep the remainder invested (Part B). The annuitization of Part A will produce a payment of $15,000/year going forward.

> For the initial year, Harold's RMD is already due for an amount of $20,000, such that his first payment of $15,000 (assuming it does in fact occur this year) will satisfy most of his RMD, and only the remaining $5,000 is due from Part B of the account.

> However, in future years after the initial year, the accounts are treated as being entirely separate. Thus, next year, if Harold's Part B account rises in value and his RMD is $11,000, he must still take the entire $11,000 from that account, and cannot count any of the $15,000 from the annuitized Part A towards his Part B RMD. This remains true even though Harold's RMD from Part A would have only been $11,000 as well, had he not annuitized the account; the "excess" $4,000 from Part A still cannot count towards Part B after the initial year.

> If Harold had not already reached his Required Beginning Date at the time of annuitization, the RMDs for Part B would always be determined entirely separately, and the RMDs for Part A would always be satisfied simply by virtue of the fact that the annuity met the requirements to be an retirement-account-annuitized contract in the first place.

Qualified Longevity Annuity Contracts Held Inside of IRAs

In recent years, there has been growing interest in what has variously been called a Deferred Income Annuity (DIA) or Longevity Annuity (see Chapter 13 for further discussion). Similar to a single premium immediate annuity, the purchaser of a longevity annuity trades off a current lump sum in exchange for a series of payments, either for a period certain, for life, or a combination of the two. However, unlike a single premium *immediate* annuity, the deferred income annuity does not begin payments until some future date, like age eighty or eighty-five. By waiting until a later start date for payments to begin, the size of the payments is significantly larger when they do begin, a combination of both the implied return on the underlying assets and the accumulation of significant mortality credits.

However, the introduction of longevity annuities inside of an IRA (or other retirement account) presents a unique challenge: how can such an annuity comply with the Requirement Minimum Distribution (RMD) rules that generally begin at age seventy and a half, if the longevity annuity is not to begin payments until age eighty or later?

To address this concern, in March of 2012 the IRS and Treasury issued Proposed Regulations 1.401(a)(9)-6, Q&A-17 to address the coordination of RMDs and longevity annuities. The regulations stipulate that a Qualified Longevity Annuity Contract (QLAC) will be treated as a separate account that inherently satisfies the RMD rules, as long as the QLAC itself complies with the regulation requirement. Thus, RMDs would continue to be due only from remaining non-QLAC-annuitized account balances.

In order to be "qualified, such a retirement-account-owned longevity annuity (the rules apply to IRAs, employer retirement plans under Section 401(a), Section 403(b) plans, and governmental Section 457 plans) must be fixed (it cannot be a variable or equity-indexed contract), it must state that it is intended to be a QLAC when issued, and also must include the following features:

1) Premiums paid for a QLAC must be the lesser of:

   a. $100,000 (adjusted for inflation) across all retirement accounts owned by the taxpayer. (Technically the limit for contributions is calculated as $100,000, adjusted for inflation, minus all the premiums previously paid for the current QLAC or any other QLACs owned by that individual in other qualified retirem-net accounts.)

   b. twenty-five percent of the participant's account balance (with all IRAs aggregated for purposes of this calculation), adjusted for previous premiums paid into that QLAC or any other QLAC purchased for the account owner in the retirement account.

2) QLAC payments to the annuitant must begin no later than age eighty-five.

3) QLAC payments must otherwise satisfy the RMD regulations when payments do begin.

4) The QLAC must not offer any commutation benefit, cash surrender, or similar features.

5)   The QLAC may only pay the following limited death benefit features:

    a.   If the beneficiary is solely a surviving spouse:

    i.   If death occurs after the annuity's starting date, the only benefit permitted is a life annuity payable to the surviving spouse in an amount no more than 100 percent of the original payment amount

    ii.   If death occurs before the annuity's starting date, the only benefit permitted is a life annuity payable to the surviving spouse that must commence no later than it would have begun to the original employee, and the amount may only exceed 100 percent of the original annuity payment if doing so is necessary to satisfy the qualified preretirement survivor annuity rules.

    b.   If the beneficiary is a nonspouse:

    i.   The only survivor benefit permitted is a continuing life annuity for the beneficiary, where the maximum beneficiary payment is a limited percentage of the original payment based on the age difference between the original owner on the benefit,[91] and those payments must begin by the end of the year following the year of death.

    ii.   In order for these rules to apply, the QLAC must also provide that either there is no pre-annuity-starting-date death benefit, or that the beneficiary of the pre-annuity-starting-date death benefit is *irrevocably* selected before the retirement account owner's Required Beginning Date.

Notably, in the end the proposed QLAC regulations are simply intended to clear the way for (qualified) longevity annuities to be made available to owners of employer retirement plans; without the regulations, purchasing such an annuity could actually have violated the RMD rules. With the QLAC regulations, it is now feasible to purchase such a contract inside a retirement plan while still complying with the account owner's RMD obligations, at least up to the limited dollar amounts permitted. Whether it is actually desirable to purchase a QLAC as a part of the individual's retirement plan depends on further details, as discussed in Chapter 13 on longevity annuities.

Roth Conversions for IRA Annuities

Where an IRA annuity is converted to a Roth, the fair market value of the annuity must be included in income for the purposes of the Roth conversion.[92] In the case of a Roth conversion, similar rules to those applicable for determining required minimum distributions must be applied to ensure that the annuity contract is fairly valued.

In final Treasury regulations issued in the summer of 2008, the Treasury indicated three allowable methods to determine the fair market value of an IRA annuity for Roth conversion purposes. These methods are:

- *Comparable Contract.* Where the insurance company currently offers annuity contracts similar to the contract owned in the IRA, the fair market value of the annuity is the cost to acquire a comparable contract from the insurer at the annuity owner's current age under market conditions available at the time. If the conversion occurs soon after the annuity is sold, a comparable contract value may simply be the premiums paid for the existing annuity.[93]

- *Reserve Method.* Where there is no comparable contract currently available in the marketplace to provide a cost comparison for valuation purposes, the fair market value may be determined based on the interpolated terminal reserve held by the annuity company on the date of the conversion, plus the proportionate part of the gross premium last paid if that premium covers a period extending beyond the conversion date.[94]

- *Accumulation Method.* As an alternative to the aforementioned methods, the taxpayer may value the annuity using the same rules applicable for determining value under the required minimum distribution rules discussed earlier. In this case, the annuity's fair market value is equal to the actual dollar value of the contract, plus the actuarial present value of any additional benefits. However, in the case of a Roth conversion valuation, the actuarial present value of all additional benefits must be included, and even a de minimis value cannot be disregarded. Furthermore, no distributions can be assumed in the process of determining the actuarial present value of benefits. Finally, any front-end loads or other non-recurring charges assessed in the twelve months preceding the conversion must also be added back into the value.[95]

In practice, most taxpayers holding deferred annuities inside of an IRA will use the third method—the accumulation method—as it is the easiest match for today's IRA annuities, especially variable annuities with various living and death benefit riders. Notably, though, the Treasury Regulations state that "if, because of the unusual nature of the contract, the value determined under [one of these methods] does not reflect the full value of the contract, that method may not be used."[96]

If the annuity contract is surrendered pursuant to the Roth conversion rollover itself, the fair market value for tax purposes will be considered to be the cash surrender value of the annuity (i.e., the net amount actually transferred), assuming no rights of the annuity are retained.[97]

The purpose of these rules is to eliminate any possibility that an IRA annuity owner can attempt to evade income taxation by artificially reducing the value of an annuity at the time of Roth conversion given that subsequent qualified withdrawals from the Roth IRA would also be tax-free.

Endnotes

1. Technically, qualified annuity refers only to an annuity purchased to fund a qualified retirement plan offered by a participant's employer, such as a pension or profit sharing plan, 403(b) plan, SEPP, etc. An IRA (either traditional or Roth) is not a qualified plan, in the strict sense of that term. However, many, but not all, of the rules governing IRAs are similar to—and in some cases, identical to—those governing qualified plans, such as the required minimum distribution rules (RMD rules of Section 401(a)(9), and very different from the rules governing ordinary savings plans, so that the terms qualified annuity and qualified money (to describe money held in a qualified plan) are commonly used in reference to an annuity purchased to fund a qualified plan or an IRA.

2. *Tax Facts on Insurance & Employee Benefits* (The National Underwriter Company, 2014), Q 402.

3. *Ibid.*

4. IRC Sec. 72(b); Treas. Reg. §1.72-3.

5. Treas. Reg. §1.72-2(b)(3).

6. IRC Sec. 72(b)(2).

7. This "exclusion ratio" treatment was confirmed for one "first generation" DIA (having no death benefit prior to Annuity Starting Date) in Let. Rul. 200939018.

8. Treas. Reg. §1.401(a)(9)-6.

9. IRC Sec. 72(e)(1)(B); *Tax Facts on Insurance & Employee Benefits* (The National Underwriter Company, 2014), Q 404.

10. *Tax Facts on Insurance & Employee Benefits* (The National Underwriter Company, 2014), Q 404.

11. *Tax Facts on Insurance & Employee Benefits* (The National Underwriter Company, 2014), Q 404; IRC Sec. 72(e)(3).

12. IRC Sec. 72(e)(4)(A).

13. IRC Sec. 72(e)(12).

14. *Tax Facts on Insurance & Employee Benefits* (The National Underwriter Company, 2014), Q 404; IRC Sec. 72(e)(5).

15. IRC Secs. 72(e)(2)(B), 72(e)(3)(A).

16. IRC Secs. 72(e)(5)(E), 72(e)(5)(A).

17. IRC Sec. 72(e)(5)(A)(ii).

18. It is worth stating, again, that the word "deferred," in the term "deferred annuity" does not refer to the tax treatment just described, but to the fact that annuity income will not commence immediately upon purchase of the contract, but will instead be deferred until some point in the future. Some deferred annuities impose a limit upon deferral by mandating that annuity payments commence no later than at annuitant's attainment of a certain age.

19. IRC Sec. 72(u)(1)(A).

20. "'Income on the contract' is the excess of (1) the sum of the net surrender value of the contract at the end of the taxable year and any amounts distributed under the contract during the taxable year and any prior taxable year over (2) the sum of the net premiums (amount of premiums paid under the contract reduced by any policyholder dividends) under the contract for the taxable year and prior taxable years and any amounts includable in gross income for prior taxable years under this requirement. IRC Sec. 72(u)(2)." *Tax Facts on Insurance & Employee Benefits* (The National Underwriter Company, 2014), Q 403.

21. IRC Sec. 72(u)(1)(B).

22. IRC Sec. 72(u)(3).

23. A qualified funding asset is any annuity contract issued by a licensed insurance company that is purchased and held to fund periodic payments for damages, by suit or agreement, on account of personal physical injury or sickness. IRC Sec. 130(d).

24. *Tax Facts on Insurance & Employee Benefits* (The National Underwriter Company, 2014), Q 403.

25. Let. Rul. 199944020.

26. *Ibid.*

27. "Although commonly discussed in the context of the legislation as a "Medicare" surtax, in practice the new tax on net investment income is not specifically earmarked for the Medicare trust fund, and instead is simply part of the general

tax revenue of the Federal government. Accordingly, some simply refer to this as a "3.8 percent surtax on net investment income" without regard to the Medicare label, though it was referred to as such in the original legislation."

28. The authors' descriptions of the Section 72(q)(2) exceptions have been abbreviated for clarity. For more detailed descriptions, see *Tax Facts on Insurance & Employee Benefits* (The National Underwriter Company, 2014), Q 405.

29. "Disabled" is defined in Section 72(m)(7), which states: "[F]or purposes of this section, an individual shall be considered to be disabled if he is unable to engage in any substantial gainful activity by reason of any medically determinable physical or mental impairment which can be expected to result in death or to be of long-continued and indefinite duration. An individual shall not be considered to be disabled unless he furnishes proof of the existence thereof in such form and manner as the Secretary may require."

30. Under IRS Notice 2004-15, 2004-9 IRB 526, taxpayers seeking substantially equal periodic payments from annuities under Section 72(q)(2)(D), may rely on the guidance of IRS Notice 89-25 1989-1 CB 662, as modified by Revenue Ruling 2002-62, 2002-2 CB 710, which provides explanation and rules regarding substantially equal periodic payments from retirement accounts under Section 72(t).

31. This provision is actually somewhat redundant. Section 72(q)(1) already indicates that the penalty will apply only to amounts includable in gross income, and Section 72(e)(5) already indicates that withdrawals allocable to investment in the contract before August 14th, 1982 will not be included in income (and thus could not be subject to penalty).

32. This prevents the imposition of a Section 72(q)(1) early withdrawal penalty on a qualified annuity that is already subject to the early withdrawal penalty rules under Section 72(t).

33. Rev. Rul. 92-95, 1992-2 CB 43.

34. Section 72(u)(4)(B) requires the annuity starting date to be no later than one year from the date of purchase to qualify as an immediate annuity—when the purchase date of the original contract must be applied under Revenue Ruling 92-95, it will almost always be beyond the 1-year period.

35. Treasury General Information Letter, issued June 29, 2001.

36. IRC Secs. 72(q)(2)(B), 72(s)(6).

37. Let. Ruls. 9204010, 9204014, and 199905015.

38. Underwood, J. Gary, "Trust Ownership of Nonqualified Annuities: General Consideration for Trustees", *Journal of Financial Service Professionals*, May, 2010. See also Treasury Regulation §1.652(b)-1 and H R Report No 99-841 (TRA 1986).

39. IRC Sec. 72(u).

40. IRC Sec. 165.

41. *Tax Facts on Insurance & Employee Benefits* (The National Underwriter Company, 2014), Q 433.

42. *Ibid.*

43. Section 844 of Pension Protection Act of 2006.

44. IRC Sec. 7702B(e)(1),

45. IRC Sec. 72(e)(11).

46. IRC Sec. 7702B(e)(4).

47. IRC Sec. 1035(a)(1).

48. IRC Sec. 1035(a)(3).

49. IRC Secs. 1035(d)(2), 1031(d).

50. Treas. Reg. §1.1035-1(c).

51. IRC Secs. 1035(d)(1), 1031(b).

52. IRC Secs. 1035(d)(1), 1031(c).

53. Let. Ruls. 8604033, 9044022.

54. IRC Sec. 72(e)(4)(A).

55. Let. Ruls. 8515063, 8810010.

56. Rev. Rul. 2002-75, 2002-2 CB 812.

57. Let. Rul. 9708016.

58. Let. Rul. 9820018.

59. IRC Sec. 1035(b)(2).

60. IRC Sect. 1035(a)(3).

61. *Conway v. Comm.*, 111 TC 350 (1998).

62. See Rev. Rul. 2003-76, 2003-2 CB 355.

63. See Rev. Proc 2008-24, 2008-1 CB 684, *superseding*, IRS Notice 2003-51, 2003-2 CB 362, Sec. 4.01.

64. Rev Proc 2011-38, Secs. 2.09, 4.01.

65. Rev Proc 2011-38, Secs. 2.07, 2.09, and also Section 2113 of the Small Business Jobs Act of 2010.

66. Rev. Rul. 85-159, 1985-2 CB 29.

67. See Rev. Rul. 79-335, 1979-2 CB 292, Let. Rul. 9245035, and TAM 9346002.

68. Rev. Rul. 2009-13, 2009-21 IRB 1029; also, *Keystone Consolidated Publishing Co* (1932) 26 BTA 1210 and *Century Wood Preserving Co v. Comm.* (1934, CA3) 13 AFTR 910.

69. IRC Sec. 72(e)(4)(C).

70. Rev. Rul. 69-102, 1969-1 CB 32

71. Treas. Reg. §1.170A-4(a).

72. IRC Sec. 170(e)(1)(A).

73. Treas. Reg. §1.170A-1(c)(1).

74. IRC Sec. 72(e)(4)(c)(ii).

75. Let. Ruls. 9204010, 9204014, 199905015, 201124008.

76. *First Nat'l Bank of Kansas City v. Comm.*, 309 F.2d 587 (8th Cir. 1962); *Estate of Katz v. Comm.*, TC Memo 1961-270; *Roff v. Comm.*, 304 F.2d 450 (3rd Cir. 1962) *aff'g*, 36 TC 818; *Arnfeld v. U.S.*, 163 F. Supp. 865 (Ct. Cl. 1958), *cert. denied*, 359 U.S. 943.

77. For example, assume an annuity with a $50,000 cost basis and a $75,000 surrender value was sold for $85,000. Perhaps this is because it provides a contractual interest rate guarantee that is more appealing than current market rates. Clearly the $25,000 gain from cost basis to surrender value must be taxed as ordinary income; however, it is not clear whether the additional $10,000 of gain would be taxed as though it were an amount not received as an annuity (i.e., ordinary income treatment), or the sale of the entire annuity contract as though it were a capital assets (i.e., capital gain treatment).

78. Rev. Rul. 2009-13, 2009-21 IRB 1029.

79. Treas. Reg. §1.1021-1.

80. *Tax Facts on Insurance & Employee Benefits* (The National Underwriter Company, 2014), Q 435.

81. IRC Secs. 671 - 677.

82. Treas. Reg. §25.2511-2(c).

83. IRC Sec. 72(e)(4)(C).

84. IRC Sec. 72(u)(1).

85. IRC Sec. 72(u)(1)(B).

86. Treas. Reg. §1.401(a)(9)-6, Q&A-12(a) & (b).

87. Treas. Reg. §1.401(a)(9)-6, Q&A-12(c)(1).

88. Treas. Reg. §1.401(a)(9)-6, Q&A-12(c)(2).

89. IRC Sec. 408(d)(2).

90. T reas. Reg. §1.401(a)(9)-6.

91. Adjustment tables provided in Treas. Reg. §1.401(a)(9)-6, Q&-17(c)(2)(iv).

92. Treas. Reg. §1.408A-4, Q&A-14(a).

93. Treas. Reg. §1.408A-4, Q&A-14(b)(2)(i).

94. Treas. Reg. §1.408A-4, Q&A-14(b)(2)(ii).

95. Treas. Reg. §1.408A-4, Q&A-14(b)(3).

96. Treas. Reg. 1.408A-4, Q&A-14(b)(1).

97. Treas. Reg. §1.408A-4, Q&A-14(a)(2).

Chapter 3

Taxation of Annuity Death Benefits

The taxation of death benefits of nonqualified annuities is a particularly difficult subject for many advisors. Most of the difficulty lies not in whether or how such proceeds are taxable, but in when and how they must be paid out to beneficiaries. The rules governing required payouts upon death are complicated and sometimes unclear. In at least one important area, when and how a nonspousal beneficiary of a deferred annuity must take death proceeds, the rules in the Internal Revenue Code appear to be contradictory (see "What About IRC Section 72(h)?" below). Fortunately, not all of the rules are this difficult. We will begin our examination with the easier stuff—the relatively straightforward rules of how death proceeds of nonqualified annuities are treated for estate tax purposes.

Estate Taxation

If the value of an annuity contract does not terminate entirely upon the death of the contract owner, leaving nothing to pass to the owner's estate or beneficiaries, any remaining value is taxable in the owner's estate for estate tax purposes.[1] Whether any value remains depends upon whether the contract is, at the time of owner's death, in payout status or not, and, if so, the terms of the payout arrangement. An annuity is said to be in payout status on or after its annuity starting date[2] – i.e., if it is either an immediate annuity or a deferred annuity that has been annuitized.

Estate Taxation of Annuities in Payout Status

What is the estate tax value of an annuity in payout status? This depends upon the payout arrangement. Let's examine each of the five possibilities:

1. If the decedent was receiving a life only annuity,[3] payments ceased with her death; thus, no property interest remains to be included in her gross estate.[4]

2. If the decedent was receiving a life annuity with a refund feature that was still operative, the value of that refund feature is includable in the decedent's gross estate.

    Example A: Decedent elected to take a life annuity, payable monthly, with a ten-year (120 month) certain refund feature,[5] commencing on June 1, 2003. She died in May, 2012, after receiving 108 monthly payments. Twelve additional payments were due under the refund feature. The value of these payments, to be included in the decedent's estate, is what the insurance company issuing the annuity would charge for a contract paying a comparable annuity—twelve payments of the specified monthly amount.[6] Value at date of death is used, even where the executor elects alternate valuation.[7]

    Example B: Decedent elected a life annuity with a cash refund feature. If annuity payments received by her, during her lifetime, were less than the value of the cash refund.[8] The value includible in the decedent's estate is presumably the amount received by the beneficiary.

3. If the decedent was receiving a life annuity with a refund feature that had expired, payments ceased with her death; thus, no property interest remains to be included in her gross estate.

    Example: Decedent elected to take a life annuity, payable monthly, with a ten-year certain refund feature, commencing on June 1, 2002. She died in August, 2012, after receiving 123 monthly payments. As the number of payments guaranteed in the refund feature had been received by the decedent during her lifetime, the refund feature had been satisfied. No payments were due to any beneficiary, and no value remained to be includable in the decedent's estate.

4. If the decedent was receiving, and was the owner of, a Joint and Survivor Annuity, the value of the survivor's annuity is "the amount the same insurance company would charge the survivor for a single life annuity [for equivalent payments for life] as of the date of the first annuitant's death."[9] The amount includable in the decedent's estate depends on who paid for the annuity and whether the joint annuitants were husband and wife. If the deceased owner-annuitant, in a nonmarried situation, contributed the entire purchase price, the full value of the survivor's annuity is includable in the

deceased's estate. If not, the annuity is includable in the decedent owner's estate only to the extent of his or her contribution.[10] If the annuity was paid for entirely by the surviving annuitant, its value is not includable in the deceased annuitant's estate.[11] If the joint annuitants were husband and wife, fifty percent of the valuation amount is presumed to be contributed by the decedent and attributable to his/her estate, although it's not entirely clear whether the consideration furnished standard of Section 2039 may trump the presumed 50%/50% split of Section 2040.[12]

5.   If the decedent was receiving a Period Certain Annuity, the value of the remaining payments includable in the decedent's estate is what the same insurance company would charge for a Period Certain Annuity for the number of payments remaining.[13]

It is worth noting that in some situations, interest rates or even mortality tables may have changed from original annuity issuance to the date of decedent's death. Consequently, the valuation of the survivor's portion of the annuity could be substantially more or less expensive than the pricing may have been at the original purchase date.

Estate Taxation of Annuities Not in Payout Status

A deferred annuity where the owner has not yet elected an annuity settlement option, or annuitization—where the owner dies before the annuity starting date—is not in payout status.[14] The death benefit of the annuity as of the owner's death, including any death benefit enhancements that adjusted the value of the annuity due to the owner's death, is fully includable in the owner's estate, either under Section 2039 (which relates to the estate taxation of annuities) or under Section 2033, which relates to property that the decedent had an interest in, for estate tax purposes.

What if the owner is not the annuitant? The annuitant of a deferred annuity not in payout status generally has no property rights under the contract. The annuity is property, and both the income tax and estate tax liabilities are those of the owner. However, because the tax code, and many annuity contracts, may refer to both the annuitant and the owner at various points, the tax rules can get very complicated, as we will see later on, where owner and annuitant are not the same individual.

Income Taxation of Death Benefits

Annuities in Payout Status: Immediate Annuities, and Deferred Annuities Where Holder Dies after Annuity Starting Date

Death proceeds of an immediate annuity or a deferred annuity that has been annuitized are governed by Section 72(s)(1)(A), which states that:

[I]f any holder of such contract dies on or after the annuity starting date and before the entire interest in such contract has been distributed, the remaining portion of such interest will be distributed at least as rapidly as under the method of distributions being used as of the date of his death.

If the death proceeds—the remaining portion of such interest—are taken by the beneficiary either as a lump sum (e.g., by accelerating the remaining payments due at death) or in installments other than payments calculated by application of a new annuity option,[15] proceeds will be excludable from income until the total amount the beneficiary receives, when added to the amounts the annuitant received tax-free, is equal to the annuitant's investment in the contract, unadjusted for the value of the refund feature.[16] Amounts received by the beneficiary in excess of the investment in the contract are taxed as ordinary income. Note that this FIFO basis first treatment of beneficiary payments is different from the standard, income/gains first treatment of annuity withdrawals and different from the pro-rata exclusion ratio treatment of annuity payments made to the contract owner. This applies only when the annuitant of an annuitized deferred annuity died when a refund element provides for continuing annuity payments to a beneficiary and where that beneficiary elects to receive those continuing payments as the annuitant had been receiving them.

If the total payments thus made to beneficiary are less than the annuitant's investment in the contract and the annuitant's annuity starting date was after July 1, 1986, the beneficiary may take an income tax deduction for any such unrecovered investment once all payments have been received.[17]

Important Note: Whose Tax Is It, Anyway—Annuitant, Owner (Holder), Taxpayer?

Unfortunately, for those trying to make sense of annuity taxation, the relevant rules in the Internal Revenue Code and the Treasury regulations, as well as many reference sources that cite case law, often refer to annuitant when applying tax rules. The often-confusing implication is that the owner and the annuitant are always the same individual and can be used interchangeably. This is generally a holdover from a time when all annuities were annuitant-driven—that is, an annuity paid a death benefit upon the death of the annuitant—and when tax law focused upon the annuitant, rather than the owner, which the Internal Revenue Code and Treasury regulations consistently refer to as the holder.

Where the annuitant and owner/holder are the same individual, there is no distinction to be made or inferred. However, where they are not, the rules—and the explanations of those rules in even the best reference sources—can be confusing. It is vital we remember that the tax liability for payments made from annuities, whether amounts received as an annuity or amounts not received as an annuity, are generally the tax responsibility of the contract owner if that owner is living—even if the payments are actually made to another individual such as a nonowner annuitant. However, if the payments are made to a beneficiary, by reason of the death of either the annuitant or owner, the tax liability is that of the beneficiary-payee.

Consider, for example, the following explanation from Question 370 of the 2012 edition of *Tax Facts on Insurance & Employee Benefits*:

> The beneficiary will have no taxable income unless the total amount the beneficiary receives when added to amounts that were received tax-free by the annuitant (the excludable portion of the annuity payments) exceeds the investment in the contract.

Strictly speaking, that ought to read "...that were received tax-free by the annuitant, or contract owner, if the owner was not the annuitant." Similarly, an observation that "proceeds will be excludable from income until the total amount the beneficiary receives, when added to the amounts the annuitant received tax-free, equal annuitant's 'investment in the contract,' unadjusted for the value of the refund feature" would be more accurate if stated as "proceeds will be excludable from income until the total amount the beneficiary receives, when added to the amounts the annuitant received without tax equal the owner's 'investment in the contract.'"

However, such precision would very likely be a cure worse than the disease—increasing, rather than reducing, reader confusion. The authors merely wish to make clear that references such as annuitant's investment in the contract should be understood to mean owner's investment in the case where the owner and the annuitant are two different individuals.

Annuities Not In Payout Status: Deferred Annuities, Where the Holder Dies before the Annuity Starting Date

The income tax rules regarding death benefits of deferred annuities not in payment status constitute one of the most difficult and confusing areas of annuity planning. Most of this confusion lies not in how taxable amounts are determined—the excess of value over investment in the contract/cost basis—but in how and when death proceeds must be received by the beneficiary under tax law. To understand these required minimum distributions from deferred annuities after death, we must first understand when death proceeds are payable—that is, whose death triggers the payment of the proceeds. In all cases, though, any amounts included in income will be taxed as ordinary income.

An annuity is said to be annuitant-driven when payment of the death benefit to the beneficiary will be made upon the death of the annuitant. When the death benefit is payable to the beneficiary upon death of the owner, the annuity is said to be owner-driven.

One might think that any annuity contract is either one or the other, but it is not quite that simple. All deferred annuity contracts issued since January 18, 1985, are owner-driven, because no annuity contract issued since that date will be treated as an annuity contract for tax purposes unless it contains language requiring the force out provisions of Section 72(s).[18] That Code provision mandates distributions from annuity contracts upon the death of the holder.[19]

Section 72(s) is entitled "Required Distributions Where Holder Dies Before Entire Interest Is Distributed." It is a very important section that should be well understood by anyone selling or offering advice on the subject of annuities. Failure to understand the rules set out in this section can be hazardous to your career! If the owner, annuitant, and beneficiary designations of an annuity are made without a clear understanding of the rules discussed below, the result could be a required distribution of that annuity at a time and in a manner never intended or desired by the client.

Before getting into a detailed examination of Section 72(s), the authors want to make three observations about it. First, it is not nearly as simple or straightforward as it may appear. Second, it applies only when the holder of an annuity contract dies. Third, holder is an exceedingly slippery term. Generally speaking, it means the owner (i.e., the individual named as owner of the annuity contract). However, when an annuity is owned by a nonnatural entity such as a trust or corporation, the Code will deem the annuitant to be the holder, even if that individual is not the owner named in the contract.[20]

With those observations in mind, let's look at what Section 72(s)(1) says:

"In General. A contract shall not be treated as an annuity contract for purposes of this title [i.e., for income tax purposes] unless it provides that:

(A) if any holder of such contract dies on or after the annuity starting date and before the entire interest in such contract has been distributed, the remaining portion of such interest will be distributed at least as rapidly as under the method of distributions being used as of the date of his death; and

(B) if any holder of such contract dies before the annuity starting date, the entire interest in such contract will be distributed within five years after the death of such holder."

We have seen the first rule (Section 72(s)(1)(A)) before in our discussion of the income tax treatment of annuities in payout status. This refers to immediate annuities and deferred annuities that have been annuitized.

The second rule in Section 72(s)(1)(B) is the default rule for annuities not in payout status (i.e. deferred annuities that have not been annuitized). It says that, upon the death of the holder, the proceeds of the annuity must be paid out within five years of holder's death. This rule applies unless an exception is available. The subsections that follow, Sections 72(s)(2) and 72(s)(3), provide the two allowable exceptions. Neither exception is available unless the annuity is payable to a designated beneficiary, which is defined by Section 72(s)(4) as "any individual designated a beneficiary by the holder of the contract."

The key word here is individual. An individual must be a natural person—a human being. A trust, for example, cannot be a designated beneficiary, because it is not an individual. It is important to note that, unlike recent new regulations regarding distributions from IRAs payable to trusts, there are no look-through provisions for trust beneficiaries of annuities; since the trust itself is not a natural person, it cannot be a designated beneficiary, even if the beneficiaries of the trusts are natural persons! Any beneficiary that is not a designated beneficiary, or a natural person, is not entitled to either of the two exceptions we are about to discuss.

The first exception to the default five-year rule allows the designated beneficiary to take the proceeds over a period longer than five years. Section 72(s)(2) permits proceeds to be distributed "over the life of such designated beneficiary or over a period not extending beyond the life expectancy of such beneficiary." Note that it does not require that the beneficiary take proceeds over his or her remaining lifetime, but merely states that the distribution period cannot be longer than that. For instance, a period certain annuity payout (e.g. Twenty-Year Certain) is acceptable, provided that beneficiary's life expectancy is at least twenty years.

If an annuity option (e.g. a life annuity with or without a refund feature or a period certain annuity) is elected by the beneficiary, the payments will be taxed according to the regular annuity rules of Section 72(b)(1). The exclusion ratio would be calculated using the deceased annuitant's remaining investment in the contract and the beneficiary's expected return. To determine the expected return in the case of a life contingency, the life expectancy of the beneficiary at the annuity starting date would be used.[21]

If the insurance company that issued the annuity permits it, the beneficiary may also elect to take death proceeds in an arrangement often referred to as a stretch annuity. This arrangement, first permitted in Private Letter Ruling 200151038, allows the beneficiary to take proceeds by using a fractional method, whereby the amount of each payment would be determined by applying divisors from the Unified Table used for Required Minimum Distributions from IRAs and qualified plans. For younger beneficiaries, the required minimum payments thus calculated are substantially smaller in the earlier years than those that would be required under any life annuity or period certain option, allowing these beneficiaries to defer receiving a greater amount of proceeds to later years. As the gain in proceeds not yet received, or constructively received, is not yet taxable, this represents an opportunity for greater tax deferral. But how should each income payment to the beneficiary be taxed? Private Letter Ruling 200151038 is silent on this point, stating:

> "Specifically, no opinion is expressed on whether payments made to the designated beneficiary under the procedures described in Requested Rulings 1, 2, and 3, above (the optional distribution procedures), are amounts received as an annuity, taxable under Section 72(a) and (b), or amounts not received as annuity taxable under Section 72(e)."

However, Private Letter Ruling 200313016 subsequently held that such payments, made in accordance with the life expectancy fraction method, will, to the extent that they do not exceed the amounts required by such calculation, qualify as amounts received as an annuity. Under such treatment, a portion of each annuity payment is excluded from tax, as a return of principal (see Chapter 2), which is more favorable that the standard gains first, to the extent of any gain treatment for withdrawals from deferred annuities.

However, a caveat should be noted with regard to this conclusion. After having elected one of three payout arrangements, of which one was the fractional method, the beneficiaries of the annuity issued by the insurance company that requested the ruling were allowed two additional options. The first option permitted the beneficiary to take, at any time, the entire remaining balance in a lump sum. The second option permitted additional partial withdrawals over and above those distributions required by the payout method. The ruling specifically stated that the result previously mentioned—that payments made to beneficiaries would be treated as amounts received as an annuity—applied only to beneficiaries who elect the first option. The remaining balance is to be taken in a lump sum. No opinion is expressed regarding those who elect the second option.

What can we say about the options that these rulings allow a beneficiary of a nonqualified annuity? First, we are obliged to note that these are only private letter rulings; consequently, they may not be relied upon by anyone other than the taxpayer to whom they were issued. Second, whether the IRS will consider fractional method annuity payments made to beneficiaries as amounts received as an annuity is moot if the issuer of the annuity will not permit such a payout arrangement. Some issuers do not permit this, as they cannot be certain that the PLR guidance will be allowable for their annuities and contract holders. It is essential that the advisor discussing this option be aware of whether the issuer of the annuity in question will permit it in the first place.

When it is permitted, the fractional method—essentially, a form of stretch annuity planning— can be extremely attractive. Many beneficiaries also select this option because it allows payments to occur across the lifetime of the beneficiary without actually requiring annuitization of the proceeds, which provides additional liquidity for beneficiaries that do not require the guarantees of annuitization, without forfeiting the tax deferral of keeping most of the money in the annuity until a future date. Furthermore, some annuity companies will allow the annuity owner, while still alive, to select a particular beneficiary payout period that the beneficiary must follow as part of the contractual annuity agreement, thus preventing the beneficiary from having fully liquid access to the proceeds at the owner's death, without necessitating the use of a trust. This may be attractive for some contract owners, especially given the lack of a stretch option for trusts as beneficiaries.

The second exception to the five-year rule of Section 72(s)(1) is available only to a beneficiary who is the surviving spouse of the holder. This exception, allowed under Section 72(s)(3), permits that surviving spouse-beneficiary to treat the decedent's annuity as her own as if she were owner of the contract from inception. It is extremely important that the advisor understand that spousal continuation applies only in the situation just stated. For example, it is not available to a surviving spouse who is trustee of a trust named as beneficiary of decedent spouse's annuity.[22] It is also not available to a beneficiary who owned an annuitant-driven annuity of which his spouse was annuitant (e.g., where H is the owner and W is the annuitant of an annuitant-driven contract, and W dies, H receives the death proceeds of the annuity he owns and must recognize the income without the opportunity to elect spousal continuation).

The Section 72(s)(2) annuitization exception to the five-year rule requires that "such distributions begin not later than 1 year after the date of the holder's death or such later date as the Secretary may by regulations prescribe." Many advisors interpret these words to mean that the beneficiary has one year from the date of holder's death to elect this option. Indeed, some insurance companies may, by current practice, allow the beneficiary up to one year to make such an election. This interpretation could pose a serious problem for clients and advisors who rely upon it. Why? Because of a Code section that is often ignored: Section 72(h).

What About IRC Section 72(h)?

Section 72(h) is entitled "Option To Receive Annuity In Lieu Of Lump Sum." It states that:

If —

(1) a contract provides for payment of a lump sum in full discharge of an obligation under the contract, subject to an option to receive an annuity in lieu of such lump sum;

(2) the option is exercised within sixty days after the day on which such lump sum first became payable; and

(3) part or all of such lump sum would (but for this subsection) be includable in gross income by reason of subsection (e) (1),

then, for purposes of this subtitle, no part of such lump sum shall be considered as includable in gross income at the time such lump sum first became payable.

What does this mean, in normal English? It means that (1) if an annuity provides the beneficiary the option to take death proceeds as an annuity, in lieu of taking a lump sum settlement, and (2) if the beneficiary exercises, within sixty days of the owner's death,[23] the option to take an annuity, and (3) if part or all of the proceeds would be includable in the beneficiary's estate if taken in a lump sum (e.g., the contract was an annuity, not qualifying for the tax-free treatment of death benefits that life insurance contracts enjoy under Section 101(a)); then (4) the entire taxable portion of this death benefit will not be taxable to the beneficiary in the year of the owner's death. The beneficiary, by electing to take the proceeds as an annuity, will, instead, be taxed on those proceeds as received, under the regular annuity rules–provided that he or she exercises such an annuitization option within 60 days of the owner's death.

This sixty-day requirement of Section 72(h)(2) appears to conflict with the one-year requirement of Section 72(s)(2)(C), even though they are not speaking of the same thing. The latter requirement concerns only when the first annuity payment must be made if regular annuity rule taxation is to be available; the former states when the exercise of the annuity option must be made to achieve that result. This suggests that the proper process is to elect to take death proceeds as an annuity within sixty days of the death of the annuitant or owner, with the first payment to commence within one year of that result, thus satisfying both rules—because the election of the annuity option is the exercise thereof. However, insurance companies typically offer beneficiaries annuity payment options only on an immediate annuity basis—where the first payment will commence one month or so from the date of election. Practically speaking, this means that the first annuity payment will probably be made much sooner than one year from death, but, in any event, the exercise of the option to receive payments must be made within sixty days.

Some commentators believe that Section 72(s) trumps Section 72(h), arguing that the former section is some twenty years newer than the latter. Moreover, it is argued, the legislative history of Section 72 shows a Congressional intent to bring parity to the rules governing required distributions from nonqualified annuities and those governing required distributions from IRAs and qualified plans. The default five-year rule—an exception for annuitization not extending life expectancy commencing within one year—and the spousal continuation provisions of Section 72(s) certainly resemble corresponding provisions in Section 401(a)(9). However, Section 72(h) was neither modified nor repealed by Congress, either when it enacted Section 72(s), or when it later amended it. Moreover, Section 72(s) says nothing about when or how distributions from an annuity must be recognized by the beneficiary as income for tax purposes; it merely mandates what distributions must occur from the contract for it to qualify as an annuity contract in the first place.

By contrast, Section 72(h) speaks directly to the taxability of death benefits, declaring basically that if a beneficiary of a contract that allows a lump sum payout as an alternative to an annuity does not exercise the option to take proceeds as an annuity within sixty days, that beneficiary will be in constructive receipt of the entire contract gain in the year of the owner's or annuitant's death. In other words, if the beneficiary has the option to take a lump sum, and does not elect an annuity payout within sixty days of the date of death, the beneficiary must recognize all of the gain, and must do so regardless of whether he actually withdraws all or any of the death benefit proceeds that year.

In the authors' opinion, a beneficiary's election to take the death proceeds of an annuity, as an annuity, must be made within sixty days of the date on which those proceeds first became available, if the contract otherwise provides for a lump sum payout. This applies to both deferred annuity and immediate annuity contracts. An insurance company may, by its current practice, permit a beneficiary to make such election as late as one year after the holder's death, and may issue tax reporting forms reflecting the availability of regular annuity rule tax treatment. But the IRS may not accept such a position, because Section 72(h) is still on the books. It may be that a late election by a beneficiary to take proceeds as an annuity will escape IRS notice, particularly if the insurance company issues Forms 1099 reflecting regular annuity rule taxation, but, to be sure of that treatment, the beneficiary should make this election within sixty days of the date of death of the original annuity owner.

It should be noted, at this point, that the apparent conflict between Sections 72(h) and 72(s) does not come into play when the annuity death benefit is paid by reason of the death of a non-owner annuitant, where the annuity contract was annuitant-driven and the nonowner annuitant died. Section 72(h) applies when the death benefit of any annuity contract is payable, as long as it provides for both lump sum and annuity payouts to the beneficiary. Section 72(s) applies only when the holder/owner of an annuity dies. But some annuities pay a death benefit upon the death of either the owner or the annuitant. What are the income tax rules in that situation?

When Section 72(s) Does Not Apply: Income Tax Treatment of Death Proceeds of an Annuity Not in Payment Status When Nonowner Annuitant Dies

Annuities that are not annuitant-driven (i.e., are owner-driven) pay a death benefit only upon the death of the owner, and the income tax rules governing those death benefits are those we have just reviewed. However, annuities that are annuitant-driven pay a death benefit upon the death of the annuitant or the owner—the annuitant under contractual annuitant-driven provisions, and the owner under required provisions as dictated by Section 72(s)(1). In the case of an annuitant-driven annuity where the annuitant and owner are different individuals and the annuitant has died but the owner has not, the rules are somewhat different.

In the situation just described, Section 72(h) applies. If the beneficiary does not elect, within sixty days of annuitant's death, to take proceeds as an annuity—if the contract even offers this option—the proceeds will be considered amounts not received as an annuity.[24] The proceeds in excess of the investment in the contract (i.e., the gain) will be taxable to the beneficiary in the year of the annuitant's death.[25] In this case, because there has been no death of a holder to which Section 72(s) might apply, there are no grounds to make an election under any time period except during the sixty-day window of Section 72(h).

If the beneficiary is the surviving spouse of either the owner or annuitant, the spousal continuation option of Section 72(s)(3) is not available in this situation, because that option applies only when the beneficiary is the surviving spouse of a deceased holder/owner. If the beneficiary is under age fifty-nine and a half, the exemptions from the ten percent penalty tax, under Section 72(q), that would apply had the owner died are similarly unavailable.

Due to all of these complications, including the time requirements of Section 72(h), loss of spousal continuation options of Section 72(s), and the potential premature distribution penalties of Section 72(q), the authors strongly caution against ever establishing an annuitant-driven contract where the owner and annuitant are different individuals.

Jointly Held Annuities

Nonqualified annuities sold to married individuals are often placed in joint ownership. Often, there are good reasons for this, but the advisor should be aware of potential problems with this arrangement. Ownership of assets held jointly, with rights of survivorship (JTWROS) ordinarily vests immediately, upon the death of one tenant, in the surviving tenant(s). This does not apply, however, to annuities owned in this manner. As we have seen, Code section 72(s)(1)(B) requires that when any owner of an annuity dies before the annuity starting date, the proceeds of that annuity must be distributed within five years, unless the exceptions of Sections 72(s)(2) or 72(s) (3) apply.

Section 72(s)(3) provides what is often termed the spousal continuation option, whereby the surviving spouse of the deceased owner may elect to treat the annuity as his or her own. In the authors' opinion, this applies only when the surviving spouse is the designated beneficiary of the deceased owner. If the annuity is owned jointly by a husband and wife, but the beneficiary is their daughter, and either of the couple dies, the distribution must be made to the daughter under the terms of Section 72(s). However, this view is not shared by some insurance companies. Both of the authors have been informed, in conversations with insurance company representatives, that the contracts of a particular insurance company provide that under the factual situation given above, that the surviving spouse-owner would be able to exercise the spousal continuation option of Section 72(s)(3). In one conversation, the insurance company representative stated that this would be so if the contract were not annuitant-driven, but that if it were, payment to the daughter as beneficiary would be required to be made, in accordance with the Section 72 rules.[26]

The authors know of no authority supporting this position, or, for that matter, the position that a surviving owner can ever elect spousal continuation if he or she is not the designated beneficiary of the deceased owner. On what basis might one assert the contrary? At least one insurance company's annuity provides that if the contract is owned jointly, the surviving owner will be deemed to be the primary beneficiary, regardless of any prior beneficiary designation. That is certainly an interesting approach, but it relies, not on any putative right of the surviving owner, but on the fact that he or she would be the primary beneficiary. The authors have heard of but have not been able to verify an annuity that defines the death benefit as payable, when the contract is owned jointly, only upon the death of the second joint owner, but would have serious concerns that this might contravene the death of any holder language of Section 72(s)(1).

The authors offer a strong suggestion to the reader to be very careful in dealing with joint ownership of annuities. If you believe that joint ownership is appropriate, and especially if a third party will be named as beneficiary, you should be certain of the insurer's policies with regard to payment of death benefits, and verify that the provisions of the annuity contract are consistent with the desired result. In addition, it is notable that in any situation where an annuity is jointly held between two individuals who are not husband-wife, the clear application of the 72(s) rules dictate that the contract must begin distributions after the death of the first owner, and no continuation will be available because the surviving owner—even if named as beneficiary—is not a surviving spouse eligible for 72(s)(3) spousal continuation.

When the Beneficiary is a Trust

Probably the most confusing area of annuity taxation is determining which distribution rules apply when (a) the annuity is not in payout status and (b) the owner and/or beneficiary is a trust and (c) either the annuitant or owner of the annuity dies. This is such a complicated area that the authors have devoted a separate chapter of this book to it (see Chapter 8, Annuities and Trusts).

Annuities and Step-up in Basis at Death

Variable annuity contracts issued before October 21, 1979 are potentially eligible for a step-up in basis at the death of the owner under Section 1014. This step-up in basis applies to contributions made to these contracts, including any contributions applied to an annuity contract after that date that were pursuant to a binding commitment entered into before that date,[27] and their attributable earnings.

> The basis of the contract in the hands of the beneficiary will be the value of the contract at the date of the decedent's death (or the alternate valuation date). If that basis equals the amount received by the beneficiary there will be no income taxable gain and the appreciation in the value of the contract while owned by the decedent will escape income tax entirely. But where a variable annuity contract purchased before October 21, 1979 had been exchanged for another variable annuity contract under IRC Section 1035 after October 20, 1979 and the annuity owner died prior to the annuity starting date, the beneficiary was not entitled to a step-up in basis.[28]

It is important to note that these rulings were written in the context of variable annuities. However, the authors have discovered no reason why fixed deferred annuities acquired prior to 1979 should not be eligible for comparable step-up in basis treatment under Section 1014, as the tax code does not otherwise make any distinctions between fixed and variable annuities for tax purposes.

Beneficiary's Income Tax Deduction for Federal Estate Tax Attributable to Annuity Gain—IRC Section 691(c)

As was noted earlier, the value of an annuity is includable in the estate of the owner for estate tax purposes, and the as-yet-untaxed gain is taxable to the beneficiary for income tax purposes. This double taxation is reduced, but not avoided entirely, by an income tax deduction available to the beneficiary under Code section 691(c), under the so-called Income in Respect of a Decedent rules:

> Income in respect of a decedent is subjected to the federal estate tax in the decedent's estate and to federal income tax in the hands of the person who receives it. Also, such income may

be subject to the generation-skipping transfer tax... Section 691(c) alleviates the hardship of the double taxation somewhat by allowing the recipient an income tax deduction for that portion of these taxes attributable to the inclusion of the net value of the income right. Where the income would have been ordinary income in the hands of the decedent, the deduction is an itemized deduction.[29]

The amount of the deduction is determined by computing the federal estate tax, or generation-skipping transfer tax, with the net income in respect of a decedent included and then recomputing the federal estate tax with the net income in respect of a decedent excluded. The difference in the two results is the amount of the income tax deduction. Thus, the amount deductible equals (a) the federal estate tax on the taxable estate, minus (b) the federal estate tax on the taxable estate less net IRD.

If two or more persons will receive income in respect of the same decedent, each recipient is entitled to that share of the total deduction that is in the same proportion that his share of income in respect of a decedent bears to the total gross income in respect of a decedent that was included in the gross estate. For example, a recipient who is entitled to one-fourth of the income is also entitled to one-fourth of the deduction. This is so, even though none of the federal estate tax is attributable to the income received by that particular recipient—for example, where his income was offset by an equivalent amount of deductions.[30]

The deduction is taken only as the income is received, and in the same proportion. For example, say that the income in respect of a decedent will be received by only one person, and will be received in equal amounts over a ten-year period. The recipient may take one-tenth of the total deduction in each of the ten taxable years.[31]

It should be emphasized that the deduction is only for the gain in the contract, and only to the extent of the federal estate tax. Any state estate or inheritance tax would not be considered for purposes of this deduction.

1035 Exchanges of Annuities after Death of the Holder

As discussed in Chapter 2, Section 1035 of the tax code allows for the exchange of an annuity for another annuity contract in a like-kind exchange, without recognition of gain. These rules allow an annuity holder to exchange one annuity contract for another, perhaps to obtain different or more appealing investment options or guarantees, while deferring any income tax liability associated with a gain.

For many years, the question often arose about whether an annuity contract can be exchanged for another under a 1035 exchange by a beneficiary, after death of the original holder. After all, the provisions that allow an annuity contract to be eligible for a 1035 exchange refer directly to a contract that depends in part on the life expectancy of the insured, and/or is payable for the life of the annuitant[32]—yet once the holder of the contract has passed away, the annuity is arguably no longer an ongoing contract of insurance, but is merely a prior contract of insurance in the process of paying out its benefits to the stated beneficiaries.

Recently, the IRS shed light on the issue by issuing a private letter ruling blessing the transaction, at least in a particular instance.[33] In the facts of the ruling, taxpayer's mother owned a series of (non-qualified) fixed and variable annuities, for which the individual taxpayer requesting the ruling was the beneficiary. After the mother passed away, the beneficiary had begun to take systematic "stretch" withdrawals from the annuity (presumably consistent with prior letter rulings[34] on that issue). Now, however, the beneficiary wanted to exchange these inherited annuities for a new variable annuity, ostensibly to take advantage of more appealing investment opportunities, and accordingly applied for a new variable annuity that included a form committing the beneficiary to continue to take distributions at least as rapidly as the prior contract (effectively ensuring the post-death Required Minimum Distribution stretch would be maintained). In addition, the taxpayer also signed supplemental forms for the new annuity that would limit any ability to transfer the contract, or make new contributions to it, to ensure that the annuity would *only* contain the prior inherited annuity funds and that they would be handled in this manner.

Given these facts, the IRS allowed the 1035 exchange, assuming that the normal 1035 exchange requirements were otherwise met, recognizing that in reality at the death of the original owner, the beneficiary effectively becomes the new owner, and thus should be permitted a 1035 exchange as any annuity owner may do. The key appears to have been the beneficiary's commitment—substantiated by new paperwork signed with the new annuity carrier—to maintain the integrity of the ongoing stretch.

While the ruling was ultimately only a private letter ruling, and thus pertains only to the specifics of the situation, its issuance appears to have at least partially opened up the marketplace for post-death 1035 exchanges of annuities. The caveat, however, is that because the ruling is not a *requirement* to offer such exchanges, nor is it even binding guidance that will continue to honor, many annuity carriers have chosen not to follow the ruling, and will not cooperate with a post-death 1035 exchange. And without the annuity carrier's cooperation, a proper 1035 exchange—including assignment directly from the old insurance company to the new one, and the associated forms to ensure the stretch is maintained—cannot be accomplished, preventing a post-death 1035 exchange from occurring.

At the time of this writing, annuity companies still appear to be split on the issue. Nonetheless, for beneficiaries of an inherited annuity who wish to change contracts, the opportunity for a post-death 1035 exchange may be worth exploring. This may be especially appealing for those who wish to escape a prior insurer with poor ratings, an undesirable contract with weak investment options, a company that won't allow post-death systematic withdrawals as a form of stretch, or simply as a way to switch from a fixed annuity (common with older investors) to a variable annuity (often more desirable to younger inheritors with long-time horizons). In some cases, an annuity company may be unwilling to facilitate an external post-death 1035 exchange, but might be willing to allow an internal one, which can resolve at least some of these issues. On the other hand, if the inherited annuity is not liquid in the first place, there will be no way to facilitate any post-death 1035 exchange—internally or externally—as an illiquid contract cannot follow the requirements for a 1035 exchange at all.

While in the end this ruling is still only a private letter ruling, and thus could be altered or even reversed in the future, nonetheless, given the IRS' relatively straightforward application of the rules—the only key requirements appear to have been that the 1035 exchange was otherwise completed properly, and that the beneficiary was obligated to continue stretch payments from the new contract in a similar manner to the old one—many annuity companies appear to feel that the standing for such an exchange is secure enough to allow the new flexibility. It is hoped the treatment will expand in the coming years as demand rises from beneficiaries who wish to maintain a different investment contract than the original owners they inherited from. On the other hand, it's notable that for better or worse, these rules apply only to *non-qualified* annuities; in the case of a qualified annuity, the ability to change contracts or companies after death will follow the rules for post-death transfers of inherited IRAs (or other retirement accounts), as well as the liquidity provisions of the annuity contract itself.

Endnotes

1. I.R.C. §§2039, 2033.
2. Also referred to as the "Annuity Commencement Date."
3. Also called "straight life annuity" or "life annuity with no refund."
4. *Tax Facts on Insurance & Employee* Benefits (The National Underwriter Company, 2012), Q 417.
5. This arrangement is variously called "Life with 10-Year Certain," "Life-10 Yr. Continuous and Certain," or the like. If annuity payments are to be made monthly, it may be called "Life and 120 Months Certain."
6. Treas. Reg. §20.2031-8(a).
7. I.R.C. §2032(a)(3).
8. The value of the cash refund guaranteed is typically less than the amount annuitized under this option.
9. *Tax Facts on Insurance & Employee Benefits* (The National Underwriter Company, 2012), q 421.
10. Treas. Reg. §20.2039-1(c), Ex. 1., and I.R.C. §2039(b).
11. Treas. Reg. §20.2039-1(c).
12. I.R.C. §2040(b).
13. Treas. Reg. §20.2031-8(a).
14. An immediate annuity is in payout status by definition.
15. If the beneficiary elects to change the amount or duration of annuity payments, this constitutes electing a new annuity option. This election would cause the payments to be taxed under the regular annuity rules. However, such a change will not be permitted if the payments would not distribute proceeds at least as rapidly as the annuitant had been receiving them. I.R.C. §72(s)(1)(A).
16. Treas. Reg. §1.72-11(c).
17. I.R.C. §72(b)(3)(A).
18. It is important to note, with regard to this owner-driven vs. annuitant-driven distinction, that certain riders and enhanced death benefits of deferred annuities may be 'annuitant-driven' and take effect only at the death of an annuitant, despite the fact that the annuity itself must be paid out to the beneficiary on the death of the owner, per Section 72(s)(1). For this

reason, the advisor should be very cautious about annuitant-driven contracts where the owner and annuitant are different individuals.

19. Section 72(s)(1) was amended by the Tax Reform Act of 1986, changing the holder to read any holder. This change had serious implications for jointly held contracts (as discussed later in the text), and applies to contracts issued since April 22, 1987. Also added were Sections 72(s)(6) and 72(s)(7), which deal with annuities held by other than natural persons.

20. I.R.C. §72(s)(6).

21. Treas. Reg. §1.72-11(e).

22. Priv. Ltr. Rul. 200323012, issued to the surviving spouse who was trustee of a joint revocable trust named as beneficiary of annuity contracts owned by that trust, of which the decedent husband was the annuitant, held that the surviving spouse/beneficiary could elect the Section 72(s)(3) spousal continuation option, but the facts of that case were unusual—the spouse had such liberal powers and access to the trust that it was as though she were the directly named beneficiary. Most commentators believe that the trustee of a trust named as beneficiary of an annuity will not be able to elect such treatment or the annuitization option of Section 72(s)(2) in all normal cases. Moreover, most insurance companies, in the authors' experience, will, at this time, not consent to such a result without, at the very least, a ruling from the IRS.

23. Presumably, the date of owner's death would be the date on which such lump sum first became payable.

24. In this instance, the sixty-day vs. one-year conflict discussed above is irrelevant. Section 72(s) does not apply, because the death benefit is paid by reason of the death of the annuitant, not the owner.

25. I.R.C. §72(e)(2)(B).

26. In addition, it is important to note that in this situation, the surviving spouse would be the owner of an annuity that must be paid to the beneficiary (the daughter), and consequently could be deemed to make a gift to the daughter of the annuity death benefit upon the death of any holder. This is not unlike the similar consequences when a husband owns an insurance policy on his wife, with his daughter as the beneficiary, and the wife dies, causing the death benefit owned by the husband to be paid to the daughter.

27. Rev. Rul. 79-335, 1979-2 CB 292.

28. *Tax Facts on Insurance & Employee Benefits* (The National Underwriter Company, 2012), Q 396. See also Rev. Rul. 70-143, 1970-1 CB 167, and TAM 9346002; Let. Rul. 9245035.

29. Rev. Rul. 78-203, 1978-1 CB 199.

30. I.R.C. §691(c).

31. *Advanced Sales Reference Service*, The National Underwriter Company, Sec. 53, ¶20.15(d).

32. I.R.C. §§1035(b)(1), 1035(b)(2).

33. Priv. Ltr. Rul. 201330016.

34. Priv. Ltr. Rul. 200151038.

Chapter 4

Basic Costs of Annuities

Thus far in this book, we have examined the basic structures of annuities and how distributions are taxed. Later, we will consider the benefits annuities can provide. In this chapter, we will focus on one of the most controversial—and often misunderstood—aspects of annuities: their costs. The controversy and misunderstanding are chiefly due to two conditions:

1. The cost factors can be very complicated and, sometimes bewilderingly so.

2. The cost factors are often poorly communicated—both from the advisor to the customer, and to that advisor from the insurance company issuing the annuity contract.

The responsibility for this poor communication is a matter of considerable debate. Some consumerists hold the advisor chiefly, if not solely, responsible for a purchaser's lack of understanding. Class-action lawsuits have asserted that the onus ultimately lies with the insurance companies, citing confusing, even allegedly misleading, training and marketing materials. The authors believe that, if an annuity purchaser can legitimately state that he or she did not understand the costs of the annuity, there is plenty of blame to go around. The same holds true with respect to the benefits of that annuity.

That being said, the costs of nearly all annuity contracts offered today are often hard to understand and appreciate fully, especially when the benefits derived from those costs are also complicated. Complex cost and benefit structures, however fully disclosed, run the risk of being misunderstood, and even the best explanations can be recalled imperfectly. The annuity advisor must have a very clear understanding of the costs and benefits of those contracts he or she deals with and be willing to spend whatever time is required in perfecting a clear explanation of both.

Cost Factors in Immediate Annuities

The least complex cost structure is that of the fixed Single Premium Immediate Annuity (fixed SPIA). These contracts generally assess no front-end sales charge or annual contract charges. A few fixed SPIAs permit commutation[1] or partial withdrawals, and may assess a charge for these distributions. Most, however, do not permit these changes to the original payout structure, but instead require that once annuity payments have commenced, no withdrawals or lump sum surrender will be permitted. The only cost component in these contracts is reflected in the payout factors, both those guaranteed in the contract and those offered on a currently available basis.

Annuity Payout Factors

An annuity payout factor, or annuity factor, is a number usually expressed with two decimal precision. It represents the dollar amount of each annuity payment, per thousand dollars of proceeds placed under the annuity option.

> *Example:* The sample table below shows that the annual payment for a life only annuity,[2] for a male age sixty-five or a female age fifty-nine,[3] will be $6.38, for each thousand dollars of annuity purchase payment. Thus, a single premium of $125,500 will purchase an annual annuity payment of $800.69 (125.5 × 6.38). The same sum would purchase an annual annuity of $672.68 (125.5 × 5.36) if payments are to persist for the greater of the life of the annuitant or twenty years (Life & Twenty Years Certain).

Male Age	Female Age	Life Only	L&10YC	L&20YC	L&Cash Ref
65	59	6.38	6.09	5.36	5.61
66	60	6.57	6.24	5.42	5.72

The amount of each payment[4] is guaranteed never to change, unless the annuity provides for a Cost Of Living Adjustment (COLA). At the time of this writing, most annuities—both immediate and deferred—do not provide for any COLA adjustments. Some offer a single fixed COLA choice (e.g., payments to increase at three percent per year). Very few, however, offer a choice of different COLA percentages (e.g., three percent or five percent), or any kind of COLA that adjusts to a specified inflation factor (e.g., the Consumer Price Index (CPI)). Fortunately for consumers, there is a trend in newer annuity contracts toward offering COLA choices. In the authors' opinion, this development is both necessary and long overdue. Annuity payout factors reflect an insurance company's estimate of life expectancy, or mortality, expenses, and interest rates, and these estimates change over time. The annuity payout factors offered to current purchasers of immediate annuities and to owners of deferred annuities choosing to annuitize their contracts can change as frequently as weekly. Of course, once one purchases an immediate annuity or elects an annuitization option in one's deferred annuity, the payout factor used to calculate the initial payment is all that matters. All future payments will be based upon that same and sole factor, which never changes once payments begin.

Fortunately for all concerned, COLA options in fixed immediate annuity contracts are becoming more common. Most allow the buyer to choose a set percentage by which the annuity payments will increase each year. Once that percentage has been chosen, it cannot be changed. Unfortunately, though, COLA provisions that link the payment increase to an external index (such as the Consumer Price Index for All Urban Consumers (CPI-U®)) are still relatively rare, which means retirees remain exposed to unexpected inflation (at least to the extent it exceeds a specific COLA increase rate).

In the authors' experience, few agents recommend immediate annuities with COLA provisions. Even where two alternatives are offered— a SPIA with COLA and one without— consumers often choose the latter because its initial payment is much higher. Often, the "break even" point (when the annual payment with COLA reaches the level of the payment without COLA) is many years after purchase.

The authors believe that agents presenting SPIAs should always present at least two alternatives (one with COLA and one without) because the impact of inflation on a nominally fixed (i.e., not inflation-adjusting) income can, in the long run, be devastating. Notably, for those most concerned about materially outliving life expectancy (where annuitization is best), research has shown that rising payment annuities may actually be superior to capitalize on the available mortality credits (for further information, see Chapter 9).

For purchasers of deferred annuities, there are two sets of annuity factors that may come into play. Every deferred annuity contract contains guaranteed minimum annuity payout factors. These are based on very conservative assumptions, and are generally considerably lower—that is, providing for lower annual payments per thousand dollars annuitized—than the current factors offered by the same insurer, for use with the same annuity. In fact, in the authors' experience, there has rarely been a time when the current factors were not significantly higher than the guaranteed ones.

Does this mean that the cost of these guaranteed annuity payout factors is wasted money? In the authors' view, the answer is no—even though these guaranteed factors have never yet been as attractive as the current ones. Americans are living longer with each passing decade. A breakthrough in gerontological medicine producing greatly increased average life expectancies, especially if accompanied by a prolonged period of low interest rates or, especially, a period of deflation, could produce future current annuity payout factors less attractive than those guaranteed in existing deferred annuity contracts. Is this likely? Perhaps not. But, as we have noted before, an annuity is primarily a risk management instrument. The presence of these guarantees allows the purchaser to manage the risk that future annuity payout rates (based on longer life expectancies or lower interest rates) will not produce sufficient income.

The other type of immediate annuity is the variable single premium immediate annuity (variable SPIA). Like its fixed cousin, the variable SPIA provides for an income commencing within one year of purchase; unlike the fixed variety, however, the amount of each annuity payment is not fixed,[5] because the annuity cash value is invested in variable subaccounts. A variable annuity, whether immediate or deferred, assesses expense charges at both the subaccount and contract (or "wrapper") levels. These charges, the form of which is generally the same for immediate annuities as for deferred ones, will be covered in the discussion on costs in variable deferred annuities.

Cost Factors in Deferred Annuities

The overhead costs of deferred annuities are considerably more complex than those of immediate contracts. Historically, fixed deferred annuities have contained fewer and simpler charges than variable deferred contracts, but, in recent years, the complexity of both types has increased substantially.

Note on Nomenclature: While immediate annuities are always purchased with a single premium, a deferred annuity, of either the fixed or variable type, may be purchased either with a single premium (Single Premium Deferred Annuity, or SPDA) or may permit, but not necessarily require, ongoing periodic premiums (Flexible Premium Deferred Annuity, or FPDA). As if this were not complicated enough, the labels SPDA and FPDA are typically used in connection only with fixed contracts, just as the term SPIA, for single premium immediate annuity is, in common practice, applied only to fixed contracts, even though it is properly applicable to variable contracts as well. To avoid adding to the confusion, the authors suggest using complete terminology (e.g., fixed SPIA, variable SPIA, flexible premium deferred variable annuity, etc.)

Fixed Deferred Annuities

Charges assessed in fixed annuities may include any or all of the following:

Front-End Sales Charge

Until fairly recently, an initial sales charge, or load—generally, a percentage of the initial premium—was a common contract expense. Very few fixed deferred annuities offered today assess such a charge, as it was notably unpopular with consumers.

Surrender Charges

A surrender charge, as its name implies, is assessed upon the surrender of an annuity contract, or upon withdrawal of more than the policy's free withdrawal amount. Typically, fixed annuities allow the contract owner to withdraw up to ten percent of the account balance, per year, without penalty. There are numerous variations of this provision, such as permitting this penalty-free amount to be cumulative or allowing a penalty-free withdrawal of all previously credited interest, but ten percent per year without penalty is fairly standard. Recently, some issuers of index annuities have pared back the free withdrawal provisions of new offerings to permit a smaller penalty-free withdrawal in the first year or so. This allows the issuer to offer increased benefits such as a higher participation rate and/or a "first year interest bonus" than would otherwise be possible.

Surrenders, or withdrawals in excess of this penalty-free amount, are generally subject to a surrender charge. While the mechanics of this charge vary widely from contract to contract, the usual format is a declining surrender charge schedule—such as six percent in the first contract year, five percent in the second, four percent in the third, and so on—until the surrender charge reaches zero. In flexible premium contracts, the surrender charge schedule may be *fixed*, terminating at the end of a specified number of years from issue, or *rolling*, applying the schedule separately to each deposit. This is a moot point with single premium annuities, which, as we have noted, do not allow subsequent deposits.

Many deferred annuities, both fixed and variable, include provisions that waive the imposition of surrender charges in certain circumstances. Most contracts waive the charges upon the death of the owner, or annuitant, if the contract is annuitant-driven. Many also provide a waiver if the owner or annuitant is confined to a nursing home, is disabled, or suffers one of several listed dread diseases.

Considering how much criticism is leveled at surrender charges by many financial journalists and those who simply don't like annuities on principle, a comment or two may be in order, at this point, on why surrender charges exist in the first place.

A schedule of surrender charges is an alternative to a front-end sales charge. Both exist to allow the issuing company to recover acquisition costs—the costs of putting the annuity policy in force. Even in today's high-tech world, this cannot be done for free. The most controversial— even notorious—acquisition cost is the selling commission paid to the agent who sells the annuity. Most annuities are sold by commissioned advisors, who are compensated in this fashion. Practically all fixed annuities are of this sort. However, not all variable annuities are commissionable. An increasing number of variable annuities are of the type usually called "low load." They pay no sales commissions. Not coincidentally, they generally assess no surrender charges.

If, at this point, you are thinking that the purpose of surrender charges is to pay the sales commission, you are basically right. The insurance company pays that commission when it issues the annuity and it needs to recover that cost. But the surrender charge almost always declines over time—after a few years, to zero. Why is that? It is because the insurance company knows that if the annuity owner keeps the policy in force for long enough, it will recover its acquisition costs from other moving parts in the annuity contract. In the case of a fixed annuity, the interest rate spread (i.e., the difference between what the company earns on invested annuity premiums, and what it credits to those annuities) will, in time, not only make up the commission cost, but make the annuity contract profitable to its issuer. In the case of a variable annuity, there's no interest rate spread, and thus it is the insurance costs that bring about this same result. A front-end sales charge would do the job, too. But front-end sales charges are unattractive to buyers, which is why most annuities no longer impose them.

So, if the sales commission is an acquisition cost, surrender charges, in lieu of an initial sales charge, pay that cost, right? Yes, for our purposes, though it's slightly more complicated than that. Essentially, if the annuity pays no sales commission, there's no need for surrender charges.

That seems simple enough, but sales commissions are not the only acquisition costs. Even when an insurance company markets a particular annuity contract through fee-only advisors as a commission-free product, it cannot produce that product for free. Not only are there development costs that any prudent company will expect to recover, but also costs of issue and administration as wells as the need to make a profit. The insurance company expects to make money selling the annuity, and prices it with that expectation. In the case of a fixed annuity, profit—and cost recovery—come from the interest rate spread. In a variable annuity, which has no such spread, they come mainly from insurance charges. Thus, insurance companies attempt to make up for the fact that there are not any surrender charges on such low load or commission-free products through other costs, or by the attempt to generate additional sales with the marketability of a low load or commission-free label.

Market Value Adjustment

There may be a Market Value Adjustment (MVA) upon surrender of the contract or upon a partial withdrawal. If so, then the surrender value or withdrawn amount is usually decreased if a benchmark interest rate—a specified, well-recognized external index—is higher when the contract is surrendered than it was at the time of issue. The surrender value will be increased if the reverse is true. The purpose of this adjustment is to compensate the insurance company for the risk that contract owners will withdraw money when the market value of the investments backing the annuity is low. In the case of fixed annuities, this generally means bonds. Since bond prices are inversely related to interest rates, the market value of the investments backing the annuity will generally be lower when interest rates have risen. Generally, this is the exact time that investors may want to withdraw their money to re-invest in a new contract with higher-than-current rates—thus the need for the insurance company to protect itself from this risk. However, MVAs are a risk-sharing feature, because, if the external index is lower at the time of withdrawal or surrender than it was at issue, and the value of the underlying bonds is correspondingly higher—again, because bond prices are inversely related to interest rates—the contract owner benefits from the adjustment. Generally, an MVA is assessed only on withdrawals in excess of the penalty-free withdrawal amount, and usually does not apply after the expiration of the surrender charge period.

Interest Rate Spread

In a fixed deferred annuity, the issuing company's profit derives chiefly from the interest rate spread, or the difference between what the company can earn on invested annuity premiums and what it will credit to the cash value of those contracts. In a sense, this spread is a cost of the contract, if one assumes that the annuity investor would otherwise be able to earn the same rate as the insurance company. And in fact, some annuity companies will forego many of the previously mentioned costs and simply drive most of their cost indirectly from interest rate spread.

Of course, it's worth noting that in nearly all fixed deferred annuities, this spread is not guaranteed for the annuity company (nor is it often even revealed directly to the contract holder), and thus represents an uncertainty at best. It may be calculated, provided one knows both the rate credited to an annuity during a certain period and the rate the insurance company earned during that same period. However, not all insurers credit interest in the same manner, or even credit interest in the same manner to all fixed annuities they have issued, and annuity investments in one contract may be pooled with the annuity company's other investments and contracts.

To understand how interest rate spread works as a contract cost, we must understand how interest is credited to fixed deferred annuities.

Guaranteed Interest Rate

All fixed deferred annuities guarantee a minimum interest crediting rate. Regardless of future conditions, interest will be credited each period to the annuity at a rate at least equal to this guaranteed rate.[6] In addition, every deferred annuity of which the authors are aware also provides for the crediting of current, nonguaranteed interest at a rate, which may be higher, but cannot be lower than the guaranteed rate.

Current Interest Rate Crediting Methods

There are four basic methods of crediting current interest to conventional nonindex fixed annuities.

1. *Portfolio Method.* For an annuity that uses this method, all contracts will be credited each period with the same current, non-guaranteed interest rate, regardless of when annuity contributions (premiums) were received, except for contracts that are still within an initial interest rate guarantee period.

2. *New Money or Pocket of Money Method.* For an annuity using this method, the rate of interest credited to all contracts will depend upon when the premiums were received.

For flexible premium annuities, this can mean that a particular annuity contract might receive, on any given interest crediting date, several different rates, each applied to the pocket of money received during the time period specified for that pocket.

Example: Mr. Jones' flexible premium annuity was issued June 30, 2009. Interest is credited each year, at a rate determined annually. On June 30, 2012, the contract is credited with the following:

a.   4.00% for all premiums received in the period 1/1/2009 – 12/31/2009

b.   3.89% for all premiums received in the period 1/1/2010 – 12/31/2010

c.   3.80% for all premiums received in the period 1/1/2011 – 12/31/2011

d.   3.56% for all premiums received in the period 1/1/2012 – 12/31/2012

3.   *Tiered Interest Rate Method: Type One*

In this method, the interest rate credited to a contract depends upon the cash value of the annuity.

Example: Ms. Smith's annuity credits interest according to the following current schedule:

a.   4.00% for the first $50,000 of cash value

b.   4.25% for the next $50,000 of cash value

c.   4.5% for cash value in excess of $100,000

4.   *Tiered Interest Rate Method: Type Two*

In this method, interest is credited at one rate if the owner annuitizes the contract and at a lower rate if the contract is surrendered. In these contracts, the value is generally reported as two separate items: (a) the annuity value and (b) the cash value or contract value. The cash value will be reduced, on surrender of the contract, by any surrender charge applicable. The amount payable at the owner's or annuitant's death may be either the cash value or annuity value, depending upon contract terms, and a surrender charge may or may not apply.

Interest Rate Guarantee Period

Sometimes the current interest rate of a newly issued fixed deferred annuity may be guaranteed for a specific period. If so, then at the expiration of this period, renewal interest is credited according to the crediting method used for that particular contract—subject, of course, to the guaranteed minimum rate.

Interest Rate Renewal History

One item that every advisor who is considering recommending a fixed deferred annuity must consider is the history of the issuing insurance company with regard to renewal interest rates. Renewal rates, except for contracts in the interest rate guarantee period, are entirely at the discretion of the issuing insurer and subject, of course, to the minimum rate guaranteed in the contract. Some insurers have a distinguished history of declaring renewal interest at competitive levels. Others, unfortunately, do not. In the 1980s and 1990s, a few insurers offered fixed deferred annuities at initial rates well above the level offered by most competitors and, as soon as the interest rate guarantee period elapsed, renewed these contracts at, or barely above, the guaranteed rate. Fortunately for consumers, most insurance companies did not play this game. Nevertheless, the risk with this sort of "bait and switching" is one that the prudent advisor must take into consideration. The authors strongly advise taking a close look at the published history of the renewal crediting rate of any insurance company whose products you are considering.[7]

A final observation on the subject of interest rate crediting is in order. It may appear to the advisor inexperienced in fixed deferred annuities that renewal interest rates, while they may drop from the initial level to as low as the guaranteed rate, may also rise at that point—even beyond that initial level—if interest rates are increasing at that time. That may appear logical, but it is not likely to happen. In the authors' experience, insurance companies rarely declare renewal interest rates at a level higher than the initial rate. This may, of course, be due to the fact that, for the past thirty years and more, interest rates have, in general, been trending downward. Nevertheless, there have been short periods, during those decades, during which rates increased. In those periods, the initial rate offered by insurance companies, on their fixed deferred annuities, did increase—but the renewal rates for existing contracts did not.

Bail-Out Interest Rate

Some fixed deferred annuities provide that, if renewal interest is ever credited below a certain specified rate, or the bail-out rate, surrender charges will be waived for a certain time period, allowing the contract owner to bail out of the contract without charges. Of course, the premature withdrawal penalty of Section 72(q) will apply if the owner is under age fifty-nine and a half and no other exception to the penalty is available. Bail-out rate annuities were very popular in the volatile interest environment of the 1980s and 1990s, but are much less common today.

Bonus Interest Rates

A policy feature that has become very popular in both fixed and variable deferred annuities is the crediting of so-called bonus interest. Typically, bonus interest is interest, over and above the current rate, that is applied to deposits in the first year or first few years,[8] and is immediately vested. That is, the contract owner is not required to keep the contract for a set period, or to annuitize, to earn it. However, it is important to note that generally the surrender charges may be slightly higher on such contracts, the interest guarantees may be lower, or the current crediting rate may be lower—in other words, the general aphorism that "there's no such thing as a free lunch" still holds true, and the insurance company likely will still find some way to make up the cost of the bonus payment.

A variation on this theme is the annuitization bonus, which provides that a certain interest rate (e.g., five percent) will be credited to the contract, in addition to the regular interest, upon annuitization.

"Bonus annuities," deferred annuities offering the crediting of an up-front interest rate bonus, have come under considerable criticism in recent years from some financial journalists and from more than a few regulators. Interestingly, it is not the additional interest crediting that has drawn the criticism, but the additional costs of these contracts. This has been especially true of index annuities. Most of the condemnation has been directed at the steeper and longer surrender charge schedules of these contracts. The authors hold no brief either for or against bonus annuities, but we do believe that any assessment of their value or appropriateness ought to balance their negatives against the benefits they offer. Typically, a bonus annuity is very much like a nonbonus annuity offered by the same insurer, except for (a) the additional interest bonus and (b) increased cost factors.

The Interest Rate Bonus

The additional interest rate offered as a bonus is typically credited to contributions made to the contract in the first year or first few years. In some contracts, this additional interest is vested immediately—that is, it cannot be taken back, even if the buyer surrenders the contract. In others, it may vest over a period of years. In some contracts, the bonus is forfeitable if the contract owner does not annuitize the contract over at least a minimum number of years. Some contracts offer as much as a 10% bonus to all contributions made during the first several years.

Often, "bonus" annuities are marketed as having a "first-year yield" equal to the first year guaranteed or expected interest rate plus the bonus. In the authors' opinion, this is a misleading practice when the "bonus" interest is forfeitable.

The Costs of the Interest Rate Bonus

All bonus annuities offer the additional interest in exchange for costs higher than if no bonus were creditable. In variable annuities, this cost is typically a higher contract charge (Mortality and Expense Charge (M&E)) and/or a steeper or longer surrender charge schedule—a schedule in which the surrender charge starts at a higher level and/or persists for a greater number of years. In nonvariable contracts, which typically assess no ongoing contract charges, the surrender charge schedule is steeper and/or longer than for a nonbonus contract; in some cases, the bonus is recouped by the annuity company in the form of a greater interest rate spread.

Many critics of annuities have focused upon contracts with very steep and lengthy surrender charge schedules as though they are, ipso facto, bad for any buyer—but, especially, for a senior citizen. Indeed, regulators in several states have banned the sale to a senior citizen of any deferred annuity with a surrender charge schedule exceeding ten years or with an initial surrender charge exceeding ten percent. Contracts allowable under this rule are known as "ten-ten" annuities. In a few states, ten-ten annuities are all that any purchaser, of any age, may buy. The rationale often given for such a rule is that no one, especially a senior citizen, ought to be subject to a loss of interest and, possibly, principal as well, for more than a decade.

This may appear entirely reasonable to many readers. Why, after all, should one have to pay a penalty for getting to one's own money, especially when that penalty endures for many years? The authors suggest that one answer to that question would be that the question itself begs another – whether the money in question is, in fact, the buyer's own. In the case of a nonforfeitable interest rate bonus, we believe that it is arguably not. The issuing insurer can afford to credit such additional interest—over and above the annual interest—only if it can be assured of having the full purchase payment of the annuity to invest, so that the excess of what it earns, above what it will pay to the contract owner each year—or what it will extract in expenses—will reimburse it for that initial bonus credited. This increased liquidity cost is, quite simply, what the buyer must accept if he or she wants that bonus interest.

Let us pose a hypothetical arbitration case, in which the plaintiff argues that the surrender charge schedule of the bonus annuity he bought was unconscionable and the sale clearly unsuitable. It is established that the surrender charge of that contract was both long and steep, declining from a first year charge of nineteen percent to zero only after fifteen years. But it is also established that the bonus paid in the first year of that annuity was ten percent of the purchase payment. The annual interest paid each year on that contract was credited to 110 percent of that buyer's actual investment.

Was this annuity unconscionable? Would it be arguably suitable for any buyer, especially a senior citizen? The authors believe that a proper answer to both questions must look at the facts and circumstances of the case. Had the advisor established the client's need for liquidity during that surrender charge period? If so, did the advisor confirm that the client had other liquid assets that could be tapped for reasonably foreseeable needs during that period and that the client fully understood and agreed to the constraints upon liquidity of his investment in that annuity? What was the purpose of the annuity—the job to be done? If the client intended to take distributions of interest only from the annuity each year, it is undeniable that interest computed on 110 percent of a given sum will always produce a greater cash flow distribution than that same rate of interest computed on 100 percent of that sum.

The authors are certainly not arguing that deferred annuities with steep and long surrender charge periods are necessarily good for a client; we argue only that for a particular client, in a particular situation, they ought not to be dismissed out of hand, without a consideration of whether they would meet that client's requirements, especially if a bonus is involved.

The authors sometimes hear the following complaint from critics of bonus annuities: "If you get the bonus, but the insurer recovers the whole bonus through increased costs anyway, why bother?" The answer is that, for a bonus annuity that differs from its nonbonus cousin only in (a) the bonus, and (b) steeper and longer surrender charges, but not actually higher ongoing costs or a reduced interest crediting rate, the owner of such a contract who does not surrender it early gets the benefit of the bonus without actually paying its cost, or the surrender charges. As noted in the hypothetical example above, for a buyer who intends to withdraw interest each year, the additional interest created by the bonus may well be worth the bother.

CD-Annuities

A relatively recent development in fixed deferred annuities is the so-called "CD annuity." This type of contract typically guarantees the initial interest crediting rate for the duration of the surrender charge period, which is typically six years or less. As its name suggests, this product was developed as an alternative to certificates of deposit. While the assurance of receiving a known interest rate for several years, with freedom from surrender charges at the end of that period, is certainly attractive, especially when the tax liability for all the interest is deferred, the existence of the Section 72(q) penalty makes this type of contract a questionable short-term savings vehicle for those who will be under age fifty-nine and a half at the end of the surrender charge/interest rate guarantee period.

Contract Charges

Some fixed deferred annuities assess an annual contract charge, though most do not. Some contracts that do assess an annual contract charge will waive that charge when the account balance exceeds a certain amount (e.g., no contract charges for annuities with a balance in excess of $50,000).

Variable Deferred Annuities

Let's look now at the costs of variable deferred annuities. As was noted, the number and complexity of charges in variable annuities is greater than those in fixed contracts, and it is the former that are usually being referred to in critics' attacks on annuity costs.

Front-End Sales Charges

Front-end sales charges are generally equally as unpopular with variable annuities as they are with fixed annuities. Interestingly, though, some issuers of variable deferred annuities are offering new contracts with a front-end sales load in lieu of surrender charges. These contracts, sometimes called A-share-type annuities, may owe their existence to the heightened regulatory scrutiny and frequent bad press aimed at B-share-type mutual funds and traditional variable annuity costs. In addition to imposing no surrender charges, they may offer smaller annual costs, including M&E charges.

Surrender Charges

Surrender charges in variable annuities work just as they do in fixed annuities, so the comments from above apply here, as well.

Insurance Charges

The insurance charges in variable annuities are just plain confusing to almost everyone. Part of this confusion stems from the practice of some commentators on annuities to refer to the total insurance costs of these policies as M&E charges. However, M&E is only one of the components of insurance expenses. In this discussion, we will use the classification employed by Morningstar, Inc., Total Insurance Expense, which works like this:

The category of Total Insurance Expense consists of three elements:

1. M&E;

2. administrative charges; and

3. distribution charges.

The M&E charge is defined by Morningstar as "the percentage of the subaccount's assets that the insurance company deducts to cover costs associated with M&E risk. Specifically, it can serve as a source of profit for the insurance company [if mortality is more favorable than expected] in addition to compensating the company for offering features such as the variable-annuity death benefit and for compensation."[9]

Administrative charges are defined by the same source as "the percentage of the subaccount's daily net assets deducted by the insurance company to cover the costs involved in offering and administering the variable annuity, such as the cost of distribution and printing of correspondence."[10]

Of distribution charges, Morningstar says, "When applicable, these fees compensate the agent, broker, or financial planner who sold the policy."[11]

What does all that mean in plain English? It means that these insurance charges are imposed:

- First, to compensate the issuing company for risks it incurs related to mortality (basically, the risk that they have underestimated longevity) and expenses (underestimation of various operating expenses, including government-imposed premium taxes); and

- Second, to pay selling and distribution expenses, including printing costs and agents' commissions.

As we have noted, these separate charges are not imposed by fixed annuities. But fixed annuities have the interest rate spread, from which the cost of these risks can be, and is, recovered.

We also need to note that M&E is but one component of total insurance expense. Some commentators, when they use the term M&E mean just that component, but others—probably most—use it to mean the total figure. It is important, when comparing different variable annuities, to be sure to compare apples with apples. One low-load annuity, for example, is reported as having an M&E charge of ten basis points, but a total insurance expense of thirty basis points. Advisors must not mix the two terms.

As if that were not confusing enough, we need, also, to be aware that the benefits paid for by the total insurance expense of one variable annuity contract may not be the same as those paid for by the total insurance expense of another contract. The minimum death benefit, for example, could be significantly different. Or there may be other optional benefits, the charges for which are included in total insurance expense.

We will look, in Chapter 5, at some of the optional benefits commonly offered in variable annuity contracts, as well as some of the enhancement features used. But, first, it is essential that we understand that, for variable annuities, the total annual overhead cost to the contract owner is not just the sum of the annual contract charge plus the total insurance expense. There is also the annual expense charge imposed at the separate account level. This charge, called fund expense, is analogous to the expense ratio of a mutual fund, and is defined in Morningstar's *Principia®* as "the percentage of assets deducted each year for underlying fund operating expenses, management fees, and all other asset-based costs incurred by the fund, excluding brokerage fees."[12]

Fund expenses vary considerably, both from contract to contract and, especially, according to the type of account. Money market and index accounts typically have the lowest fund expense, with bond accounts somewhat higher, general equity accounts even higher, and specialty accounts (e.g., natural resources, real estate) with the highest fund expense.

The sum of (a) fund expense and (b) total insurance expense equals the total annual overhead cost to the annuity contract owner. Well, almost. There may also be an annual contract charge, but that is usually about $30 per year, and is often waived for contracts with balances exceeding specified levels, not a percentage of the annuity balance.

What do these various charges and expenses amount to, in percentage terms? The average M&E expense for variable annuities, according to Morningstar (2012) is 1.25 percent.[13]

The average fund expense was 0.97 percent, and the average total expense (total insurance expenses plus fund expenses) was 2.35 percent. This does not count the contract charge, which is measured in dollars, or the surrender charge, as the surrender charge is payable only on surrenders or withdrawals in excess of the penalty-free amount.

L Share Annuities

Recently, annuity companies have begun to offer an L Share contract providing the same features and benefits as their standard variable annuity contract, but with a shortened surrender charge schedule. Typically, the initial surrender charge is the same as the standard share class, but it declines to zero more rapidly. The trade-off for this benefit is typically a higher annual M&E charge.

> *Example*: One insurer's standard share class variable annuities impose the following surrender charge schedule—seven percent, six percent, six percent, five percent, four percent, three percent, two percent, zero percent. Surrender charges cease in year 8. The M&E charge for that contract, assuming a standard death benefit, is 1.25 percent. The L share variant of that contract imposes surrender charges of seven percent, six percent, five percent, zero percent. Surrender charges cease in year four. The M&E charge, for the same standard death benefit is 1.50 percent.

Is the shortened surrender charge period worth an additional annual cost of 0.25 percent? For some clients, it may be worth it. For others, it may not.

P Share Annuities

Some clients may be willing to bear longer surrender charge schedules in return for lower annual costs. The so-called P share variant offers this trade-off. The insurer cited in the above example issues a P share contract with surrender charges of eight percent, eight percent, eight percent, seven percent, six percent, five percent, four percent, three percent, two percent, zero percent. Surrender charges cease in year ten. The M&E charge, for the same standard death benefit, is 1.15 percent.

Is the longer and heftier surrender charge schedule worth the lower annual cost? Again, some clients will prefer this option; others will not. The relative importance of surrender charges, in the overall value proposition represented by a deferred annuity, whether fixed or variable, is almost always a matter of client perception. For an investor who does not intend to take distributions from her annuity until many years after buying it, surrender charges may be of little importance. She may be happy to bear higher and longer charges, and assume a greater liquidity risk in exchange for lower annual costs. For another investor, however, being able to get at his money whenever he wants, without charges, may be a prerequisite. The L Share contract and free withdrawal provisions were devised to be more attractive to him—as were no-commission zero surrender charge contracts. In any case, the prudent advisor should consider that a deferred annuity is, generally speaking, a long-term investment and that regulators and broker-dealer compliance officers certainly consider it as such.

Endnotes

1. Commutation is the right of an annuity contract holder to surrender a policy in payout status for a lump sum, in lieu of the remaining annuity payments. This is generally determined as the present value of remaining payments, with some minor adjustments to compensate the insurance company for the change.

2. A life only annuity pays for the life of the annuitant. Payments cease at the annuitant's death, regardless of when death occurs.

3. Most annuity contracts are issued on a sex-distinct basis, recognizing that females live longer, on average, than males. A few contracts use unisex rates—where the payout factor for a male is always the same as for a female of the same age. These are usually employed in group retirement plans where sex-distinct annuity factors have been judged to be discriminatory.

4. The payout factors are examples. They may be more or less than actual payout factors.

5. Variable SPIAs typically offer a fixed account option, which does provide for fixed amounts. The present discussion refers, however, to amounts placed under the variable payout option.

6. Conventional fixed deferred annuities typically credit interest annually. Some index annuities do as well. However, some index annuities may credit interest every two or three years or, in the case of term end point contracts, only at the end of the initial term period (see Chapter 7).

7. This applies, not just to annuities, but also to other products—notably, universal life policies. Many insurance companies publish their interest rate crediting history. In addition, an excellent, and unbiased, source for such information is A.M. Best (www.ambest.com).

8. Some contracts provide for the payment of bonus interest at certain policy anniversaries (e.g., at the end of the fifth and tenth years).

9. Morningstar® *Principia®* software, Variable Annuity/Life module. Quoted from the online help section.

10. *Ibid.*

11. *Ibid.*

12. *Ibid.*

13. http://awgmain.morningstar.com/webhelp/glossary_definitions/va_vl/pol_M_E_Risk.html.

Chapter 5

Optional Benefits in Variable Annuities

The total insurance expenses described in Chapter 4 are the standard costs for the standard features of a typical variable deferred annuity. The principal benefits typically purchased by these expenses are:

1. The guaranteed death benefit provided by the contract, without election of optional, extra-cost riders. An interesting development in the annuity marketplace has been the decision by a few annuity providers to offer variable contracts with no death benefit guarantee whatsoever—not even a return of premium provision. Most variable annuities, however, offer at least that level of death benefit guarantee.

2. The guaranteed annuity payout factors, providing a minimum annuity payment if the contract is annuitized under one of the annuity payment options, regardless of future changes in longevity or interest rates.

Most deferred variable annuities marketed today offer additional, optional benefits at additional cost. New policy enhancements are introduced by one company or another nearly every month, and the variety—and complexity—of options available is downright staggering. Some relate to the guaranteed value at the death of the annuitant or owner and are generally termed death benefit enhancements, discussed at the end of this chapter. Others—indeed, most of the recently introduced options—fall into the category of living benefits.

Living Benefits

The living benefit riders offered in deferred variable annuity contracts refer to benefits that a contract holder can exercise while still alive. They are not triggered by the death of either the annuitant or owner. Strictly speaking, the term should include benefits such as the guaranteed annuity payout factors, the availability of the various investment sub-accounts and cost-free transfers among those sub-accounts, dollar cost averaging, and automatic rebalancing. However, in practice, living benefits[1]—especially when the reference is to enhanced living benefits— generally means any of these four enhancement features:

1.   Guaranteed Minimum Income Benefit (GMIB);

2.   Guaranteed Minimum Accumulation Benefit (GMAB);

3.   Guaranteed Minimum Withdrawal Benefit (GMWB); and

4.   Guaranteed Lifetime Withdrawal Benefit (GLWB). This is similar but not an identical alternative to the GMWB.

Availability of Enhanced Living Benefits

Some variable annuity contracts permit these enhanced living benefit options to be elected only at the time of contract issue. Others permit them to be added later. Some contracts permit election of only one of these benefits. After electing one of these benefits, the contract owner may or may not be permitted to discontinue it and cease paying its cost.

Guaranteed living benefit riders are also available in many fixed index annuities. The costs and benefit levels are different from the costs and benefits of these riders when applied to a variable annuity. A discussion of these differences, and possible differences in efficacy, appears at the end of this chapter.

Guaranteed Minimum Income Benefit

The Guaranteed Minimum Income Benefit (GMIB) guarantees a minimum income to the annuitant, regardless of adverse investment performance of the variable annuity contract. The amount of the guaranteed income is typically calculated by applying a guaranteed interest rate (usually five to seven percent) to the initial payment to produce a benefit base[2] from which the GMIB payments are calculated. It is extremely important that the advisor understand that this rate does not guarantee a future account balance that may be withdrawn as a lump sum! The only thing guaranteed by a GMIB benefit is that the benefit base can be annuitized at certain guaranteed payout factors, ultimately providing a certain level of income the annuitant is guaranteed to receive in the future. Advisors must understand that this guarantee comes only with certain conditions.

Annuitization Generally Required

Variable annuity contracts offering a GMIB benefit generally require that the benefit base (and thus the entire contract) be annuitized for the GMIB to be applicable. Usually, the annuitization must be for the life of the annuitant and, in some cases, must be elected within a thirty- or sixty-day window each year (typically, immediately following a contract anniversary), following the expiration of a waiting period, which is usually seven to ten years. Annuitization that uses the GMIB benefit base is not available during the waiting period. Often, the GMIB provision will also require an annuitization age setback—typically, from three to seven years—where the actual age of the annuitant will be reduced, by the number of years specified in the setback requirement, and the special GMIB annuity factor for that adjusted age is used to determine the annuity amount. It is important to note that the downward adjustment of the annuitization age will spread payments over a longer period of time, resulting in a lower payment amount. This represents an indirect cost of utilizing the GMIB rider.

Calculation of the GMIB

The GMIB is calculated by using special annuity payout factors that are generally significantly lower[3]—that is, they produce lower annuity payments per dollar of principal applied—than the factors the insurer offers to owners of deferred annuity contracts wishing to annuitize on a regular basis, using the cash value or annuity value of their contracts.[4] The special GMIB payout factor for the payout option chosen (e.g., Life & Ten-Year Certain) and the annuitant's age—or adjusted age, if applicable—is applied to the benefit base, rather than the cash value or annuity value of the contract, to determine the guaranteed income under the GMIB provision.

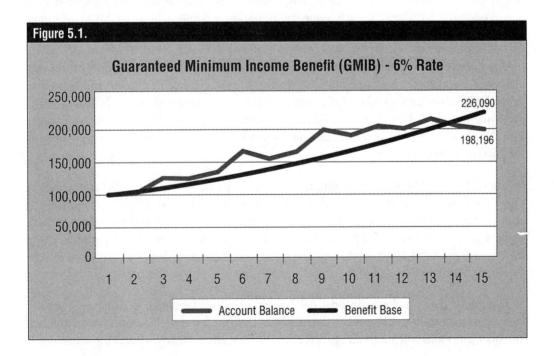

Figure 5.1.

Guaranteed Minimum Income Benefit (GMIB) - 6% Rate

Obviously, electing the GMIB payout with its reduced annuity factors would not be advisable if the contract annuitization value exceeds the benefit base or if the investment performance has produced a cash value available for annuitization that is greater than the initial premium, compounded at the GMIB guarantee rate.[5] However, if the benefit base exceeds the actual account balance (the cash value or annuity value), that greater amount is used to produce the GMIB annuity amount. In Figure 5.1, the account balance at the end of fifteen years is $198,196, and the benefit base is $226,090. This represents the primary potential benefit of the GMIB rider: the ability to elect to annuitize a lifetime stream of payments based on a higher benefit base if contract performance turns out to be unfavorable, thereby guaranteeing a certain income stream in the future regardless of market performance, while still providing the investor with the opportunity to participate in the investment potential of the variable subaccounts selected.

What is not so obvious is that the election to annuitize using the GMIB may not be advantageous for the contract owner even if the benefit base is higher than the account balance. This is because the lower payout factors used in the GMIB, and the age setback, if applicable, may produce a lower annuity amount than the higher regular payout factors applied using the annuitant's actual age to the annuitization value. In this situation, regular annuitization would be more profitable. To avoid unintentionally annuitizing for a lower payment under the GMIB, some contracts will always pay, upon the owner's election to annuitize under the GMIB, the higher of (1) the regular annuity payout factor chosen, applied to the regular annuitization value, or (2) the GMIB payout factor, applied to the GMIB benefit base. However, from a practical perspective, if the annuitization payment available under the GMIB is inferior, the client will simply make a decision to utilize the existing annuity cash value in whatever manner desired (e.g., systematic withdrawals, cash value annuitization regardless of the GMIB, or simply continued accumulation/deferral).

The income guaranteed under a GMIB annuitization is an option. The contract owner may always elect not to exercise that option, for reasons such as the income amount is unattractive, or the GMIB annuitization, like regular annuitization, is generally irrevocable. In that scenario, some might argue that the cost of the GMIB was wasted money. However, the authors disagree. The GMIB option, like an option traded on the stock market, is not worthless simply because the purchaser never exercises it.

The GMIB typically requires annuitization on a fixed basis. That is, the special annuity factor used creates an income stream that is not only guaranteed, but also fixed in amount. Some annuity contracts however, also offer the GMIB with variable annuitization, using variable annuity units. In the authors' opinion, the choice is a valuable one, particularly for those who are especially worried about future inflation rates, who anticipate a lengthy retirement income period, or both.

Because of the complexity in how the benefit base is determined, and the even greater complexity in how the GMIB annuity payments are calculated, due to the application of different annuity factors and potentially an age setback, it is often advisable to focus on the actual dollar amount of the guaranteed annuity payment at a particular point in the future. By comparing actual guaranteed dollar payments at a particular point in the future, it becomes easier to compare the GMIB benefit to other income options in the contract or to GMIB riders of other variable annuity contracts. Some companies may offer a lower interest rate applied to the benefit base but higher annuity factors, or apply an unusually high interest rate to the benefit base but include a substantial age setback. By viewing the GMIB benefit in terms of the actual dollar payments that will be received, evaluation may be easier, and clearer, despite all of the moving parts. But the prudent advisor should be careful to consider the inherent time value of money when evaluating guaranteed payments in the future based on a lump sum deposited today.

Withdrawals and the GMIB

GMIB options often permit the contact owner to make withdrawals before, or even after, exercise of the GMIB option. Such withdrawals reduce the benefit base from which the guaranteed minimum income is calculated. Two methods of reduction are used:

1. Dollar-for-dollar reductions adjust the benefit base downward by one dollar for each dollar withdrawn. Usually, this dollar-for-dollar treatment, if offered, is available only for withdrawals up to a specified percentage of the prior year's account balance or benefit base. Withdrawals in excess of this percentage then reduce the benefit base proportionally. However, for older GMIB contracts (e.g., prior to 2002), dollar-for-dollar treatment often applied up to the entire value of the annuity contract.

2. Proportional reductions (also called pro rata reductions) adjust the benefit base downwards by the proportion that the withdrawal represents of the current account value.

Where the benefit base exceeds the account value, the proportional method will produce a greater reduction in the benefit base than a dollar-for-dollar method, which is less favorable for the annuity holder. Conversely, where the benefit base is less than the account value, the proportional method will produce a smaller reduction in the benefit base than the dollar-for-dollar method.

These same two methods are used in the guaranteed minimum death benefit discussed below. See that discussion for an example.

Step-Up and the GMIB

Often, the GMIB rider includes a step-up option. This allows the contract owner to step-up, or increase, the benefit base if the account balance has grown to exceed it. Typically, the comparison between the account balance and the benefit base is applied on the contract anniversary. In the chart in Figure 5.2, the GMIB benefit base is stepped up to the greater account balance in year six. This option is typically subject to restrictions as to the number and timing of step-ups.

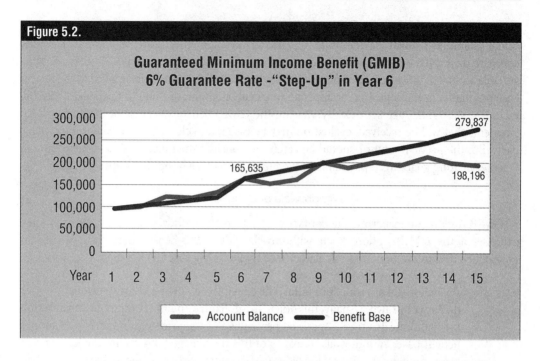

Figure 5.2.

Guaranteed Minimum Income Benefit (GMIB)
6% Guarantee Rate -"Step-Up" in Year 6

Some GMIB provisions require the contract owner to elect to step-up the benefit base; others will step-up that value automatically, at specified intervals, if the contract value at those times exceeds the previously established benefit base. Typically, a step-up in the benefit base— particularly if it is optional and requires a voluntary election—imposes a new waiting period before that new benefit base may be applied under the GMIB payout option.

The interaction between riders for a contract that includes both a step-up feature and a growth rate on the benefit base will depend on the contract. For some contracts, the growth rate will only apply to the original contributions. In other cases, it will apply to whatever the current benefit base is, thereby accruing the growth rate on top of any recent step-up adjustments. This difference can be significant and reminds us that it is critical to read the details of the provisions regarding living benefit options as they appear in the prospectus. Reading the brochure designed for the client or even the agent's guide is simply not enough.

Withdrawals under the GMIB

Most GMIB riders permit the contract owner to make contract withdrawals up to a specified percentage of the account balance or benefit base on a dollar-for-dollar basis. Thus, any withdrawals will reduce both the contract cash value and the GMIB benefit base by the amount withdrawn, thus reducing both the lump sum surrender value and the amount that can be annuitized under the GMIB guarantee. It is very important that the advisor understand the impact of withdrawals in excess of the specified percentage, which is often 6 percent. Some contracts provide that, while withdrawals up to that percentage will reduce the GMIB benefit base on a dollar-for-dollar basis, any excess withdrawal will reduce that benefit base proportionally. For a contract that has been significantly depleted—where the annuity owner is relying on the guarantee—a pro-rata excess withdrawal from a contract with little remaining cash value can catastrophically reduce the benefit base.

In other contracts, typically older ones, an excess withdrawal will reset the benefit base to the then-current contract cash value—perhaps even if a withdrawal exceeds the specified percentage by only a dollar! Excess withdrawals have a similar effect on the guaranteed death benefit in most variable annuities (see "Impact of Withdrawals on Death Benefit," later in this chapter). In short, the authors recommend that advisors be very cautious in considering any withdrawal from a GMIB rider in excess of the annual specified percentage, particularly in situations where the annuity's cash value is significantly below the benefit base.

Cost of the GMIB

The current cost of a GMIB rider varies from contract to contract, but is generally about one hundred basis points per year.[6] In some contracts, this cost is assessed against the account value; in others, it is assessed against the benefit base. In some contracts, the GMIB charge, as a percentage of the benefit base or account balance, is fixed; in others, the charge may be increased. It is often difficult to tell. For example, one major insurer's prospectus says, "Currently, we deduct a charge equal to 0.5 percent per year of the average Protected Income Value for the period the charge applies." The word "currently" at the beginning of the statement suggests, to the authors, at least, that the percentage charged is not guaranteed. However, representatives of that insurer assured one of the authors that it has never been, and will not be, changed. We suggest that advisors make sure that such assurances are in writing.

Fourth Edition Update

Since the release of the third edition of this book in 2012, the GMIB has become much less popular (and, as a result, less available). However, existing contracts with this benefit are still in force and the income planning options exercisable under it may still be valuable. The authors strongly suggest that advisors whose clients own annuities with this, or any, optional living or death benefit carefully review the options available before making any recommendations regarding those annuities.

Guaranteed Minimum Accumulation Benefit

The Guaranteed Minimum Accumulation Benefit (GMAB) is the second of the four basic types of optional living benefits offered in variable deferred annuity contracts. As with the other three enhanced living benefits, the GMAB consists of several moving parts.

Guarantee Period

Unlike the GMIB, which promises a future minimum income value, the GMAB guarantees a future account value. It does not do this by guaranteeing a minimum growth per year, but by promising that the account balance will be equal, at a minimum, to the GMAB guarantee amount at the end of the guarantee period,[7] which is typically seven to ten years. Thus, if the account value is less than the GMAB guarantee amount at the end of the guarantee period, the account value will be adjusted upwards to equal the GMAB guarantee amount.

The guarantee amount is generally the initial investment, in the case of single premium contracts, or all contributions made during the guarantee period in flexible premium contracts. This guarantee of principal is sometimes referred to as the base guarantee of the GMAB provision. The base guarantee may also incorporate an interest bonus by guaranteeing a percentage greater than one-hundred of such amounts (e.g., 120 percent of premiums, or 120 percent of premiums paid within the first 120 days of the contract).

Step-Up Provision

The step-up provision in a GMAB rider operates to provide additional downside guarantees in the event that the cash value of the annuity rises above the initial principal amount. Note that this is different from how step-up provisions work with GMIB riders. The opportunity to step-up the GMAB guarantee amount to the current cash value may be available every certain number of years, every year, or at any policy anniversary where the current value exceeds the prior anniversary's value by a certain percentage. When a step-up option is exercised, a new guarantee period begins, and the new, stepped-up value guarantee is not applied to the contract to adjust the account value until the end of this new period (see Figure 5.3). However, the original benefit amount, or the contract owner's contributions, is in many contracts, guaranteed indefinitely from the end of the original guarantee period.

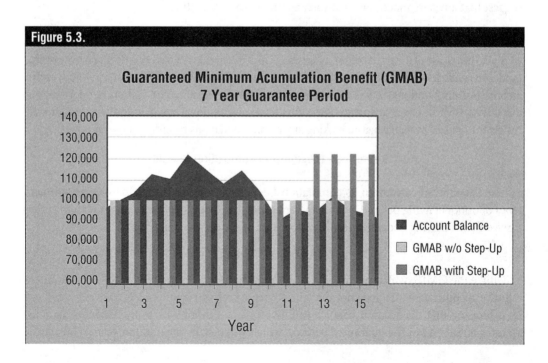

Figure 5.3.

Guaranteed Minimum Acumulation Benefit (GMAB)
7 Year Guarantee Period

Figure 5.3 illustrates a GMAB where the policy owner elected to step up the GMAB benefit base to the cash value at the end of the fifth year. The GMAB had a seven-year guarantee period, meaning that the greater of the original contribution or this stepped-up amount was available at the end of the twelfth policy year. Typically, GMAB riders do not require annuitization.

Asset Allocation May Be Required

Most insurers manage the risk inherent in the GMAB by imposing restrictions upon the asset allocation permitted to contract holders who purchase the GMAB rider. Often, funds with high volatility are not available, and many contracts require that the contract owner choose one of several defined model portfolios. Alternatively, the insurer may reserve the right to move funds from the variable subaccounts chosen to the fixed account or more conservative separate accounts. The conditions under which this may occur are not always clear from a reading of the prospectus, and point of sale marketing materials often ignore this issue entirely. However, it is a crucial distinction; in practice, one of the primary benefits of using such guarantees is that it can make the investor more comfortable with more aggressive growth-oriented investments, and having asset allocation restrictions makes this impossible. In addition, given that annuity fees are generally charged on the entire amount, even though only a portion may actually be invested in volatile assets, an asset allocation restriction results in an "indirect cost" to the investor in the form of buying guarantees on assets that arguably aren't volatile enough to have really needed such a guarantee in the first place.

Withdrawals

Withdrawals may be, but are not always, permitted from contracts in which the GMAB rider has been purchased. If so, they may reduce the guarantee amount on a dollar-for-dollar basis, a proportional basis, or a combination of the two (e.g., dollar-for-dollar for withdrawals not exceeding five percent of the guarantee amount; proportional, for any excess).

Annuitization Generally Not Required

Unlike the GMIB, the GMAB generally does not require annuitization. If the GMAB guarantee amount is greater than the contract's cash value at the end of the GMAV waiting period, the difference will be added, by the insurer, to the cash value, in the form of additional accumulation units of the sub-accounts chosen, and the GMAB rider, and charges to same, will cease. The increased cash value may then be re-allocated to any of the contracts' available sub-accounts, as the GMAB asset allocation restriction will no longer apply. It is worth noting that if the GMAB rider is applied at the end of the guarantee period, the account value itself is typically adjusted upwards as appropriate immediately, providing additional amounts invested for future growth in the contract from that point forward.

Cost of the GMAB

The cost of the GMAB, like the cost of some other enhanced living benefits discussed, varies considerably. Some contracts charge about twenty-five basis points per year, but others charge as much as one hundred. This cost is typically assessed against the annuity account value. Some insurers offer an enhanced GMIB that includes a principal guarantee similar to a GMAB. While many variable annuity contracts offered a GMAB only a few years ago, few do so, as of December, 2011. No index annuities of which the authors are aware offer it, which simply makes sense, given that the principal of an index annuity is guaranteed anyway.

Fourth Edition Update

The GMAB, like the GMIB, is less popular today than in earlier years. Few insurers currently offer a GMAB on a stand-alone basis, but contracts including this benefit may still be found.

Guaranteed Minimum Withdrawal Benefit

The third of the basic enhanced living benefits is the guaranteed minimum withdrawal benefit. This can be a confusing benefit for at least two reasons. First, the structure of this benefit is, in almost every contract, fairly complicated. Second, there are two variations of this benefit: (1) what the authors call the True Guaranteed Minimum Withdrawal Benefit (GMWB), and (2) The Guaranteed Lifetime Withdrawal Benefit (GLWB). Regretttably, the first label is sometimes used, usually by academics and journalists, to describe either type.[8] The GMWB and GLWB are, in fact, different provisions. To avoid this confusion, the authors suggest that the GLWB be considered as a fourth type of living benefit; the first three being the GMIB, GMAB, and GMWB.

The True GMWB

Strictly speaking, the term Guaranteed Minimum Withdrawal Benefit (GMWB) describes a contract provision that guarantees only the return of principal, or of a protected withdrawal value, (or benefit base) over time, through systematic withdrawals. It does NOT guarantee an income for life. That is how we will use the term in this book. The amount guaranteed to be available via withdrawals may be the owner's total contributions to the annuity (the principal) or a greater protected withdrawal value, such as the annuity cash value at the time of the first withdrawal.

The GMWB specifies a maximum percentage, typically between five and seven percent, of the protected withdrawal amount that may be withdrawn without resetting, or adjusting downward, that protected withdrawal amount. The benefit of the GMWB to the contract owner—and the risk to the issuing insurance company—is that the insurer must permit withdrawals, not exceeding the specified percentage, of the remaining principal or the protected withdrawal amount, even if the annuity cash value has fallen to zero due to adverse investment performance. This means that the annuity holder may be able to deposit an amount to the annuity contract and withdraw that entire principal amount at a specified percentage annually until all principal has been recovered, regardless of investment performance, as can be seen in Figure 5.4.

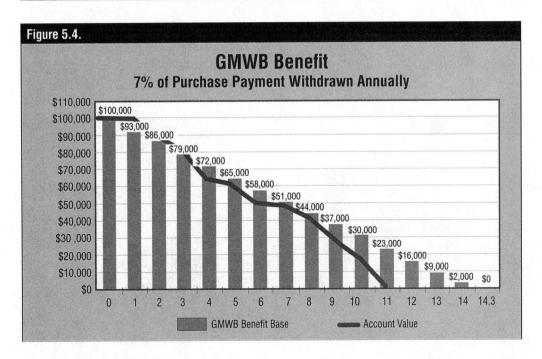

Figure 5.4.

GMWB Benefit
7% of Purchase Payment Withdrawn Annually

GMWB Benefit Base — *Account Value*

It is vitally important that the advisor know the impact upon the GWMB guarantee if the contract owner makes withdrawals exceeding the specified percentage. Some contracts will, in this circumstance, reset the protected withdrawal amount to the then-current cash value, which in a declining market—while withdrawals are also occurring—could be substantially lower. In some contracts, this reset can occur if any excess withdrawals occur, even if that excess is only a dollar.

When does the presence of a GMWB add value? Some commentators suggest that the GMWB rider provides value only if the investor's account balance falls to zero before the expiry of the GMWB period. As shown in Figure 5.5, the rider guarantees the contract owner the right to take withdrawals up to seven percent per year until the guarantee amount is exhausted. In this case, that is approximately 14.3 years (100/7). If actual contract performance results in cash value remaining at the end of that period, the GMWB could be said to have been worthless. However, in the authors' view, that is rather like saying an insurance policy has been worthless to any insured who has not submitted a claim. The assurance of a benefit if certain bad things happen must surely have value even if those bad things don't happen.

Moreover, most GMWB riders issued today guarantee a benefit base greater than the investor's total contributions, either by an interest bonus applied to each contribution or by compounding contributions by a specified rate of interest until the earlier of the first withdrawal or a specified year, which is often year ten.

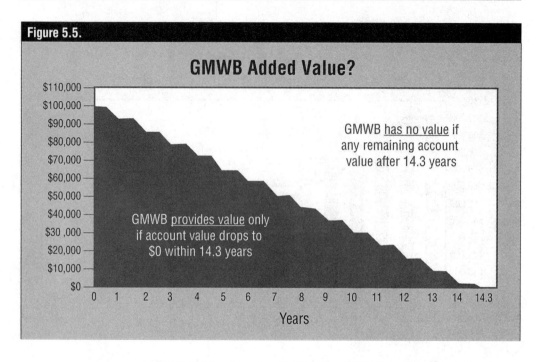

Figure 5.5.

GMWB Added Value?

GMWB has no value if any remaining account value after 14.3 years

GMWB provides value only if account value drops to $0 within 14.3 years

GMWB May Require No Waiting Period

Typically, GMWB provisions do not require a waiting period before withdrawals can begin under the guarantee, although some contracts impose such a requirement.

Asset Allocation May Be Required

Some GMWB provisions, like most GMAB provisions, impose restrictions on the investment choices available to the contract owner. Certain variable subaccounts—typically, those having high price volatility—may be unavailable, or election of a diversified model portfolio may be required. As noted earlier, this can limit the value of the rider and/or indirectly increase its cost, forcing the investor to purchase the annuity guarantee on assets that may not be volatile enough to have otherwise merited a need for the guarantee in the first place.

Reset Option

Most GMWB provisions allow the contract owner an option, similar to the step-up option often permitted by GMIB provisions, to reset the protected withdrawal amount to the annuity cash value if that value has risen due to investment gains. The owner may, thus, lock in these gains and is entitled to take the stepped-up benefit base by withdrawals not exceeding the specified percentage (in this example, seven percent per year) until that benefit base is exhausted, regardless of how long that takes. See Figure 5.6. In some contracts, a step-up option is available only at certain contract anniversaries. In others, it is available each year until a certain age. In this example, only three step-up elections are shown, for clarity.

Figure 5.6.

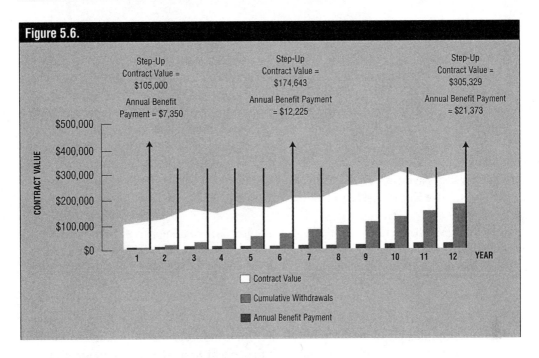

GMWB with Step-Up Provision

In so doing, the contract owner who has elected the GMWB option ensures a greater guaranteed withdrawal amount, because the GMWB withdrawal percentage will apply to this greater protected withdrawal amount. Reset may be permitted only at certain option dates, such as every five years, on each contract anniversary, or at any anniversary where the annuity cash value has increased by at least a certain percentage over the previous year's value. Recently, the frequency of step-up option dates has increased significantly. Some contracts permit step-ups annually, or even more frequently, but only if the account balance exceeds the previously established benefit base amount.

Cost of GMWB

The current cost for the GMWB option is typically between sixty and ninety basis points per year; the maximum cost is in the range of 120-150 basis points per year. Some contracts waive this cost if no GMWB withdrawals are made within a specified period (e.g., seven years) following election of the option, but will continue the GMWB provision in force. Most insurers reserve the right to increase the rider cost to a specified maximum or to the then-current cost if the benefit base is stepped-up. The true GMWB, with no guarantee that income payments will persist for life, is far less popular today than when it was introduced.

Fourth Edition Update

The "true" GMWB is rarely seen today. Virtually all deferred annuity contracts (either variable or indexed) with a minimum income benefit guarantee that minimum income for life (GLWB).

Guaranteed Lifetime Withdrawal Benefit (GLWB)

The other type of withdrawal benefit that is sometimes referred to, misleadingly, as a GMWB or lifetime GMWB is the Guaranteed Lifetime Withdrawal Benefit. The GLWB, although less popular than in past years, is still the most frequently elected rider in deferred annuities.[9] It is similar to the GMWB, but with one very significant difference. Here, the operative term is lifetime. The contract owner is guaranteed the right to withdraw up to the specified percentage of the benefit base each year for life, even if the account balance falls to zero, and even if cumulative withdrawals exceed the original benefit base, or protected value. By contrast, the GMWB guarantees such payments, even if the annuity account value falls to zero, but only to the point where cumulative withdrawals equal, or have exhausted, the benefit base.

Like the GMWB, the GLWB typically does not impose a waiting period before withdrawals can be made. However, the guaranteed compounding component of the benefit base generally ceases upon the later of the first withdrawal or the expiration of a specified period, which is often ten years.

In some contracts, the GLWB is an option within the GMWB rider. In those riders, if withdrawals commence prior to a specified age, the contract owner is guaranteed the right to withdraw up to the specified percentage of the benefit base, which may be stepped-up if that option was elected or is automatic, until that benefit base is exhausted. At that point, the guarantee ceases. If withdrawals commence after a specified age, withdrawals up to a specified percentage, which may be different from the percentage permitted for earlier withdrawals, are guaranteed for life, or for the joint life of policy owner and spouse.

The utility of a step-up option in a GLWB, once withdrawals have begun, is rarely made clear from either prospectus language or point of sale marketing materials. It is true that, in many contracts, if the account balance exceeds the remaining benefit base, at a step-up option date, that benefit base may be increased to the level of the account balance. However, the likelihood of such a scenario is questionable. Typically, withdrawals reduce the benefit base. For a step-up to be profitable, or even available, to the contract owner, the account balance must have increased by more than the sum of the annual withdrawals taken and the GLWB rider cost since the last step-up option date. For example, if the GLWB withdrawal percentage is five percent and the total annual costs of the VA total three percent (e.g., an M&E charge of 1.4 percent, subaccount fees of 0.6 percent, and a GLWB rider cost of one percent), the contract must grow by at least eight percent.[10] This is certainly possible, even with the asset allocation restrictions typically imposed when the GLWB is chosen. If it occurs even once, the contract owner will benefit from the resulting step-up every year from that point on, for life. But the step-up election may increase the GMWB rider cost, making the hurdle the account balance growth must overcome even higher for future step-ups.

The authors are not suggesting that the step-up provision in the GLWB is not worth it. To a particular client, who has been informed as to how it works and what is required for it to be available, it may well be worth it. But the key word here is informed. In the authors' experience, variable annuity marketing materials generally do not address the issue just described. For the contract owner to know, the advisor must know, and be willing to educate her client. It may be best—for both client and advisor—to think of the GLWB income, once it has commenced, as being a flat amount since the risk in an adverse market is that the market will decline and, thus, no future step-up may ever apply.

GLBs Expire at Annuitization

It is vitally important that the advisor understand that all of the living benefit guarantees described above (GMIB, GMAB, GMWB, and GLWB) operate only in the accumulation phase of the annuity—that is, prior to annuitization. When the contract owner elects an annuity payout option, whether fixed or variable, all of these guarantees expire. Of course, in the case of the GMAB and the GMIB, it may be more appropriate to say that the benefits mature. If the GMAB value exceeds the cash value of the contract and the waiting period has passed, the annuitization value of the contract will be the GMAB value because the cash value will have been stepped-up to the GMAB value at the end of this waiting period. If the GMIB value exceeds the cash value, the higher (former) value may be used as the annuitization value, but this will require use of the special GMIB payout factors. As noted above, these factors are usually significantly less than the regular payout factors available to contract holders wishing to annuitize the cash value. This could result in a lower annuity payment than would be payable by annuitizing the lower cash value, using the regular payout factors, except in contracts guaranteeing the higher of the two income amounts.

Guaranteed Living Benefits and Prospectus Changes: A Troubling New Trend for Existing Variable Annuities

Over the past fifteen years, the variable annuity industry has experienced a tremendous amount of change—from the explosive rise of variable annuities with guaranteed living benefit riders for retirement income leading up to the fall of 2008, to the dramatic pullback of many insurers away from such offerings in the aftermath of the financial crisis. While ultimately many annuity owners who purchased contracts prior to 2008 have been happy with their contracts and the guarantees, the same has not been true of the annuity companies who offer them, as a rising number of insurers have been offering buybacks to annuity owners that offer contract value increases or outright cash in exchange for releasing the company from their guarantees in order to reduce exposure.

In a disturbing new trend, though, several annuity companies have begun to make changes to the investment offerings, ostensibly to simply change the lineup of funds being offered, but done in a way that increasingly appears to change the rules of the game for existing annuity holders after the fact. In the spring of 2013, one insurer, in the process of rotating investment offerings in a 'routine' prospectus change, indirectly defaulted a large number of annuity holders into more conservative investments than they may have originally selected (and often into their own affiliate-managed funds to boot). In an even more concerning shift, another insurer decided to change its investment offerings as well—and actually required policyowners to voluntarily adopt the new investment offerings or lose their annuity guarantees! In other words, owners of contracts with ostensibly lifetime guarantees were forced to complete a "renewal" process (changing their investment options in a specified manner, but with a requirement to take a proactive step to do so) or permanently lose their lifetime income protection!

These insurer moves were not popular. However, the reality is that because some of the companies that made those changes are no longer in the business of offering variable annuities, the potential fallout, in damage to their brands, is arguably limited. Nonetheless, this emerging trend to alter annuity contracts after the fact by changing the prospectus and attaching requirements to continue the guarantees puts new pressure on advisors to monitor *existing* annuity contract on behalf of clients. Even advisors who didn't originally sell the annuity might still be liable if they're engaged for ongoing monitoring of the client's comprehensive financial plan and miss a crucial change to the guarantee! As a result, advisors will need to be increasingly diligent in reviewing client annuity contracts, or look to outsource to due diligence services that can help to support the process.

Assessing the Value of a Guaranteed Living Benefit

In 2008, the TIAA-CREF Research Institute published a paper that sought to determine the value of a guaranteed lifetime withdrawal benefit.[11] It concluded that there is little, if any value, to this rider in nearly all situations.[12] The paper asserts that:

> "This product only has value if the performance of the underlying funds is extremely poor. For example, if the S&P index has a zero percent return for twenty years, and the policyholder is still alive, then the $5,000 income guarantee has value; at that point the account balance is zero but annual payments of $5,000 will continue for life. But the vast majority of the time, the investor is only receiving his or her own money back, along with its investment earnings. And for this, he or she is paying as much as seventy-five or even one-hundred basis points per year. In addition, as we will demonstrate later, annuitization is a better way to guarantee lifetime income. We think this point is important enough that it bears repeating. If market performance is similar to the past few decades, the buyer is paying for an insurance feature that has little value."

We believe that this reveals a fundamental misunderstanding of the subject. The first two sentences state that the only way this contractual provision can have value is if it pays off. That's investment logic, and it's quite correct—when applied to an investment problem.

However, the GLWB is not an investment feature. It's a risk management feature. It's insurance. The investor is paying to transfer to the insurance company the risk that the annuity investment performance will not produce at least a certain level of income.

The TIAA-CREF authors say that this is a bad deal because the probability that the GLWB will produce more income than the annuity without such a benefit, where both are invested identically, is so small that it's not worth the cost. But can the economic value of an insurance guarantee be reckoned purely by examining the probability that the event insured against will occur? We do not believe that is an appropriate way to analyze the value of a GLWB, or, indeed, any insurance feature. The benefit to the buyer of insurance isn't a probability, but a certainty. For someone who ran out of money yesterday, because she bought a variable annuity without a GLWB and investment losses caused her account balance to fall below the level needed to support the distributions from that contract that she required, it doesn't matter what percentile of the whole population she ended up in, or that the statistics predicted that she probably would not have run out of money. Nor does it matter that most people in her age cohort haven't (yet). What really matters is that she's now one-hundred percent broke!

Other studies of GLWBs have addressed this issue in a way that recognizes that an insurance feature cannot be analyzed merely by assessing its profitability to the buyer.

In October, 2007, Ibbotson released a study entitled *Retirement Portfolio and Variable Annuity with Guaranteed Minimum Withdrawal Benefit (VA+GMWB)*, comparing four traditional portfolios (Conservative, Moderately Conservative, Moderate, and Aggressive) with a variable annuity having a GMWB component, invested in a Moderate Aggressive model. The *VA+GMWB* allocation had a higher equity exposure than the average of the portfolios on the other side of the comparison, but that higher allocation did not, in the authors' opinion, translate into a higher risk to income level because the GMWB hedged that risk. It should be noted that this study ignored the risk that the insurer might not be able to pay the income guaranteed by the GMWB.

More recently, Garth Bernard and David Blanchett have published analyses of the value of the GLWB that are well worth reading. Blanchett's article,[13] published in the July, 2011 issue of the *Journal of Financial Planning*, compares the probability of a retiree's actually needing income from a lifetime withdrawal rider with the net cost of that rider, which Blanchett, like TIAA-CREF refers to as a GMWB. He finds that that probability of needing income is approximately 3.4 percent for males, 5.4 percent for females, and 7.1 percent for a couple, given current prevailing lifetime distribution factors, or guaranteed withdrawal rates. The rider will pay off, he notes, only if both of two conditions are true: (a) that the portfolio can no longer sustain the guaranteed withdrawal rate, and (b) the annuitant is still alive. The net cost of the rider, from the perspective of the annuitant as a percentage of annuity total value, is approximately 6.5 percent for males, 6.1 percent for females, and 7.4 percent for couples. Thus, he concludes, "the guaranteed income in [an annuity containing a GLWB rider] may be a relatively inexpensive form of 'longevity insurance.' Just because the overall expected net value of a longevity protection strategy is negative, does not mean that it does not offer a valuable benefit to a retiree. This is a fundamental truth that is either overlooked or ignored by many critics of annuity protection features, who often fail to recognize that, in Blanchett's words, "the cost of any insurance product should be expected to be negative."

Garth Bernard's article,[14] in the March, 2010 issue of the *Journal of Financial Service Professionals*, makes this same point—that any insurance product will not pay off, on average. That is, that the buyer cannot expect to profit from purchasing insurance protection, because if the average insured experiences a profit, the insurer issuing the coverage will go broke.

Bernard concludes that:

- the younger the purchase age, the more valuable the [GLWB] rider;

- the sooner withdrawals begin, the less valuable the rider;

- the rider may never produce the insurance company's own money; that is, that the rider is in the money, on average, only after several decades;

- a SPIA may produce better results if withdrawals are to begin immediately; and

- a longevity annuity may produce better results if income is to commence after many years.

Bernard's first two conclusions are self-explanatory. The fourth and fifth conclusion illustrate that either an immediate or future annuitized stream of income, providing the contract owner with no right to discontinue payments and take the annuity cash value in a lump sum, will generally provide a higher rate of income than a GLWB which does provide such a right. But what does that third point mean?

In February, 2013, a paper by H. Huang, M. Milevsky, and T. S. Salisbury, entitled "Optimal Initiation of a GLWB in a Variable Annuity: No Arbitrage Approach," created quite a stir in the financial services industry. The paper focuses "exclusively on the problem from the perspective of the individual (retiree) who seeks guidance on when to initiate or begin withdrawals from the guaranteed living withdrawal benefit (GLWB)." In their approach, the authors assume that "the individual [the annuity buyer] is trying to maximize the cost of the guarantee to the insurance company offering the GLWB. The optimal policy is the one that is most costly to the issuer." In other words, the optimal approach, from the perspective of the buyer, is the one that provides the most of "the insurer's money."

Using sophisticated stochastic analysis, the authors came to a conclusion that may strike many, especially agents who sell variable annuities with GLWB benefits, as counterintuitive. Many such agents emphasize the "rollup" feature of the GLWB, suggesting that the longer the buyer waits before electing payouts under this option, the more benefit he will receive from the increased ("rolled up") benefit base. The authors of this paper, however, found that "given current design parameters in which volatility (asset allocation) is restricted to less than 20%, while guaranteed payout rates (GPR) as well as bonus (roll-up) rates are less than 5%, GLD's that are in-the-money should be turned on by the late 50s and certainly by the early 60s." In other words, the optimal strategy is to begin to take guaranteed withdrawals as soon as possible – *even if the money isn't needed* – to try to work through the policyowner's own cash value as quickly as possible and get to claiming against the insurer's money instead.

This rule of thumb does not apply in every case, the paper notes. "Given current product features, typically it is optimal to initiate immediately, exceptions being poor particularly young individuals, individuals within a short time of a rise in withdrawal rates, or individuals holding products with extreme return characteristics (e.g. very high volatility [maximum permissible allocation to equities] or bonus rates)."

When is the GLWB in the Money?

Bernard calculates that for a GLWB with a roll up rate of seven percent (i.e., that the benefit base is guaranteed to increase by seven percent per year), guaranteeing a lifetime withdrawal rate of five percent of the benefit base at the time withdrawals commence, and where underlying investments earn seven percent per year, the annuity account value will fall to zero after thirty years. Of course, the rider provides that income payments will continue for the lifetime of the annuitant, even if that makes payments persist beyond thirty years. Nonetheless, payments under the GLWB return only the contract owner's own money for the first thirty years[15] until his/her own cash value is depleted, and only then is the contract in the money by actually paying the insurance company's money out to the annuitant. Other studies have calculated a different in the money point, which is to be expected, as that result will vary, depending upon the assumptions made as to roll up rate, guaranteed withdrawal rate, and return on investments.

The Guaranteed Lifetime Withdrawal Benefit in Index Annuities

While guaranteed living benefit riders have been offered in variable annuities for about fifteen years, they have only recently been available in index annuities. By far the most popular guaranteed living benefit in index annuities is the lifetime withdrawal rider (GLWB). A few contracts offer a Guaranteed Minimum Accumulation Benefit (GMAB) rider; to the authors' knowledge, no index annuity offers a GMWB or GMIB rider.

Garth Bernard observes[16] that GLWBs in index annuities work in identical fashion to GLWBs in variable contracts. He argues that they both exhibit the same potential benefits and shortcomings, but that the key distinguishing characteristic is the level of fees. Fees for the GLWB rider on an index annuity are typically substantially less than those for the same rider on a variable annuity. Bernard argues that there are two key implications to the principal protection and fee differences between the two types of contracts:

1. "When the total fees in a VA with a GLWB are taken into account, the reduction in the expected performance of the VA may bring it closer to what would be expected of a fixed annuity. It becomes more bond than equity.

2.   A GLWB with a given feature-set (i.e., annual increase on the income base and guaranteed withdrawal factor), costs substantially less to deliver on an FIA platform than a VA platform."

While the first point is arguable, the second is certainly true. The issuer of a GLWB rider on an index annuity does not face the same hedging costs as the issuer of a VA with that same rider, as the value of an index annuity cannot decline due to market losses. These lower costs are reflected in the lower charge for the rider in index annuity contracts.

Which is better—a GLWB in a VA or one in an index annuity? Bernard's answer is "it depends." "Clearly," he writes, "one cannot make a valid comparison simply by looking at the design features of the GLWBs and the underlying products to be compared—there are just too many moving parts." The authors agree. Indeed, the question of whether a variable annuity with a GLWB rider is better or worse than an index annuity, with or without that rider, is a difficult one. Perhaps more importantly, it seeks to compare two very different instruments. A variable annuity, particularly one in which the cash value is invested in equities subaccounts, has a distinctly different risk/ reward potential than an annuity in which there is no risk of loss of principal.

The authors are often asked by advisors why a guaranteed living benefit rider would make any sense in a deferred annuity that guarantees both principal and a minimum rate of return, such as an index annuity. In the case of either a GMIB or GMWB, the answer is "it would make no sense, which is why no index annuity offers such a benefit." However, GLWB riders are available in many index annuities. They will provide a benefit if the net return on the annuity is less than the roll up rate guaranteed by the rider.

> *Example*: Using a software tool called "The Annuity Bulldozer" (www. annuitybulldozer.com), we compared two hypothetical *fixed* annuities. Both were assumed to produce 4 percent growth per year. Both included a GLWB rider, costing ninety-five bps/year, with a guaranteed payout percentage (of the benefit base) that increases with the age at first withdrawal (but which remains constant once withdrawals begin). The "rollup" rate was assumed to be six percent for the earlier of ten years or the first withdrawal.
>
> The first scenario was for taking withdrawals immediately (at age fifty-five, when the guaranteed withdrawal percentage was four percent). The second was for taking withdrawals at the end of ten years (when the payout percentage was five percent).
>
> The software computed the implied yield of the annuity with the GLWB, both at the end of forty years (age ninety-five) and when the contract value fell to zero. In the "take in year one" scenario, the contract value never fell to zero, and the implied yield at the end of forty years was 3.01 percent. In the second scenario, the contract value fell to zero in nineteen years after withdrawals began (twenty-nine years from annuity purchase). The implied yield at the end of forty years, in that second scenario, was 4.48 percent—greater than the assumed return on the annuity itself.

What should one make of these examples? The authors suggest that one lesson to be learned is that the question of "which alternative is better?" should almost always be answered by "it depends." Individual facts and circumstances always affect the result. In this comparison, the annuities were not variable contracts. There could be no loss years. Therefore, the optimal strategy described by Huang et al. of exhausting the annuity cash value in order to get into "the insurer's money" as soon as possible could not be aided by negative investment returns. Clearly, the six percent "rollup rate" and the twenty percent greater guaranteed payout percentage achieved by waiting ten years before initiating withdrawals both contributed to the greater implied yield in the second scenario. One of the authors has run multiple cases using the "Bulldozer" software, varying the assumed interest rate and "rollup rate," and found that in most of the cases the "wait ten years" scenario produced higher implied yields. That said, the question of whether to begin withdrawals immediately using a GLWB or to wait and allow the benefit base to increase over time is not simply a matter of implied yield. When the income is *needed* must surely be a factor, and the reader can probably think of others (tax considerations, etc.).

Death Benefit Enhancements

The industry standard death benefit in variable annuities was, for many years, the greater of (1) the amount originally invested less any withdrawals, or (2) the account balance at death. Often, surrender charges were waived upon death, and most contracts offered today contain this waiver.

Most variable deferred annuity contracts available today offer much more liberal death benefit guarantees, though these enhanced death benefits are generally available only at extra cost, either by additional cost for the rider, or by incorporating the guarantee into the base contract for a higher M&E cost. Some contracts offer a choice of several death benefit provisions.

The typical enhanced death benefit of a modern variable deferred annuity is a guarantee to pay the highest value of:

1. total contributions made, or less withdrawals;

2. the cash value at the time of death, usually without regard for any surrender charges;

3. the highest cash value as of certain prior dates, such as of any prior policy anniversary or as of the fifth, tenth, fifteenth, or twentieth policy anniversaries. This is often referred to as a ratcheted death benefit, and is typically restricted to policy anniversaries prior to a certain maximum age (e.g., age eighty-five).

4. total contributions made, or less withdrawals, accumulated at a specified rate of interest (e.g., five percent). This option typically provides that accrual cease at a certain maximum age (e.g., age eighty-five).

Figure 5.7.		

ANNUITY BULLDOZER	Comparison Report	INCOME ANNUITY TOOLBOX
Client	Testcase for CUNA	Testcase for CUNA
Case	take in yr 1	take in yr 11
Description	4% growth 4% payout	4% growth 5% payout
Solve For	Income	Income
Roll-Up Calculation	Compounding	Compounding
Premium Available	100,000.00	100,000.00
Pre-Tax Income	4,240.00	9,491.49
Tax Rate	25.0000	25.0000
After-Tax Income	3,180.00	7,118.62
Rider Bonus	0.0000	0.0000
Rider Roll-Up	6.0000	6.0000
Rider Withdrawal Rate	4.0000	5.0000
Roll-Up Years	10	10
Proj Annual Return	4.0000	4.0000
Fee - Account Balance	0.9500	0.9500
Fee - Benefit Base	0.0000	0.0000
Fee - Highest Balance	0.0000	0.0000
Income Begins in Year	1	11
Years to Retirement End	40	30
Deposit to Achieve Target	100,000.00	100,000.00
Total Income Received	169,600.00	284,744.70
Rider Guaranteed Withdrawal	4,240.00	9,491.49
Balance at Retirement End	7,370.42	0.00
Implied Yield at Retirement End	3.01	4.48
Years to Annuity Value Zero	42	19
Implied Yield, Annuity Value Zero	3.03	3.06

The cost of such an enhanced death benefit is typically thirty-five basis points or less per year. As with some living benefits, the cost may be calculated based on the annuity account value, or the guaranteed death benefit amount. Typically, this cost is the same for all contract owners, regardless of sex, health status, or age up to the allowable maximum. This makes the benefit a significantly better deal for some than for others.

Impact of Withdrawals on Death Benefit

An extremely important provision in any variable deferred annuity contract is the one specifying what adjustments will be made to the death benefit as a result of any partial withdrawals. Some contracts reduce the death benefit by withdrawals made, on a dollar-for-dollar basis. Others reduce it proportionally, by the percentage that the withdrawal represents of the cash value.

If the death benefit equals the current cash value, these two formulas will produce the same result. However, if the death benefit does not exceed the current cash value, the proportional method produces a higher remaining death benefit after withdrawal. The death benefit may be less than the current cash value if:

1. the death benefit is a basic return-of-premium death benefit and the contract has appreciated since inception;

2. the death benefit is a guaranteed return on contributions structure where the subaccounts have outperformed the guaranteed interest rate; or

3. the death benefit is an annual step-up option, and the contract value has increased since the last anniversary step-up occurred, but the increase will not be credited until the next anniversary.

**Example: Where Death Benefit
Does Not Exceed Current Cash Value**

Total Contributions to Annuity	$100,000
Current Cash Value	$150,000
Death Benefit Guarantee	$125,000
Withdrawal	$10,000
Dollar-for-Dollar Reduction in Death Benefit	
$125,000 – $10,000 = $115,000 (Death Benefit following withdrawal)	
Proportional Reduction In Death Benefit	
$10,000 / $150,000 = 6.7%	
$125,000 × 6.7% = $8,333	
$125,000 – $8,333 = $116,667 (Death Benefit following withdrawal)	

Example: Where Death Benefit Exceeds Current Cash Value

However, when the death benefit exceeds the current cash value, the dollar-for-dollar method results in a higher after-withdrawal death benefit than the proportional method. In the following example, the annuity owner invested $100,000. At one point, a later policy anniversary, the cash value had grown to $150,000. Subsequently, the cash value dropped to $75,000 due to poor investment results. The annuity offers an annual ratchet death benefit guarantee, whereby that earlier high water mark of $150,000 was locked in as the guaranteed death benefit.

Total Contributions to Annuity	$100,000
Current Cash Value	$75,000
Death Benefit Guarantee	$150,000
Withdrawal	$10,000

Dollar-for-Dollar Reduction in Death Benefit
$150,000 – $10,000 = $140,000 (Death Benefit following withdrawal)
Proportional Reduction in Death Benefit
$10,000 / $75,000 = 13.3%
$150,000 × 13.3% = $20,000
$150,000 – $20,000 = $130,000 (Death Benefit following withdrawal)

This distinction can be very important if the client is concerned with the amount to be left to heirs. It is particularly significant when a client is considering making a partial tax-free exchange of an existing annuity to a new annuity under Section 1035. If the existing contract uses a dollar-for-dollar method for reducing the death benefit, and the account value is less than the death benefit, then a partial withdrawal of all but the minimum amount necessary to maintain the existing contract can leave much of that contract's death benefit intact while allowing the client to invest most of its former cash value in a new, and better, annuity. It is presumed that the client, and his advisor, would not consider making the exchange unless the new annuity is significantly better, for the client's purposes, than the existing one.

Whose Death Triggers the Death Benefit Guarantee?

As was discussed in Chapter 3, all annuities issued since January 18, 1985 must provide that the contract value will be paid to the beneficiary upon the death of the contract owner/holder, in accordance with rules specified in Code section 72(s). This rule of tax law mandates only that the contract value be paid upon the death of the contract owner. However, it does not necessarily mean that the guaranteed minimum death benefit of the contract will be payable. Whether that is the case is not a matter of tax law, but, rather, depends upon the terms of the annuity contract. Some, but not all, contracts are annuitant-driven; that is, they state that the contractual death benefit, including any optional, or enhanced death benefit guarantees, will be payable only upon the death of the annuitant. In such contracts, if the annuitant and the owner are different individuals, the owner's death will trigger payouts of the contract value, under Section 72(s), but will not trigger payment of the guaranteed minimum death benefit, which is payable, in annuitant-driven contracts, only upon death of the annuitant. Of course, where annuitant and owner are the same individual, this point is moot. But where they are not, it is extremely important that the advisor and the client know whose death will trigger the death benefit minimum guarantee—and who will receive that benefit. As noted in an earlier chapter, one annuity contract provides that, upon the death of an annuitant, the death benefit will be paid to the beneficiary named in the contract. But upon the death of a nonannuitant owner, the contract value will be distributed to (a) the contingent owner, if named, or (b) to the surviving joint owner, if named, otherwise, (c) to the estate of the owner! The authors doubt that any prospective purchaser of that annuity—or most advisors—would expect such a result.

Death Benefit Guarantee is Not Applicable after Annuitization

A point that may be overlooked in many sales presentations is the fact that the guaranteed minimum death benefit—a point often emphasized in these presentations—is operative only when the annuity contract is in the accumulation phase; that is, before the owner has exercised an option to annuitize the contract. Upon annuitization, the death benefit guarantees described above cease to exist. If the advisor is emphasizing the advantages to the client, and the client's family, of the death benefit guarantees in a deferred annuity, it is essential that he or she make clear when those guarantees are no longer operative. This is of particular importance if the client has chosen a GMIB rider because electing to annuitize the benefit base will terminate any guaranteed death benefit.

IRD Tax Offset Benefit

As the GMAB can be said to preserve principal against market loss, a rider in some variable annuities is designed to preserve earnings against loss wrought by annuity taxation. As discussed in Chapter 3, the undistributed and untaxed earnings, or gain in a deferred annuity is subject to tax, both if distributed to a living contract holder and to a beneficiary, following holder's death. Sometimes called an Earnings Preservation Benefit, this rider adds to the death benefit otherwise payable an additional amount to offset the reduction in the death benefit represented by income—and perhaps estate—tax due from the beneficiar(ies). Typically, this amount is a percentage of the contract earnings. For example, if Dave buys an annuity for $100,000 that has a death benefit of $200,000 at his death and the contract contains a forty percent Earnings Preservation Rider, the total death benefit would be $240,000 ($200,000 death benefit plus forty percent of $100,000).

Structured Product Based Variable Annuities

Recently, a new type of variable annuity has entered the marketplace. Often described as a "hybrid," it is technically a variable annuity but has return characteristics similar to a fixed index annuity or a "structured product." A structured product "provides an agreed level of income or growth over a specified investment period and displays the following characteristics:

(a) the customer is exposed to a range of outcomes in respect to the return of initial capital invested;

(b) the return of initial capital invested at the end of the investment period is linked by a pre-set formula to the performance of an index, a combination of indices, a "basket" of selected stocks (typically from an index or indices), or other factor or combination of factors; and

(c) if the performance in (b) is within specified limits, repayment of initial capital invested occurs but if not, the customer could lose some or all of the initial capital invested."[17]

In the past, these "structured products" have typically been offered as a form of bond or investment note where the return of the bond is a formula tied to some underlying index (thus they are often called "structured notes"). For example, a structured note might specify that the investor will receive eighty percent of the upside of the S&P 500 up to a maximum of twenty percent in a year, with a maximum downside of only ten percent. Notably, this risk/return profile is not unlike many types of fixed index annuities, with the caveat that there is often some downside component (i.e., principal is not entirely guaranteed).

The currently available structured product deferred annuities (as of February, 2014) are all variable contracts. They differ from conventional variable annuities in that the purchaser does not invest in mutual fund-like "separate accounts" but chooses one or more indices

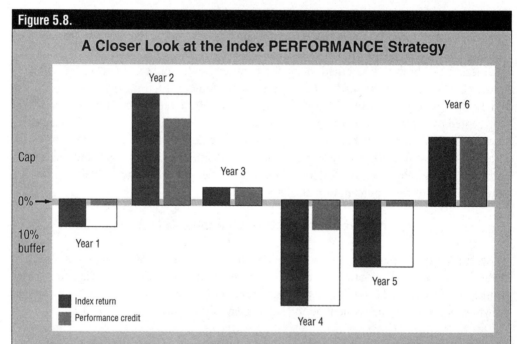

Figure 5.8.

A Closer Look at the Index PERFORMANCE Strategy

- **YEARS 1 AND 5:** In these years, the index return was negative, but it was within the 10% buffer. So there was no positive or negative performance credit.

- **YEAR 2:** In this index year, the index return exceeded the declared cap. So a positive performance credit equal to the cap was applied.

- **YEARS 3 AND 6:** In these years, the index retrun was positive, but it was less than the declared cap. So the positive performance credit was equal to the index return.

- **YEAR 4:** Here, the index return was negative and exceeded the 10% buffer. So there was a negative performance credit equal to the amount of negative returns in excess of the buffer.

The 10% buffer does not change after your contract is issued. The cap is subject to change annnually on the Index Anniversary. The minimum annual cap is 1.50%.

(S&P 500®, etc.), the performance of which will determine interest to be credited, subject to certain limitations of potential caps, spreads, and/or participation rates. In this respect, they resemble index annuities; however, unlike traditional index annuities, structured product-based variable annuities may subject the purchaser to the risk of at least some loss of principal, typically limited by a "buffer" (a percentage of loss that will be absorbed under the annuity contract before the investor bears further losses).

For example, one insurer's contract offers a choice of two strategies (in both strategies, the term over which performance is measured and interest is credited is one year):

(a) A "performance" strategy, in which the interest credited is based upon the performance of the chosen index or indices and is limited by a "cap," declared annually. Should the value of the index or indices chosen decline over the period, the investor will not bear the first 10 percent of the loss (the "buffer"); however, any loss in excess of ten percent will be borne by the purchaser. (For instance, if the index was down fifteen percent,

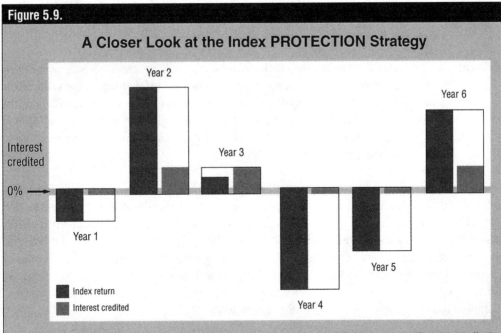

Figure 5.9.

A Closer Look at the Index PROTECTION Strategy

- **YEARS 1, 4, AND 5:** In these years, the index return was negative. So there was no interest credited.
- **YEARS 2, AND 6:** In these two years, the index had a significant positive return. So the interest credited was limited by the cap even though the index return exceeded the credit.
- **YEAR 3:** In this year, even though the index return was less than the interest credited, the fact that it was positive means the entire interest credited was received even though it was more than the index return.

The minimum annual interest credited is 1.50% for the life of the contract. This is subject to change annually.

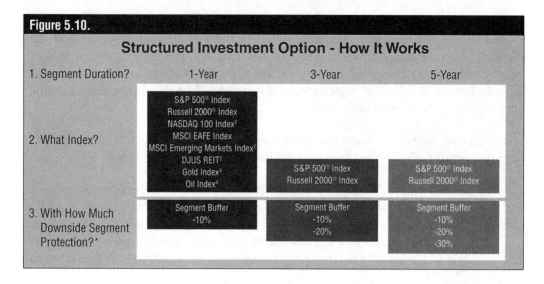

Figure 5.10.

Structured Investment Option - How It Works

	1-Year	3-Year	5-Year
1. Segment Duration?			
2. What Index?	S&P 500® Index Russell 2000® Index NASDAQ 100 Index² MSCI EAFE Index MSCI Emerging Markets Index² DJUS REIT² Gold Index³ Oil Index⁴	S&P 500® Index Russell 2000® Index	S&P 500® Index Russell 2000® Index
3. With How Much Downside Segment Protection?*	Segment Buffer -10%	Segment Buffer -10% -20%	Segment Buffer -10% -20% -30%

the investor would lose five percent; if the index was down nine percent, the investor would lose nothing.)

   (b)   A "protection" strategy, in which the contract will be credited with a specified percentage return, declared each year and "locked in" for that year if the value of the index or indices chosen is equal to or greater than the value at the beginning of the period. A decline in the value of the index/indices will result in interest crediting of zero percent. This strategy is similar to the "trigger" index crediting method used in some index annuities.

Another insurer's product allows the purchaser to divide his investment among segments of different duration (one, three, and five years) and to choose among the available indices for each segment and the available "buffers" for each segment. The one-year segment of this product allows the greatest choice of indices and only one buffer (ten percent); the three-and five year segments allow a more restricted choice of indices but greater choice of buffers (ten or twenty percent for the three-year and ten, twenty, or thirty percent for the five-year segment). Cap rates for each segment are declared at the beginning of the period and are locked in for that period's duration, but the buffers will remain at the chosen level.

Both insurers' products impose both annual fees and surrender charges typical of variable annuities. The chief appeal of this product design appears to be to those purchasers whose risk tolerance permits annual losses up to, but not exceeding, a specified percentage of the contract value. In exchange for accepting these losses, the purchaser gets greater potential annual growth (higher "caps" and/or participation rates) than would be available in a product guaranteeing no losses, such as an index annuity.

Endnotes

1. While the guaranteed living benefits in annuity contracts are, strictly speaking, living benefit riders—because they're optional provisions that ride on the basic contract—the term living benefits is almost universally used to describe these riders, and the authors use that term to avoid confusion.

2. This value is also known as the Income Base or Protected Value.

3. The interest rate used in calculating these special payout factors is less than the rate used to calculate the regular payout factors. Often, this special interest rate is 2.0 or 2.5 percent, although it may be as high as 3.5 percent in some older GMIB riders.

4. See "Annuity Payout Factors" in Chapter 4.

5. In many contracts, the annuitization value is equal to the cash value. However, in some, a separate, and higher, account balance is available upon annuitization. This may result from the annuitization value's being computed using an interest rate higher than that used for the cash value or from the insurer's including an initial bonus interest in the annuitization value, but not the cash value available on a lump sum surrender. Some deferred annuities do not offer a lump sum surrender option. These contracts may never be cashed in, but must be placed under an annuity payout option. This is rare in variable contracts, but less so in either conventional or "indexed" fixed annuities.

6. A basis point is 1/100th of a percent. Therefore, 30 bps = 0.30%. Basis points are useful terms for describing the magnitude of difference between two values, each of which is expressed in percentage terms. For example, if A = 6% and B = 4%, B is 200 basis points less than A. To say that "B is 2 percent less than A" would be incorrect, literally speaking. (100% - 2% = 98%, and 98% of 6% is 5.88%).

7. Also called the waiting period or vesting period.

8. For example, in October, 2007, Ibbotson released a paper entitled Retirement Portfolio and Variable Annuity with Guaranteed Minimum Withdrawal Benefit (VA+GMWB). The GMWB provision studied was a lifetime income benefit, in which income payments would not cease if the protected amount (benefit base) fell to zero.

9. The percentage of VA and IA contracts issued with this rider elected has declined from more than ninety percent to roughly seventy-five percent. Source: Advantage Compendium, 2014.

10. The growth rate required for a step up to be triggered may be even greater than that described if the rider cost is based on the benefit base rather than upon the account value. In that situation, the cost of the rider, relative to the annuity cash value, could be greater than its nominal cost, which is stated as a percentage of the account balance.

11. TIAA/CREF Research Institute, "The 5% Guaranteed Minimum Withdrawal Benefit: Paying Something For Nothing?," April, 2008. Available at https://www.tiaa-crefinstitute.org/public/institute/research/dialogue/5percent-gmwb.

12. Many studies of the guaranteed lifetime withdrawal rider refer to it as a GMWB, which may confuse readers who are aware that GMWB is, in most industry marketing material, used to describe the Guaranteed Minimum Withdrawal Benefit, a minimum withdrawal benefit guaranteed only to return the benefit base through a series of withdrawals. Strictly speaking, a GMWB does not guarantee that those payments will persist for the life of the recipient. By contrast, the term GLWB, or Guaranteed Lifetime Withdrawal Benefit, describes a minimum withdrawal benefit where payments are guaranteed for the lifetime of the recipient (or, if a joint rider is elected, for the lifetime of the recipient and his/her spouse). It is that benefit that the TIAA-CREF paper describes.

13. Blanchett, David, "The Expected Value of a Guaranteed Minimum Withdrawal (GMWB) Rider," Journal of Financial Planning, July, 2011

14. Bernard, Garth, "Measuring the Value of a Guaranteed Lifetime Withdrawal Benefit," Journal of Financial Service Professionals, March, 2010

15. Bernard, Ibid,, p. 39

16. Bernard, Garth, "The GLWB Conundrum" (unpublished white paper).

17. Financial Services Authority, "Retail Product Development and Governance – Structured Product Review," November, 2011.

Chapter 6

The Variable Annuity as an Investment

In earlier chapters, the authors have made the point that an annuity is primarily a risk management tool and only secondarily an investment. Arguably, there are exceptions. A short-term CD annuity and, perhaps, an index annuity, might properly be viewed as primarily a savings instrument. On the whole, however, many—if not most—deferred annuities are purchased and sold as investments, and this is particularly true of variable deferred annuities.

Because the variable deferred annuity is typically sold as an investment, in this chapter we will examine it as an investment, using as our framework a model that one of the authors uses to describe the process of financial and estate planning. Then we will relate various characteristics of the variable annuity to three key aspects of the overall planning process, focusing on the extent to which these characteristics provide solutions to the needs that cause consumers to purchase financial instruments—investments—in the first place.

The Model

The process of financial and estate planning may be described as a three-legged stool. The three legs are:

1. accumulation;

2. conservation; and

3. distribution.

From the standpoint of the planning process, each leg, or aspect, represents a need, or combination of needs, that must be satisfied if the plan is to be successful. From the standpoint of a deferred variable annuity, each aspect is reflected in one or more characteristics of the annuity that are designed to satisfy the need in question. We will examine each leg, first as a component of the planning process and, then, as a need for which certain features of the variable annuity were designed to provide a solution.

Leg One: Accumulation

The accumulation goal, as many investors perceive it, is to amass as much capital as possible, by achieving the highest investment returns possible, consistent with acceptable risk. The authors believe that, while this may be a valid investment objective, it is not a good planning objective. Rather, we think, one should aim for maximizing the probability of achieving one's goals. Often, goals are expressed in the form of income. To satisfy these income goals, a tool designed specifically to create income may be more efficient than one designed to create a future lump sum that can then be tapped to create income. There is good evidence that a combination of (1) instruments designed for pure wealth accumulation and (2) purely income instruments can produce higher probabilities of overall plan success than pure accumulation instruments by themselves.[1] In so doing, a combination is actually addressing both the client's accumulation goal and his or her conservation goal.

That said, let's stay focused on the accumulation goal, and ask, "How can a variable annuity help the investor to achieve this goal?"

The Variable Deferred Annuity as an Accumulation Instrument

The efficient accumulation of wealth is the object of all investment methodologies, including the widely used and popular Modern Portfolio Theory (MPT). This theory holds that, to achieve the highest returns possible, with the least amount of investment risk—or, viewed another way, to minimize the investment risk necessary to achieve a given portfolio rate of return—one should construct a diversified portfolio, composed of asset classes, that:

1. offers the opportunity, through a broadly diversified portfolio, to achieve the return necessary to achieve planning goals with the least amount of risk where risk is traditionally defined as volatility—usually measured by standard deviation.

2. reduces risk by constructing the portfolio efficiently from components that represent asset classes that are, to the extent possible, as weakly correlated—or even negatively correlated—as possible. This requires that the investment vehicle provide a sufficient variety of asset classes to allow construction of such a portfolio.

3. can be adjusted periodically. Many theorists believe that periodic rebalancing of the portfolio is essential, by selling those components that have outperformed expectations

and buying those that have underperformed, so as to bring the proportions of the components back to the original optimum mix. How often such rebalancing should occur is a matter of considerable debate.

4.   can be adjusted with as little expense (e.g., transaction costs, taxes, etc.) as possible.

How Does a Variable Annuity Allow the Investor to Build Such a Portfolio?

1. A Broadly Diversified Portfolio.

Early variable annuities offered only limited investment choices, often managed by the issuing insurance company. Today's contracts typically provide the policy owner access to a wide variety of investment subaccounts,[2] managed by several different independent money management firms, in addition to a fixed sub-account, which acts much like a fixed annuity, and for which separate management charges are not assessed. Some variable annuities offer thirty or more variable subaccounts from dozens of money managers. Generally, these subaccounts are actively managed and are sometimes said to be clones of mutual funds offered outside the annuity by the money manager.

However, it is very important that the advisor understand that the term clone, in this connection, is misleading. For example, an annuity may contain a subaccount called Atropos Growth Opportunities, managed by, say, Olympia Capital Investments. Olympia may offer, outside the annuity, a mutual fund with the exact same name. But this does not mean that they are managed by the same individuals or that they have precisely the same investment objectives or investment policies. Nor does it mean that the fees and expenses are the same. Even when the same individual manages both, and when the investment policies of both are essentially the same, that manager may employ different strategies in the annuity than for the mutual fund. Tax considerations alone might suggest the use of different strategies. Realized gains in a mutual fund must, by law, be distributed to shareholders of a mutual fund and are currently taxable even if reinvested.

Consequently, advisors should avoid referring to these subaccounts as clones and, most certainly, should never use the performance history of one when discussing the other. Moreover, as noted in Chapter 1, the pricing of a variable annuity subaccount is different from the pricing of a mutual fund. Reinvested gains in a mutual fund purchase additional shares having, at the time of distribution, the same value as the original shares. By contrast, gains in a variable annuity subaccount do not purchase additional shares; instead, the value of the shares is adjusted to reflect those reinvested gains.

Similarly, though, most variable subaccounts are actively managed, as are most mutual funds. Recently, more and more variable annuities have added passively managed subaccounts designed to match the performance of an external index such as the S&P 500.

2. An Efficient Portfolio.

The availability of a wide variety of investment subaccounts, representing many asset classes, may allow the owner of today's variable annuity to construct a portfolio that is not only diversified but theoretically efficient. It is comprised of asset class components that are weakly, or even negatively, correlated, such that they do not perform in lockstep with one another. We say "may allow" because few, if any, variable annuity issuers provide the annuity owner, or his or her advisor, for that matter, with a tool to construct such an efficient portfolio. This construction is usually done by means of a technique known as Mean-Variance Optimization, and the software tool used to employ it is usually known as an optimizer. As of this writing, the authors know of no variable annuity issuer that provides either the client or the client's advisor with an optimizer, either on a website or in illustration software.

Of course, the client's advisor may have access to such an optimizer, either incorporated in a financial planning software package or a standalone software package. However, even access to this tool will not suffice unless the advisor also knows some vitally important data about the subaccounts to be used to create the optimum portfolio. The required data includes:

- the expected mean return of the asset class;[3]

- the expected volatility of the asset class, as measured by its Standard Deviation (SD);

- the coefficient of correlation of the performance of every subaccount to be considered to the performance of every other subaccount to be considered; and

- the historical time period to which these data refer.

Few, if any, variable annuity issuers provide all of this information. All provide historical return data, however, and an advisor who has access to an analysis tool such as Microsoft Excel®, expertise in using its statistical functions, and historical return data for all subaccounts to be considered for a common time period of significant duration (we suggest at least ten years) can derive the remaining data, which can then be plugged into an optimizer.[4]

Realistically, though, few advisors will do this. First, because it requires statistical expertise that many advisors do not possess, and, second, because there is a much easier way to do the optimization—or, at least, there appears to be.

Some advisors will choose specific investment subaccounts within the annuity to represent asset classes (e.g., Olympia Giant Growth to represent large cap growth stocks) and create an optimized portfolio from those accounts, using optimizer software and the statistical data, such as Mean, SD, and coefficient of correlation, supplied with the software, representing the asset classes themselves. The subaccounts will, in this procedure, be acting as proxies for the asset classes.

Use of an optimizer program in this way is fairly common among advisors seeking to build optimized portfolios from actively managed mutual funds. Applying it to actively managed variable annuity subaccounts is not much different, and the results should be no less credible. The problem is the results will not be credible—whether it is mutual funds or variable annuity subaccounts that are being optimized—if they are actively managed.

The manager of an actively managed fund or variable annuity subaccount seeks to distinguish the performance of the account from its peers, hopefully, by outperforming them. That is what sells the fund and that is what produces the manager's bonus. If the benchmark for a fund is a particular index, the fund manager will seek to outperform that index. But the whole idea of using a proxy for something is to obtain results as close as possible to the values that would be produced if that something were the thing used. The very idea of a proxy, a substitute— deliberately managed to produce results different from the object for which it is substituted—is self-contradictory.

In the authors' opinions, use of Mean-Variance Optimization (MVO) has its uses, but it is not nearly the ideal tool that many advisors suppose it to be when it's used as just described. By definition, any fund or subaccount with a low R-Squared value,[5] in relation to the asset class for which it is standing proxy, will not perform in accordance with the expectations for that asset class. The lower the R-Squared value, the greater the dissonance. The authors believe that MVO is a much more reliable and credible tool when the correlation between the asset classes chosen— to which the return, SD, and coefficients of correlation apply directly—and the proxies chosen to represent those asset classes is as close as possible. There is a fairly simple way to accomplish this objective: the proxies should be designed to mirror the asset classes they represent. If the asset class is, say, U.S. Small Cap Growth, as measured by the Russell 2000 Growth Index, then an excellent proxy would be an index fund or subaccount deliberately constructed to perform like that index.

Until a few years ago, index subaccounts were rarely offered in variable annuities. Recently, however, many contracts have added them, though usually only one or two broad, well-followed indices, such as the S&P 500. A few contracts also offer Exchange-Traded Fund (ETF) accounts, which are also designed to mirror various indices. The expense ratio of both types of accounts is generally much lower than that of their actively managed cousins, and one might wonder why, in light of the frequent criticism of variable annuities as being too expensive, we do not see more of them in the variable annuity marketplace. It's possible that they are less profitable to the annuity issuer than actively managed accounts. It may also be that passively managed accounts are incompatible with the culture of many insurers, whose marketing usually highlights the investment managers available for their products. Whatever the reason, the debate between actively managed and passively managed still rages. Many commentators and a few scholars argue that active management can provide additional value, over and above the value expected from the asset class to which a fund is most closely related. For those who agree with this argument, a variable annuity offers a significant benefit that is often under-appreciated.

As noted earlier, many variable annuities offer dozens of separate subaccounts managed by perhaps a dozen or more money management firms. Often, these managers are chosen by the insurance company because they represent a specific style expertise. Olympia Capital Investments, for example, may be a highly respected growth manager that is particularly adept and successful at managing client money using that style. By contrast, Asgard Asset Management may be well known and respected as a value manager. Another management firm may be highly successful at bond investing. By including all three firms in its stable of managers, an annuity offers the policyholder the opportunity to choose, not only those asset classes that comprise the most appropriate portfolio for his or her goals, but to select managers for each class that are unusually good at managing that particular kind of investment.

3. Periodic Adjustment.

Nearly all variable annuities allow the switching of money among the various subaccounts without cost.[6] Moreover, such a transfer is not a taxable event for income tax purposes. This allows the annuity owner to adjust her portfolio to reflect changed objectives or time horizons, because a manager has consistently underperformed, or to rebalance the portfolio, to return the investment mix to original, or revised, percentage allocations. Most variable annuities offer the policy owner the opportunity to elect such re-balancing automatically, at various intervals; typically, annually, semi-annually, quarterly, or monthly, or when the existing percentage allocation of a holding varies from its target by at least a certain amount or percentage. Typically, there is no charge for this feature.

A related benefit allowed by many variable annuities is sometimes referred to as dollar cost averaging. This feature allows the contract owner with a lump sum to invest, who may be concerned about the risk of investing in the market at the wrong time (i.e., when share prices may be ready to fall), to deposit the lump sum into the fixed account of the annuity in an arrangement where a portion of this lump sum will be automatically transferred, each month, to variable subaccounts that she has selected, so that the entire sum will be transferred evenly across a certain time period, which is typically, six months or one year. Often, an annuity issuer will offer contract holders who elect this feature a higher-than-market interest rate on the funds remaining in the fixed account, which will, by operation of the feature, be entirely invested in the separate accounts at the end of the period.

4. Low Annual Cost.

The owner of a modern variable annuity can construct a portfolio of many individual subaccounts, representing a wide variety of investment types and managed by a diverse stable of professional money managers with different styles and expertise. She can adjust this portfolio periodically—in some contracts, as often as desired—at no cost and with no tax consequence, and may elect to have adjustments made automatically, at no cost. These are powerful and attractive portfolio management benefits, rarely available to regular taxable accounts, which are all too often ignored when the variable annuity is considered as a wealth accumulation tool.

Leg Two: Conservation

The second leg of our three-legged stool model is wealth conservation. Here, the investor's goal is to keep his accumulated assets as safe as possible from loss, including loss due to:

- poor investment performance;

- taxes;

- bankruptcy or other failure by the institution holding the investment; or

- attacks by creditors.

How can a variable annuity help the investor achieve this goal?

1. Protection from Loss from Poor Investment Performance.

Loss due to poor investment performance can adversely affect both the annuity owner during his or her life and the owner's beneficiary, if the owner dies before the contract is surrendered or annuitized. Today's variable annuities contain several risk management features that can help the annuity owner manage the risk of such losses.

As described in Chapter 5, the living benefits in modern variable annuity contracts provide the contract owner with four basic assurances:

1. a guarantee of a minimum future accumulation value, through the guaranteed minimum accumulation benefit;

2. a guarantee of a minimum income, through the guaranteed minimum income benefit;

3. a guarantee of no loss of principal through a guaranteed minimum withdrawal benefit; or

4. a guarantee of a minimum income for life through a guaranteed lifetime withdrawal benefit.

Newer combination riders, incorporating elements of more than one of these benefits, provide these same assurances while offering greater flexibility.

As discussed in Chapter 5, the guaranteed death benefit in today's variable annuity contracts assures the owner that her beneficiary will receive at least the amount originally invested, plus depending upon policy terms, a minimum rate of return on that investment or all or part of previously credited gains.

Both the living and death benefits are, of course, insurance features. They are, however, arguably relevant to a proper evaluation of the variable annuity-as-investment, for anyone whose overall financial planning goals include a desire for conserving his invested wealth.

2. Protection from Loss Due to Taxes.

One of the most-cited benefits of any deferred annuity, including a deferred variable annuity, is that undistributed gain is not subject to current income taxes. Indeed, tax deferral is often said to be the main attraction of deferred annuities. This, in the authors' opinion, is unfortunate for two reasons.

First, this narrow focus ignores the many benefits offered by deferred annuities that have nothing to do with taxation. The investment aspects of a variable annuity just described may be sufficiently attractive to an investor to justify the annuity costs, irrespective of tax deferral. Moreover, an annuity is the only financial instrument that can guarantee its owner an income that he or she cannot outlive.

Second, the argument that tax deferral is the main benefit to be gained from owning a deferred annuity necessarily implies that anyone purchasing a deferred annuity inside an IRA or qualified plan foregoes that main benefit. It is certainly true that the holder of an IRA annuity does not get tax deferral, by reason of owning the annuity, because the IRA itself provides such deferral. However, there are other reasons why one might wish to fund an IRA, or qualified plan, with a deferred annuity.

All that being said, however, the tax deferral enjoyed by annuities is clearly a benefit. Dollars that would otherwise be lost to annual income tax are, in a deferred annuity, able to earn further gain. The miracle of compound interest, in which gain on an investment can, itself, earn yet more gain, is enhanced by yet another layer, producing what is sometimes called triple compounding. This is when: (1) the principal earns gain, (2) the after-tax gain earns gain, and (3) the gain that would otherwise be surrendered to pay tax can also earn further gain.

Notably, this tax-deferral value is increasingly valuable as tax rates on investments increase. Thus, the introduction of a new top twenty percent rate on long-term capital gains and qualified dividends under the American Taxpayer Relief Act of 2012 made using a variable annuity for tax deferral more appealing; the value is further enhanced for those subject to the "new" 3.8 percent Medicare surtax on net investment income under the Patient Protection and Affordable Care Act of 2010, along with the impact of the Pease limitation which phases out itemized deductions and the Personal Exemption Phaseout as income rises (which both function as a small additional surtax on income).

Of course, tax deferred does not mean tax-free! The untaxed gain will eventually be taxed, either to the living annuity holder or to the beneficiary. It will also be taxed as ordinary income. Whether the trade-off of tax deferral now, or a benefit, for ordinary income treatment later, which might be considered a cost of that benefit, is attractive or problematic depends upon a number of variables. This includes assumptions as to tax rate, for both the annuity and the alternative, investment return rate, and, most importantly, how the money will eventually be distributed. A comparison of a hypothetical variable annuity with a hypothetical mutual fund portfolio, taking into account all of these factors and some others, appears at the end of Chapter 12. Many annuity versus investment alternative comparisons are pure accumulation scenarios. They reckon the worth of each side of the comparison in terms of an after-tax future lump sum. In the authors' opinion, such an analysis is inherently faulty. The benefits of a deferred annuity include guaranteed annuity payout factors—assurance that, regardless of future investment conditions or life expectancies, the annuity owner is assured of receiving at least a specified income, every year—or more frequent payment interval—for each dollar that is annuitized. This benefit does come at a cost, which is part of the M&E charges of a variable annuity. Moreover, the annuity owner may elect to annuitize, using the greater of the current, nonguaranteed payout factors or the payout factors guaranteed in the contract. While the latter have, historically, been less attractive and thus, rarely if ever used, they do represent minimum guarantees that might be of value in the future. In summary, the question of whether the benefit of *guaranteed* annuitization rates is worth its cost is certainly arguable. To the authors' knowledge, there has rarely been a time when the guaranteed payout rates contained in an existing deferred annuity contract have been as attractive as payout rates available in Single Premium Immediate Annuity (SPIA) contracts.

Nonetheless, in some cases it may still be appealing to utilize a variable annuity for pure tax deferral alone (versus a comparable pure accumulation scenario without the annuity). This is especially true in scenarios where not all the investments that might be held inside of a variable annuity for tax deferral were going to be eligible for (long-term) capital gains treatment anyway, such that creating ordinary income may not be adverse. For instance, more actively traded investment strategies, or in general investments that have greater turnover, have limited value to being held in a taxable account and may benefit more from tax-deferred compounding. In addition, many types of "alternative" asset class investments that have appealing risk/return and diversification characteristics can be relatively tax-inefficient and/or generate mostly or entirely ordinary income. Thus, in some cases using a variable annuity to shelter investments for tax-deferred compounding growth is simply a matter of absorbing the cost of the annuity and its guarantees in exchange for tax-deferral on investments that are already high-return, ordinary income, and tax-inefficient. In this context, the variable annuity essentially becomes an "asset location" vehicle, which can be used to create tax-deferred growth for those who do not already have sufficient tax-preferred accounts to shelter high-return tax-inefficient investments, especially if the annuity contract can be held at a reasonably low cost.

Purchasing a Deferred Annuity vs. Accumulating in Existing Investments, Then Purchasing a SPIA

The holder of any nonannuity investment wishing to convert his accumulated wealth to a guaranteed income stream could elect to purchase a SPIA. However, the success of this scenario, as compared to investing in a deferred annuity at the outset, depends upon two assumptions:

1.   that the payout rates in SPIA contracts will always be more attractive than those guaranteed in today's deferred contracts;

2.   that the after-tax value of the accumulated wealth—invested in the alternative being considered—will, when invested in the SPIA, produce a greater income than the annuitized deferred annuity. If the alternative investment contains any as-yet-untaxed capital gains, the tax on that gain must be paid on the surrender of the investment. By contrast, the entire future value of the deferred annuity, including all untaxed gain, could be available to purchase the same SPIA, if the deferred annuity is exchanged for the SPIA in a tax-free exchange under Code section 1035.[7] Or the deferred annuity could be annuitized using the then-current payout factors available for holders of that contract, if they are more attractive than those of every SPIA the investor might consider. While that situation has not, to the authors' knowledge, occurred in the past, it might well occur in the future, if average longevity increases.

A comparison of a variable annuity versus an investment alternative that addresses which alternative is better, purely in terms of an after-tax future lump-sum, does not consider the potential advantages of an exchange of such annuities. Moreover, it does not allow for even the possibility that the guaranteed payout factors in the deferred annuity might be more attractive than future SPIA rates. Whatever one believes, as to the latter possibility, it should be taken into account. Any comparison that ignores a benefit that is contractually guaranteed by one alternative but is absent in the other is hopelessly flawed, unless one is prepared to decree that benefit to be utterly worthless—now, and at every time in the future.

3.   Protection from Loss Due to Bankruptcy or Other Failure of the Institution Holding the Investment.

All investors are, or should be, concerned with the extent to which they may lose money as a result of the bankruptcy, or other failure, of the institution holding that money. Investors in annuities should be aware that the cash value in their contracts is not insured by the FDIC. Fixed annuities are backed by the general assets of the issuing insurer and are subject to the creditors of that insurer. The situation with variable annuities is somewhat different. The investments in the variable subaccounts are not held by the insurer, are not protected from loss other than by operation of any living benefits elected by the annuity owner, and are not subject to the insurer's general creditors. However, the contractual guarantees—including annuity payout factors, guaranteed minimum death benefits, and guaranteed living benefits—are, like the cash value of a fixed annuity, backed only by the financial resources of the issuing insurer. The advisor recommending—or even discussing—an annuity with a client should exercise special care to ensure that the client understands these limitations. That said, most alternative investments are not guaranteed against loss due to bankruptcy or insolvency, as many holders of stock and bond issues can attest. We mention the issue only because annuities are sometimes marketed by depository institutions whose regular accounts are insured, and because of frequently cited regulatory concerns that the inapplicability of such insurance to annuities sold by those institutions—or by advisors not connected with such institutions—is not well understood by consumers.

That said, in all fifty states, as well as Puerto Rico and the District of Columbia, there are guarantee funds to reimburse owners of annuity and life insurance contracts from losses resulting from insurer insolvency. The coverage provisions and limits of these funds vary by state. Information on this topic is available at: www.annuityadvantage.com/stateguarantee.htm.

    4.   Protection from Loss to Judgment Creditors.

A serious concern for many investors is the extent to which their assets may be attached by judgment creditors. Many advisors are unaware of the special protections afforded annuities by the laws of many states. Unfortunately, the extent to which annuity cash values receive creditor protection and the limitations on such protection vary widely, and simple answers are—in this context—more than usually dangerous. Two sources of insightful information on this subject are the websites of the law firm of Donlevy-Rosen & Rosen (protectyou.com) and *Quatloos!*, the marvelously informative and surprisingly humorous self-described "Cyber Museum of Scams & Frauds" devoted to estate planning and tax protestor and creditor protection scams (http://quatloosia.blogspot.com).

Leg Three: Distribution

The third leg of the planning stool is distribution. Here, there are typically two goals involved:

1.   during the investor's lifetime, to create income—in the amounts required—from accumulated capital;

2.   at the investor's death, to ensure that the wealth passes, as efficiently as possible, to those intended.

How can a variable annuity help our investor to realize these goals?

Income

Annuities are particularly useful in meeting a goal of required income because income is what annuities are all about. Their effectiveness as accumulation instruments notwithstanding, annuities were originally developed for one purpose—to produce income. When the desire is for an income that will, in any and all events, last as long as the life of the recipient—however long that might be—an annuity is arguably the perfect instrument because it is the only instrument that is guaranteed to do so. Furthermore, all annuities can do so.

What a variable annuity can do in this regard, that no other financial instrument can, is produce an income stream that (1) is guaranteed to last for the lifetime of the annuitant, assuming a life annuity payout option is elected, and (2) will fluctuate in amount—that is, the amount of each payment will vary—reflecting the performance of the underlying investments. This is the so-called variable annuity payout option in a variable deferred annuity contract and the basic structure of a variable immediate annuity.

Why is such a variable payout desirable? Well, initially it should be admitted that for some investors, it is not. Some investors will desire a guarantee—that annuity payments will never change. For those individuals, a fixed annuity payout is indeed more appropriate. This option is available in variable deferred annuity contracts, just as it is in their fixed cousins. On the other hand, however, many investors are concerned with the impact of inflation on their retirement income. They know that, whatever the nominal value of their income, it is the purchasing power that buys groceries.

But is a payout arrangement where the amount of each payment varies, not with the cost of living, but with the performance of the annuity investments, truly the best way to keep pace with inflation? If keeping pace with inflation is the sole objective, probably not. After all, the investments could suffer a loss—resulting in a decrease in the amount of the annuity payment—at the same time that inflation is increasing, further eroding the purchasing value of each dollar of that payment. A better solution would be a life annuity where the amount of each annual payment is adjusted in accordance with some index of inflation, such as the Consumer Price Index. Unfortunately, very few insurance companies offer such a contract. A few insurers offer fixed annuities where the amount of each year's payment will be increased by a specified percentage, typically, one percent to three percent; at the time of this writing the authors know of no company offering an annual adjustment of more than five percent. For the inflation fearful, a guaranteed increase of a few percentage points each year is better than nothing, but it is probably not what they would prefer. Of course, the initial payment of the increasing annuity will be lower than that of the level one. The greater the guaranteed annual increase, the greater this difference will be. *Fourth Edition Update:* The value of annuitization is discussed at length in Chapter 9.

For those individuals, the choice, at the present time, comes down to purchasing a truly inflation-indexed annuity from an insurer that offers one that may not contain all the features the investor wants, or electing a variable payout in the hope that the performance of the annuity investments chosen will enable annuity payments to rise with, or even beyond, the rate of inflation. The authors hope that more insurers will choose to offer genuinely inflation-indexed annuities, both as immediate contracts and as payout options in deferred ones.

The scenario described above is one in which the investor's goal is for an income that is guaranteed both to last a lifetime—or for the lifetime of investor and someone else—and to keep pace with inflation. But what if the goal is to outperform inflation? Many consumers, and probably all advisors, know that lifestyles are not carved in stone. Some retirees wish to do better every year—in real dollar terms. For these individuals, an inflation-indexed payout may not be so attractive. If they believe that a properly designed portfolio, which probably consists mostly of equities, is more likely than not to outperform inflation, a variable payout may make more sense. In any event, the guarantee that the income, whether level or varying with investment performance or inflation rate, cannot be outlived is a powerful benefit.

But annuity payout factors are not the only mechanism by which a variable annuity can generate income for the investor. Living benefits can do so as well. The Guaranteed Minimum Income Benefit (GMIB) guarantees a minimum income based on a guaranteed benefit base that is unaffected by any investment losses within the annuity. The cost of this benefit is, however, not only the contractual charge assessed, but also the fact that the GMIB income stream usually requires annuitization using payout factors less attractive than those available to contract holders not electing this benefit (see Chapter 5).

The guaranteed partial withdrawal benefit also provides a guarantee of a minimum income, but it is really a guarantee of principal irrespective of adverse investment performance, provided that principal—or benefit base, if higher—is accessed via withdrawals not exceeding a certain limit each year.

Passing Wealth to Those Intended

Annuity proceeds are paid to the contract owner's designated beneficiary. They generally pass outside of probate, avoiding the potential cost and time delays that may be associated with that process. In addition, annuity proceeds usually enjoy special creditor protection—the level of protection varying with state law.

Furthermore, special restrictive beneficiary designations offered by some carriers can allow the contract owner to limit the beneficiary's access to proceeds, by either requiring a fixed systematic withdrawal schedule or imposing limits on the amount that the insurer will release each year.[8]

The variable annuity, viewed strictly as an investment, is a remarkably potent vehicle. While many proponents and critics see it purely as an accumulation device, it offers benefits designed to address the needs implicit in all three legs of the financial and estate planning stool.

Endnotes

1. Two of the best demonstrations of this conclusion are in "Making Retirement Distributions Last a Lifetime," by Ameriks, Veres, and Warshawsky, *Journal of Financial Planning*, Dec. 2001, and "Merging Asset Allocation and Longevity Insurance: An Optimal Perspective On Payout Annuities," by Chen and Milevsky, *Journal of Financial Planning*, June 2003.

2. These variable subaccounts are sometimes referred to as separate accounts.

3. For purposes of projecting possible future values, the arithmetic mean is generally considered to be a better factor than the geometric mean. Published historical performance figures generally report the geometric mean, which is always equal or lower—often, significantly lower—than the arithmetic mean.

4. As noted earlier, most historical returns information, when including mean return, use the geometric mean—as that is the best measure of average performance in historical data. If that geometric mean is used as an input in an optimizer software program that expects the user to supply an arithmetic mean—a better measure of the average when forecasting future values—the results will be theoretically inaccurate.

5. R-Squared (R2) is a measure of the extent to which change in one variable can be explained by changes in another, the model. It is often said to be a measure of goodness of fit.

6. Many contracts limit the number of transfers that may be made without cost per year. A few allow switching as often as daily.

7. Deferred annuities are commonly exchanged for SPIAs when the annuity owner decides to annuitize and the current payout factors in the deferred annuity are less attractive than those available from a SPIA. Because this practice is so common, the authors suggest that the often-cited statistic that "only about 2 percent of deferred annuities are ever annuitized" is probably misleading—perhaps very misleading. Any deferred annuity exchanged for a SPIA would be considered as not annuitized, although the result of the Section 1035 exchange produces that result.

8. Such options are particularly appealing for deferred annuity owners that do not necessarily want to deal with the cost and hassle of using a trust to accomplish the same goals. In addition, the use of an individual beneficiary, albeit with restrictions, may be more income-tax-favorable that naming a trust as a beneficiary.

Chapter 7

Index Annuities

In Chapter 1, we observed that one of the ways to classify annuities is to distinguish how the cash value is invested between fixed annuities and variable annuities. Some commentators suggest that that there is also a third type—index annuities. While this might seem reasonable—after all, index annuities certainly look different—it is not correct. An index annuity is a type of fixed annuity. Indeed, it is, in every respect, a fixed annuity, because its value is expressed in dollars, not units that vary in value according to the underlying investments. It is not, in any respect, a variable annuity. To understand why, we must examine how an index annuity works.

But first, it is important to understand the sometimes troublesome matter of its name. Index Annuities (IAs) are also referred to as Equity Index Annuities (EIAs) or Equity-Linked Index Annuities (ELIAs). This is because the interest[1] credited to an IA is linked to an external index, which is usually, but not always, an equity index—typically, but not always, the S&P 500.[2] The nature of this linkage—that is, the extent to which changes in the index will be reflected in the amount of interest credited to the index annuity—varies, and often greatly from one IA product to another. There are several—or many, depending upon how closely one wishes to differentiate—basic index annuity designs and dozens of methods of crediting interest. But all of them link the interest to be credited to the annuity contract to changes in the index used for that contract.

A serious problem with the terms equity index annuity and equity-linked index annuity, according to Jack Marrion, probably the foremost expert in IAs, is that both imply a greater degree of correspondence between movement of the underlying index and interest credited to the index annuity than actually exists in any of the IA designs. Holders of IA contracts may, in attending to those two terms, come to expect the same level of returns—specifically, positive returns—that they could enjoy by holding a more nearly direct investment in the index, such as an index mutual fund, or an exchange-traded fund such as the S&P 500 SPDR.[3] Moreover, both terms virtually ignore two of the most attractive benefits enjoyed by IA owners by virtue of the fact that an IA is a fixed annuity—namely (1) a guarantee of principal and (2) a guarantee of a minimum rate of interest.

For these reasons, Marrion prefers to use the term index annuity, or, better yet, "Fixed Index Annuity" (FIA). In the authors' opinion, Marrion's concerns are valid. The last thing any advisor should want is a label for any savings or investment product that is misleading. So, we will dispense with both EIAs and ELIAs. But, with all due respect to Jack, we'll stick with the term index annuity because it is in common usage. It's also shorter.

Basics of Index Annuities

An IA is a fixed deferred annuity. Like all fixed deferred annuities, it offers a guarantee of principal and a guaranteed minimum rate of interest.[4] However, unlike traditional fixed annuities, the IA offers the potential for excess interest based, not on whatever the insurer decides to declare, but on the performance of the underlying index. An IA gives the buyer some of the gains achieved by the stock index and none of the losses. What do we mean by some? The extent to which the annuity owner participates in the gains realized by the underlying index and when those gains are credited to the annuity, in the form of interest, depends upon the design of the annuity. We will examine the basic designs later in this chapter, but, first, we need to clarify some of the special terminology used in index annuities and to understand the various moving parts that go into the construction of these contracts.

Index Annuity Terminology[5]

Indexing Method

The indexing method is the approach used to calculate the change in the underlying index, for the purpose of determining the interest to be credited to the annuity.

Term or Index Term

The term or index term of an IA is the period over which index-linked interest is calculated. It is important to understand that "index term" does not mean the duration of the annuity contract itself. The contract duration is the period from inception (issue) to the *maturity date*, which is often age ninety-five or one hundred. The maturity date is that date at which the accumulated value of the contract must be paid out, either as a lump sum or in the form of regular annuity payments. Many consecutive index terms can occur over the span of the duration of the contract itself.

Participation Rate

The participation rate is a method—but not the only method—used to determine how much of the increase in the underlying index will be credited as interest to the annuity. For example, if the index growth over the index term was ten percent and the participation rate is seventy percent, the interest credited will be seven percent (10 percent of 70 percent). The participation rate may be guaranteed by the issuer for a period of time, from one year to the entire term, or may be changeable by the insurer at any time. Some contracts guarantee that this rate will never fall below a stated minimum. The participation rate is one of the moving parts in an IA, allowing the issuing insurer to adjust the interest crediting formula to reflect changes in interest rates and the cost of equity options[6] over the term period.

Yield Spread or Term Asset Fee

The yield spread is another method of reducing the amount of index gain that will be credited as interest to the annuity, thus reducing the risk to the insurer, another of the moving parts. If the annualized growth of the index, over the index term, was ten percent and the yield spread is three percent, the interest credited will be seven percent (ten percent minus three percent). Yield spread is simply another way of limiting the insurer's risk and annuity owner's gain—an alternative to the participation rate.

Cap Rate or Cap

Some index annuities put a maximum value on either the interest rate that will be credited, known as the interest rate cap, or the amount of index gain recognized in calculating the equity-linked interest, or index cap. The marketing material for some IAs that use a cap do not make entirely clear whether an interest rate cap or an index cap is being used. It is vitally important that the advisor, discussing an IA with a cap, understand which method is being employed. Here's why. Assume the underlying index gains 20 percent in a given year:

1. An IA with a 70 percent participation rate and a 12 percent interest rate cap will credit 12 percent. 20 percent × 70 percent = 14 percent, but the cap limits the interest credited to 12 percent; therefore, the interest credited is 12 percent.

2. An IA with a 3 percent yield spread and a 12 percent interest rate cap will credit 12 percent. 20 percent – 3 percent = 17 percent, but the cap limits the interest credited to 12 percent; therefore, the interest credited is 12 percent.

3. An IA with a 70 percent participation rate and a 12 percent index cap will credit 8.4 percent interest. The cap recognizes no more than 12 percent of the index movement—12 percent × 70 percent = 8.4 percent.

4. An IA with a 3 percent yield spread and a 12 percent index cap will credit 9 percent interest. The cap recognizes no more than 12 percent of the index movement—12 percent – 3 percent = 9 percent.

Does this mean that IAs with index caps are not as good as those with interest rate caps? Not necessarily, because IAs with index caps frequently offer higher participation rates or lower yield spreads than contracts with interest rate caps. As Marrion and John Olsen explain in their book *Index Annuities: A Suitable Approach*, "caps are used to boost participation rates or minimize yield spreads. Since they limit upside exposure, the cost [to the insurer] of providing the index-linked interest is less, so participation in caps up to the cap are higher. Caps enable one to get 'more of most' instead of 'less of more.'"[7]

Notably, though, this does represent a trade-off, and depending on the composition of the underlying returns may turn out better or worse; for instance, if returns are routinely greater than the cap in a volatile investment, getting "less of more" (but participating in *all* of the upside) can still net better results than getting "more of most" (if some is routinely left on the table). Ultimately, advisors trying to decide whether to recommend solutions with higher or lower caps (and the associated participation rates) should consider the return potential relative to the volatility of the underlying investment used to calculate those returns.

Index Annuity Designs

IAs have been around since the mid-1990s. Initially, the designs (the ways in which contracts recognized and credited interest) were few and relatively simple. With changes in the stock market and consumer attitudes, new designs were introduced. By November, 2000, there were over forty different interest crediting methods.[8] In recent years, most of those designs have fallen by the wayside. Currently, the great majority of IAs sold use one of just a few basic methods.

Annual Point-to-Point (APP)

Like a fixed rate annuity—a conventional fixed annuity—the annual point-to-point method, credits interest each year. The amount of interest credited each year is based on the movement of the underlying index during that year, calculated from the ending balance of the index for the previous year (thus, "point to point"). An essential characteristic of annual reset index annuities is that losses are ignored. If the index movement in any year is negative, the contract treats that loss as a zero percent gain and credits zero interest for that year. Another essential characteristic is that, because gain is measured from the index value at the end of the previous year, an annual point-to-point IA can credit interest based on index gain even if that gain is only a recapture of some of previous losses. This is due to the "annual reset" that occurs each year. The beginning-of-year index value, for purposes of determining interest, is "reset" from the prior year's value (and the reset can be up *or down* from the prior year!). The annual point-to-point method is usually abbreviated as (APP) and is sometimes referred to as the "ratchet" or "annual reset" method.

Figure 7.1 illustrates the hypothetical performance of a $100,000 APP annuity with a sixty percent participation rate, and a five percent interest rate cap. In the first three years, the index lost over forty percent; in each of those years, the annuity was credited with zero percent interest (because loss years in the APP crediting method are treated as zero percent gains). In the fourth year, the index gained over twenty-six percent, but that gain had not erased all of the first three years' losses. Nevertheless, the annuity was credited with five percent interest (due to the five percent cap).

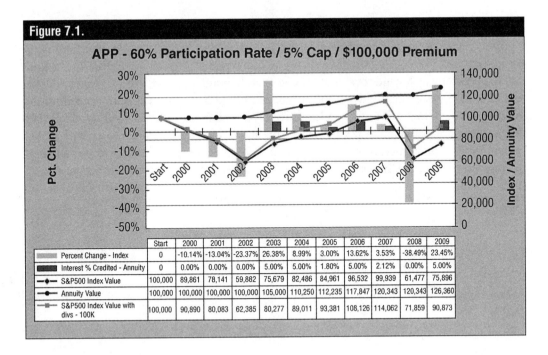

Figure 7.1.

APP - 60% Participation Rate / 5% Cap / $100,000 Premium

	Start	2000	2001	2002	2003	2004	2005	2006	2007	2008	2009
Percent Change - Index	0	-10.14%	-13.04%	-23.37%	26.38%	8.99%	3.00%	13.62%	3.53%	-38.49%	23.45%
Interest % Credited - Annuity	0	0.00%	0.00%	0.00%	5.00%	5.00%	1.80%	5.00%	2.12%	0.00%	5.00%
S&P500 Index Value	100,000	89,861	78,141	59,882	75,679	82,486	84,961	96,532	99,939	61,477	75,896
Annuity Value	100,000	100,000	100,000	100,000	105,000	110,250	112,235	117,847	120,343	120,343	126,360
S&P500 Index Value with divs - 100K	100,000	90,890	80,083	62,385	80,277	89,011	93,381	108,126	114,062	71,859	90,873

At the end of the tenth year, the index value was almost twenty-five percent less than at the start; even with dividends (which aren't used in the index annuity crediting calculations), the ending value was nearly ten percent less. By contrast, the annuity value was more than twenty-six percent higher. The S&P® numbers shown are actual historical values from January, 2000 through December, 2009. So, does this mean that one can expect an index annuity to outperform the index itself?

Definitely not. First, stocks in an equity index may produce dividends, which, as noted earlier, are not taken into account in IAs, but would be received by investors holding a mutual fund or ETF based on that index. Moreover, this hypothetical illustration, which uses actual values of the S&P 500 Index, is of a highly volatile period, and happens to start from what turned out to be a significant market peak. APP IAs do very well in such a climate, if an investor should be lucky enough to start investing when such a volatile market environment occurs.

Averaging – Monthly or Daily

The use of averaging can "smooth out" market highs and lows and drive credited interest to the middle-of-market performance during the crediting period. Thus, in a generally rising market, averaging usually produces a lower value than a point-to-point design and, in a falling market, usually produces a higher value. Similarly, an averaging formula can protect the annuity buyer from a dramatic end-of-term market decline, but also may forgo fully benefitting from a dramatic end-of-term market rally.

Monthly Averaging

The amount of interest credited under a monthly average is calculated by first finding the average (monthly) value of the index over the crediting period (typically, one year), determined by simply adding up the index value at the end of each month and dividing by the total number of months. The beginning index value at the start of the period is then subtracted from this monthly average to produce the "index difference." The index difference is then divided by the beginning index value to produce the gross interest rate. The gross interest rate is then multiplied by the participation rate (often, in monthly averaging contracts, one-hundred percent) to produce the interest rate to be credited to the annuity contract for that period.

Exhibit 7.1.	
Example:	
Beginning Value	100
Value Period 1	102
Value Period 2	103
Value Period 3	105
Value Period 4	107
Value Period 5	104
Value Period 6	106
Value Period 7	109
Value Period 8	112
Value Period 9	111
Value Period 10	108
Value Period 11	107
Value Period 12	110
Average over all periods	1284/12 = 107
(Average Index Value) – (Beginning Index Value) = (Index Difference)	
107 – 100 = 7	
(Index Difference) / (Beginning Index Value) = (Gross Interest Rate)	
7 / 100 = .07	
(Gross Interest Rate) × (Participation Rate) = (Interest Earned)	
.07 × 100% = 7%	

Daily Averaging

Daily averaging is done in the same way as monthly averag ing, except that the index values are added on a daily basis and the number of data points (to divide by, to determine the average) is the number of days in the year having index values.

Monthly Sum (Monthly Cap on Gains, but not Losses)

This method was borrowed from a Wall Street principal protection securities idea.[9] It sums the monthly gains and losses, after applying a cap to each monthly gain. Monthly losses are not subject to such capping. The resulting sum is the interest rate that will be credited to the annuity contract. This method is sometimes called "monthly point-to-point," which can be confusing because, unlike a true APP method, the values in this method are not locked in each month;[10] thus, intra-year losses in some months actually can offset gains in other months, though if the total year's loss is negative the policyowner still receives a zero percent (non-negative) return due to the principal guarantee of the annuity.

Exhibit 7.2.		
Example: MONTHLY CAP 2%		
MONTH	*Actual Return*	*Capped Return*
January	+2%	+2%
February	+1%	+1%
March	–3%	–3%
April	+4%	+2%
May	+2%	+2%
June	–4%	–4%
July	–3%	–3%
Aug	+1%	+1%
Sept	+5%	+2%
Oct	+3%	+2%
Nov	–1%	–1%
Dec	+3%	+2%
AVERAGE	10%	CAPPED AVERAGE 3%
3% interest would be credited to the contract.		

"Trigger" Method (AKA "Performance Trigger")

In this method, the index annuity will be credited with a stated interest rate (declared at the beginning of each year) if the index value at the end of the period (typically, one year) is equal to or greater than the value at the beginning of the period, regardless of the size of that index gain. For example, if the beginning index value is 100 and the ending value is 102 (a gain of two percent), the annuity will be credited with the declared rate whether that rate is more or less than the actual index gain. If the index declines, no interest is credited.

"Inverse Performance Trigger" Method

This method is similar to a Put Option. If the ending index value is equal to *or less than* the beginning index value, the stated interest rate (declared at the beginning of each year) will be credited to the contract. If the index rose during the period, zero percent interest will be credited.

Notably, neither the performance trigger method, nor the inverse performance trigger method, can produce an interest credit of other than the stated rate or zero.

"Rainbow" Method

As Marrion and Olsen note, the rainbow concept has been used for years in the investment world. The rainbow method is an option basket whose best-performing indices are weighted more heavily than those indices that performed less well. It is a "look back" method because the contract value is allocated based on the ranking of the indices' performance after the period is over.

Exhibit 7.3.	
Example: A Rainbow Method using allocations of 35%, 35%, 20%, and 10%.	
US Stock Index	up 20%
Bond Index	down 10%
Foreign Stock Index	up 18%
Emerging Markets Index	up 5 %

The best performer was the US Stock Index with a twenty percent gain. The rainbow method uses the highest allocation for that index, thirty-five percent, and credits seven percent. The next best performer, also allocated thirty-five percent, is the Foreign Stock Index at plus eighteen percent and produces a credit of 6.3 percent.The third performer, Emerging Markets, allocated twenty percent, was up five percent, producing plus one percent interest. The worst performer, the Bond Index, was down ten percent, producing, with an allocation of ten percent, a minus one percent credit. The sum of the credits is 13.3 percent, which is credited to the contract, as shown below:

Exhibit 7.4.		
US Stock Index	up 20% × 35%	= + 7%
Foreign Stock Index	up 18% × 35%	= + 6.3%
Emerging Markets Index	up 5% × 20%	= + 1%
Emerging Markets Index	up 5% × 20%	= + 1%
Bond Index	down 10% × –10%	= –1%
Total:		**13.3%**

Other Interest Crediting Methods

Term End Point

The Term End Point design measures index movements over a period greater than one or two years and does not calculate or credit interest each year. The investor's return is not known, and cannot be estimated, until the end of the term period, which is typically seven to ten years. The index gain is calculated by dividing the index value at the end of the term by its value at the beginning and then subtracting 1. For example, if the index is 100 at the outset of the contract, and ten years later is 180, the index gain is eighty percent [(180 ÷ 100) − 1]. That gain is then adjusted by applying any participation rate and the resulting interest percentage is multiplied by the initial contract value to produce the interest to be credited. For example, at a seventy percent participation rate, the cumulative interest credited would be fifty-six percent (80% × 70%). Such an annuity, purchased for $100,000, would be worth $156,000 at the end of ten years.

A variation of this design, called *Term Yield Spread*, works similarly, in that interest is neither calculated nor credited until the end of the period. However, the yield spread is not simply subtracted from the index gain, because the yield spread is an annual figure and the index gain is a cumulative one. Instead, the interest is credited by applying the yield spread to the annualized return of the index over the time period, using this formula:

Exhibit 7.5.

Interest Credited = R − Y

$R = (E \div S)^{(1/n)} - 1$

E = Ending Index Value

S = Starting Index Value

n = number of years in period

Y = Yield Spread

Using the facts above and a yield spread of 3 percent, the interest credited would be 3.054 percent per year [$R = (180 \div 100)^{1/10} - 1 = 6.054$; interest credited = R-Y = 6.054 − 3.00 = 3.054]. The annuity, at the end of ten years would be worth $135,098 [$100,000 \times (1 + .0354)^{10}$]. What if the index were lower at the end of ten years than at the outset (or higher, but less than the guaranteed value)? Then the contract would not use that final index value, but would, instead credit the guaranteed interest rate to the initial index value for each year of the term.

The APP and Term End Point designs are the two basic types of IAs. However, there are many variations on those themes. We will not attempt to describe all of the variations out there,[11] but we will look now at certain features that are common to several, or even all, IAs.

High Water Mark

In this variation on the Term End Point design, index-linked interest, if any, is credited based on the difference between the starting index value and the highest value of the index—usually, at policy anniversaries—during the period. This method is rarely used in currently issued contracts because the cost of the options is higher, and so index participation would have to be much lower than for other interest crediting types.[12]

Index Annuities Provisions

Guaranteed Interest Rates

Some IAs guarantee the crediting of a minimum amount of interest to the owner's entire investment. Others guarantee it to only a percentage—often, eighty percent or ninety percent—of that investment. The latter arrangement can produce confusion as to the minimum interest the annuity owner is guaranteed to receive. For example, many older contracts guarantee three percent interest on ninety percent of the amount invested. (Newer policies have lower guarantees, such as two percent interest on 87.5 percent of premium). This may appear to mean that the interest rate guaranteed is an annual compound rate of 2.7 percent credited (90% × 3%) to the amount invested. This is not correct! The principal on which the three percent interest is credited is only ninety cents for each dollar invested. Thus, on a $100,000 single premium, the guaranteed future value at the end of ten years would be $FV = PV \times (1 + i)^n = \$90,000 \times 1.03^{10} = \$120,952$. The compound rate of return required to produce $120,952 at the end of ten years, if one invests $100,000 today, is 1.92 percent $[(120,952 \div 100,000)^{1/10} - 1]$. The effective guaranteed minimum rate on the entire amount invested is, thus, 1.92 percent, not 2.7 percent.

Will that guaranteed minimum interest be paid if the owner of the annuity surrenders the contract before the end of the term? No, because guaranteed interest is almost always credited at the end of the surrender period and not each year. The owner surrendering an annuity that is not an annual reset design, or one that otherwise vests interest—as some high water mark designs do—will generally receive no index-linked interest, if surrender occurs prior to the end of the term. In this case, the individual would simply receive a return of the original premiums paid, and any guaranteed interest payable if applicable. Moreover, surrender charges may apply.

It should be noted that the crediting of only guaranteed interest to an index annuity contract is very unlikely. Over a period of many years, an index annuity has only to experience a few good years in order for its average return to exceed the guaranteed minimum. Average returns have been substantially higher.

Advantage Compendium, a firm owned by Jack Marrion, tracks such returns and the following data were taken from his reports.

Exhibit 7.6.	
Actual Annualized Returns for Index Annuities	
2008–2013	4.9%
2007–2012	3.27%
2006–2011	4.06%
2005–2010	3.89%

This does not ensure, of course, that future returns will be in the same ranges. Nonetheless, through a range of market outcomes, the contracts all had at least a few years good enough to beat the minimum guarantee.

Surrender Charges

Surrender charges in IAs work just like the surrender charges in other annuity contracts. However, the size of the charges, and the length of time during which they apply, is generally higher in IAs. Some IAs do not impose surrender charges as such, but base the surrender value on the guaranteed minimum amount, based on crediting of interest to less than the full investment. This has the same effect as a declining surrender charge over the first few years of the contract.

Free Withdrawals

As is typically the case with both conventional fixed and variable annuities, IAs usually permit withdrawals of up to a specified percentage of the cash value each year without imposing surrender charges.

However, if the prospective buyer of any deferred annuity feels that there is a significant likelihood of a need to tap the money in that annuity before the expiration of the surrender charge period, we suggest that a deferred annuity may not be appropriate in the first place. As was noted, surrender charges in IAs typically are higher and last longer than those in other annuity contracts, so an early distribution in excess of the amount permitted under the free withdrawal feature could be subjected to a stiff penalty. Moreover, any distribution, whether surrender charges apply or not, could be subject to the ten percent early distribution penalty. Furthermore, as discussed earlier, an early partial surrender could cause forfeiture of any accumulated equity-linked interest, or guaranteed minimum interest, to the extent attributable to the withdrawal taken. In short, the authors believe that annuities in general, and IAs in particular, are of questionable appropriateness when liquidity is an issue.

Premium Bonus

Many IAs offer a premium bonus, whereby the contract owner is credited with an additional percentage of the premium actually paid, which will earn interest on the same basis as paid premium, provided that the contract is not surrendered before the end of the term. However, this bonus is not free. Often, contracts offering a premium bonus require higher surrender charges, longer surrender charge periods, or a lower participation rate compared to contracts without the bonus. In some contracts, the difference is not reflected in lower benefits for the owner, but rather, in a lower commission paid to the selling agent. See the discussion on bonus annuities in Chapter 4.

Required Annuitization

Some IAs require the contract to be annuitized for certain benefits to be payable, or provide lower levels of benefits, such as participation rate, for contracts that are surrendered for a lump sum—even if held to the end of the required term. The value of annuitization is, as will be discussed in a later chapter, a very controversial issue in the financial services community.

Notwithstanding the controversial aspects of annuitization (which some take so far as to suggest annuitization is "never" appropriate), the authors do not subscribe to the widespread belief that it is always a bad decision. However, it seems only logical to observe that, whatever value the annuity owner places on annuitization, an obligation to take proceeds in that form would not be attractive to a rational investor in the absence of some benefit not available without that requirement. A few contracts not only require annuitization for the contract holder to receive the entire account balance; that is, they impose surrender charges on withdrawals and lump sum surrenders that never expire, but impose that same requirement upon beneficiaries. Fortunately for consumers—and, in the authors' opinion, for the insurance industry, too—such contracts are becoming increasingly rare.

How Can the Insurance Company Do All This?

A question often asked by consumers is, "how can the insurance company do all this?" This, meaning the guarantee principal plus a minimum rate of interest and participation in exceptional upside movements in the underlying index. Where's the catch? When this question is asked, it usually means that the advisor has done a poor job of explaining how the index annuity works. It may look too good to be true. This is certainly true when the advisor has said something like "with this annuity, you get the upside of the equity market, but with no downside risk."

That is just not true! The index annuity owner does not "get the upside of the equity market," but only a portion of that growth. The portion of any index growth an individual gets is determined by the various limiting factors, or the moving parts, in the contract design. These moving parts are essential for the issuing insurer to limit its loss exposure. After all, it is guaranteeing the purchaser's principal from any loss of principal and a minimum rate of return, if the contract is held for the full term.

Typically, the insurer purchases a combination of bonds and call options on the underlying index to guarantee the funds required to meet its obligations under the contract. The greatest part of the purchaser's premium is invested in bonds, in sufficient amount to provide the dollars needed to meet the insurer's minimum obligations. The remainder is used to buy those call options. The price of the call options, to fund the indexed-linked interest, and the cost and yield of the bonds, to fund the contractual guarantees, together determine how many options the insurer can purchase with a given premium. If option prices at a particular time are low— because expected index volatility is low—and bond yields are high, it might be possible for the insurer, at that time, to purchase enough index options to provide the annuity owner with one-hundred percent of the performance of the index, in addition to guaranteeing principal and the minimum interest rate.

But in the last few years, such has not been the case. Interest rates are near historic lows and option prices are relatively high, because index performance is expected to be more than usually volatile. So, at this time, insurers do not have enough left over from an IA purchaser's premium, after purchasing the bonds required, to buy enough index options to give that purchaser one-hundred percent of the index performance on the premium invested. For that reason, today's participation rates and cap rates are relatively low and yield spreads are relatively high, although both are better today (from the perspective of a potential buyer of an IA) than they had been only a few years earlier. Issuers of IAs are still not purchasing options for all possible growth at this time because they can't. But they don't need to because today's participation rates, caps, and yield spreads limit the amount of that growth they're obliged to credit to their annuities.

This is precisely why, when an annuity owner is limited to a sixty percent participation rate or a cap of, say, five percent, and the index goes up fifteen percent, the insurer does not keep the excess return above the nine percent it would credit under a sixty percent participation rate or the five percent it would credit under the cap. And it does not purchase enough options to get one-hundred percent of the growth on the entire amount of that annuity owner's premium. There is no need to do so, nor is there enough paid-in premium left over, after purchase of the bonds, to do so. The insurer does not keep that excess because it does not receive it.

But why can't the insurer guarantee the level of the various moving parts (e.g., the cap rate, participation rate, and yield spread)? It may guarantee some of these factors, but it cannot guarantee all of them and expect to remain in business. Why?

It is because financial markets change. Interest rates change and, with them, the cost of the bonds the insurer will purchase to meet minimum contractual guarantees. Likewise, the cost of index options also change, increasing with the volatility, or expected volatility, of the index and the length of time over which they are exercisable. If an insurer chooses to guarantee the participation rate, cap rate, or yield spread for the entire term, it cannot offer as high a participation rate and cap rate, or as low a yield spread, as if it reserves the right to adjust those factors periodically because it will not be able to purchase as many options since the cost of those options will be higher. For these reasons, nearly all IAs do not guarantee all of the moving parts for the entire term. This is particularly true of annual reset contracts, where the insurer will need to continue purchasing call options in the future at an unknown cost.

Because the issuing insurer can adjust these moving parts periodically, to reflect changing economic realities, it is essential that the advisor choose an insurer with a good record of renewing these rates so as to treat existing contract holders fairly. The authors strongly suggest that advisors ask the issuer of any IA, or fixed annuity for that matter, they are considering for a history of renewal rates.

Which Index Annuity Design Is Best?

Perhaps the most common question asked by advisors who are considering IAs for their clients is, "which kind is best?" In the authors' opinion, the only reasonable answer is, "it depends". As Marrion and Olsen point out, any crediting method can produce the best return for a given period. There are, however, certain general observations that one can make regarding index annuity policy designs.

Annual Point-to-Point

With an annual reset index annuity, the purchaser knows how much her annuity is worth at the end of each year. Interest is calculated, credited, and locked-in each year. Future decreases in the index will not reduce the annuity value. The biggest trade-off to this is that the participation rate, cap rate, or yield spread is likely to be lower than in other designs. These contracts generally excel in markets with high volatility, although such volatility tends to increase option costs and reduce participation rate or increase yield spread.

High Water Mark

The high water mark design protects the annuity owner from a decline in the index at the end of the term, which could wipe out much, or even all, of the gain previously experienced, but not credited. However, the rates for the various moving parts are likely to be less attractive than for a contract with a point-to-point design with the same term.

Term End Point

The Term End Point design does not allow the purchaser to know the value of the annuity until the end of the term. However, the rates for the moving parts are likely to be greater than for other policy designs with the same term. In addition, because many or all of the bonds and call options are put in place when the contract is acquired, point-to-point contracts tend to have fewer moving parts that may be changed after the contract is initially acquired.

Averaging

Crediting methods using averaging generally have higher participation rates and/or caps than those methods without averaging. On the other hand, averaging drives numbers to the middle. In a generally rising market, averaging usually produces lower interest crediting than would be produced using the final value (an unaveraged point-to-point design). The reverse is also true; in a declining market, averaging will produce greater interest crediting than the unaveraged point-to-point method.

In practice, this creates a challenge as to when averaging methods are appropriate. If, during the index crediting period, the index rises substantially over most of the period but declines sharply at the end, averaging performs well. In the reverse scenario, averaging performs worse (than a straight point-to-point design).

Monthly Sum

In the Monthly Sum method, the "best case" scenario would be where the index increases each month by *precisely* the cap rate. With a two percent cap, that scenario would produce an annual crediting of twenty-four percent. A "worst case" scenario would be a "raging bull" for eleven months—a fifty percent gain, for example—followed by a disastrous December—a decline of twenty-two percent or more. The maximum "capped" gain would be twenty-two percent (eleven months x two percent), which the December decline would wipe out entirely.

In general, investors should avoid the monthly sum methodology if they are bearish on markets, as a significant decline can wipe out most or all of a year's worth of monthly-capped gains. Monthly sum contracts will tend to perform best in environments with less volatility and a gentle upward tilt to market returns.

Which Index Crediting Method Will Perform Best?

The authors are often asked this question by advisors. Of course, the question of "which crediting method will perform best?" presumes that there is a "best" method. In the authors' opinion, the most that one can say is that in certain scenarios, some methods may outperform others. If the investor has a very specific view about the direction of markets, it may be possible to align a crediting method to certain anticipated market scenarios, though this isn't always feasible.

For instance, in a raging bull market, an interest crediting method that gives the greatest percentage of index growth but as little recognition as possible of index losses should perform best. The APP method, especially if the "interest rate spread" rather than a participation rate is used, should do well, and either should do better than the monthly averaging method. In this scenario, the Monthly Sum method COULD produce even better results if there are no months of significant losses. (e.g., a "best case" scenario for the monthly sum method with a three percent cap on gains could produce a thirty-six percent return, but that is extremely unlikely (we did say that this scenario is a "RAGING bull" one).

In a mediocre, "sideways" market, Monthly Averaging may perform well because that method typically has higher caps than the Monthly Point-to-Point method. By contrast, the APP method may do poorly (especially if the final ending value is either less than, or only slightly higher than, the beginning of year value). The Monthly Sum method would likely do poorly in this scenario, especially if the loss months are greater than the gain months. If monthly gains and losses are quite small, the Trigger method should do best if the stated interest rate (payable if the month-end value is at least equal to the beginning-of-month value) is higher than the actual monthly gains.

In a "bear" market, the Inverse Performance Trigger method will perform best, as it credits interest when there are monthly losses, but not when there are gains, while an APP is unlikely to create much value (if the end-value is anticipated up front to be below the starting value). Of course, we should recognize that if one expects an extended bear equities market, a fixed rate annuity or bonds might make more sense in the first place.

Jack Marrion and John Olsen also address this issue of comparing various crediting methods in their book, Index Annuities: A Suitable Approach (Olsen & Marrion LLC, 2010). The following excerpt is used by permission.

Different Methods & Different Markets

IAs have been around for less than twenty years and several individual crediting methods have an even shorter history, so we do not know how the different crediting methods would have performed over the long term. However, we can calculate the hypothetical returns of different reset structures over the past fifty years to get an idea of how they would have performed. While we do not know what crediting rates might have been over the last fifty years, we do know that annual reset point-to-point structures have often had actual participation rates of forty-five percent or less for quite a while. So by plugging a forty-five percent participation rate into every up year of the last fifty years of S&P 500 returns (annual reset index annuities treat down years as zeroes), we can determine that the annualized average return over all of the ten-year calendar year periods is 5.2 percent. We can then use this average return for the Annual Point to Point (APP) design and see how high the index participation rates for other designs would need to be in order to equal the return produced by the 45 percent APP method. There is not a particular reason for using ten year periods; we simply picked ten years for illustrative purposes.

If you could have purchased an index annuity for every ten-year period since 1960, with this forty-five percent APP annual reset structure, your annualized interest rate would have been 5.2 percent, and your overall effective rate would have been seventy-four percent. The chart below gives examples of other types of IA interest crediting factors that would have given the same annualized return and effective rate. This gives us a "level playing field" of existing interest crediting factors all would have earned an annualized 5.2 percent interest rate.

For example, if you had purchased an annuity with a one-hundred percent APP and an 8.45 percent interest cap (where you would never have earned more than 8.45 percent interest in a given year), your overall annualized return would have been 5.2 percent. An index annuity using monthly averaging with a seventy-six percent participation rate would have also averaged a 5.2 percent annual return. We can do this analysis for other crediting methods, including daily and monthly averaging:

Exhibit 7.7.

What Is Required to Produce the Same Annualized Return

Crediting Method		Effective Rate
Annual Pt-to-Pt	45%	74%
Monthly Averaging	76%	74%
Daily Averaging	80%	74%
Annual Pt-to-Pt	100% with 8.45% cap	74%
Monthly Cap	3.05% cap on monthly gain	74%
Monthly Averaging	100% less 2.75% yield spread	74%

If we could have deposited the same amount of money into annuities using each of these different index annuity crediting methods over the last fifty years, our overall returns would be the same for each crediting method. We are not saying this is what the index participation would have been; only that these crediting factors all yield the same returns over the last half-century of market data.

The lesson here is that simply choosing the annuity with the lowest spread, the highest rate, or the best cap will not ensure you of getting the highest return.

Guaranteed Living Benefit Riders

Given the enormous popularity of Guaranteed Living Benefit riders in variable deferred annuity contracts, it was only a matter of time until issuers of fixed annuities—including IAs—got into the game. In 2006, the first Guaranteed Lifetime Withdrawal Benefit was offered as a rider on an index annuity. By the end of that year, seven index annuity carriers were offering GLWBs, with more carriers considering the addition of these benefits.[13] As of February, 2014, GLWB riders are offered in many index annuities and are very popular. (See "Guaranteed Lifetime Withdrawal Benefit in Index Annuities," in Chapter 5.)

It should be noted that payments from all GLWB riders will, for many years, represent only a return of the investor's own principal. With the limited volatility and principal guarantees applicable to IAs in the first place, investors may not actually end up "ahead" (receiving more than their own contract values) with such guarantees unless their withdrawal periods are long enough (possibly several decades) to fully recover principal and any growth that could have been obtained with fixed income investments anyway.

As to other living benefits in IAs, no IA, to the authors' knowledge, offers a Guaranteed Minimum Income Benefit (GMIB) because the guarantee of principal in an IA makes a guaranteed minimum annuitization benefit unnecessary.

Endnotes

1. The gain realized in an index annuity is interest, not dividends or capital gains.

2. The S&P 500, or S&P 500 Composite Price Index, was created by the Standard & Poor's Company in 1923. The S&P 500 is "calculated using a base-weighted aggregate methodology, meaning the level of the Index reflects the total market value of all component stocks relative to a particular base period. Total market value is determined by multiplying the price of its stock by the number of shares outstanding." See "S&P 50th Anniversary" at: http://www2.standardandpoors.com/portal/site/sp/es/la/page.topic/indices_500anniv/2,3,2,2,0,0,0,0,0,1,1,0,0,0,0,0.html.

3. SPDR is the exchange symbol for the S&P 500 Index Fund, an exchange traded fund, and stands for Standard & Poor's Depository Receipt.

4. The guaranteed rate of return for IAs can sometimes be as low as zero percent. Most guarantee a rate of at least three percent, which might be credited to only a percentage, such as eighty percent or ninety percent, of the premiums received.

5. Some of the material in this section was taken from *the Buyer's Guide To Equity-Indexed Annuities*, prepared by the National Association of Insurance Commissioners, reprinted by the Illinois Division of Insurance at: www.ins.state.il.us/Life_Annuities/equityindex.htm.

6. Purchase of equity call options is the usual mechanism used by issuers of IAs to guarantee the funds to pay the equity-linked interest. However, other methods may be used, or the insurer may go naked and self-insure that equity-linked interest payment liability. See Marrion and Olsen, *Index Annuities: A Suitable Approach* (Olsen & Marrion, LLC, 2010, www.indexannuitybook.com), Chapter 2.

7. Marrion and Olsen, *ibid.*, p. 59.

8. Advantagecompendium.com.

9. Marrion and Olsen, ibid.,

10. Marrion and Olsen, ibid.

11. See Marrion and Olsen, ibid.. for a detailed discussion of the different types of interest crediting methods..

12. Marrion and Olsen *ibid.* p. 51

13. Jack Marrion, *A Look At Annuity And Securities GLWBs* (Advantage Compendium, August, 2008, available at www.indexannuity.org).

Chapter 8

Deferred Income Annuities ("Longevity Annuities")

The *deferred income annuity* (also called the "longevity annuity") is a relatively new type of annuity contract, different from both the deferred and immediate types. Like an immediate annuity, it provides only a guaranteed stream of income for life or a certain period of time (or both) and typically has no account balance that may be accessed other than by annuitization. However, where income payout from an immediate annuity must commence within one year of purchase, the payout from a longevity annuity is generally not available until the annuity starting date chosen by the buyer, which may be many years after purchase. The longevity annuity appeared as a concept called the high protection annuity in a 1978 paper by James Stephenson.[1] The authors have been told that one major insurer had developed a longevity annuity over twenty years ago, but that, as there was little interest in it, the product "sat on the shelf" until very recently, despite some serious *academic* interest in the concept.

In a 2004 article[2], Moshe Milevsky referred to the product as an "Advanced Life Deferred Annuity" (ALDA). In 2006, Scott, Watson and Hu called it a "delayed payout annuity" and argued that it affords the buyer with far more efficient annuitization than an immediate annuity.[3] Although there is still no universal agreement, in today's marketplace this type of annuity is most commonly called a "Deferred Income" or "Longevity" annuity, though the ALDA and "delayed payout" annuity labels are sometimes still used as well.

How Does a Deferred Income Annuity Work?

A deferred income annuity might be viewed as a hybrid of a deferred annuity and an immediate annuity. Like the former, it is purchased in advance of the annuity starting date—typically, well in advance—such that payments will not begin until many years into the future. Like an immediate annuity and unlike a deferred annuity, the original version of the deferred income annuity (often labelled the "longevity annuity") typically offers no cash accumulation and exists only to provide an income benefit. The amount of that income benefit is a guaranteed amount at the time of purchase, payable either for a period of years or a certain period of time.

A typical version paying a stated income for life might specify that payments will not begin until the annuitant reaches the annuity starting age (usually an advanced age, often age eighty-five). If the annuitant dies before reaching the annuity starting date, the contract terminates without value. (It was this type in particular usually referred to when it first appeared as a "*longevity annuity.*") If the annuitant dies after reaching the annuity starting date, the payments may stop immediately (if payments are purely life contingent) or may continue for some fixed period of time (if the annuity has a period certain payment feature) given that the annuity starting date had been reached. One contract, currently offered by a major U.S. insurer, requires annuitization only at age eighty-five or later and provides no death benefit or commutation feature. This is an example of the "pure longevity" annuity and is similar to Milevsky's concept product, except that Milevksy envisioned that annuity payments would be inflation-adjusted.

The second type, which first appeared more recently, provides for some benefits even if death occurs before the annuity starting date—either a death benefit, a cash value, or both—and may allow the contract owner to make withdrawals prior to the annuity starting date, accelerate payments, or (rarely) commute remaining payments. For example, another contract, offered by that same insurer that provides the aforementioned "pure longevity" annuities, allows annuitization at the earlier of age fifty or two years after purchase, with a maximum annuitization age of age eighty-five (allowing the annuitization to occur anywhere in that time period). It includes a death benefit equal to premiums paid plus three percent interest if the investor dies prior to annuitization, and permits the investor to commute the annuity (to take a lump sum in lieu of remaining income payments) within sixty days following the annuity starting date. This *one time only* commutation feature is the only way in which the owner of this contract may liquidate it for a lump sum once purchased.

This latter type is often referred to as a "*deferred income annuity*" (although some commentators refer to both types as "longevity annuities" or both types as "deferred income annuities"). Some insurers offer both types of contracts. While most deferred income annuities are non-variable ("fixed"), at least one insurer offers a variable version.

Although there is still some variability by company, "pure" *longevity annuities* (the first contract type) typically permit only a single purchase payment while *deferred income annuities* (the second contract type) often permit ongoing premiums. In addition, while longevity annuities often (but not always) provide payments for life (but only for life), deferred income annuities often allow payouts either for life or for a specified period of years (Period Certain). In those contracts that allow ongoing premiums, each premium purchases a specified amount of guaranteed annual income to commence at the annuity starting date chosen by the buyer. As the amount of annual income purchased by a given premium will vary with the purchaser's age, number of years before annuity starting date, and current interest rates, each annual premium will likely purchase a different annual annuity benefit, even if recurring premiums are identical.

Until recently, few deferred income annuity contracts offered inflation protection. Currently, several carriers offer the option of level annual income payments or annually increasing payments. Typically, the amount of annual increase is chosen at the time of application and is a set percentage increase annually (usually, no more than six percent), but a few carriers offer annual increases tied to an external index, such as the Consumer Price Index. Notably, though, such increases generally do not apply *until* payments actually begin at the annuity starting date; as a result, there may be inflation protection beyond the point that payments begin, but not necessarily during the waiting/deferral period.

Death benefit, withdrawal, and commutation options are, as of December 2013, becoming more varied and more numerous, in much the same way that "guaranteed living benefit" riders on variable annuities proliferated a few years ago. Consumers are becoming more aware of the existence of deferred income annuities and financial advisors are, in the authors' experience, increasingly more willing to consider incorporating these instruments into their clients' financial plans. More insurance companies are offering deferred income annuities and sales have increased dramatically; for the first nine months of 2013, deferred income annuity sales grew 132 percent to $1.5 billion,[4] although they are still a very small part of the overall market, with those nine months of sales representing less than one percent of just the fourth quarter, 2012, annuity sales.[5]

Where does a deferred income annuity fit in the retirement income picture? A few years ago, one of the authors talked with several financial advisors, none of whom was familiar with deferred income annuities, about the "pure version" of longevity annuities. The almost unanimous opinion of these advisors, on first hearing of the general provisions of this type, was a mix of incredulity and distaste. "Why would anybody buy one of those?" was the consensus. Why, indeed? What's it good for?

Milevsky calls a longevity annuity "a close relative of a defined benefit pension, and intended for those who don't have one."[6] This is a vital observation that goes to the heart of the deferred income annuity concept. It's all about the assurance of a known level of income, starting in the investor's old age—a *risk management* tool. Yet the advisors who view the fact that the annuity will terminate without value if the investor fails to live to age eighty-five as unacceptable are employing a very different mindset. They are applying investment thinking to what is fundamentally a risk management problem. Milevsky speaks to this difference. "From a slightly different perspective," he writes, "this type of product is akin to buying car, home or health insurance with a large deductible, which is also the optimal strategy—and common practice—when dealing with catastrophic risk."[7] Walter Updegrave, a senior editor at *Money* magazine, describes the longevity annuity in similar terms, observing that, "In effect it's like buying a homeowners or health insurance policy that has a very large deductible. You're insuring yourself against a catastrophic risk you can't handle on your own—in this case, running out of money late in life—while holding your premium to a minimum."[8]

Strictly speaking, the risk is not really running out of money at just any point in retirement. If there's truly not enough money to support retirement, the annuity cannot create it out of thin air. The distinction, though, is that if a retiree is depleting funds because he is living beyond life expectancy and his anticipated retirement time horizon, an annuity—including a deferred income annuity—can provide outsized payments for those additional years beyond life expectancy, funded indirectly by the "mortality credits" that are generated under an annuity contract from those who did not live as long. Jason Scott, in his article *The Longevity Annuity: An Annuity for Everyone?,*[9] distinguishes between funding a retirement income by saving (or investing) in a portfolio that will provide that income and purchasing insurance that will do so. He makes the point that funding a retirement income portfolio with investment assets amounts to setting aside the full replacement cost of the income stream, which is essentially self insurance. He observes that "with self insurance, the money is set aside whether or not the insurance event occurs." (Scott, *Ibid*) The longevity annuity—the insurance solution, if you will—differs in that the payout, or the benefit, is contingent upon the insured's survival, without which the risk in question does not occur. In other words, if a retiree will need significantly higher than expected investment returns to provide income if he lives well beyond life expectancy, a longevity annuity is uniquely suited to provide those additional income payments through the morality credits that will apply in that situation.

In the conventional model of retirement income funding, we save for an event—reaching late retirement age, when we'll need the money—rather than insure against it. In this savings model, the money we save is ours, and is always available—either to us or to our heirs—whether the event for which we're saving (reaching late retirement age) occurs or not, with the risk that if the unexpected event occurs—incredibly long life—we may find out after the fact that our expected retirement time horizon was incorrect and that our assets are depleting. When we purchase a pure longevity annuity, we invoke a different model. In this insurance model, we buy a contract that will pay off only if the event insured against actually occurs: that we do, in fact, live to old age. It is this *contingency* of payoff that makes the longevity annuity so cost-effective.

One problem with this two-model view is that it characterizes the investor during the savings period wholly as an accumulator. When we save for an event, the money we save is available to us, whether the event occurs or not, because it's always been our money. When we insure against an event, we pay a premium to an insurance policy in exchange for a promise to pay us a much larger sum in the event that the event actually occurs. We do not accumulate that larger sum, because it is not ours until it is paid to us. If it is never paid to us, the insurance company uses the premiums we contributed to pay the claims for someone else in the pool, making the overall cost of pure protection lower for everyone involved. But our clients are not mere accumulators; they're also consumers. They have lifestyles, and those lifestyles cost money. Accordingly, with a deferred income annuity, we can also take into account that certain asset allocation, income distribution strategies, and spending choices could be attractive to an investor who is assured of a certain income on reaching the annuity starting age, but unattractive to an investor having no such assurance, who may otherwise need to create an additional reserve (save more money) against the potential of unexpected long life (or take the risk of depletion).

What lifestyle and investment choices may become available to our investor if she has an assurance that her retirement portfolio need not persist beyond age eighty-five because the deferred income annuity will take it from there?

This certainty—that once the investor reaches a certain age, the retirement income need will be met (to the extent of the benefit purchased) for the rest of that investor's life—totally reconfigures the retirement income planning problem. Without the longevity annuity in place, the problem is one of ensuring an adequate income over *an indefinite period*—a "longevity contingent" problem. With the longevity annuity, the period to be funded by withdrawals from a retirement portfolio is known in advance. It begins at the age of retirement and ends at the longevity annuity's starting date—a "period certain" problem. These are not merely different scenarios; they are wholly different investment paradigms.

One might argue that there is another risk in play here. If one buys a pure longevity annuity and does not survive until benefits are payable, the purchase payment may be viewed as lost. But that is the same risk borne by anyone who purchases an automobile, medical expense, disability income, or term life insurance policy. If the insured peril does not occur, no benefit is payable. The purchaser, in that situation, will still have received value—the absolute assurance of the specified benefit had the insured peril materialized.

That said, some advisors will insist upon viewing the premium paid for a pure longevity annuity as a loss in the event of the insured's death prior to annuitization. For this reason, some insurers offer contracts with a pre-annuitization death benefit. The cost of this benefit is the difference between the income guaranteed by that contract and the income guaranteed by the "pure longevity" variant. In any such product, this difference can be significant, and the greater the period between purchase and annuitization date, the greater the difference in the annual benefit provided by the two variants. If you require a refund of your investment if you don't live to age eighty-five, for example, you'll get less income when you reach that age then you would have if you hadn't required that refund, and that income reduction will last as long as you do.

In the authors' opinion, buying a longevity annuity with a pre-annuitization death benefit (the *deferred income annuity* type) is like buying term life or disability income insurance with a return of premium benefit. One is not only insuring against the occurrence of a specified peril (death or disability), but also insuring the economic value of the premium payments themselves. By adding an ancillary benefit, one reduces inexorably the leverage in the underlying insurance itself. To some purchasers and some advisors, this may make sense. To the authors, though, it is not prudent risk management. The purpose of insurance is to protect only against risks that the individual otherwise could not afford to manage without such protection. If the premium is so unaffordable that it would require its own insurance (just for the cost of the premium), it may be time to revisit the decision to purchase longevity, or any other kind, of insurance in the first place.

Another way of viewing the potential loss of premium would be to compare the current purchase of a pure longevity annuity with saving for the purchase of an immediate annuity at the longevity annuity's annuity starting date. The example below outlines one such comparison using one insurer's rates as of December, 2013:

> *Example:* A sixty-year-old male client can purchase a pure longevity annuity today for $100,000 and be assured of receiving $7,259 per month ($87,108 per year) for life upon reaching age eighty-five. An immediate annuity at today's rates, paying $7,259 per month for life, for an eighty-five-year-old male, would cost roughly $585,000.[10] What rate of return must we earn on the $100,000 we are considering using to buy the longevity annuity to produce $585,000—that will produce the same annual income as the annuity—in twenty-five years? The answer is 7.32 percent. (Taxes are ignored for simplicity.)

What does this answer tell us? It *does not* tell us that the longevity annuity produces the same result we'd get if we were assured of earning that computed interest rate every year from investing that $100,000, because, in the "save for" scenario, the invested funds are ours. We can take that money at any time, or leave it to our heirs. The longevity annuity has no cash surrender value or, indeed, any value whatsoever unless and until we reach age eighty-five.

On the other hand, the goal—income for life, commencing at age eighty-five—is guaranteed in the annuity scenario. It is merely projected in the "save for" scenario, and our projection makes two huge assumptions. First, that we will, in fact, earn the projected return each and every year. While that may be possible, in the case of the deferred income annuity it is effectively guaranteed (at least to the extent of the credit quality of the insurance company), and a 7.32 percent "guaranteed" fixed income return is arguably *quite* appealing relative to comparable market rates at the time this quote (and book) is being published. (And in general, the rate will always be appealing, as it represents a combination of both investment returns on the insurance company's asset portfolio, and the accumulation of mortality credits for the survivor who reaches the annuity starting date.)

Second, even if we were to grant that our earnings assumption will be realized, we cannot be sure that the "save for" scenario will produce the required income at eighty-five, because immediate annuity rates are sensitive to both interest rates and longevity.

Is the certainty that $100,000 today will buy us $7,259 per month, (or whatever income could be purchased at the time you read this chapter) for life, if and only if we reach age eighty-five, worth locking away that money, perhaps never to get it back? That's not an easy question to answer. Our quantification example provides a baseline for the comparable return we must earn on our investments over the next twenty-five years to achieve the future lump sum required, which obliges us to note that earning an average return as high as 7.32 percent will entail some investment risk itself. Moreover, when we employ that baseline, we must remember that the longevity annuity pays off if and only if (though guaranteed if that point is reached).

Part of the difficulty stems from the fact that our computation makes the valuation of the longevity annuity an investment problem. In the "save for" scenario, we've calculated how much money our investor would need to have accumulated at age eighty-five to obtain the amount of income that could be guaranteed *today* by a longevity annuity if he does, in fact, live that long. But only one of the two alternatives can occur. The real risk against which the longevity annuity provides insurance is that our investor will live longer than anticipated, and that his assets may not be enough to produce a sufficient income over an unexpectedly long life. Arguably, if he doesn't live to that age, he won't need the money, because that long-life, or superannuation, risk never materializes. To put it bluntly, dead people don't require income and probably don't mind an unfavorable investment result that only occurred because they're no longer around to witness it.

What if we modify the problem, using a longevity annuity that guarantees a return of all premiums paid if the annuitant dies prior to the annuity starting date? As of December, 2013, one insurer's longevity annuity guarantees that a sixty-year-old male, contributing $100,000 in a single payment, will receive $4,993 per month for life at age eighty-five (and that all premiums will be paid to the annuitant's beneficiary if he dies before age eighty-five). At that company's current rates, a "life only" (no refund) SPIA for $4,993 per month will cost an eighty-five-year-old male about $402,000. What rate of return is required for $100,000 to grow to $402,000 after twenty-five years? The answer is 5.72 percent. Why is this computed interest rate significantly lower than the 7.32 percent computed in the "no death benefit" scenario? The answer is that the *leverage* in a longevity annuity with a death benefit is less than that of a longevity annuity with no death benefit; the potential annuity accumulates fewer mortality credits when a portion of funds must be held aside by the insurer to fund the refund guarantee for those who pass away early.

From a practical standpoint, we ought to note that the premium cost of a longevity annuity that might be lost if the investor doesn't live to the annuity starting age should never be more than a fraction of that investor's total portfolio for at least two reasons.

First, because a higher cost is not necessary. The premium required to guarantee a given level of income, commencing at age eighty-five, with a longevity annuity is but a fraction of the money that would be required to accumulate sufficient capital to produce that same income at age eighty-five *with total certainty*. Scott states that "the spending benefit a retiree could achieve with a ten percent allocation to a longevity annuity typically exceeds the benefit from a fifty percent allocation to an immediate annuity."[11] Our earlier example showed similar results. This significant difference occurs because the insurance company can pool the money for all those who don't live to age eighty-five with those who do receive payments past age eighty-five, allowing the insurer to transform the liquidity that the purchaser gives up into an increased guaranteed benefit amount. This is what actuaries call a morality credit, and it's what makes the longevity annuity so efficient.

Second, because retirement income might not be the investor's only goal. He or she may also have estate planning and legacy goals for heirs. In this case, the authors recommend that the client may be able to maximize both retirement and legacy goals by obtaining a pure longevity annuity to minimize the expense of insuring against an unexpectedly long life, while locking in the maximum leverage inherent in such a contract. The money freed up by this strategy is thus available for other uses, such as legacies.

What about Inflation?

One major carrier offers two versions of its longevity annuity—one with a death benefit and one without—but both provide only a level annual benefit. That is, there is no inflation increase or Cost-Of-Living-Adjustment (COLA) feature. Another insurer's product offers consumers a choice of an annual increase ranging from one percent to five percent of the annual benefit, but the increase begins only in the second year of payout.

In other words, there is no protection against unexpected inflation occurring from policy purchase until the first payout year, which may render the first payment already insufficient to provide for the desired purchasing power of the retiree. Moreover, an individual longevity annuity owner who receives annuity payments over many years will see the value of those payments eroded by the inflation occurring during that payout period if there aren't at least scheduled increases that will begin once payments *do* begin.

In the third edition of this book, the authors wrote that "The lack of inflation protection in most of the longevity contracts currently offered is worrisome." Fortunately, in the two years since we made that comment, the situation has changed somewhat for the better. More insurers are offering longevity annuities and more of these contracts are offering inflation protection. A few contracts offer cost-of-living adjustments tied to the CPI-U, while most COLA provisions require the buyer to choose the rate (typically, no more than six percent) at which annual annuity payments will increase. The authors strongly encourage advisors to be very cautious in recommending longevity annuities with no cost-of-living adjustments as such contracts will almost certainly fail to provide a sufficient level of real (after inflation) income to meet the client's entire future needs. Unfortunately, though, the authors are aware of no longevity annuities that provide a full inflation guarantee that addresses both the period between the purchase of the annuity and the annuity starting date, and inflation adjustments *after* the annuity starting date. One method of dealing with this problem, where the longevity annuity being considered offers no inflation protection for the deferral period, might be to estimate the future (inflated) level of income required and to recommend that inflated amount. Obviously, this assumes at the least that payments under the contract will be inflation-adjusted once the payout period begins;

otherwise, calculating the future inflated income need but allowing that it will degrade every year thereafter is at best only a partial solution.

Another option might be to purchase a series of longevity annuities, such that the investor is buying additional protection as the need for it becomes apparent. Newer "Deferred Income Annuities" often provide the buyer with the opportunity to "lock in" future annuity values with each recurring premium as well as some flexibility in changing the annuity starting date after purchase. One U.S. insurer offers a longevity rider to one of its variable annuity contracts in which the rider premium is paid by installments, as a percentage of the total premiums paid into the annuity contract.

None of these solutions is, in the authors' opinion, as satisfactory as choosing a longevity annuity that offers protection against inflation occurring during both the payout and deferral periods. The authors hope that we will see such contracts as the market for this product matures.

The Importance of a Death Benefit Feature

In conversations with marketing executives at two major insurers currently offering longevity annuities, one of the authors has been told that the overwhelming majority of advisors considering these products prefer a version offering a death benefit. In conversations with dozens of financial planners and insurance agents, the authors have heard the same thing. Apparently, most advisors believe that a client will not pay money for a product guaranteeing a substantial income at, say age eighty-five, if it pays no benefit if the client dies beforehand.

Viewed one way, this makes sense. Why would one invest one's money in something that might never pay off, essentially risking a potential total loss (a negative one-hundred percent return)? Yet this viewpoint is, in the authors' opinion, fundamentally misdirected for a very simple reason: A longevity annuity is not, in any way whatsoever, an investment. It is wholly a risk transfer instrument, a pure insurance play.[12] The retiree is not facing the risk of a negative one-hundred percent *investment* return, but instead is simply making a *premium payment* for an *insurance guarantee* against a risk.

What is the risk in question? It is the possibility that you live longer than expected, such that your portfolio proves to be insufficient to fund your retirement with the time horizon that is longer than originally planned (such that retirement assets are depleted). That's the risk. If that possibility so concerns you that you're willing to part with a substantial insurance premium now to preclude it, even if that will mean losing that money if you never reach old age, then transferring that risk to an insurer by making that premium may make good sense to you—just as you find it sensible to buy medical expense insurance knowing that if you don't get sick, that insurance will never pay off.

The authors believe that the reason that some advisors don't like longevity annuities without a death benefit is that they're applying investment analysis to a product that isn't an investment, or even an insurance product with investment features. The longevity insurance purchase decision should be, functionally speaking, identical to the thought process involved in purchasing a property and casualty product, where a premium is paid purely to insure a risk with no other benefit but the risk protection—and it should be evaluated as such.

Regrettably, that is not how it has been marketed, if the brochures from the few insurers offering it are any indication. Most point-of-sale and agent training materials typically speak of the longevity annuity as an income investment product, which is half right and half dead wrong. A longevity annuity is all about guaranteeing income in the event of long life, but it's nothing about investment, except to the extent that it's a trade-off *against* using an investment approach instead. Until insurance marketers understand this, their producers (insurance agents and financial advisors) never will. Until we advisors do, our clients won't either. Fortunately, a few insurers have realized this and their marketing material speaks more to risk transfer than to "investment."

Implications of the Longevity Annuity for Retirement Income Planning in General

In the authors' opinion, the Longevity Annuity (or "Deferred Income Annuity") concept has the potential to redefine the landscape of retirement income planning. Traditionally, the problem facing planners is to construct and manage a portfolio that will provide, at least to a minimum level of confidence, required levels of income throughout retirement. We make projections to model how various asset allocations and income distribution patterns will perform to that end. In doing so, we take into account numerous variables. That, by itself, isn't hard, given the formidable computer software tools now available. The difficulty lies, of course, in the uncertainties. Even when we prescribe the levels of net real income required and assume particular tax and inflation rates, we're left to deal with two fundamental uncertainties: (1) the level and sequence of investment returns; and (2) the length of the period over which income will be required.

Various methodologies have been developed to help us do this. Stochastic techniques, such as Monte Carlo simulation, historical back testing (which uses actual returns over a specified earlier period), and "historical bootstrapping" (using actual historical returns, chosen randomly for each analysis year) are all in common use. Each method has its proponents and critics, but each must acknowledge that we do not know for certain: (1) what investment returns our client will earn each year; or (2) for how many years returns will be needed. The influence of each of these uncertainties upon our overall confidence is considerable, but the product of both—of these uncertainties compounded, if you will—exerts a profound impact upon the confidence we feel about our results.

How much more confident could we be if one of these two uncertainties were removed—if, while we must guess at investment returns, we could know, for certain, the number of years over which those returns will be required to generate income? To the extent that a longevity annuity will provide, with certainty, the level of income our client needs on reaching a particular age—age eighty-five, for example—it transforms our "longevity continent" problem to one of a "period certain." By incorporating this instrument in the client's overall plan, we can know that his or her remaining assets will be required to last only until age eighty-five—because the longevity annuity will take it from there. (Though as noted earlier, the solution may be imperfect in today's marketplace, due to the lack of contracts that provide a full inflation guarantee during both the deferral and payout periods.)

What kind of asset allocation decisions can now be made with regard to those remaining assets in the light of this new certainty regarding the retirement investment time horizon? Even more importantly, what kind of lifestyle choices may the client now make, with confidence?

Longevity annuities are still relatively new to the marketplace. Most insurers do not offer even one. But more and more are seeing the light. Newer contracts (which are usually called "Deferred Income Annuities") frequently offer contract owners far greater flexibility in choosing the annuity starting date (often from age eighty-five to as soon as two years after purchase), the right to change the annuity starting date (usually, only once), and the opportunity to make additional contributions (which will purchase additional guaranteed income). As a result of this increased flexibility, and because "Deferred Income Annuities" have gotten much greater attention from financial journalists, more and more advisors are coming to realize the benefits that these contracts offer to their clients.

In February, 2012, the U.S. Treasury Department and the Internal Revenue Service proposed a series of Treasury Regulations designed to make it easier for participants in employer-sponsored retirement plans and IRAs to invest in longevity annuities. Under the "Qualified Longevity Annuity Contract" (QLAC) rules, retirees will no longer have to deal with the Required Minimum Distribution aggregation of accounts rules and, under certain circumstances, will be able to postpone the application of those rules until the longevity annuities begin payout. These proposals represent a good start, but widespread acceptance of these tools has a long way to go.

Which is Best—a DIA or SPIA, or maybe a GLWB?

The authors are often asked this question by attendees of our presentations on retirement income planning. It's an understandable question; financial advisors are always looking for the best solutions for their clients' needs. But the only answer to this question can be "it depends", because the "best" solution will always be a matter of individual facts and circumstances. Moreover, the question of "Which tool is best?" seeks a single solution when the optimal solution may be a combination of tools. In many planning scenarios, the solutions may include deferred income annuities working alongside and *in combination with* SPIAs or lifetime withdrawal riders (GLWBs).

One planning tool that incorporates such combinations is Curtis Cloke's "THRIVE® Income Distribution System" (available at www.thriveincome.com). It uses the familiar "buckets of money" approach, by dividing the client's required income streams into "buckets" and funding each bucket with either a SPIA, a DIA, or a GLWB (see Figure 8.1 below). This same process can be done in other financial planning software by subtracting from the client's chosen asset account or accounts the cost of the proposed annuities and entering the income from those annuities as income streams. (In the case of a GLWB, you must be careful not to count both the accumulation value of the annuity contract containing the GLWB and the guaranteed income payments from that rider).

Figure 8.1.

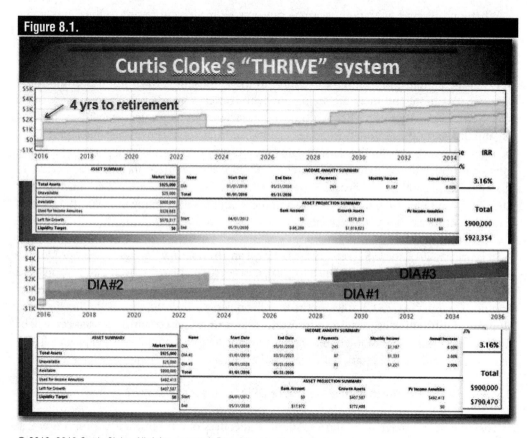

The Contingent Annuity

Recently, a number of Private Letter Rulings[13] have addressed an entirely new type of annuity: the contingent annuity (also known as a contingent deferred annuity, or CDA). Essentially a stand-alone guaranteed lifetime withdrawal benefit rider without the underlying deposit to an annuity itself, the contingent annuity is a contract between an issuing insurance company and a customer, or the annuitant holding an investment account at a sponsoring organization and the sponsor. Once purchased, the customer will have a benefit base, similar to a GLWB in an annuity, that may be either the greater of the account balance, the balance on specified prior dates as a high-water mark, or the balance at inception accumulated at a specified rate of interest. As the customer takes withdrawals from his/her own account balance, so too are the withdrawals applied against the benefit base. And as with the GLWB, if withdrawals under this benefit result in the account balance falling below zero, the insurance element of the contingent annuity would come into play, and the insurance company will continue payments of the same amount to the annuitant for life; or, if a joint benefit is elected, the joint lifetime of the annuitant and his/her spouse. Again, though, the funds themselves remain invested in the customer's own account balance, and not an annuity contract; the contingent annuity essentially forms a benefit base "wrapper" around the account, and costs for the guarantee—but only the guarantee—are paid from the account directly.

Unlike payments under the GLWB, payments by the insurer under a contingent annuity (in the event that payments kick in after the account balance has been depleted) will, based on the letter rulings cited, enjoy regular annuity rules taxation, where a portion of each payment is considered a tax-free return of principal under the exclusion ratio rules. Moreover, the investment account would not be considered an annuity contract, and returns in the investment account being protected by the contingent annuity would still be eligible for capital gains taxation.

There remains considerable confusion as to whether a contingent annuity is, in fact, an annuity contract. Contingent annuity contracts have been filed with insurance regulators in many states; in some states, they have been approved as annuity contracts. In others, they have not. In November 2011, the NAIC formed a working group to study the marketing of these instruments. As of October 30, 2013, the status of these contracts was still under review by the NAIC's Life Insurance and Annuity Committee and the CDA (Contingent Deferred Annuity) Working Group. The NAIC's website includes the following update:[14]

Status

The NAIC Life Insurance and Annuities (A) Committee charged the Contingent Deferred Annuity (A) Working Group with evaluating the adequacy of existing laws and regulations as applied to CDAs and whether additional solvency and consumer protection standards were required. At the 2013 NAIC Spring National Meeting, the CDA Working Group adopted a memorandum and recommendations for adoption by the A Committee regarding the future regulation of CDAs.

The CDA Working Group concluded that: CDAs do not easily fit into the category of fixed or variable annuity and should have their own definition; continuing review of solvency and consumer protection standards is appropriate; and tools to assist states in the review CDA product filings and solvency oversight of CDAs should be established. The Working Group also identified issues to be addressed by other NAIC committees and working groups with specific subject-matter expertise.

Endnotes

1. Stephenson, James B., "The High Protection Annuity," Journal of Risk and Insurance, 45, no. 4 (1978): 593–610.

2. Milevsky, Moshe, "Real Longevity Insurance with a Deductible: Introduction to Advanced-Life Delayed Annuities." Managing Retirement Assets Symposium, 2004, published in North American Actuarial Journal (9)(4): 109–122.

3. Scott, Jason S. and Watson, John G. and Hu, Wei-Yin, "Efficient Annuitization with Delayed Payout Annuities" (working paper, November 2006), available at http://ssrn.com/abstract=932145

4. Gladych, Paula Aven "Fixed-rate Deferred Annuity Sales Jump," benefitspro.com, Nov. 21, 2013, http://www.benefitspro.com/2013/11/21/fixed-rate-deferred-annuity-sales-jump

5. "LIMRA: Deferred Income Annuity Sales Reach $1 Billion; Fixed Indexed Annuity Sales Hit Record High in 2012," (LIMRA News Release, Feb. 21, 2012), available at: http://www.limra.com/Posts/PR/News_Releases/LIMRA__Deferred_Income_Annuity_Sales_Reach_$1_Billion;_Fixed_Indexed_Annuity_Sales_Hit_Record_High_in_2012.aspx.

6. Milevsky, ibid.

7. Milevsky, ibid.

8. Updegrave, Walter "Sure Income for the Very (Very) Long Haul" money.cnn.com, January 21, 2008, available at: http://money.cnn.com/2008/01/21/pf/long_haul.moneymag/

9. Scott, Jason S. "The Longevity Annuity: An Annuity for Everyone?" (working paper, June 2007), available at: http://papers.ssrn.com/sol3/papers.cfm?abstract_id=992423

10. Rates for both immediate and longevity annuities vary considerably by age and sex and by insurer. The results of this comparison might be very different for a client of a different age and/or sex, or if contracts from a different insurer were used.

11. Scott, ibid.

12. See Olsen, John L., "Longevity Annuities Could Redefine the Retirement Income Planning Landscape," Life Insurance Selling (January, 2009), available at: http://www.lifehealthpro.com/2009/01/09/longevity-annuities-could-redefine-the-retirement.

13. See Priv. Ltr. Rul. 200949007 (July 30, 2009), Priv. Ltr. Rul. 201002016 (Oct. 6, 2009), and Priv. Ltr. Rul. 201129029 (March 17, 2011).

14. Available at: http://www.naic.org/cipr_topics/topic_contingent_deferred_annuities.htm

Chapter 9

Exploring the Benefits and Challenges of Immediate Annuitization

Buying an immediate annuity that pays out for a *period certain*, where a lump sum is exchanged for an annuitized series of cash flow payments over a known and finite number of years is essentially a process of liquidating that lump sum. Each payment received is a combination of the original principal and the interest/growth earned on that principal. Similar to structuring a bond ladder, the underlying investments are arranged in a manner that the appropriate amount of cash is available on a year-by-year basis, until eventually the entire combination of principal and interest has been received over the intended time period.

However, a unique feature of annuitization is that payments are not always just payable for a specific period of time. Payments can also be *life contingent*, which means the payments will continue for the lifetime of the annuitant, however long that may be.

From the perspective of a self-liquidating pool of money, the potential that payments must continue "for life" without knowing how long any particular individual will live is a significant challenge, because it is impossible to determine the correct amount of ongoing principal and income payments without knowing the time horizon involved in the first place. Fortunately, though, while it's almost impossible to know how long any specific person will live, it turns out that it's much easier to estimate the percentage of people that will survive from a large group of individuals.

The reason is a theorem known as the *law of large numbers*, a staple of probability theory that shows while it's impossible to predict the outcome of a single random event (like one throw of the die or how long a particular person will live), the randomness averages out with enough events such that in the aggregate, the probabilities are measurable with a significant degree of accuracy. This is why, for instance, we know that if rolled enough times, the average score of a six-sided die will be 3.5 (even though the available numbers are only one, two, three, four, five, and six!), and the long-term probability of rolling snake eyes (two ones) on a pair of dice is 2.78 percent (or 1/36). In the context of annuitization, the law of large numbers means that while it's impossible to know how long an individual will live, it's very possible to know with reasonable accuracy how many people from a large group will still be alive over time (even if we don't know which specific people will survive or not).

This application of the law of large numbers is crucial and essential in allowing insurance companies to provide payments "for life" yet still pay for (and be able to invest and manage to) a "known" time period, because with a large enough pool of annuitants, it really *is* possible to estimate what payment amounts will be due over time, and therefore what amounts need to be set aside to cover those payments.

However, allocating annuitization payments based on a large group aggregated together for calculating mortality/longevity has an additional opportunity as well: not only can their survival rates be pooled together to have a better estimate of how long payments must last, but their actual dollars can be pooled together. Why does this help? Because the benefit of combining the lump sums from each individual into an aggregate pool of money from which all annuitization payments are made is that the average payment to each participant can be larger than what that individual could afford otherwise, due to mortality credits.

Understanding Mortality Credits

To understand the role of mortality credits, an example might be helpful.

Imagine for a moment that an individual has $1,000 to invest, and needs to generate cash flows. At a five percent fixed return, the individual could simply take withdrawals that would amortize the account down to $0 at the end of their time horizon. If the individual believes that the longest he could live is twenty-five years, then annual payment over a twenty-five-year time horizon would be $70.95/year, a combination of interest and principal that shifts as the account balance is liquidated, as shown below.

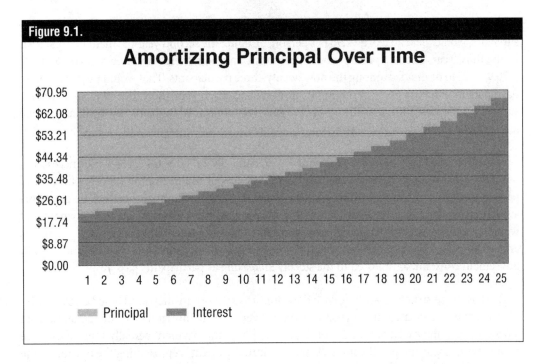

Figure 9.1.

Amortizing Principal Over Time

Legend: Principal, Interest

Of course, the caveat in the above example is that the individual might not even live for twenty-five years, and it could turn out that this payment stream was too conservative. However, without otherwise knowing what the time horizon will be, and having only personal assets to rely upon, the best-case scenario is simply to spend conservatively with a conservative longevity time horizon.

Now imagine instead that our individual comes together with twenty-four other individuals, to form a pool of $25,000 of available assets (twenty-five people total, with each contributing $1,000). Assume as well that while we don't know when any particular person is going to die, we know that on average one person will die every year for the next twenty-five years. Given this simplified mortality assumption, the entire group will have passed away at the end of the twenty-five-year time horizon, even without knowing who individually will be the survivor in the twenty-fifth (or any other) year. (This simplified example is for illustration purposes only. In the real world, we would need thousands of individuals to estimate mortality this accurately, and the mortality rate tends to rise with time instead of being evenly spread across twenty-five years.)

In this pooled-assets-and-pooled-mortality scenario, the payment structure will look a bit different. In the original example, if the individual passed away before the end of twenty-five years, the account balance is simply left over, ostensibly as an inheritance. In the pooled scenario, any remaining principal for those who do not survive can be reallocated to those who do, to support their higher payments—which, again, can be modeled predictably as long as we have enough people to let the law of large numbers take hold.

For instance, if the payments started at the individual-style $70.95/year, when someone passed away in the second year, that person's $70.95 payment for that year (and every year thereafter) could be re-distributed to the others. Dividing that amount among the twenty-four survivors, would yield an extra $2.96 per person, bringing the second year payment up to $73.91. In the third year, another person would pass away, and now there would be an extra $141.90 ($70.95 × 2) to be divided among the now twenty-three participants. That would raise everyone's payments by an extra $6.17, bringing it up to $77.12. Each year thereafter, the payments for survivors would rise further as the number of survivors continued to shrink. By the final year, the last survivor would receive everyone's final payment, or a single payment of $1,773.75!

Of course, this rising stream of payments—technically called a tontine—is not necessarily useful as a planning tool, as the payments are very low at the beginning (and for those who pass away early), and "unnaturally" large by the end. Yet knowing that there *will* be payments available to redistribute every year means that it's also possible to determine a *level* payment that would keep payments for all participants constant across the time horizon; the early payments are higher than in the tontine (knowing that some people will not survive the whole time period), but remain constant, as opposed to the steeply increasing as participants pass away.

This payment structure—where cash flows for the survivors are increased based on those who pass away, but calculated in a levelized manner over the time horizon—is what an annuitized stream of cash flows actually is. Accordingly, each ongoing payment actually represents three components: the principal, the interest, and a "mortality credit" representing the portion of the payment for the survivors funded by those who didn't survive. The contribution of these three components of the annuity payments over time for our hypothetical twenty-five people over twenty-five years scenario above is shown in the chart below.

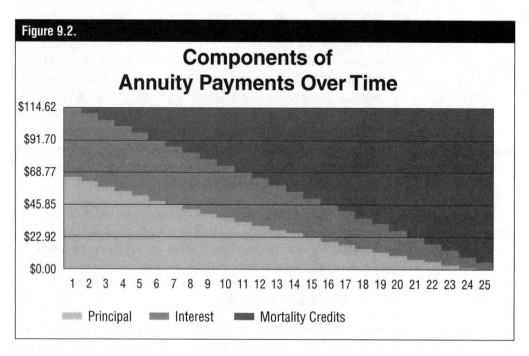

Figure 9.2.

Properly annuitized, the total amount of each payment in this annuitization scenario would be $114.62, which is significantly higher than the $70.95 that the individual could have produced simply by spending down his/her own asset base. The $43.67 difference in the payments is the unique contribution of the mortality credit, which is an increasingly large component of each annuity cash flow over time, but allocated in a 'smoothed' manner across the time horizon (to avoid the exponentially growing tontine style of payment).

Ultimately, this potential for a mortality credit is a unique contribution that annuitization offers, unlike what can be produced by an investment strategy alone. If the individual tried to spend $114.62/year, the money will be depleted before the end of the twenty-five-year time horizon, yet the *group* receiving annuity payments can sustain a $114.62 per person annual payment, knowing that there is enough money for all the participants (even without knowing *which* participants will be alive to receive it).

The mortality credit itself, along with the fact that annuitization can effectively pay a certain amount that self-liquidates appropriately over a time horizon that is unknown for an individual but known in the aggregate, represents an entirely unique value propositions that simply cannot be replicated by an investment portfolio alone. This can be especially appealing for those facing the dual retirement challenges of an unknown time horizon and difficulty creating returns that can be sustained through the retirement time period.

Using Annuitization to Generate Retirement Cash Flows

All else being equal, annuitization has the potential to both generate greater cash flows than merely using a comparable-risk bond portfolio alone (due to the contribution of mortality credits), and resolve the classic "unknown time horizon" challenge of generating retirement income. A life contingent annuitization by definition is a payment stream that cannot be outlived, while a fixed portfolio time horizon does face such a risk. Accordingly, a popular retirement income strategy is to annuitize a significant portion of a portfolio to efficiently secure a "base" or "floor" of income, most commonly by aligning the annuitization amount to the anticipated target "base" retirement income need (e.g., the essential household expenses in retirement).

In fact, retirement researchers in the world of economics have long observed that an inflation-adjusted annuity appears to be the "perfect" retirement income vehicle, providing superior risk-adjusted returns (via mortality credits) and an efficient solution to the uncertain-time-horizon challenge (at least for those without any bequest motives).[1]

However, a significant complication arises in practice when attempting to execute this strategy: while annuitization may provide the most efficient liquidation of a lump sum to provide cash flow needs, this is only true when cash flow needs are stable. In an environment where more uneven cash flows may be necessary—for instance, to deal with unexpected health shocks in retirement—the annuitization solution becomes less efficient.

Accordingly, a recent working paper by Reichling and Smetters (2013)[2] found that, contradictory to Yaari's earlier work, annuitization may actually not be optimal for most retirees, due to the challenge of health care and long-term care cost shocks that can occur in retirement. On the one hand, the relatively moderate income of most households can ill afford the danger of outliving household assets in retirement. On the other hand, households in retirement can also be the most prone to a 'liquidity crisis' and be unable to fund health care needs if most/all household income is annuitized. Ironically, Reichling and Smetters actually found that the households most suited to annuitization may be those who have such wealth they don't actually *need* to annuitize, but may nonetheless find full or at least partial annuitization appealing because there is enough wealth to afford the cost of health care shocks even if they do occur. They also found that many households would actually be better off with "negative" annuities—i.e., life insurance—that increase in implicit value. When health shocks occur and life expectancy is reduced, "negative annuities" can be used to fund the expenses of that health shock.

While Reichling and Smetters did indirectly find a benefit of at least partial annuitization for a subset of more affluent households, standalone studies on at least partial annuitization of a portfolio have also found benefits to the strategy in the form of higher sustainable withdrawal rates for the overall household than just portfolio-based strategies alone. For instance, Ameriks, Veres, and Warshawsky (2001)[3] found that while a moderate growth portfolio has a 12.6 percent chance to be depleted at a 4.5 percent inflation-adjusted initial withdrawal rate after thirty years, the probability of depletion falls to 7.8 percent when twenty-five percent of the portfolio is annuitized and 3.3 percent when 50 percent is annuitized.

However, a more recent study by Kitces and Pfau (2013)[4] found that a portion of the benefits previously attributed to partial annuitization may actually be a result of the liquidation strategy that it creates, rather than a benefit of the annuitization itself. For instance, Kitces and Pfau observed that in a scenario where a portion of wealth is annuitized and spending occurs from the annuitized cash flows first and only then from the portfolio, the net effect is that the fixed-income portion of household wealth is spent down first (as the remaining value of the fixed annuitization payments depletes over time), while the portion of household wealth in equities rises as the portfolio can grow. While this is clearly a beneficial effect, as it essentially reduces the exposure to "sequence risk" of equities by reducing the need to draw on the portfolio much (if at all) in the early years, the reality is that such a liquidation strategy where bonds/fixed income is reduced first while equities are allowed to grow can be implemented without actually annuitizing.

Accordingly, Kitces and Pfau tested this form of "rising equity glidepath" (where the portion of household wealth in equities drifts higher as spending occurs disproportionately from the fixed income investments) by using portfolio allocations that mimicked the equivalent allocation from the annuitization scenario, and found that throughout the first half of retirement, the beneficial improvements of partial annuitization were explained almost entirely by the glidepath liquidation effect, and not annuitization itself. At life expectancy, the majority of benefits from annuitization were still actually attributable to the liquidation/glidepath effect. It was only for those that lived materially beyond life expectancy that eventually the unique contribution of an annuity's mortality credits became the dominating factor for improving the success rate and portfolio longevity. In turn, Kitces and Pfau also showed that in scenarios where mortality credits performed favorably—those living well past life expectancy—the best results were achieved by using inflation-adjusted "real" annuitization, rather than "nominal" annuitization with flat dollar payments. For the subset of individuals who do live well beyond life expectancy, the rising payments better leverage the available mortality credits.

Logically, this result should not be entirely surprising. As shown in Figure 2 earlier, while mortality credits can provide some benefit—relative to a bond-based liquidation strategy alone—throughout retirement, the contribution of mortality credits on an aggregate basis is far greater in the later years than the early years (and especially for annuities that provide the largest payments in those later years). At the individual level, the situation can be even more severe— unless some form of period certain or refund guarantee is procured (which in turn reduces the payments themselves). Annuitants must live a significant number of years just to generate *any* effective rate of return on their cash flows. While technically each payment is partially attributable to mortality credits by the second year for the group in the aggregate, until an individual fully recovers his/her original contributions, the *individual's* internal rate of return is negative. It's only in the later years that the internal rate of return on annuitized payments finally turns positive, eventually becoming a significantly positive and favorable "fixed" yield relative to comparable alternatives. For instance, the chart below shows the internal rate of return of cash flows over time for a sixty-five-year-old married couple that purchases a $100,000 immediate joint-and-survivor annuity with a $5,832/year lifetime payment.

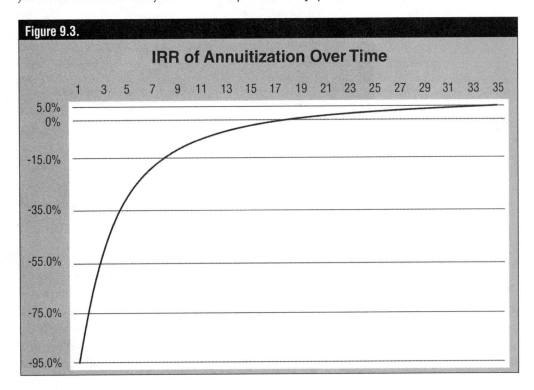

Figure 9.3.

IRR of Annuitization Over Time

Of course, straight annuitization (even for a married couple) produces a rather extreme potential loss, for the highly-unlikely-but-possible untimely death of both members of the couple in the first few years. Accordingly, most annuitants purchase at least some amount of period certain payments. The chart below shows a comparison of the straight $5,832/year joint life payments to an actuarially equivalent $5,796 with fifteen-year certain, and is also compared to the available yield on a government bond over an equivalent time horizon.[5]

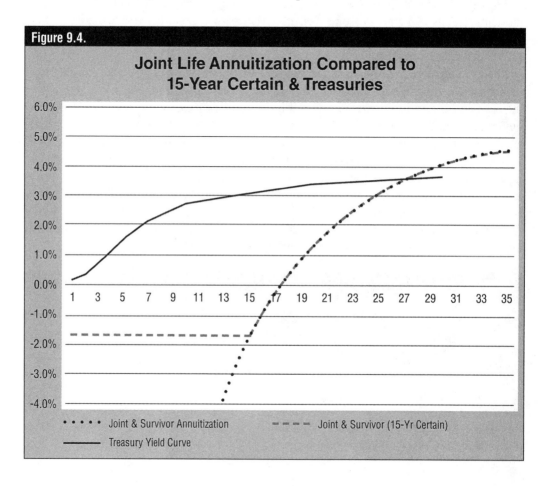

Figure 9.4.

Joint Life Annuitization Compared to 15-Year Certain & Treasuries

• • • • • Joint & Survivor Annuitization   – – – – Joint & Survivor (15-Yr Certain)
——— Treasury Yield Curve

As the results reveal, the period-certain payments give up very little over time, but secure the "worst case scenario" loss at an IRR of only about -1.7 percent (represented by the horizontal orange line portion of the graph). However, it still takes many years before the effective internal rate of return of the annuitization payments even turns positive, much less catches up to comparable available Treasury bond yields that could be achieved by simply investing in a portfolio for a comparable time horizon. However, in the later years, the annuitization payments eventually provide superior returns, as the relative contribution of mortality credits grows larger and larger and the yield exceeds what could be produced by fixed income portfolio alternatives alone (in addition to the fact that Treasuries themselves do not extend beyond thirty years). Notably, though, producing the "maximal" internal rates of return from annuitization at the end of the chart would 'require' at least one member of the couple to live thirty-five years, until age one hundred!

Challenges of Annuitization

One of the biggest challenges to the decision to annuitize is simply the question of whether, in the end, annuitization will necessarily provide greater retirement income than simply investing in a balanced portfolio, systematically rebalancing, and taking ongoing withdrawals that are modest enough to survive market downturns and the time period until they recover.

For instance, historical research has indicated that a "safe" withdrawal rate is an initial withdrawal of approximately four percent to 4.5 percent of the starting account balance, with subsequent cash flow distributions adjusted annually for inflation. This 4 percent withdrawal rate has been shown[6] to survive all available historical return periods in the U.S. over a thirty-year time horizon, and generally shows an approximately ninety-five percent probability of success on a Monte Carlo basis (which hypothetically includes an ever wider range of returns than the ones seen in "just" the limited data set of available U.S. historical data going back for the past century or so).

Similarly, available rates for an inflation-adjusted immediate annuity for a sixty-five-year-old couple are generally in the range of 3.5 percent to 4.5 percent, which means the available payments for annuitization (at least in a low-return environment) are not materially greater than simply spending conservatively over a conservative time horizon. Yet for providing what is arguably a "comparable" floor, annuitization payments generally leave no remaining legacy at death or the end-of-the-time horizon (unless a period certain guarantee applies), while a four percent safe withdrawal rate has been shown in historical data to also have a ninety-six percent probability of leaving over one-hundred percent of starting wealth at the end of the thirty-year time horizon (in addition to sustaining inflation-adjusted withdrawals for the whole time period), and a median wealth of more than quadruple the starting balance at the beginning of retirement.[7] On the other hand, some research has suggested that the safe withdrawal rate may be even lower in today's somewhat unprecedented current low-yield environment,[8] has been somewhat lower in international studies using the historical data of other countries,[9] and still ultimately carries some risk that the retiree may outlive even an arbitrarily conservative time horizon.

Beyond the difficulty of simply comparing annuitization to portfolio-based withdrawal alternatives, most additional challenges to annuitization strategies are centered upon one of three issues:

1.   risk of untimely death;

2.   (irrevocable) illiquidity; and

3.   limited upside.

Risk of Untimely Death

As shown earlier in Figure 3, the danger of untimely death is relatively straightforward—if payments are to be made "for life" but death occurs early on, the annuitant (or rather, his/her beneficiaries) can face a significant financial loss. While a period certain guarantee can help to mitigate the magnitude of the loss, the guarantee may still not necessarily provide a one-hundred percent return of principal and will certainly bear a 'loss' of opportunity cost relative to even Treasuries as an investment alternative. On the one hand, some annuitants may decide that this is an acceptable risk, especially given the morbid reality that if he/she passes away early, the funds weren't actually "needed" for retirement after all; the only real consequence is a loss of legacy assets to bequeath to heirs, which may or may not have been a significant planning concern. With those for whom leaving a legacy is a concern, annuitization may still be appealing as a trade-off for giving up a legacy (if death occurs early) in exchange for more certainty about retirement income itself and eliminating the risk of turning a legacy into a burden (if assets are outlived). Ultimately, many choose to partially mitigate the risk by purchasing annuitized payments with some form of period certain or other refund guarantee, trading off somewhat smaller payments—in essence, fewer mortality credits—to avoid the risk of a total loss due to untimely death.

(Irrevocable) Illiquidity

In some cases, the challenge of the irrevocable and illiquid decision to annuitize can also be mitigated by obtaining an immediate annuity that provides for some form of commutation option, where anticipated remaining payments can be commuted back into a lump sum. In practice, though, such commutations are not always available, and may have significant limitations attached to them.

Limited Upside

The third challenge for many considering annuitization is that while life contingent payments by definition cannot be outlived—reducing the shortfall risk in the event of unusually long life—the payments also will not rise unless the annuitization option chosen provides for an annual increase in the annuity payment. But even if that option is chosen, the annuitant cannot be certain of receiving an income that will rise at the rate of inflation, as most such provisions limit the annual increases to a set percentage (which may be more or less than the actual inflation rate) and to the authors' knowledge none provide a guaranteed real return above the rate of inflation. For some, this may lead to an "As Good As It Gets" syndrome, where the prospective annuitant is daunted by the fact that with annuitization there is no possibility of improvement in the future (beyond the annual increase, if chosen), even though it's simply a trade-off for the fact that there's less downside as well. This challenge and "danger" in turn can be at least partially mitigated by choosing partial annuitization instead of full annuitization (or by choosing the less common form of variable immediate annuitization), even though choosing partial (or variable) annuitization may also limit access to the core guaranteed payment floor and risk management benefits that annuitization was intended to provide in the first place. (Of course, investors can also choose to adopt a safe withdrawal rate approach to establish a spending floor that seeks out more upside as well.)

Trade-Offs

From a practical perspective, these trade-offs—period certain or refund guarantees to protect against early death, commutation to protect against illiquidity, and partial annuitization to allow for some potential future upside—create a significant challenge for prospective annuitants. The difficulty is that the annuitant's assumption of these risks (limited or no liquidity, no opportunity for growth) is necessary for the insurance company to effectively provide the benefits of mortality credits in the first place. After all, if annuitants can commute their remaining payments and walk away at any time—especially if there is also a period certain or refund guarantee attached as well—the annuitized payments essentially *have* been converted back into a normal investment account like any other (and of course with partial annuitization, funds that aren't annuitized remain in the investment account as well). In other words, if various guarantees ensure there are no funds to be lost in the event of death, there are also no funds to be added to the mortality pool and generate mortality credits. Trying to mitigate all of the "risks" and challenges of annuitization undermines the very essence of purchasing an annuity in the first place! The annuity company cannot attach any mortality credit to dollars that aren't annuitized at all, or to dollars investing into an immediate annuity contract that allows the owner to opt out of annuitization or has enough guarantees that few if any dollars will be available for the mortality pool following the death of the annuitant!

Practical Implications for Annuitization Strategies

From a practical perspective, the findings of the current research on annuitization, its benefits, and its associated challenges and risks, suggest a series of common strategies and best practices for implementing annuitization, including:

- If you want to annuitize, then annuitize. Be cautious about purchasing immediate annuities that provide so much flexibility and guarantees that the contract has little or no mortality credits and has essentially reverted back to an investment account rather than a true annuity. However, some moderate amount of period certain guarantee may be appealing to protect against at least the most extreme consequences of an unlikely but highly adverse early death, especially if there are any legacy concerns.

- Annuitize some, but not all. Given the real risk of health care and/or long-term care shocks in the later years, most households should not fully annuitize all available wealth. Instead, partial annuitization strategies allow for at least some balancing between managing the risk of outliving assets and managing the risk of needing access to a significant amount of liquidity. Notably, effective medical insurance and long-term care insurance can help to mitigate this need, though even with effective insurance full annuitization would not be appealing for those who have at least some legacy goals (whether for heirs or with charitable intent).

- Maximize mortality credit opportunities. Given that in the end, the primary benefit of annuitization is the leverage of mortality credits, especially for those who live materially past life expectancy, choose annuitization payment structures that maximize payments in later years. Rising payment streams—either with a fixed increase, or those that are directly inflation-adjusted—have the potential to provide the greatest internal rate of return when it's needed most (for those who live a very long time). This is an important trade-off to recognize, because rising payment streams generally have lower initial payments, and the annuitant may have to wait many years just to reach a "crossover" point and breakeven; however, in the years beyond, rising payments begin to accrue exponentially more for the long-lived annuitant, making the approach especially effective as a longevity hedge. Notably, in the coming years, deferred income annuities (also known as longevity annuities) may provide further opportunities to leverage mortality credits in this regard for those who are especially long-lived (see Chapter 8 for further discussion).

- Use annuitization to manage longevity risk. While the primary benefit of annuitization is mortality credits, the primary situation in which mortality credits accrue is when retirees live well beyond life expectancy. For those who are concerned about outliving their assets just trying to get to life expectancy, the value of annuitization is limited at best, and may be managed with other (non-annuitization) liquidation strategies. Annuitization functions best when it is matched not only to someone who is concerned about outliving available retirement assets, but specifically those who are concerned about living materially beyond life expectancy and not having the assets to sustain such a long time horizon, where the contribution of mortality credits can help to provide the additional (absolute and risk-adjusted) return necessary to make the retirement income goal succeed.

- Coordinate with other guaranteed income sources. For some retirees, an available pension may already represent a significant source of annuitized income (or conversely, the decision to "annuitize or not" may actually be the decision about whether to convert a pension to a lump sum, not whether to convert a lump sum to an annuity). In addition, most retirees will also have access to Social Security benefits, which themselves are a form of "forced annuitization" (and spending assets to fund retirement while delaying Social Security benefits can itself be an effective form of "purchasing an annuity"). As a result, retirees who already have access to these forms of guaranteed income sources may find annuitization to be less necessary. Conversely, those who do not have access to such income sources may find annuitization more appealing to provide a base of guaranteed income in the face of what would otherwise be a retirement funded solely by available portfolio assets.

The bottom line is that annuitization continues to provide two unique benefits: payments that can be made "for life" (however long that may be) and payments that are a liquidation of not only principal and interest but also mortality credits from those who did not survive as long. These benefits of annuitization are balanced against associated illiquidity and mortality risks, but this is the inherent trade-off of annuitization in the first place. For those who are concerned about unexpected longevity damaging their ability to support their retirement, and are struggling to generate a sufficient return to fund a retirement that extends past life expectancy, annuitization continues to offer a unique solution as at least part of the retirement income picture.

Endnotes

1. Yaari, Menachem, "Uncertain Lifetime, Life Insurance, and the Theory of the Consumer," Review of Economic Studies, 32 (2) (April 1965), pp. 137–50.

2. Reichling, Felix and Smetters, Kent, "Optimal Annuitization with Stochastic Mortality Probabilities," NBER Working Paper Series, 2013-05 (July, 2013).

3. Ameriks, John; Veres, Robert; and Warshawsky, Mark, "Making Retirement Income Last a Lifetime," Journal of Financial Planning 14, 12 (December, 2001) 60–76.

4. Kitces, Michael and Pfau, Wade, "The True Impact of Immediate Annuities on Retirement Sustainability: A Total Wealth Perspective," Retirement Management Journal (Fall, 2013).

5. Treasury Yield Curve and Annuitization payment estimates based on available yields/rates as of 2/22/2014.

6. Bengen, William, "Determining Withdrawal Rates Using Historical Data," Journal of Financial Planning (October, 1994). Cooley, Philip; Hubbard, Carl; and Walz, Daniel, "Retirement Savings: Choosing A Withdrawal Rate That Is Sustainable," AAII Journal (1998) 10, 3: 16–21.

7. Kitces, Michael, "What Happens If You Outlive Your Safe Withdrawal Rate Time Horizon," Nerd's Eye View blog (June 20, 2011).

8. "Finke, Michael; Pfau, Wade; and Blanchett, David, "The 4 Percent Rule Is Not Safe in a Low-Yield World," Journal of Financial Planning (June, 2013).

9. Pfau, Wade, "An International Perspective on Safe Withdrawal Rates: The Demise of the 4 Percent Rule?," Journal of Financial Planning (December, 2010).

Chapter 10

Annuities and Trusts

As a financial asset, an annuity is necessarily part of the overall financial and estate plan of its purchaser. However, it is sometimes not well coordinated with the other components. Indeed, the ownership and beneficiary arrangement of an annuity may be inconsistent with—or even in conflict with—the rest of a client's plan. Not uncommonly, this results from an advisor's decision to employ the annuity in connection with a trust without a full understanding of the rules governing both. In the following discussion, we will examine some of the problems advisors may encounter when annuities are owned by, or made payable to, a trust, and the rules (i.e., the tax rules and the contractual provisions and administrative policies of annuity issuers) that are not well understood.

For most of the following discussion, we will be concerned only with deferred annuities. Not only are most annuities sold of this type, but the Internal Revenue Code (Code) provisions that cause most of the difficulties where annuities are owned by or payable to a trust (Section 72(u) and certain paragraphs of Section 72(s)) do not apply to immediate annuities. We will also be concerned only with nonqualified contracts, because qualified annuities, or annuities used to fund IRAs, cannot be owned by a trust other than the trust for the type of retirement plan being funded.

Problematic Annuity Structuring with Trusts

Problems can arise when a deferred annuity is:

- owned by and payable to a trust;

- owned by a trust and payable to another party;

- owned by another party and payable to a trust.

When an annuity is owned by a trust, the holder of the annuity is deemed by Section 72(s)(6)(A)[1] to be the primary annuitant.[2] It is vital that the advisor understand that this provision applies with regard to distributions required to be made from the annuity upon the death of the holder by Section 72(s), if the annuity is to be considered an annuity for income tax purposes. However, what if a particular annuity does not provide for payment upon the primary annuitant's death when the annuity is owned by a trust? The result is a conflict—an incongruity, which can pose serious problems as will be discussed later in this chapter.

Also, as was discussed in Chapter 2, an annuity owned by a trust, or other nonnatural person, will not be considered an annuity for income tax purposes unless the owning entity is acting as the agent of a natural person.[3] This requirement, too, is a source of potential problems. Although many trusts qualify as such agents, not all do (see Chapter 2).

When a trust is the beneficiary of an annuity, that annuity is subject to distribution requirements different from those applying when the beneficiary is an individual, or a natural person. These requirements apply whether or not the trust is also the holder of the annuity.

Annuity-Trust Situations

Where Trust Owns Annuity

1.   The Annuity Is Owned by a Revocable Living Trust.

A curiosity that advisors frequently encounter is a deferred annuity contract owned by a client's Revocable Living Trust (RLT). It is curious, because there is often little reason for it. Sometimes, the annuity was transferred into the RLT because someone felt that "everything ought to be in the trust." But there can be some problems with this arrangement.

First, we should ask, what is to be gained by owning a deferred annuity inside an RLT? RLTs avoid probate, of course, which is often a main reason for establishing these trusts. But annuity death benefits pass to beneficiaries outside probate anyway by operation of the annuity contract, so probate avoidance is not a good reason for putting an annuity in an RLT. Another, and better, reason might be a desire to have annuity death proceeds distributed under the terms of that trust, which terms can be far more flexible than a normal beneficiary designation. But that does not require that the annuity be owned by the trust, merely that it be *payable to* the trust under the beneficiary designation. Another reason might be to avoid problems that could arise upon the annuity owner's becoming incompetent. Yet a properly drafted durable power of attorney may suffice for this purpose.

Thus, nearly all of the benefits just described can be achieved by other means or by virtue of the annuity itself, without inviting the problems connected with naming the RLT as the annuity owner (most significantly, that the annuitant becomes the holder for tax purposes, which can create significant complications if the annuitant is not the same as the grantor of the RLT).

2.   The Annuity Is Transferred to Owner's Irrevocable Trust.

A common reason for an owner to transfer ownership of a deferred annuity to his irrevocable trust is to remove its value from his/her taxable estate (and/or to shelter future growth from the estate). Can this create problems? Perhaps. Section 72(e)(4)(C) says that:

> "If an individual who holds an annuity contract transfers it without full and adequate consideration, such individual shall be treated as receiving an amount equal to the excess of:
>
> (I)   the cash surrender value of such contract at the time of transfer; over
>
> (II) the investment in such contract at such time, under the contract as an amount not received as an annuity."

In other words, such a transfer will trigger recognition of all the gain in the contract at the time of the transfer. The only statutory exception to this rule is a gift to holder's spouse.[4]

What if the receiving trust is a grantor trust? Under the original grantor trust rules and subsequent rulings, a *sale* of property from an individual to his/her grantor trust does not trigger recognition of gain because it is not deemed to be an income tax event, because under Revenue Ruling 85-13 the trust is not viewed as a separate entity from the grantor capable of entering into a taxable sales transaction.[5] Since Section 72 is an income tax provision, some contend that under those rules, an individual holding a highly appreciated deferred annuity could theoretically transfer ownership of that annuity to a grantor trust and avoid income tax gain recognition, while also enjoying the benefit that the value of the annuity will not be includable in the estate for federal estate tax purposes if the trust is otherwise not includable, e.g., in the case of a so-called Intentionally Defective Grantor Trust (IDGT).

However, such a transfer for less than adequate consideration is probably a gift—certainly, in the case of a IDGT—and thus may trigger the aforementioned language of Section 72(e)(4) (C) simply on the basis that a transfer has occurred, and by definition it was without full and adequate consideration because it triggered a gift tax event. In essence, the interpretive challenge is whether the word "transfer" in Section 72(e)(4)(C) is to be applied using an income tax framework, or a gift tax framework. From an income tax perspective, a transfer to a grantor trust should be exempt from the income tax event by virtue of the principle that a transaction between a taxpayer and his/her grantor trust is a transaction between the same tax entities and thus does not constitute an income tax transfer. However, if the term "transfer" is interpreted from a *gift* tax perspective, then any transfer that would be construed as a transfer for gift tax purposes (e.g., a gift to an IDGT) would cause an income tax event under Section 72(e)(4)(C). In point of fact, under the gift tax framework, in theory even an incomplete gift due to a retained interest may still trigger income taxes upon the transfer of an annuity, because the transfer would still be for less than *full* and adequate consideration.

Moreover, it is not clear that a grantor trust transaction would apply in the case of a transfer of an annuity to an IDGT, in the manner that it applied to a sale of property to a grantor trust under Revenue Ruling 85-13. It is significant—in the authors' opinion—that the Ruling cited Section 1.675-1 of the Income Tax Regulations, noting that the Section "treats the grantor as the owner of a trust if, under the terms of the trust instrument, or the circumstances attendant to its operation, administrative control is exercisable primarily for the benefit of the grantor rather than the beneficiaries of the trust." In reviewing the applicability of Section 675, the Ruling observed that "In all of these cases, the justification for treating the grantor as owner is evidence of substantial grantor dominion and control over the trust."

In the authors' opinion, such justification is arguably not present when a taxpayer gifts a deferred annuity to an irrevocable trust of which he is not trustee. Prior to making the gift, that taxpayer could exercise unfettered control over the annuity; afterwards, he cannot. Control of the annuity has shifted, but the tax liability should not. Gary Underwood argues[6] that the most common sensible approach would be to assume that the grantor trust provisions prevail, and that Section 72(e)(4)(C) simply doesn't apply because no transfer has taken place for income tax purposes. We are not so sure that the grantor trust provisions of the Code and Revevue Ruling 85-13 can be safely stretched to cover the facts of the present scenario and that the plain language rule of Section 72(e)(4)(C) can be ignored.

Unfortunately, as of this fourth edition, neither the IRS nor the Treasury have issued definitive interpretation or guidance on this particular issue. To say the least, however, practitioners should be extremely cautious about any transfer of an annuity to an irrevocable trust that may constitute some form of gratuitous transfer.

An alternative to avoid these rules might be the *sale* of the annuity to the trust, perhaps in exchange for a balloon note, private annuity, or Self-Canceling Installment Note (SCIN). Such a sale would more clearly not trigger recognition of any gains in the annuity under the grantor trust rules[7] as it is clearly not treated as a sale for income tax purposes—under Revenue Ruling 85-13— nor a gratuitous transfer (because a sale actually *did* occur). Such an approach would furthermore allow the owner to avoid gift tax consequences on the transfer in exchange for the cash flow and estate tax consequences of using such devices. While a sale of an annuity might avoid the Section 72(e)(4)(C) problems that a gift can trigger, it's notable that this transaction structure, too, may have its risks. The issue is that as Revenue Ruling 85-13 viewed the sale-to-grantor-trust transaction nontaxable because it was the equivalent of an exchange of property for a promissory note between a grantor and grantor's trust (i.e., as an indirect borrowing of the property), and Section 72(e)(4)(A) states that a loan—even indirect—against an annuity, as well as the pledge or assignment of an annuity as collateral for a loan, triggers income tax consequences as though the amount were withdrawn. To say the least, there is no clear consensus about the proper treatment even in this context, with plausible arguments on both sides of the case.

It is also worth noting that the transfer of an annuity to the owner's trust might produce different results with regard to the death benefit of the annuity, especially in the case where the owner is not the annuitant. We will examine this scenario later as we consider the implications of having a trust named as beneficiary of a nonqualified annuity.

3.   The Annuity Is Owned by an Irrevocable Grantor Trust and the Grantor Is Not the Annuitant.

Let us suppose that George establishes an irrevocable grantor trust and that the trust purchases a deferred annuity. The trust is named owner and beneficiary. The primary annuitant is George's daughter, Sally. Whose death triggers payout of the contract? The answer is not clear. Some authorities state that Sally's death must cause payout. Others insist that George's death must do so.

Does Sally's death trigger payout? Code section 72(s)(6)(A) declares that when an annuity is owned by a nonnatural person, the primary annuitant shall be deemed, for purposes of post-death distribution requirements, to be the holder, or owner. Thus, the death of Sally, the imputed owner, will trigger payout under the provisions of Section 72(s). Of course, if the annuity contract is annuitant-driven, the contract will be paid out upon Sally's death—that is, the death of the annuitant—even if 72(s)(6)(A) were not implicated.

Does George's death trigger payout? Some authorities insist yes, that the grantor trust rules require that the annuity be paid out upon George's death, even though George is neither the annuitant nor the owner named in the annuity contract or deemed owner by application of Section 72(s)(6)(A). Gary Underwood observes that:

> "Although no authority explicitly addresses this issue [of triggering death distribution rules], distribution at the death of the grantor is the most logical choice. Since the grantor is the owner of grantor trust assets for income tax purposes, and the death of the owner is the primary trigger for annuity distributions at death, then the death of the grantor should trigger the death distribution requirements. It seems incorrect to assert that the grantor is the owner of the annuity for income tax purposes, but the grantor is not the owner for the income tax requirement of distributions at death under IRC Sec. 72. Although some insurance companies treat the death of the grantor as a distribution event, it is possible that other insurance companies may not be aware of the death of a nonannuitant grantor and may not have reporting procedures in place to trigger a distribution."[8]

The authors have been unable to find any authority as to which position is correct, or even any case law dealing with this issue. In practical terms, it appears that the correct answer is whatever the issuing insurer decides is correct, because that insurer will take action, or not take action, depending upon its interpretation, and if the trustee disagrees, the trustee will be compelled to request a Private Letter Ruling to dispute the reporting the insurer issues on the Form 1099-R. Thus, if it is the policy of that insurer to distribute the value of the annuity on the death of the primary annuitant, as Section 72(s)(6)(A) mandates, it will make such distribution, and apply the restrictions of Section 72(s), even if Mr. Underwood's interpretation is correct.

Moreover, if the trust is beneficiary of the annuity as well as the owner—which many insurers require—most insurers will require full distribution of the contract within five years, as the trust is not a designated beneficiary under Code section 72(s)(4), as discussed further below.

If, on the other hand, the issuing insurer's policy follows Mr. Underwood's interpretation, it will not require payout upon Sally's death unless the annuity is annuitant-driven, but will do so upon George's death. In conversations with representatives of several insurers, the authors have learned that some insurers follow the rule of Section 72(s)(6)(A) and will require payout on George's death, while others agree with Mr. Underwood's interpretation, and will require payout if Sally dies first.

It is vital that everyone involved in such a scenario—in this case, George, Sally, the Trustee of George's trust, and all advisors offering counsel regarding the annuity—know, before anyone dies, what the issuing insurer will require in the event of either George's or Sally's death.

Where a Trust Is Beneficiary of an Annuity

Naming a trust as beneficiary of a nonqualified deferred annuity is even more common than naming the trust as owner of that annuity. As was noted above, the transfer is sometimes for no other reason than a belief that "everything should be in the trust." Often, however, the reason is deliberate: because trusts allow greater dispositive control of assets on behalf of beneficiaries after death of the grantor. The settlement provisions of most annuity contracts are fairly standardized; a trust can provide far greater flexibility to direct the timing and distribution of assets.

What is often not well understood—or, in some instances, understood at all—is that when an annuity is payable to a trust, or to any beneficiary other than a natural person, the Internal Revenue Code imposes special restrictions as to when and how distributions must be made and a special rule as to whose death will trigger such distributions. We noted, in Chapter 3, that Section 72(h) governs payments to beneficiaries of annuities and when those payment elections must be made. However, Section 72(h) is not the only subsection that addresses beneficiary payments. As also mentioned in Chapter 3, Section 72(s) imposes its own requirements. So let's review the rules of Section 72(s) that apply to all payments of annuity proceeds to any beneficiaries.

Section 72(s) says that any annuity contract issued since January 18, 1985, in order to be considered an annuity in the first place, must provide that, upon death of the annuity holder, proceeds will be distributed in accordance with the following rules.

Distribution Requirements for Annuity Contracts

Section 72(s)(4) states that the proceeds of a deferred annuity not yet annuitized must be distributed within five years of the holder's death, unless one of the exceptions applies, as discussed in Chapter 3.[9] The exceptions include allowing the beneficiary to take proceeds over life expectancy, or a period not exceeding life expectancy;[10] however, this requires that the annuity be payable to, or for the benefit of, a designated beneficiary.[11] Section 72(s)(4) says, quite plainly, that "for purposes of this subsection, the term 'designated beneficiary' means any individual designated a beneficiary by the holder of the contract."

The key word, here, is individual. An individual is a natural person, and a trust is not a natural person.

Trusts under the Annuity Distribution Rules

So what happens if the deferred annuity is payable to a trust? A trust is not an individual and, thus, cannot be a designated beneficiary, and it certainly cannot be a spouse eligible for spousal continuation. Thus, must a trust that is the beneficiary of a nonqualified annuity take proceeds within five years, with no opportunity for stretching out payments based on a life expectancy?

Some commentators believe that other alternatives are available. One argument asserts that because Section 72(s)(2)(A)—in defining when the annuitization option of Section 72(s)(2)(B) will be permitted—requires only that the holder's interest be "payable to (or for the benefit of) a designated beneficiary," then (1) if the trust is acting as the agent of a natural person, and (2) if that natural person is the sole beneficiary of the trust, it follows that the trust is acting for the benefit of that designated beneficiary. Therefore, the trust should be able to take proceeds over a period not exceeding the life expectancy of that designated beneficiary, so long as payments commence within one year of death.

However, the authors believe that the agency argument just stated, however elegant, avoids the fact that Section 72(s)(4) is really quite precise. It says:

> "For purposes of this subsection, the term 'designated beneficiary' means any individual designated a beneficiary by the holder of the contract."

There is no opportunity for agency here, as there is under Section 72(u) for tax-deferral treatment of an annuity based on the nature of the owner (while the owner is still alive). To be a designated beneficiary, an individual must be designated as such by the holder of the contract. He or she may not acquire that status by imputation. Section 72(s)(4) does not state that a designated beneficiary may be "any individual, or a nonnatural agent for that individual." If the beneficiary shown in the annuity contract and appearing on the application for that annuity is a trust, the trust is the party designated as a beneficiary. But a trust cannot be a designated beneficiary because that term, in the very specific context of Section 72(s)(4), must be an individual. As the trust, the only entity that was actually designated by the holder to be the beneficiary, is not an individual, and, therefore, not a designated beneficiary, the annuity has no designated beneficiary. Therefore, the annuitization option of Section 72(s)(2) is unavailable.

Another argument for the availability of the Section 72(s)(2) option holds that Congress, in enacting Section 72(s), intended to provide parity between the rules governing distributions from qualified plans and IRAs and those governing distributions from nonqualified annuities. The legislative history of Section 72 shows such intent, and the structure of that section certainly resembles that of Section 401(a)(9). Therefore, it is only logical that we look-through the trust to the individual trust beneficiaries in applying the required distribution rules, in the same manner that existing regulations permit a look through of a trust named as beneficiary of a qualified plan or IRA.

It may be logical for us to want to look-through to the individual trust beneficiaries for an annuity, but the authors do not believe that existing rules offer any authority for such a position. Unfortunately, the IRS has not seen fit to provide much guidance in this area, and there are no conforming Treasury Regulations for Section 72 to match those promulgated under 1.401(a)(9)-4 for the see-through treatment of trusts payable to IRAs. In addition, it is important to note that the existing Treasury regulations that allow look-through trust treatment are fairly new[12] in the context of a section of the Internal Revenue Code that has existed for much longer. Furthermore, the IRS has explicitly noted other situations where the provisions that apply to retirement accounts are intended to apply to annuities,[13] and its failure to announce any such parity regarding look-through trust treatment should inspire caution.

However, there is one holding[14] that affirms not only the availability of the annuitization option Section 72(s)(2), but also the spousal continuation option of Section 72(s)(3), where the beneficiary was a trust. However, the fact situation was extremely unusual. The surviving spouse/grantor/trustee had, according to the ruling, such complete control and dominion over the trust assets, which included two annuity contracts, that she was permitted to treat herself, individually, as the designated beneficiary of the annuities and exercise the spousal continuation option of Section 72(s)(3).[15]

What does this ruling suggest about the willingness of the IRS to ignore the existence of other trusts named as annuity beneficiaries and to look through to the trust beneficiaries in applying Section 72(s) rules? In the authors' opinion, very little. This ruling is an anomaly. The fact situation was, as we noted, very unusual. In a normal context, trusts established for other individuals will not allow complete dominion and control over the trust and consequently will not be able to apply the facts of this ruling. Otherwise, one might contend, why establish the trust in the first place? Moreover, we have been unable to locate any other ruling regarding annuities that arrived at a similar conclusion. Despite arguments that Congress intended parity between the rules governing nonqualified annuities and qualified plans, and that a trust as a beneficiary is merely an agent acting for the benefit of individuals who should be deemed to be designated beneficiaries, in the authors' opinion existing law and rulings support only a conclusion that a trust named as beneficiary of a nonqualified annuity will not be able to elect the annuitization option of Section 72(s)(2) or the spousal continuation option of Section 72(s)(3). Moreover, most insurance companies are unwilling to permit trust beneficiaries to elect these options.

A few insurers have taken the position that where a trust having characteristics that would conform to the Treas. Reg. 1.401(a)(9)-4 rules is named as beneficiary of one of their deferred annuities, those companies will honor a request by the trustee to pay death proceeds of the annuity to the trust over the lifetime of the oldest trust beneficiary. These companies effectively believe that it is safe to interpret the implied parity between Section 401(a)(9) and Section 72(s) as being sufficiently reliable as to authorize treating trust beneficiaries similarly, whether those beneficiaries are receiving distributions from a retirement account or a nonqualified annuity. Whether this represents the beginning of a trend, we do not speculate. Most insurers insist that death proceeds payable to a trust be fully paid out within five years of the annuitant's death, and will not cooperate with a beneficiary that wishes to stretch through a trust until the IRS issues more definitive guidance allowing such treatment, or unless the trust submits its own Private Letter Ruling to request guidance based on a specific fact pattern at the time of death. In any event, it is important to note that even where an insurer will comply with a more favorable interpretation and allow a trust beneficiary to stretch out payments, there is no guarantee that the IRS will acquiesce to that treatment on discovering it, given that the IRS still has not definitively provided final guidance on the issue.

At this point, the authors want to make clear—and emphasize—that Section 72(s) does not say how death benefits will be paid from any particular annuity contract. The contract itself will govern, and Section 72(s) merely dictates what *minimum* payout provisions must be in an annuity contract—issued since January 18, 1985—if that contract is to qualify as an annuity for income tax purposes in the first place. It is entirely possible that an annuity contract may contain provisions that are perfectly legal and enforceable (i.e., they do not violate principles of contract law, public policy, etc.), but that might violate the requirements of Section 72(s), such that the contract would not qualify as an annuity under that subsection.

Let's look at an example of such a potential conflict—specifically of the congruity or incongruity between when death distributions from an annuity owned by a trust must be made by law and when they will be made under terms of the annuity contract.

Annuities and Consistency with Section 72(s)

Annuity contracts issued since January 18, 1985, must require distribution of proceeds, in accordance with the rules of Section 72(s), upon the death of the holder. All annuities issued since that date require distribution of the annuity proceeds to the beneficiary upon the death of the owner of the annuity contract.[16] These are called owner-driven contracts. Some, but not all, annuities will also pay a death benefit upon the death of the annuitant. These are called annuitant-driven contracts. In actuality, they are both owner-driven and annuitant-driven.

When either type of annuity is owned by an individual, the death of the owner will always trigger payment of a death benefit[17] under the terms of the annuity contract (i.e., by the terms of a provision the annuity contract must contain under the death-of-holder rules of Section 72(s)). Here, owner and holder refer to the same individual, and when that individual dies and a payout occurs, the requirements of Section 72(s) that the owner's entire interest in the contract be distributed at the owner's death are satisfied.

But where the annuity is owned by a trust, the triggering event for the distribution required under Section 72(s) may not be the same as the event causing payment of any death benefit under the terms of the annuity contract. Section 72(s) mandates a distribution upon the death of the holder of an annuity. Where an annuity is owned by a trust or other nonnatural person, Section 72(s)(6)(A) deems the holder of the annuity to be the primary annuitant for purposes of this subsection.[18] Thus, for Section 72(s) purposes, that is, for purposes of "Required Distributions Where Holder Dies Before Entire Interest Is Distributed," an annuity owned by a trust, must, by its terms, require that the entire interest in the annuity will be distributed upon the death of the annuitant.

The problem—the incongruity—is that in the authors' experience, some annuity contracts do not contain this requirement. Some annuities state that where the contract is owned by a trust, the contract value—but not necessarily the guaranteed minimum death benefit—will be distributed upon the death of the primary annuitant. No problem here. But at least one contract the authors have read contains language that appears to contravene the rule stated above, that an annuity owned by a trust, must, by its terms, require that the entire interest in the annuity will be distributed upon the death of the annuitant. In the section on Death Benefit in the prospectus, this particular contract states:

> "If the Annuity is owned by one or more natural persons, the Death Benefit is payable upon the first death of an Owner. If the Annuity is owned by an entity, the Death Benefit is payable upon the Annuitant's death, if there is no Contingent Annuitant. If a Contingent Annuitant was designated before the Annuitant's death and the Annuitant dies, then the Contingent Annuitant becomes the Annuitant and a Death Benefit will not be paid at that time. The person upon whose death the Death Benefit is paid is referred to below as the 'decedent'."

Note that while this provision does direct that the death benefit be paid upon the death of the primary annuitant if no contingent annuitant had been named, it denies a payment when a contingent annuitant had been named, and elevates that contingent annuitant to the status of primary annuitant and continues the contract without a death benefit payout. Whatever the reason for this provision, the authors believe that it clearly violates the requirements of Section 72(s), which effectively requires payout at the death of *any* (i.e., the first) holder (or the first annuitant in the case of ownership by a trust); as a result, the IRS could declare that every annuity issued with these terms fails to qualify as an annuity for income tax purposes.[19] Is this likely? The contract in question has been marketed since 2000, and the IRS has not, to the authors' knowledge, raised this issue. Moreover, the legal department of the issuing insurance company evidently believes that the provision does not violate the Section 72(s) rules.

Is this merely nit-picking on the part of the authors of this book? Perhaps it is. But we believe it is more than that. Whether the contract provision cited above actually does violate the required distribution rules of Section 72(s) or not, is just one issue and perhaps the authors' conclusion is wrong. But that cited provision is also an example of another issue—one that is absolutely vital to the financial well being of financial advisors who sell or offer counsel about annuities and the clients of those advisors. That issue is this:

> The contractual provisions of every annuity you deal with will determine how the various benefits of that annuity will be provided or not provided. If you, the advisor, do not understand what those provisions say—and what they mean—you cannot tell your client when—or whether—he will receive those benefits.

When a Deferred Annuity Is Purchased by a Special Needs Trust

A deferred annuity is sometimes recommended as an investment for a Special Needs Trust. This may be a suitable recommendation for several tax and non-tax reasons. If the trust qualifies as the agent of a natural person, the annuity would enjoy tax-deferral; given the compressed tax rates to which such trusts are sometimes subject, such deferral may be a significant advantage.

However, in the case of so-called (d)(4)(A) Medicaid payback trusts, the situation is more complicated. To the extent there are required paybacks to the state by the trust of Medicaid benefits made to the trust beneficiary, the state could be held to constitute a beneficiary's interest. If the state is a remainder beneficiary of the trust, such a trust may not qualify as the agent of a natural person under Section 72(u), because it is no longer being held solely as an agent for natural person beneficiaries, causing annual gains in the annuity to be taxable as earned—as ordinary income, at compressed trust tax rates.

Thus, generally speaking, third-party special needs trusts that do not require Medicaid payback—and therefore should only have natural persons as beneficiaries—are more likely to withstand scrutiny as the owner of an annuity that can be deemed an agent of a natural person. Caution is merited, though, if a special needs trust that is a (d)(4)(A) Medicaid payback trust acquires ownership or otherwise invests funds into a deferred annuity.

When a Deferred Annuity Is Owned by a QTIP Trust

A deferred annuity presents unique complications as an investment for a QTIP trust, because undistributed gains in the annuity may not, in the laws of some states, be considered income and thus may not have to be distributed to the spouse beneficiary. If the purpose of the QTIP was to maximize income to the spouse, this may be an issue; conversely, the spouse may potentially force the liquidation of the annuity, to convert it to income-producing property. Otherwise, the trustee may potentially be caught in a conflict between a spouse who wants to increase income distributions from the trust, and a remainder beneficiary who wants to maximize the expecting corpus remaining behind.

Either way, though, if the beneficiary of the QTIP is under the age of fifty-nine and a half the early withdrawal penalty tax of Section 72(q) may apply, making a QTIP trust with a younger-than- fifty-nine and a half beneficiary unappealing, even if the income aforementioned allocation rules are not an issue.

Best Practices When an Annuity Is Being Used in Connection with a Trust

Many advisors rely upon the marketing materials, home office marketing representatives, or external wholesalers of insurance companies for their understanding of those companies' insurance products. To be sure, these sources can be very helpful. But they may not be sufficient. Sometimes, they are either unclear or just plain wrong.[20] Those of us who are not licensed attorneys cannot, and should not, practice law. But we can, should, and must exercise due care in our advisory activities. Therefore, with regard to annuities, the authors strongly recommend that advisors consider the following caveats:

1. Avoid naming a trust as annuity owner unless:

    a. there is *very* good reason for doing so; and

    b. you are sure of all of the results of structuring the contract ownership this way—including when (i.e., due to which deaths) the insurance company will pay a death benefit and under what conditions any death benefit enhancements will be payable.

2. Avoid naming a trust as beneficiary, for the same reasons, unless there is truly no need or desire to stretch the payments of the annuity after death and a post-death liquidation of the annuity under the five-year rule will not cause a tax hardship.

3. Avoid naming different individuals as owner and annuitant, for the same reasons (and in the case of a trust, be cautious if the grantor and annuitant are different persons).[21] This is a good rule to observe, whether a trust is involved or not.

4. If the owner and annuitant will be two different individuals, know whether the contract you are considering is annuitant-driven or not.

The above list is not a complete recitation of things to know and avoid about annuities, but merely the authors' suggestions of the most vital caveats to consider when annuities and trusts are both involved. A better general caveat might be:

Be sure that you understand how, and under what conditions, the annuity you are considering will deliver, or not deliver, all the benefits provided by that annuity.

Endnotes

1. This provision applies to any annuity owned by an entity other than a natural person, including a corporation, partnership, or trust.
2. Primary annuitant is defined by Code section 72(s)(6)(B) as "the individual, the events in the life of whom are of primary importance in affecting the timing or amount of the payout under the contract."
3. IRC Sec. 72(u).

4. IRC Sec. 72(e)(4)(c)(ii).

5. IRC Secs. 671-677; Rev. Rul. 85-13, 1985-1 CB 184.

6. Underwood, "Trust Ownership of Nonqualified Annuities: General Consideration for Trustees," *Journal of Financial Service Professionals* (May, 2010), footnote 45.

7. There are no income or gift tax consequences of transfers from a taxpayer to himself, whether by gift or sale.

8. Underwood, *Ibid.*

9. IRC Sec. 72(s)(1)(B).

10. IRC Sec. 72(s)(2).

11. IRC Sec. 72(s)(2)(A).

12. Amendments to Treasury Regulation §1.401(a)(9)-4 became effective on April 15, 2002.

13. For example, IRS Notice 2004-15, 2004-9 IRB 526, explicitly established cross-application of the rules under Code section 72(t)(2)(A)(iv) regarding substantially equal periodic payments from retirement accounts to the same type of payments under annuities and Section 72(q)(2)(D).

14. Let. Rul. 200323012.

15. In addition, the spouse was permitted to make a tax-free exchange of the annuities, under Code section 1035, for new annuity contracts owned by herself.

16. An exception to this general rule exists where an annuity is jointly owned. See Chapter 3.

17. We have said a death benefit, rather than the death benefit because annuitant-driven contracts typically pay the contractually-guaranteed guaranteed minimum, or enhanced death benefit only upon the death of the annuitant. In these contracts, the amount payable to the beneficiary upon the death of the owner is only the cash value of the annuity, and, in some contracts, a surrender charge may apply.

18. "This subsection" refers to Code section 72(s).

19. Presumably, the most immediate consequence would be that all these contracts were not in fact tax-deferred, and that income attributable to the contract for prior years should be declared as taxable income, with retroactive interest, and potential penalties, applicable to any years not closed by the statute of limitations.

20. Most experienced advisors have at least a few horror stories of home office marketing representatives or wholesalers who made statements about the operation or tax treatment of an insurance product that were totally inaccurate. The authors have more than a few of these stories as well.

21. The potential problems resulting from different individuals named as the annuitant and owner are so common and serious that some insurance companies refuse to issue contracts on this basis.

Chapter 11

Annuities in Estate Planning

Chapter 8 examined the annuity as an investment, in the context of a three-legged stool model. This chapter will focus on how various kinds of annuities can work in a more specific context—that of estate planning.

Avoidance of Probate

One of the estate planning reasons often cited for buying, or recommending, an annuity is that values in such contracts generally pass to beneficiaries directly, through the beneficiary designation, and are not subject to the probate process. This is true, but one does not need to purchase an annuity to achieve this result. Assets held in trust or taxable accounts titled as Payable on Death (POD) or Transfer on Death (TOD) also bypass probate.[1]

However, annuity beneficiary designations and the beneficiary designations permitted by state laws regulating POD and TOD accounts typically do not allow the degree of dispositive flexibility offered by a well-drafted trust. Moreover, values in an annuity may be includable, under state law, in the owner's augmented estate and subject to a surviving spouse's elective share.[2] If includable, an election by such spouse to take such share could cause the annuity value to be subject to probate, and to pass other than by the beneficiary designation to someone besides the named beneficiary. To determine whether this is an issue for their clients, advisors should check the rules in those jurisdictions in which they practice.

That said, the fact that annuity values do generally pass directly to named beneficiaries, outside of probate, is significant, and may be a valuable advantage for many clients.

Providing Guaranteed Income to Heirs

A principal goal of many estate plans is to provide income to the estate owner's heirs. This goal can often be achieved by using either immediate or deferred annuities. Where the goal is to provide heirs with an immediate income, an immediate annuity may be the ideal mechanism, especially if the income is to continue for the recipient's lifetime. The certainty afforded by such a contract is sometimes more important than the amount of each income payment or the fact that the annuity income does not preserve principal. This may be particularly appropriate to satisfy specific beneficiary lifetime income bequests from a portion of assets while the remainder passes to another beneficiary.[3]

Where the desire is for the heir's income to increase over time—perhaps to keep pace with inflation—an immediate annuity providing for known annual increases is often attractive. While most insurers do not offer immediate annuities with cost-of-living increases tied to some index such as the Consumer Price Index (CPI), some do, and more are likely to be offering such contracts in the future in response to a demand that appears to be increasing. An additional attraction is that annuities enjoy creditor protection in most jurisdictions.

A disadvantage to immediate annuities, in this context and others, is their inflexibility. Most immediate annuities, once begun, do not permit modification of the payment amount or commutation, although an increasing number of contracts do.

Purchase of a SPIA by a Credit Shelter Trust

One application of immediate annuities that may be of interest to estate planners is their use to solve the trustee's investment dilemma. Often, a trust (e.g., a credit shelter trust) is established to provide both an income to an income beneficiary—perhaps the surviving spouse—and growth of principal, for the benefit of remainder beneficiaries (perhaps the children and/or grandchildren). The dilemma for the trustee is satisfying the opposing desires of these beneficiaries. The income beneficiary wishes to receive as much income as possible, and would prefer that trust monies be invested to provide that goal. Remainder beneficiaries are interested in capital accumulation, and prefer that the trust be funded with growth investments. The problem, of course, is that investments that provide high current income rarely offer good long-term growth, and vice versa.

This conflict has always presented problems for trustees. A possible solution might be for the trust to purchase an immediate annuity, naming the income beneficiary as annuitant, in an amount sufficient to provide the income the beneficiary requires—perhaps increasing over time—and to invest all remaining trust assets solely for growth, without regard for whether they produce any current income. Adverse results in the growth investments will have no effect upon the income beneficiary. This strategy does not always work, of course. Financially, its attractiveness may appear to be directly proportional to the age of the income beneficiary/ annuitant, because, the older the annuitant, the greater the income that each dollar of premium will purchase; or, viewed another way, the less premium required to produce each dollar of income. This is assuming that the annuity is to continue for the annuitant's life. However, older income beneficiaries are likely to die sooner, and an annuity that expires without value at the beneficiary's death may be perceived as a bad deal. The existence of a refund element may reduce this objection.

Whether a refund feature should be included in the annuity is, however, problematic. A *life-only* annuity will require a smaller premium than one providing a benefit to another beneficiary if the annuitant, or the income beneficiary of the trust, should die prematurely. This would allow a greater percentage of the trust corpus to be allocated to growth investments, for the benefit of remainder beneficiaries. However, many people, including many advisors, find an annuity that provides no further benefit if an annuitant dies shortly after income payments commence unacceptable. The perception is that the insurance company keeps this extra money. This perception is false; the money is not retained by the insurer, but is paid out by that insurer to other members of the risk sharing pool, or annuitants who lived longer than their expected lifetimes. That said, the perception may be its own reality. Most people will not buy a life only annuity and would probably prefer that such an annuity not be purchased for anyone of whom they might become remainder beneficiary. Moreover, recommending a life-only annuity may subject an advisor to a greater risk of litigation. The heirs of a decedent named as annuitant in a life-only annuity may complain if that annuitant died shortly after annuity payments began. One of the authors has served as an expert witness in numerous annuity-related litigations and has seen plaintiffs complain, in that situation, that a life-only annuity was *ipso facto* unsuitable, especially when the annuitant was elderly and the "break even" point (when cumulative annuity payments equaled the amount annuitized) was beyond life expectancy.

Purchase of an Immediate Annuity for Heirs Outside of a Trust

Sometimes, an estate owner's goals include providing a specific and certain income for specified heirs, apart from the overall dispositive provisions of the estate plan. Here, an immediate annuity is arguably the perfect instrument. Without the certainty of the annuity, a trustee or executor must take into account the market risk involved when invested assets must be accessed each year to make payments to the beneficiary. Thus, the use of an annuity may allow the trustee/executor to invest more money immediately on behalf of the other beneficiaries while still guaranteeing that the income beneficiary will receive all promised payments.

Purchase of a Deferred Annuity for Heirs

Where estate planning goals include providing a certain income for heirs to begin at some future time, a deferred annuity may make sense. Advantages include tax deferral of current gains, which can be of considerable importance if the annuity is owned by a trust subject to the compressed tax rates applicable to nongrantor trusts,[4] creditor protection (to the extent allowed by relevant law) where the annuity is owned outside a trust, and the risk management and investment characteristics of deferred annuities discussed at length in earlier chapters of this book. Disadvantages include the overhead cost of the annuity, which may be higher than that of alternative investments, surrender charges (if applicable), the fact that all distributions from an annuity are taxed at ordinary income rates, and the unavailability of a step-up in basis for annuities owned by a decedent.

Purchase of a SPIA to Coordinate Legacy Planning

Impact on the Attractiveness of Making Lifetime Gifts to Heirs

A primary goal of most retirees is to ensure income for themselves for their lifetimes. This goal often surfaces in discussions between clients and advisors when considering lifetime gifts in an estate planning context. "I might need that money" is perhaps the most common objection raised by many clients to suggestions that they utilize the gift tax annual exclusion[5] in making lifetime gifts to heirs.

SPIAs can be used in this context to help coordinate retirement and legacy goals. For retirees and their spouses, an assurance of required income during their lives may make the option of annual gifts to heirs, which may be made for any number of reasons, far less worrisome. If securing this required income by purchasing an immediate annuity helps a client feel more comfortable about making lifetime gifts, the result can be both greater net wealth transferred to heirs—due to lower transfer tax and estate clearance costs—and greater emotional satisfaction. Retirees can live to see his heirs enjoy lifetime gifts, and can also monitor how well such gifts are managed. For the parent or grandparent concerned about sizeable inheritances spoiling the kids, being able to see how well those kids deal with the money can be both gratifying and informing. If the kids mishandle such gifts, estate plans can be changed, perhaps by adding additional spendthrift provisions.

Implications for the Retiree's Asset Allocation Decisions

Even where lifetime gifts are not a concern, adequate income for the estate owner(s) is usually a key estate planning goal. "We want to provide for the kids and grandkids, but first we've got to take care of ourselves" is a refrain familiar to all estate planners. Allocating a portion of one's retirement portfolio to a deferred or immediate annuity designed specifically to produce income can help an advisor achieve this key planning objective by making the allocation of remaining assets easier and less worrisome. Chapter 9 goes into more detail about when annuitization maximizes the overall value of retirement (and, indirectly, the estate that may be left over).

Using a Variable Deferred Annuity to Provide a Death Benefit for an Uninsurable Estate Owner

A deferred annuity is not life insurance. Section 101 of the Internal Revenue Code taxes the death benefit of a contract qualifying as life insurance (under Section 7702) differently than the death benefit from a contract qualifying as an annuity (under Section 72). The two chief differences are:

1. All gain—or excess of contract value over adjusted basis—in an annuity will be taxed as Ordinary Income, either to the living contract holder or to the beneficiary.[6] By contrast, the death benefit of a life insurance policy is generally received income tax free by the beneficiary.[7]

2. Distributions to the living owner of a life insurance policy are generally taxed under a first in, first out basis. All distributions are considered a return of principal until all contract gain has been distributed.[8] Distributions from an annuity (issued since 8/13/82) are taxed on a last in, first out basis, or as gain until all gain has been distributed. This same treatment also applies to life insurance policies that are modified endowment contracts.[9]

A variable deferred annuity often provides a death benefit in excess of the contract's cash value, whereas the death benefit of most fixed deferred annuities is limited to the cash value. The advantage of this additional death benefit in a variable annuity can be significant, especially for an individual who cannot obtain life insurance, or for whom the rates would be unacceptably high, for one simple reason: while the contract owner does not escape taxation on the death benefit of an annuity, he or she does escape insurance underwriting. The annuity death benefit is available to anyone who is willing to pay the standard cost charged for it.

How large might that benefit be? Some variable annuities offer an enhanced death benefit that pays the greatest of (a) the contract value at death; (b) total contributions, accumulated at a specified rate of interest (often six percent) until a maximum age, which is sometimes, as late as age ninety-one, this is often called the rollup value; or (c) the contract value as of the highest annual, monthly, or even daily, valuation date, prior to some maximum age. If investment performance of the annuity is good, the resulting death benefit can be far greater than the amount invested, or the cash value otherwise available at the individual's death. Even if performance is poor, the second of those two factors produces a constantly rising floor under the contract death benefit.

Many advisors recommend variable annuities with enhanced death benefit guarantees for this reason. Yet even this strategy might be improved by splitting the annuity investment into more than one annuity contract, as can be seen from the following examples:

Example 1: Ms. A invests $100,000 in a single variable deferred annuity with an enhanced death benefit. She selects a diversified asset allocation model, consisting of fifty percent equities and fifty percent bonds. At Ms. A's death six years later, the account balance is larger than at any prior valuation date, and is also larger than her contribution of $100,000, compounded at six percent—despite the fact that in the two years prior to her death, the stock market dropped significantly, while the bond market flourished. Her beneficiaries will receive the date-of-death account balance as a death benefit.

That balance includes the appreciated value of those subaccounts that did well (the bonds), and the value of those equity subaccounts that lost money. The losses of the latter are netted against the gains of the former to produce the total account balance.

Example 2: Mr. B splits his $100,000 into $50,000 contributions for each of two different variable deferred annuities, each with the same enhanced death benefit. He also allocates his overall annuity holdings in a fifty percent equities/fifty percent bond mix. He allocates all the equities to the first $50,000 annuity and all the bonds to the second. At his death, the account balance of the first contract is lower than at a prior valuation date—due to the decline in the stock market—so the greater prior value is paid as a death benefit. The date-of-death balance of the second contract—containing the bonds that did well—becomes the death benefit of the second contract.

The losses in the first contract are not netted against the gains in the second. Indeed, the losses in the first are ignored, because the rollup death benefit value is used. Thus, Mr. B's heirs receive more money at Mr. B's death in this example because they receive all of the appreciation from the contract holding bonds and the rollup death benefit of the contract holding equities.

Sadly, many advisors are unaware of this strategy. Some even insist that an advisor's sale of two annuities instead of one is inherently bad. Often, this is because they believe it results in a higher commission, which it does not.

There is yet another reason, having nothing to do with the death benefit, why two deferred annuities can be better than one. To understand it, consider this example, which uses both fixed and variable contracts and has nothing to do with the death benefit.

Example: Ms. A invests $100,000 in a single deferred annuity. Two years later, she decides to withdraw $20,000 from the contract, which is now worth $120,000. Her entire withdrawal consists of gain and is, therefore, fully taxable. Had she bought two identical contracts for $50,000 each and achieved the same investment results, she would now have two contracts of $60,000 each. She could withdraw the $20,000 from only one contract, and only half ($10,000) of the withdrawal would be taxable as gain, with the other half being considered a return of principal. It is important to note that due to the annuity anti-abuse rules, all annuities purchased from the same insurance company in the same calendar year will be treated as one contract, requiring gains to be aggregated for withdrawal purposes.[10] Consequently, a $20,000 withdrawal would still be treated as being withdrawn from an aggregate contract worth $120,000, resulting in the same $20,000 gain as the first scenario. Thus, to apply this strategy, the annuity purchaser would need to purchase each annuity from different insurance companies, or in different calendar years.

Using the Guarantees in a Deferred Annuity to Provide Portfolio Insurance

A fixed deferred annuity provides three guarantees to its owner:

1. a guarantee of principal because the money invested in a fixed deferred annuity is guaranteed against loss by the insurer;

2. a guaranteed minimum rate of return; and

3. guaranteed annuity payout factors.

The first two guarantees provide a known minimum return, on the portion of one's portfolio allocated to the annuity, which has the effect of lowering the overall principal and interest rate risks of the entire portfolio. Moreover, the assurance that this known future value can be converted into an income stream that will provide at least a certain amount of money each year can make future cash flow projections less problematic.

A variable deferred annuity does not offer the first two guarantees to the living policy owner, except to the extent that annuity values are invested in the fixed account. However, the guaranteed death benefit provides assurance that the heirs—not the living policy owner—will receive, at a minimum, the amount originally invested or the account balance at death, if greater. Enhanced death benefit guarantees, common in newer variable contracts, can even assure heirs of some other potentially higher minimum amount; perhaps the account balance at some policy anniversary prior to death, or the original investment compounded at some specified rate of return. If the minimum amount that will pass to heirs is a serious estate planning concern, the guaranteed death benefit may be worth its cost.

The guaranteed living benefits in today's variable deferred annuities may provide even more comfort for the estate owner in making his asset allocation decisions, precisely because of the refrain noted earlier—namely: "we want to provide for the kids and grandkids, but first we've got to take care of ourselves." The guaranteed minimum income benefit, guaranteed minimum withdrawal benefit, guaranteed minimum accumulation benefit, and provisions combining all three features can assure the estate owner that, irrespective of the performance of the investments in the annuity, certain minimum income and/or future lump sum values will be available.

Many critics contend that the costs for these provisions outweigh the benefits that they are likely to provide. The mathematics supporting such a conclusion—if any are supplied—often rely upon historical averages and probable life expectancies. This is not to say that all such criticisms are invalid, or that the logic and mathematics are never valid or persuasive. They may be both. However, it is the authors' contention that the certainties these riders provide can be very important to many estate owner clients on an emotional level. These certainties, with regard to that part of an individual's portfolio invested in annuities providing them, can enable him to make asset allocations with regard to money that he might not otherwise feel comfortable making. In addition, it's important to note that even though this individual may come out with less money in the long run on average, he is still receiving a guarantee that a particular minimum amount will be available, which may be more consistent with his goals than merely having the most dollars at death by investing heavily in equities.

Many individuals, especially older ones, are often wary of putting too much in the stock market, even though they know that equities have historically provided significantly better returns than fixed dollar investments such as CDs and bonds. To the extent that such a conservative (or risk averse) person's equity investments can be held in an investment account that guarantees minimum future lump sum and present and future income values, that person may be willing to allocate more of his portfolio to such equities, and remain invested in them longer than if no such guarantees were available. For the client whose portfolio is not large enough to generate required income with reasonable certainty if invested very conservatively, this increased equity exposure might make the difference between an adequate income and just getting by, or even running out of money. Why might this be? He or she might only be willing to invest substantially in equities if there are underlying guarantees, and would otherwise choose a much more conservative portfolio, with lower expected risk and return.

Using the Guaranteed Income of an Immediate Annuity to Reduce Retirement Portfolio Failure Rate

As noted, the risk management benefits of either a fixed or variable deferred annuity may allow some clients to invest their retirement portfolios—the portion invested in those annuities, but also, perhaps, more of the nonannuity portion—more aggressively, and with more confidence, than they might in the absence of these guarantees. The result of such a change in allocation should, over time, be an increase in the income produced, despite the expenses of the annuity. For retirees living on less than the amount their portfolios earn, this translates to greater capital accumulation, ultimately providing more wealth to transfer to heirs.

Yet many retirees do not live on less than what their investments earn. For all too many clients, the most important issue is not how much will be left to heirs after they die, but whether their portfolios will produce enough for them to live on, for as long as they live. Indeed, this uncertainty represents what one of the authors refers to as the one big risk in retirement income planning, namely: "What are the chances that my account balance will fall to zero before my blood pressure does?" This risk can be managed, with considerable effectiveness, by use of immediate annuities.

As was noted in Chapter 9, there is mounting evidence that allocating a portion of one's retirement portfolio to a mechanism providing immediate, certain income can produce a significant increase in the probability that the portfolio as a whole will be able to provide required income for the retiree's entire lifetime, however long that may be. The purchase of a life annuity, either for a level or especially for an increasing annual benefit, can offset—to an extent proportional to the percentage of required retirement income provided by the annuity—the effects of negative dollar cost averaging, where more shares must be liquidated to provide a set amount of income after a decline in the value of those shares than would have had to be sold if the share price remained level or increased. The strategy is most effective for those who live materially beyond life expectancy, where the mortality credits of annuitization can become very significant.

However, a life annuity is not the only way to implement this strategy. Laddered bonds or laddered period certain annuities may also be used (especially for those who do not expect to live long enough to accrue significant mortality credits).

Whatever the implementation, this strategy can offset negative dollar cost averaging, decrease the probability that the retirement portfolio will be exhausted during the retiree's lifetime—or produce declining income levels—and provide greater emotional comfort, although only an annuity guarantees that payments will continue even if an individual lives much longer than anticipated. In addition, this strategy may foster greater willingness to make lifetime gifts to heirs and/or gifts—lifetime, testamentary, or both—to charities.

Using Annuities to Maintain Tax Deferral, and Control, from Beyond the Grave

Ensuring Tax Deferral of Gain beyond the Annuity Owner's Lifetime

The income tax on annual gain in a deferred annuity is generally deferred until it is distributed (see Chapter 2), and distributees of annuity proceeds can benefit from even further tax deferral if those distributions are considered amounts received as an annuity (see Chapter 3). If so, a portion of each payment is excluded from tax as a return of principal under the regular annuity rules of Code section 72(b). This treatment applies to annuity payments whether made to an annuitant or to a beneficiary. Thus, if a deferred annuity is structured so as to ensure that the beneficiary or beneficiaries can, or perhaps must, take proceeds in the form of an annuity, the benefits of tax deferral will survive the annuity owner. This can be done utilizing a concept known as the stretch annuity.

What is a stretch annuity? In its broadest sense, one might say the term describes any annuity where the beneficiary designation allows, or requires, the beneficiary to stretch death proceeds and the benefits of tax deferral of undistributed gain over as long a period as possible. Deferred annuity contracts nearly always allow the beneficiary to take proceeds in the form of an annuity, either over lifetime or for a period of years. If the beneficiary is the surviving spouse of the owner, he or she is typically granted a spousal continuation option, allowing an election to treat the contract as if it were his/her own from inception,[11] and to name new beneficiaries, who will themselves be able to choose to take proceeds as an annuity. Moreover, many contracts permit the owner to ensure that death proceeds will be eligible for the favorable tax treatment of the regular annuity rules by allowing the owner to require that death proceeds be taken by the beneficiaries as an annuity. This election is usually made on the beneficiary designation form, or by election of a special contract option. Such election is usually revocable by the contract owner at any point before death, but not by the beneficiary after the owner dies.

However, election of a regular annuity payout option, whether by the owner or beneficiary, is not necessarily the only way to achieve this post-death tax deferral. As was noted in Chapter 3, the IRS has indicated that payment of annuity death benefits using the life expectancy fraction method, rather than the payout factors of a regular annuity option, can satisfy the requirements of Code section 72(s). The undistributed gain would not be constructively received (and would, therefore, enjoy tax deferral until it is distributed).[12] In other words, a beneficiary may take systematic withdrawals as the beneficiary of an annuity, without annuitizing, and still stretch the payments—and tax on the gain—over the beneficiary's lifetime.

In a subsequent letter ruling the IRS went even further, to hold that, under certain circumstances, payout to a beneficiary using this method or the amortization or annuity factor methods[13] will qualify as amounts received as an annuity.[14] As such, the regular annuity rules of Section 72(b) would be applicable, whereby a portion of each annuity payment is excluded from tax as a return of principal. It must be noted that the ruling that permitted this tax result did so on the basis of case-specific facts. Advisors should not assume that this result is available for any particular client without a ruling from the Internal Revenue Service. Moreover, many annuity contracts do not permit the life expectancy fraction method to be used.[15] Finally, insurers that do permit this option may issue a Form 1099-R to beneficiaries indicating that the payments made are amounts not received as an annuity. That is, they may not apply the regular annuity rules exclusion ratio, but will report such payments as fully taxable, to the extent of any remaining gain in the contract.

Of the three optional methods referred to above (amortization, annuity factor, and life expectancy fraction), the last offers the most stretch of tax deferral, because it permits smaller payments in the early payout years. It also offers beneficiaries the greatest flexibility. Most annuitizations are irrevocable. The beneficiary is stuck with the arrangement for the duration of the payout, which may be for that beneficiary's entire lifetime.

By contrast, the fractional method permits the beneficiary to take only the relatively small amounts required under that method and the freedom to take amounts over and above those required at any time. Moreover, undistributed proceeds will remain invested in the chosen sub-accounts and any gains earned will continue to enjoy the benefit of tax deferral.

As noted, the life expectancy fraction method of payout offers the most stretch. Thus, a more restrictive—but, in the authors' opinion, better—definition of stretch annuity is any annuity contract that guarantees for the beneficiaries the right to take proceeds according to this life expectancy fraction method. This definition might be refined even further, to include only contracts that waive surrender charges upon death.

A few caveats should be noted. First, as was noted above, not all deferred annuity contracts allow the beneficiary to use the life expectancy fraction method or, for that matter, the other two optional methods described in Notice 89-25. Many, especially older contracts, restrict the beneficiary to the use of regular annuity options. Second, not all contracts that do make the life expectancy fraction method payout arrangement available to beneficiaries permit the policy owner to restrict beneficiaries to using only that option. But is that necessarily a bad thing?

An annuity owner's right to restrict beneficiaries to some form of stretched payout of death proceeds does offer the benefit of post-death tax deferral. But it does so at the cost of flexibility. What if the beneficiary has extraordinary, unanticipated financial needs such as uninsured medical bills? An irrevocable annuity income will be of little help in meeting such expenses.[16]

Some flexibility and post-death control may be offered by the use of special beneficiary designations or contractual options. One key benefit of these is that annuity owners can place certain limitations on how beneficiaries receive the money after death, without having to go through the cost and trouble of having a lawyer draft a trust to accomplish that goal. Of course, it should be noted that a trust can provide much greater flexibility to accomplish goals than use of a beneficiary designation, which, no matter how special, cannot.

However, a nonqualified annuity payable to a trust will generally be required to make a full distribution under the five-year rule (as discussed in Chapter 2), while the same annuity payable to an individual beneficiary with a restricted beneficiary designation may provide for similar restrictions while still allowing the beneficiary to stretch withdrawals and income tax consequences over his/her lifetime. Consequently, so long as trusts are not considered to be designated beneficiaries, owners and their advisors must weigh the income tax consequences with the flexibility allowed by trusts in determining an appropriate course of action.

> *Example:* One major insurer offers a Predetermined Beneficiary Payout Option that permits the owner to restrict the beneficiary to a payout over his/her lifetime calculated only in accordance with the Single Life table of Treasury Regulation Section 1.401(a)(9)-9, Q&A 1, and, upon reaching a specified age, access to any distributions above the minimum specified by that table.

However, some deferred annuities do not offer such provisions. It is essential that the advisor know what stretch provisions are permitted by the annuity contract being considered. Whether the law permits a payout option is a moot point if the issuing insurer does not offer it. It is also crucial that the advisor knows whose death will result in the payment of the contractually guaranteed death benefit of the annuity being considered. In annuitant-driven contracts, the death of a nonannuitant owner will force distribution (per the requirements of Section 72(s)), but any guaranteed death benefit exceeding the cash value in the contract will not be payable. See Chapters 1 and 3.

Using a SPIA to Provide for a Longtime Household Employee

Often, wealthy clients wish to provide benefits, at their deaths, to longtime household help. They may be concerned that the employee might lack the skills to manage a lump sum bequest, or might squander it. A direction, in the estate planning documents, to purchase an immediate annuity for the benefit of that employee can address these concerns, without the hassle of establishing a standalone sub-trust for such purposes. A SPIA would ensure an income for that employee for lifetime; moreover, the cost of a life-contingent immediate annuity for a specified amount of income decreases with the age of the annuitant at issue. Thus, the longer the estate owner lives, the older the employee will be when the annuity is purchased, and the lower the cost of the annuity.[17]

Using a SPIA to Fund a Small Bequest

Similarly, a SPIA might be used to fund a small bequest to someone not a beneficiary under the client's trusts, where there is concern that the recipient might be unable or unwilling to manage the bequest prudently and where the amount of the bequest is less than the minimum that professional trust managers will accept. Of course, this assumes that the SPIA bequest itself would still produce a large enough monthly or annual payment to be a meaningful bequest in the eyes of the decedent.

Purchase of a SPIA by a Trust for the Benefit of Children not His and Hers

As Mancini, Olsen, and Warshaw note,[18] "when a trust is created at the death of an individual for the benefit of his or her spouse and children, if the children are not also the surviving spouse's children, tension can develop over the trust's investments. One solution might be for the trustee to be directed to purchase one or more immediate annuities for the benefit of that deceased spouse's children and manage the balance for the benefit of the other trust beneficiaries. Of course, this does separate out the trust principal at the time of the first death, making such principal, and its interest, unavailable to the surviving spouse while he/she is still alive, but it avoids the cost of drafting multiple trusts to accommodate all the heirs."

Using a Deferred Annuity to Fund a QTIP Trust

In some estate planning situations involving trusts, the use of an annuity may be problematic. Gary Underwood writes:

Annuities may not be appropriate investments for QTIP trusts for a reason associated with state law definitions of income. In most states, the undistributed gains inside of an annuity are not defined as income, and therefore may not have to be distributed to the income beneficiary. Income would only be recognized to the extent the trustee made withdrawals of gains from the annuity. If the trustee made no withdrawals, then there may be significantly less trust income to distribute to the surviving spouse. The trustee could be placed in an unenviable position between the surviving spouse who may want to maximize income and the children who want to maximize principal for later distribution. Unless the trustee and all beneficiaries agree on specific parameters for any annuity withdrawals, an annuity may present problems.[19]

Some of the aforementioned problems highlighted by Underwood can be mitigated by a clear drafting of the QTIP trust before the first death (i.e., to clearly state what constitutes income and whether/how income with respect to the annuity will be classified for income distribution purposes). In some cases, the treatment of an annuity may be preferable to alternatives, if the specific goal is actually to minimize income distributions to the surviving spouse. On the other hand, if the spouse is not happy with such an arrangement, the spouse could potentially have the annuity liquidated, under the required right of a spouse under a QTIP trust, compelling the trustee to convert QTIP assets to income-producing property. If such a conversion occurs after many years, the trust could be compelled to recognize significant accrued taxable gains in a single year. Accordingly, it may ultimately be wise to avoid the use of deferred annuities inside of a QTIP trust, unless the spouse income beneficiary is clearly supportive of the arrangement, and unlikely to have his/her mind changed.

Using a Variable Annuity to Fund a Charitable Remainder Unitrust

One commonly used application of a variable annuity is in funding a charitable remainder unitrust (CRUT). In fact, the variable annuity has often been touted as the perfect funding instrument for the so-called spigot NIMCRUT—especially by those marketing variable annuities. Is it? The following discussion will examine the pros and cons of such a strategy. But first, some terms need to be defined. What is a spigot NIMCRUT?

A CRUT is a type of Charitable Remainder Trust (CRT)—a split-interest trust with a charitable remainder beneficiary and one or more noncharitable beneficiaries with rights to payments each year during the term of the trust. Often, the estate-owner client is the noncharitable beneficiary. The CRUT provides that the noncharitable beneficiaries will receive a unitrust amount each year (i.e., a certain percentage of the trust value, as revalued each year). CRTs that pay specified amounts each year are called Charitable Remainder Annuity Trusts.

The NIM stands for Net Income with Makeup. Net income means that each year the trust will pay the lesser of the net income or the payout percentage specified in the trust to the noncharitable beneficiary. The makeup part means that whenever net income is less than the payout percentage, the shortfall is credited to a makeup account, which can be tapped later on if the trust's net income exceeds the specified payout percentage, but only to the extent of that excess.

The spigot part means that the payment stream can be turned on and off, as with a spigot. Typically, this works by having a special independent trustee instruct the trust administrator to turn the payment stream on or off, as needed by the noncharitable beneficiary.

Proponents of the variable annuity-funded spigot NIMCRUT sometimes assert that only with a variable annuity can the noncharitable beneficiary be sure of being able to tap the makeup account, which may have been created deliberately by having the trust invest in the early years in vehicles that produce only capital gains, but no trust income.

This is not necessarily true. First, the Principal and Income Act of the state in which the trust is sited may permit allocation of post-contribution capital gains as either income or principal, each year, as the trustee sees fit. Secondly, there are certain types of investments that can produce income on demand, so to speak, such as a Limited Liability Company (LLC). Some commentators have described a one person LLC as the ideal spigot NIMCRUT instrument, where state law permits such entities.

There are also some fundamental disadvantages to using variable annuities to fund this type of CRT. First, there's the fact that beneficiaries of a CRT are generally taxed under a four-tier system in which trust income is deemed to be (1) ordinary income, (2) realized capital gains, (3) tax-exempt income, or (4) principal, in WIFO order (Worst In, First Out). All distributions from an annuity are always ordinary income. A CRT funded with an annuity can never receive capital gains treatment on any gains from that annuity.

A second disadvantage is that a variable annuity owned by a NIMCRUT is not considered to be owned as an agent for a natural person.[20] Consequently, annual gain in the annuity—even if not distributed—is taxable. Although the NIMCRUT itself is a tax-deferred entity, insurance companies have recently adopted the practice of issuing a Form 1099-R to the CRT/owner, showing the annuity gain to be currently taxable. Previously, many insurers did not issue a Form 1099-R to report undistributed gain if the contract owner was a CRT, since it is already a tax-exempt entity. For this reason, and because charitable trust accounting is very complex, advisors recommending or considering a variable annuity to fund a NIMCRUT should be aware that the services of an accountant or tax attorney experienced in charitable trust accounting will be essential.

A third disadvantage is the wrapper cost of the annuity, which was discussed earlier. These overhead costs can serve as a drag on investment performance, especially if the insurance charges produce benefits only for the charitable remainder beneficiary and if the client's interest in benefiting the charity is secondary. It should be mentioned, here, that the first word in the term charitable remainder trust is charitable, and that advisors and clients probably ought to keep that in mind.

Critics of using variable annuities to fund spigot NIMCRUTs often harp on these disadvantages, often without acknowledging that there might be advantages in the bargain. This is neither fair nor accurate.

Ordinary trust accounting rules treat realized capital gains as additions to trust corpus, not as income. However, a CRT can be drafted so as to allow the trustee to treat capital gains as income. Regardless of which rule is applicable, if the trust investments include, say, a stock that has appreciated in value in the trust, but which is now performing poorly, the trustee, or a special trustee, of a spigot NIMCRUT may have an unpleasant decision to make if the income beneficiary doesn't happen to want income at the time. If the stock is sold, the gains are additions to principal, which will not benefit the income beneficiary. If the trustee treats the capital gain as income it may come at a time when the beneficiary doesn't want income.

On the other hand, a spigot NIMCRUT funded by an annuity can be drafted so as to define distributable income as any distribution from the annuity used to fund the trust, provided state law permits such language. Buys and sells within the annuity aren't income unless actually distributed. When income is desired, the distribution may be taken in the amount desired— limited, of course, by the actual gain the annuity has produced—provided that there is gain in the annuity. There can be no distributable income from the annuity unless its value exceeds its basis (the amount originally invested). If no gain exists in the annuity, no income exists to be distributed to the income beneficiary, because of how trust accounting rules define income. This last point is all too often not fully understood by clients, or advisors.

It's also important to understand that when a spigot NIMCRUT defines distributable income, that definition of income—or the definition under the state's Principal and Income Act—may be different than taxable income earned by the trust. This is specifically applicable when a NIMCRUT owns a variable annuity, because the trust's nonnatural person ownership causes annual gains on the contract to be taxable. Consequently, even when a NIMCRUT receives a Form 1099-R for taxable income attributable to annual gains on the contract, it does not necessarily mean that the trust must distribute that amount of income under its net income requirements, if the definition of income states otherwise.

The bottom line answer to the question of whether a variable annuity is the best funding instrument for a spigot NIMCRUT or not is, as one might expect, dependent on several factors. These include what the client's state Principal and Income Act permits, how flexible a spigot the client requires, and the size of the annuity wrapper costs, just to name three factors.

Endnotes

1. POD and TOD are types of financial accounts with designated beneficiaries, where account values pass directly to those beneficiaries, generally bypassing the probate process. POD accounts are often bank accounts, while securities or investment accounts are typically TOD.

2. That share which, by state law, is the surviving spouse's by right, regardless of decedent spouse's provisions to the contrary.

3. For example, a decedent wants to leave $50,000/year, for life, to one beneficiary while leaving the remaining estate assets to other beneficiaries (e.g., children).

4. Such tax deferral is possible only if the trust owning the annuity can qualify as an agent of a natural person. See Chapter 2.

5. I.R.C. §2503(b).

6. See Chapter 2 for further discussion of the taxation of annuities.

7. I.R.C. §101(a)(1).

8. I.R.C. §72(e)(5)(C).

9. I.R.C. §§72(e)(5)(C), 72(e)(10), 72(e)(2)(B).

10. I.R.C. §72(e)(11).

11. For the tax implications of this decision, see Chapter 3.

12. Priv. Ltr. Rul. 200151038 (Sept. 25, 2001).

13. These are the three methods set forth in Q&A-12 of Notice 89-25, 1989-1 CB 662, 666, as modified by Rev. Rul. 2002-62, 2002-2 CB 710.

14. PRiv. Ltr. Rul. 200313016 (Dec. 20, 2002).

15. According to Rick Bueter (www.rickbueter.com), an industry expert on stretch annuities, only a fraction of contracts currently available permit the use of the life expectancy fraction option.

16. It should be noted that firms exist that will purchase an annuitant's right to an annuity income—or a structured settlement—for a lump sum, but the lump sum is usually discounted at a rate of interest much greater than the rate used to create that income stream. Moreover, such a purchase may be barred by contractual provisions or local law.

17. Mancini, Mary Ann; Olsen, John; and Warshaw, Mel, "Annuities in Estate Planning," *Private Wealth* (Nov., 2011).

18. Mancini, Olsen, and Warshaw, *ibid.*

19. Gary Underwood, "Trust Ownership of Nonqualified Annuities: General Consideration for Trustees," *Journal of Financial Service Professionals* (May, 2010).

20. Priv. Ltr. Rul. 9009047 (Dec. 5, 1989).

Chapter 12

Summary: The Annuity as a Planning Tool

We have examined, in this and preceding chapters, how annuities work, how they are taxed, and their special provisions. In the next couple of chapters, we will discuss some of the arguments made in favor of, and in opposition to, the use of annuities in financial, estate, and retirement planning. The authors have tried to treat the subject fairly, and to present the pros and cons of annuities as planning tools as objectively as we know how. It is, of course, up to the reader to decide whether we have been successful in that effort. The authors are neither for nor against annuities. Annuities are merely tools, and are appropriate or inappropriate to the extent that they do the job better or worse than available alternatives.

The value of any annuity, as a planning tool, depends upon the planning objective. Where that objective involves managing certain risks, the annuity may well be the right tool, for an annuity is not only an investment but also a risk management instrument. As such, its performance should be assessed in the light of how well it performs in both areas. If a particular investor has no want or need for some of the risk management features of an annuity, the cost for those features can reasonably be considered to be investment overhead cost. However, where the benefits provided by these features have value to the investor, the cost of those benefits should not be charged against investment performance, as is often done, especially when the annuity is compared to an instrument that neither provides these benefits nor charges for them. The risk management benefits, to the extent that they are wanted and needed, should be related to the charges for that benefit and a cost/benefit decision should be made. If, for example, the guaranteed death benefit in a variable annuity costs twenty-five basis points per year, its value might be ascertained by the consumer asking, "would I rather have the investment performance of the contract without this benefit and risk leaving my heirs with whatever the account balance happens to be on the day I die, or is having the guaranteed values I've just examined worth my giving up one-quarter of one percent of investment returns every year?"

This procedure can be done with each of the risk management features of the annuity that are not offered by an alternative investment. Where the benefit is perceived to be worth less than its contractual cost, that difference may be viewed as an additional cost of the annuity. However, where the investor values the benefit and has determined that it is worth so many basis points per year in reduced returns, a proper comparison of the annuity with an alternative would require that the return for that alternative be reduced by the cost of the valued benefit, which is not provided for on the alternative side of the ledger. On the other hand, the assumption by many marketers of annuities, that the risk management features of these contracts are worth the charges imposed for them is no more valid than the assumptions of critics that such features are of little or no value. Value is in the eye of the beholder, and should be measured as it applies to any unique client situation.

Variable Deferred Annuities

Not all variable deferred annuities offer the same risk management features. Some offer no guaranteed living benefit riders and/or only a basic return of principal guaranteed death benefit. These contracts typically assess often much lower annual costs than contracts offering living benefits and enhanced death benefits and, in some cases, impose no surrender charges. In the extreme, some variable deferred annuities do not even provide a death benefit guarantee at all, and simply provide the current cash value to a beneficiary and the feature of tax deferral.

The authors believe that these bare-bones variable annuities represent a cost/benefit proposition fundamentally different from that offered by their all-the-bells-and-whistles counterparts. While the investment benefits and costs are similar in both types, the risk transfer benefits, or the insurance benefits, and the costs of those benefits in the bare-bones contracts are far smaller. In a deferred annuity having no living benefits and offering only a return of principal as a guaranteed death benefit—or in some cases not even a death benefit guarantee—the only risk that the purchaser is transferring to the insurance company is superannuation, when the contract owner might outlive his/her money. The insurer underwrites this risk by including guaranteed annuity payout factors in the contract. The contract owner may annuitize the contract, using these payout factors, at any time, even if then-current payout rates for immediate annuities are less favorable. If life expectancies continue to lengthen, it is certainly possible that these guaranteed annuity payout factors will become valuable, but they have not proven so in the past. There has rarely been a time, to the authors' knowledge, when the payout factors guaranteed in a deferred annuity were as attractive as factors for the same payout arrangement available in the immediate annuity marketplace. But we cannot say, with certainty, that this will hold true in the future. The purchaser of any deferred annuity transfers to the insurer the risk that later economic conditions might not permit a regular annuity amount as high as that guaranteed in the contract, by application of those payout factors. If there are any death benefit guarantees associated with one of these bare-bones contracts, those risks are also transferred to the insurance company on behalf of the beneficiaries.

A bare-bones variable deferred annuity gives very minimal and basic risk transfer opportunities, for which the contract owner pays a typically very modest Mortality & Expense (M&E) charge. A bells-and-whistles contract gives the contract owner those same opportunities, as well as the risk transference afforded by its guaranteed living benefits and enhanced guaranteed death benefits. For all of that, the owner pays both the M&E charge and the costs of any additional guaranteed living and death benefits selected. The total risk transfer benefits and costs of these two types of variable annuities can be hugely different. Yet the investment benefits—the variety and quality of investment subaccounts, the opportunity for dollar cost averaging, portfolio rebalancing, etc.—are basically the same.

Regrettably, many comparisons of annuities with investment alternatives either assume that the special annuity benefits are worth their cost or that they are not. Some proponents of annuities assume that tax deferral is always better than current taxation even when the trade-off is the unavailability of capital gains taxation. Often, the unattractive tax implications for beneficiaries of nonqualified annuities are either ignored or dismissed as unimportant. Critics of annuities frequently assume that the investor will take his accumulated money in a lump sum at the end of the comparison period, which implicitly condemns both the guaranteed payout factors as worthless and ignores the favorable taxation of annuitized benefits. Even worse, many comparisons contain serious analytical errors, including stacking the deck by applying one set of assumptions on the annuity side of the ledger and different assumptions on the other side.

The problem with The Great Annuity Debate is that it is, all too often, less a debate than a feud. Balance and logic give way to mere polemic, and the result is not analysis, but diatribe. No one benefits by this, least of all, the consumer seeking honest and impartial advice and a decent understanding.

When, and In What Planning Situation, Does an Annuity Make Sense? When Does it Not?

As advisors who often talk about annuities to financial advisors, the authors are often asked whether we like annuities. To that question, our standard answer is that we neither like nor dislike them—because they're just tools, which work well in certain circumstances and do not work well in others. Occasionally, that response will elicit what may appear to be a better follow-up question:

> *"When—that is, in what planning situations—does an annuity make good sense and when does it not make good sense?"*

That's a core question, and one that might be in the mind of you, our reader, as you hold this book. What's our answer? One answer might be that "it depends... on the specific facts and circumstances of the case." That's a reasonable and rather obvious reply, and what our audiences often expect to hear. But it's not our answer. Our answer to that question is that the question in unanswerable—until we know what the questioner means by an annuity. Are we talking about a variable deferred annuity or a fixed immediate annuity? As we've seen in earlier chapters, those contracts are hugely different. Each is an annuity but the two contract forms are designed to meet completely opposite needs. Generalizations, always hazardous, are especially unproductive when used with annuities. A true statement about fixed annuities is likely to be false when applied to variable ones, and vice versa. The same is true when the annuities are immediate versus deferred. Yet many, if not most, consumers—and all too many advisors—routinely generalize about annuities, often to the extent that their conclusions are so flawed as to be worthless.

This is not to say that all generalizations about annuities are without value, but merely that we should avoid lumping together, in a summary judgment, things that are more different than alike. "Immediate annuities are usually inflexible" is a fair statement because most immediate annuities do not permit either a change in the pattern of payouts or commutation of the contract, or surrender for a lump sum in lieu of remaining annuity payments. By contrast, the statement that "deferred annuities are risky" is misleading at best, because the risks borne by the owner of a fixed deferred annuity are mostly, but not entirely, different from those borne by a variable annuity owner. Both generally assume a temporary liquidity risk, due to surrender charges, but the former enjoys a guarantee of principal while the latter does not, with regard to amounts invested in variable subaccounts.[1] The former is subject to interest rate risk while the latter must shoulder market risk.

If we bear in mind this caveat—that we must generalize only when our assessment can be generally accurate—can we now attempt to answer the question posed earlier: "When, and in what planning situations, does an annuity make good sense and when does it not make good sense?" The authors believe that we can, and should, construct bright line tests to help us determine when an annuity is likely to be suitable for our client. In the following discussion,[2] we'll examine some of the most common goal situations and how well or poorly annuities may work in those situations. Where a particular type of annuity is clearly suitable or unsuitable, the authors suggest suitability rules, or bright line tests.

Where the Goal is Immediate Income

When immediate income is the primary goal, an immediate annuity may be appropriate, so long as it is understood that it may provide no benefit at the annuitant's death. Indeed, if the annuitant lives beyond the point where any refund element is payable, an immediate annuity will not provide any death benefit. As an immediate annuity consists of the amortized distribution of both earnings and principal, and as it will terminate without value at the later of the annuitant's death or the end of the period certain, if elected, it is not appropriate when all—or even some—of the amount invested must remain at the end of the income period (e.g., to satisfy other legacy goals). On the other hand, if there is no need or desire for having any invested amounts remaining at the end, annuitized income provides the unique opportunity to boost income with the contribution of mortality credits, which are not available in other annuity contract forms (or from non-annuities at all).

A deferred annuity is not designed to produce income immediately. Indeed, many deferred annuities do not permit distributions during the first contract year. Those contracts that do permit distributions in the first year may limit such distributions to contract gain. Thus, if income must commence within a year of the investment, a deferred annuity is usually inappropriate. And either way, distributions from a deferred annuity other than those made under an annuity payout option do not incorporate mortality credits.

There are, of course, exceptions to the use of a deferred annuity for income. For example, if the contract permits withdrawals of up to ten percent of contract value each year without penalty, and the purchaser does not anticipate needing more than that level of income, a deferred annuity may make sense. If the contract contains a Guaranteed Minimum Withdrawal Benefit, or Lifetime Benefit, that is designed to support withdrawals that commence immediately, a deferred annuity may make more sense than an immediate one. As always, individual facts and circumstances trump rules of thumb.

Where the Income Amount Must Be as High as Possible on a Guaranteed Basis

Where the primary goal is income and where the amount of that income must be as high as possible on a guaranteed basis, an immediate annuity is ideal. The key word, here, is guaranteed. Where the income period is a fixed number of years, a Period Certain fixed immediate annuity will generally provide a greater amount than can be assured from any investment alternative because the non-annuity alternative must preserve principal. Where the income period is for the entire lifetime of the recipient and where no part of principal must remain at the expiry of that period, and where the amount of each income payment must be assured in advance and be as high as possible, a fixed immediate annuity is not just the most appropriate solution; it is the only solution, because it will be the solution with the greatest income in the long run, due to the contribution of mortality credits.

This is true not only when the amount of each payment must be the same, but also when the amount of each year's payment must increase, by either a fixed percentage or by an index such as the Consumer Price Index (CPI). It should be noted that not all fixed immediate annuities offer such an increasing amount option and that few offer increases tied to an external index such as the CPI, though such choices are increasingly available in today's marketplace.

Where the amount of income payments must be guaranteed in advance and be as high as possible, and where no principal must remain, a fixed immediate annuity is the ideal solution. For maximizing overall income in the long run, though, especially for those who anticipate or wish to plan for outliving life expectancy, annuitization with rising income benefits may actually be superior (for further detail, see discussion of annuitization in Chapter 9).

Where the Goal Is Accumulation of Capital

Where the goal is capital accumulation, an immediate annuity is clearly not suitable, but a deferred annuity may be. If preservation of principal is a requirement, a fixed deferred annuity might be appropriate, but a variable one, in the absence of a Guaranteed Living Benefit rider,[3] might not. This is because a variable annuity, except to the extent that its cash value is invested in the fixed account, does not offer safety of principal.

With the addition of this rider—or, if the purchaser is willing to regard a return of purchase payments in installments as a guarantee of principal, a Guaranteed Minimum Withdrawal Benefit (GMWB)—a variable deferred annuity can serve as an instrument for capital accumulation with safety of principal. Indeed, the GMWB provision of many contracts includes a step-up feature that not only assures the return of the original investment in installments, but also any contract gain accrued as of the point where the step-up option may be exercised. However, it is important to emphasize that in this context, the safety of principal provided by the deferred annuity exists only if the annuity owner accesses the principal according to the terms of the guarantee. In the context of a GMWB, this means that principal is not guaranteed, unless the annuity owner is willing to extract that principal as a series of periodic payments over a span of many years.

If safety of principal is not required, or if the riders described have been added, and the timing and nature of the principal guarantee fit the client's protection goals, a variable annuity can certainly serve as an instrument for capital accumulation. Whether it's the right instrument, however, depends upon several factors.

First, we must account for and evaluate both its protection (insurance) and accumulation (investment) features. If the protection features offered, and charged for, in a variable deferred annuity are desired, then we must decide whether the cost of those features is acceptable. If it is, then the cost of those protections should be accounted for on both sides of any comparison with an alternative. As described above, we might adjust our comparison ledger by adding those annual costs to the annual expense ratio of the alternative—which neither offers nor charges for those protection benefits—or by deducting them from its assumed return.

If we do not value the protection features or consider them overpriced, the extent of the overcharge could be reckoned as overhead cost of the annuity, requiring no adjustment on the other side of our comparison ledger.

Example: If the enhanced guaranteed death benefit of the annuity is something we want, but we believe it's worth only twenty-five basis points (bps) per year rather than the sixty basis points actually charged, we might, in comparing the projected value of the annuity with some alternative, add twenty-five basis points to the expense ratio of the alternative or reduce its assumed return by that same amount.

Second, we must understand how the costs—both explicit and implicit—of deferred annuities impact investment returns and pay for insurance protection.

In a variable annuity, the M&E charge pays for both the basic death benefit guarantee, or guarantee of principal, and the guaranteed annuity payout factors. In a fixed annuity, these insurance features are not charged for directly, but are paid for from the interest rate spread, or the difference between what the insurer realizes by investing the premium and what it pays the contract owner. In comparing the variable annuity with alternatives, we can account for those insurance features and their impact on returns in the manner described above. But as a fixed annuity doesn't charge us directly for these features, we must look to the difference between the interest rate we expect to receive from the annuity and what we might otherwise get from a comparable alternative (e.g., a CD or bond). If the expected return from the fixed annuity exceeds that of the alternative, we might consider that the insurance provided by the annuity payout factors is free.

It's not free, of course—not literally. Rather, it's paid for, ultimately, from the difference between what the insurer expects to get from investing our premium and what we would expect to get by investing those same dollars. Yet where such a difference exists, where the expected return from the annuity exceeds that of our comparable investment, one might argue that the insurance benefit of the guaranteed annuity payout factors in a fixed annuity is pure value added and, in effect, free.

A variable annuity, on the other hand, charges us directly for both the basic guaranteed death benefit and the guaranteed annuity payout factors, neither of which is typically available from a comparable alternative investment. Here, as with an enhanced death benefit, we can determine what we believe these combined protections are worth to us. If we decide that's sixty bps/year and the M&E charge of the variable annuity is 140 bps/year, we can adjust the annual expense of the alternative upward by eighty bps or reduce its assumed return by the same amount.

Some critics of variable annuities ask why an M&E charge is even necessary. After all, they assert, a fixed annuity offers both a guarantee of principal, of all accrued and credited interest, and guaranteed annuity payout factors. The answer is simple. In a fixed annuity, the issuing insurer invests the contract owner's premium and is entitled to whatever return it can earn on those dollars. As was noted, it is from those investment earnings that the insurer pays for the guarantees of principal and minimum annuity payout it offers, and is also where the insurer earns some of its profits.

The issuer of a variable annuity, on the other hand, receives no return from investing the contract owner's premium except to the extent that the premium is invested in the insurer's fixed account. Investments in the separate accounts are, literally, separate. They are invested directly with the managers of those accounts. The insurer cannot pay for insurance benefits from the earnings it receives on those dollars; it must charge for them directly, and it does.

But the dollars invested in the fixed account do generate investment earnings for the insurer, which is precisely why no variable annuity contract assesses the M&E charge against funds invested in the fixed account.

All variable deferred annuities offer a fixed account and many advisors recommend allocating a portion of the client's money to them. There are two advantages to this strategy, in addition to the obvious diversification advantage. First, holding a portion of one's annuity money in a fixed account guarantees both safety of principal and a minimum interest rate with respect to that portion. Second, as was noted, M&E charges and any optional rider charges are assessed only against the value of separate, nonfixed accounts. That said, it should be noted that the current interest rate of the fixed account in some variable annuities is less than the current interest rate offered by the same insurer in its fixed deferred annuities. Funding a variable annuity entirely with the fixed account may be less attractive than simply buying a fixed annuity.

With regard to comparisons, it should also be noted that, in variable contracts, the *net* return available to the purchaser is the gross rate earned by the underlying investments, less the operating costs at the investment subaccount level—comparable to the expense ratio of mutual funds—less the contractual charges. If one assumes, for purposes of comparison, that the gross return on a portfolio of variable annuity subaccounts is the same as that of a comparable portfolio of mutual funds, the annuity imposes an additional level of costs, which inevitably results in a lower net return in the annuity.

Where All That is Wanted is Capital Accumulation

Where the goal is purely accumulation of capital, with no concern for assuring a minimum income later on or for a guaranteed minimum death benefit, a fixed deferred annuity may be appropriate, but, in the authors' opinion, a variable annuity is probably not.

As discussed earlier, this is primarily because variable annuities impose additional charges to pay for mortality and other guarantees. These costs, and the benefits they provide, must be carefully assessed when considering a variable annuity for accumulation purposes. If the insurance benefits are not desired—that is, that the investor does not value the annuity guarantees or the basic death benefit guarantee—then the charges for those benefits should be considered overhead costs that will inexorably drive down investment returns. Of course, not all investors consider annuity and minimum death benefit guarantees to be meaningless. For those who do, however, a bright line test emerges with regard to variable deferred annuities that do not include Guaranteed Living Benefits:

To the extent that the investor considers the insurance benefits purchased by the M&E cost of a variable annuity, that cost is more overhead, or a drag on investment performance.

An analogous bright line test for the suitability of a fixed deferred annuity might be:

To the extent that the investor can obtain a fixed deferred annuity with a rate comparable to available fixed income alternatives, and is willing to take on the reduced liquidity of the annuity—in terms of pre-59½ tax treatment and potential surrender charges—a fixed deferred annuity may be appropriate for capital accumulation.

But what about those investors who wish the upside potential of returns possible from a portfolio of equity, or equity and bond, investments, but with some downside guarantees? That's where the newer Guaranteed Living Benefits, available in newer variable deferred annuity contracts, can be very attractive. These benefits are discussed further in Chapter 5.

Where the Goal is Tax Deferral

The true value of tax deferral in a deferred annuity is a subject of considerable debate. Annuity proponents have argued for years that tax deferral is an unalloyed good thing. The authors agree that, *where all other factors are equal*, the opportunity to pay a dollar of tax next year is certainly preferable than a requirement to pay that dollar of tax today. But is that really the choice? How often are all other factors truly equal?

Critics of variable deferred annuities point out that all taxable distributions from these contracts, whenever and to whomever made, must, under current law, be taxed at ordinary income rates. By contrast, they insist, investors in stocks, real estate, mutual funds, and other instruments that qualify for long-term capital gains taxation often enjoy much lower tax rates on a significant portion of their profits. The real choice, such a critic might suggest, is not paying a dollar of tax today versus paying that dollar of tax later, but, rather, paying tax on a dollar of income today, versus paying tax on that dollar of income later.

The difference, of course, is that in the latter case, the rate at which the tax is payable may be different. Long-term capital gains (LTCG) rates are, for all investors, lower than ordinary income rates. A taxpayer holding a stock or share of a stock mutual fund will enjoy LTCG rates on much, or, in some cases, all profit from that investment. In addition, regardless of whether some income may be taxed as ordinary income, taxpayers face the risk that their marginal tax rates will be higher in the future, resulting in potentially higher tax burden by deferring income.

Moreover, tax deferral of investment gain can be obtained from buying an investment other than an annuity. If one buys a share of stock and holds it, there is no current tax liability in any year, other than on the stock dividend, if any, which may still be taxed at preferential qualified dividend rates under current tax law. If one holds a stock mutual fund, there may be current capital gains liability, due to turnover in the fund, and dividends, if any. However, some mutual funds are managed for tax efficiency—to reduce short-term or overall capital gains distributions, and commensurate current tax liability, and increase the percentage of total return eligible for LTCG taxation and/or for overall tax deferral.

Of course, not all gain from investments in a nonannuity account will get such treatment. Some dividends are not eligible for qualified dividend treatment, and taxable interest (e.g., from bonds) has never received such favorable treatment. Even those distributions from a mutual fund that are eligible for LTCG treatment are taxable in the year received.

The choice, then, is not simply "pay a dollar now or pay it later," but instead is more complicated. In a comparison of a variable deferred annuity with a nonqualified mutual fund invested partly or wholly in equities, it's a trade-off between the total tax deferral offered by a variable annuity, regardless of the types of investment subaccounts held, with all gains receiving all ordinary income treatment and tax deferral until the funds are withdrawn, versus mutual fund or ETF gains that at least receive some LTCG treatment and potential for deferral until those gains are turned over and distributed by the mutual fund and that are never subject to the ten percent penalty imposed on annuity distributions by Code section 72(q). As the tax rate (and associated tax drag) on the taxable accounts increases, and the turnover rate of tax-*inefficiency* increases, the variable annuity can become compelling for tax deferral purposes, though it may still take a material number of years—and sometimes, decades—for the tax deferral to become worthwhile, which means investors and advisors should be cautious to ensure the investor's time horizon matches the breakeven period.

It should be noted that this tax deferral vs. all ordinary income treatment trade-off exists for a variable annuity, but not for a fixed annuity. This is because the alternatives reasonably comparable to a fixed annuity (e.g., CDs, bonds) are, themselves, subject to all ordinary income treatment. On the other hand, using a variable annuity for tax deferral may also become more appealing in cases where the underlying investments might have already produced ordinary income tax treatment as well, for instance in the case of many alternative investments.

Of course, it's important to remember that the Section 72(q) penalty tax applies to distributions from both fixed and variable deferred annuities.

Where the Goal Is Market-Like Returns with Downside Guarantees

Amounts invested in the separate accounts of a variable deferred annuity[4] enjoy neither safety of principal nor a guaranteed minimum return. The value of these accounts varies directly with the performance of the underlying investments chosen. The purchaser assumes the investment risk inherent in these accounts, in exchange for the potential reward associated with such holdings. However, many investors want and need the returns possible when their money is in the market, but are unwilling to assume all the risks commensurate with that choice. To satisfy these investors, issuers of variable deferred annuities have developed optional riders to their contracts, the so-called Guaranteed Living Benefits. See Chapter 5 for a further discussion of these contract riders and how they may be applied in certain client situations.

Endnotes

1. Some guaranteed living benefit riders provide a guarantee of principal, or principal plus specified interest, either in a lump sum or through periodic withdrawals or regular annuity payments.

2. The material in this section was adapted from *"Annuities and Suitability: Reflections on the State of the Debate,"* by John L. Olsen, *Journal of the Society of Financial Service Professionals* (November, 2006).

3. While the Guaranteed Minimum Withdrawal Benefit rider available in most variable deferred annuity contracts guarantees the purchaser at least a return of the amount originally invested, that return must be taken in installments. In the authors' opinion, most consumers equate guarantee of principal with the right to take that principal in a lump sum. An assurance that one will receive, in installments, one's original investment is not the same thing. Moreover, it ignores the time value of money.

4. Separate accounts—sometimes termed investment subaccounts—are invested in pooled equity and/or bond accounts the value of which can, and usually does, change daily. There is no safety of principal or Minimum Guaranteed Return in such accounts. Amounts invested in the fixed account of such contracts are invested in the general account of the issuing insurer and do enjoy guarantees, both of principal and of a minimum interest rate.

Chapter 13

The Great Debate: Are Annuities Good or Bad? Part One: Arguments in Favor of Annuities

For many years, annuities have been the subject of considerable debate among financial planners, insurance agents, financial journalists, and academics. While some of this discussion is dispassionate, a surprising amount of it is not. Much of what is written on the subject—especially by those opposed to annuities—is outright polemic. The debate has become, for many, a feud—as if one must be either for annuities or against them.

This is both unfortunate and absurd. It is unfortunate because the tone and level of discussion regarding the appropriateness and value of annuities in financial planning often sinks to the point of mere diatribe, in which the search for genuine understanding is abandoned for the sake of making one's case. In that sort of debate, as in war, the first casualty is truth. It is absurd because it rests upon an absurd premise—that an annuity, which is simply a financial tool, can be, in and of itself, inherently good or bad.

The authors of this book neither are in favor of, nor opposed to, annuities. They view, and strongly encourage the reader to view, an annuity, or any annuity, as a tool, the appropriateness and value of which necessarily depends upon how well it does the job to be done, and how well it accomplishes the planning objectives compared to other tools that are available. In these two chapters, we will evaluate some of the more commonly advanced arguments for and against annuities and attempt to supply some balance.

Arguments in Favor of Deferred Annuities

The Benefits of Tax Deferral

Many proponents of deferred annuities point to tax-deferral as a great advantage of these instruments. Indeed, many commentators have stated, flatly, that tax deferral is the main attraction of deferred annuities—implying that it must be the main reason for purchasing one. Others have argued that the real value to such deferral is the control it gives the contract owner. Because there are no required minimum distributions applicable to deferred annuities, and because the contract owner can decide when, and in what amounts, to take distributions, the deferred annuity has been labeled by some as the perfect tax control device.

Certainly, tax deferral has value. Some commentators have observed that it enhances even further, the miracle of compound interest. Jack Marrion refers to this enhancement as "triple interest crediting."

> Money that remains inside an annuity grows free from current income taxes. Not only does the principal earn interest (simple interest at work), and the interest earns interest (compound interest at work), but the money that would have gone to Uncle Sam also earns interest (tax-advantaged interest at work).[1]

Moreover, the control over the timing of taxation of gain enjoyed by the owner of a deferred annuity is unquestionably worthwhile. The annuity owner may choose to take distributions in years of unusually low income or when such distributions can be netted against ordinary income losses. Moreover, the income earned in an annuity, but not yet distributed, is not countable for purposes of the alternative minimum tax or the taxability of Social Security benefits.

Yet the tax deferral and tax control provided by a deferred annuity are not entirely free. There are costs to these benefits, and the costs are not always acknowledged by those who proclaim the benefits. What are these costs?

Insurance Charges. These apply only to variable annuities. The insurance charges, or the sum of the mortality and expense (M&E) charge and any separate Administrative Expense charge, are usually the largest component of the overhead cost in a variable annuity. These charges are discussed in detail in Chapter 4.

Surrender Charges. Many deferred annuities assess surrender charges for distributions exceeding a specified amount or a percentage of the account value, if taken during the surrender charge period. These charges are a limitation upon the control the annuity owner enjoys over the money invested in his annuity.

Early Distribution Penalty. In addition to any contractual surrender charges, the Internal Revenue Code imposes a penalty tax on distributions taken from a nonqualified annuity by an annuity owner who is under age fifty-nine and a half, unless the distributions qualify under certain very specific exceptions. See Chapter 2. The penalty is equal to ten percent of the taxable amount of such distributions.[2] Like surrender charges, this penalty tax is a limitation on the tax control enjoyed by the annuity owner.

Ordinary Income Treatment. All distributions from an annuity are taxed as ordinary income. The preferential tax treatment of Long-Term Capital Gains (LTCG), and qualified dividends, enjoyed by many other investment alternatives, is not applicable to the gain in an annuity. This is true for all distributions—partial withdrawals, total contact surrenders, or death benefits—to the extent that there is gain in the contract, and it applies whether a distribution is taken as a lump sum or in the form of annuity income.

Does ordinary income treatment constitute a disadvantage of deferred annuities? If someone is comparing a deferred *variable* annuity to investments such as stocks, commodities, or mutual funds, the answer might be yes. Much of the gain derived from these investments will, if the investment is held for at least one year, qualify as LTCG, and/or may receive qualified dividend treatment, both of which enjoy taxation at rates significantly lower than ordinary income rates—especially for high-income investors. In addition, qualified dividends on stocks—or mutual funds holding stocks—may also be eligible for preferential tax treatment lower than ordinary income tax rates. The difference in net, after-tax, accumulated wealth and net after-tax income, wrought by the differential between these two tax regimes, can be profound. *See Chapter 12 for a comparison of a deferred variable annuity with a nonqualified mutual fund portfolio.* On the other hand, it's important to note that one material benefit of the tax-deferral structure for annuities holding equities is the fact that the investor can change equity allocations without realizing capital gains and generating a current income tax liability. Thus, for portfolios with high enough turnover, the benefits of tax deferral can still theoretically outweigh the less favorable ordinary income treatment.

In addition, with the introduction of a new top LTCG and qualified dividend rate of twenty percent in 2013 as a part of the American Taxpayer Relief Act of 2012, along with a new 3.8 percent surtax on net investment income for higher income taxpayers, the potential "tax drag" associated with holding investments in taxable accounts is greater than ever. Over long periods of time, even a modest level of turnover with relatively limited trading can significantly erode compounding—so much, in fact, that it's quite possible for the investor to end out ahead, *even if* the LTCG and qualified dividends are converted to ordinary income at a fairly low turnover rate.

Furthermore, it's important to note that not all investments held for growth are eligible for preferential LTCG and qualified dividend treatment. Foreign equities may pay nonqualified dividends, more actively managed strategies may generate short-term (rather than long-term) capital gains, and many types of alternative investments (from high-income REITs to many types of commodities funds) also generate ordinary income treatment. In such cases, the decision to "wrap" a variable annuity around such investments will not convert income at all—it's already ordinary income—but will simply create an appealing tax-deferral wrapper. At higher growth rates and upper income tax brackets, the "breakeven" period for when the cost of the annuity is outweighed by the economic value of tax deferral can be quite short;[3] in other words, it takes very few years inside a variable annuity for the tax deferral to be worthwhile at high tax and growth rates for investments already subject to ordinary income treatment. While such high-return tax-inefficient investments might ideally be located in retirement accounts already, for those who do not *have* retirement account assets available, a variable annuity thus presents an appealing "asset location" alternative.

On the other hand, when comparing a deferred *fixed* annuity to investments such as certificates of deposit or bonds, the ordinary income treatment of annuity distributions may not represent a disadvantage at all, simply because the interest earned on CDs and bonds is taxed in exactly the same way. In such a scenario, taxation will be subject to ordinary income treatment either way, yet the annuity's ordinary income gains are at least tax deferred.

It should be noted that the benefit of tax deferral in a deferred annuity is not limited to the accumulation phase, or the period from contract inception to the point where the owner begins taking distributions. Distributions taken as an annuity are taxable only to the extent that the annuity payment exceeds the excludable portion, calculated according to the annuity rules of Section 72(b). Gain not yet received, by this method, continues to enjoy tax-deferral until all gain has been distributed, which occurs when the annuitant reaches life expectancy or the end of a period certain term.

This opportunity for tax deferral of annuity growth, even during the distribution phase of a deferred annuity is often overlooked by critics of annuities, who often compare the annuity to some investment alternative assuming that both will be surrendered at some future point in a lump sum. The advantage of continuing tax deferral during the distribution period can be very substantial, as was noted in a study conducted in 2002 by Price Waterhouse Cooper, entitled "The Value of Lifetime Annuitization."[4]

> **No Step-up in Basis for Inherited Annuities**. As was noted above, the gain in a deferred annuity is always taxed as ordinary income, even when distributed to a beneficiary as death proceeds, with the exception of original pre-1979 contracts, as discussed in Chapter 3. When received by a beneficiary, such gain is considered income in respect of a decedent. Most other types of investments held by a decedent at death enjoy, under current law, a treatment known as step-up in basis, in which the cost basis, for income tax purposes, of the investment passing to an heir is stepped-up to its value as of the date of decedent's death.[5] Thus, a stock, which the decedent paid $1,000 for, but which is worth $2,000 at his death, passes to his heir with an income tax cost basis of $2,000. If that heir subsequently sells the stock for $2,500, he will pay tax only on a gain of $500.

If, however, the decedent had bought a deferred annuity for $1,000 and died without taking any distributions, when the annuity was worth $2,000, the beneficiary would be liable for the tax on the entire $1,000 of untaxed gain, at ordinary income rates.[6]

The authors suggest that, where net wealth passing to heirs is a major planning goal, far better instruments than a deferred annuity may be available. For example, life insurance offers far better tax treatment, if the individual is insurable. The beneficiary of a life insurance policy can receive, free of income tax, not just the full cash value of the policy, but the greater—often, far greater—death benefit.

An Annuity Is the Only Vehicle that Can GUARANTEE an Income for Life

One of the most commonly advanced arguments in favor of an annuity is that it is the only vehicle guaranteeing, for a given investment amount, an income that (a) is certain as to amount and (b) cannot be outlived. Strictly speaking, this is not true. Perpetual bonds guarantee an interest rate in perpetuity, in addition to invested principal, but these bonds are sufficiently rare as to qualify as exotic investments. Ordinary bonds cannot guarantee an income indefinitely, because all ordinary bonds have a fixed duration. Most instruments considered by investors desiring a certain income either have fixed durations or generate income only through dividends or interest that are not absolutely guaranteed. Deferred annuities also have a maximum maturity date, by which the owner must either surrender or annuitize the contract, so the claim stated above really applies only to immediate annuities or deferred annuities that will be annuitized.

That being said, there is a huge difference between the income generated by an immediate annuity, or a deferred annuity that has been annuitized, and that produced by any nonannuity alternative. By definition, an annuity is an income stream representing earnings, the systematic liquidation of principal, and mortality credits. To compare the income produced by an annuity with the income produced by some alternative using only earnings on principal (or earnings plus the liquidation of principal) is to compare totally dissimilar instruments. Unless it is made clear that one alternative preserves principal while the other exhausts it, such a comparison is utterly misleading; and even then, there's a distinction of mortality credits.

Yet if income is the only goal for a particular investor, the fact that no principal will remain at the annuitant's death—or at the end of the annuity period, if a period certain payout is contemplated—may not be as important as the amount of the income. For older clients, the annual annuity payment may be significantly greater than that realistically obtainable from any alternative, given the same lump sum investment. The additional income may, for these clients, be worth the cost of spending the kids' inheritance. Moreover, a comparison of a life annuity with an alternative investment need not contemplate that all of the investor's capital will be placed under either alternative. Allocating part of someone's assets to a life annuity might, in some situations, produce an income that is both certain—with all the emotional satisfaction that certainty provides—and sufficiently larger than might otherwise be achievable. The investor then might feel comfortable allocating his remaining assets to more conservative investments, to reduce investment risk, or to more aggressive ones, to achieve even greater total income or final wealth. In either scenario, the annuity would be performing, not only as an investment, but also—the authors would say primarily—as a risk management tool.

If one grants the advantages to annuitization just described, there remains the question of when the annuity needs to be purchased to achieve these advantages. Would it not make sense for our investor to put his money into some instrument that offers more growth opportunity than a fixed annuity or lower overhead costs than a variable one and simply sell that instrument to purchase an immediate annuity when the time comes to begin taking income?

Many commentators and advisors will answer "yes." Supporting this conclusion is the fact that the annuity payout factors guaranteed in a deferred annuity have rarely been as attractive as the payout factors available in the immediate annuity marketplace. Moreover, many investment alternatives may be taxed at LTCG rates and may even enjoy some degree of tax deferral. For example, the profit from an investment in a nondividend-paying growth stock will be taxed only when that stock is sold, and, then, at LTCG rates.

These are valid points. Tax deferral is not the sole province of annuities, and annuities never get capital gains treatment. However, the guarantee of principal, of a minimum rate of return in fixed annuities, and the guaranteed living benefits available in today's variable contracts provide a degree of downside risk protection that should not be overlooked. Whether that protection is worth the tradeoffs involved is a question well worth serious consideration. But it is not actually an investment question, even though most critics view it as such. It is really a risk management question.

As to whether investing in some alternative that perhaps offers LTCG tax treatment, during someone's wealth accumulation phase and then surrendering that investment to purchase an immediate annuity is preferable to locking in guaranteed annuity rates is a question we should consider in the light of longevity trends. Americans are living longer with each passing decade. Is it not possible that medical breakthroughs may so lengthen the life expectancy of the average American that immediate annuity rates, decades hence, will be less attractive than those payout rates guaranteed in today's deferred annuity contracts? If so—and, especially, if those future annuity payout factors are significantly lower than today's guaranteed ones—the result could be a significantly lower income, for every year of the investor's retirement, for each dollar annuitized.

Can we know which scenario is more likely? Not unless we have a functioning crystal ball. Without one, we can either make a bet that future Single Premium Immediate Annuity (SPIA) rates will be at least as attractive as today's guaranteed rates and that the risk management features of the deferred annuity will cost us more than the benefits they guarantee, or we can insure against those risks.

Furthermore, it is important to remember that if the alternative investment has created substantial gains over the years, a tax liability will be due upon the conversion of that asset from its nonannuity form to an annuitized payout. This foregoes the opportunity for additional tax deferral. Consequently, it may be more beneficial to accumulate funds within an annuity with the plan of future annuitization, because of the tax-deferral achieved not only during the accumulation phase, but also the tax further deferred by spreading the income recognition treatment across a lifetime of annuity payments.

Perhaps most significant in the decision to wait, though, is the recognition that part of the payout of annuitization includes not *only* payments of principal and the (tax-deferred) accumulation of interest, but also the payment of mortality credits for those buyers who have since passed away. This accumulation of mortality credits only begins once the investor buys into the annuitization stream of income (either with payments beginning immediately, or delayed to a future point in the case of a longevity annuity). Thus, investors who delay the onset of annuitization also delay the point at which mortality credits begin to accrue.

On the other hand, in the long run, the greatest contribution of mortality credits comes for those who live materially past life expectancy (see Chapter 9 for further discussion of the benefits of immediate annuitization). Accordingly, the reality is that the decision to annuitize is really best for those who anticipate (or wish to hedge against) living to advanced ages, and in such scenarios the contribution of mortality credits becomes so significant that (for those who really do live long enough) traditional investment portfolios simply cannot generate a comparable risk-adjusted rate of return.

The Guaranteed Death Benefit in a Variable Annuity Provides Protection Alternative Investments Do Not Offer

A feature of modern variable deferred annuity contracts often cited by their proponents is the guaranteed death benefit. It offers the annuity investor assurance of a minimum amount that will pass to his heirs, regardless of the performance of the underlying investment subaccounts. If the annuity owner happens to pass away after a severe market decline, the beneficiaries will not suffer from that decline, but will receive a guaranteed minimum amount. The standard minimum death benefit is typically the greater of (a) the account balance at death, or (b) the amount originally invested, less cumulative withdrawals. Most contracts also offer an enhanced death benefit for an additional charge. The enhanced death benefit may provide that the beneficiary will receive the greater of: (a) the amount originally invested, less any withdrawals; (b) the account balance at death; (c) the original investment, less withdrawals, compounded at some specified rate of interest; or (d) the highest account balance at any of certain specified prior policy anniversaries. Some contracts will include only one of the last two factors.

For investors who are greatly concerned with maximizing the amount passing to their heirs, this guarantee may be very important. Moreover, those investors might, having the assurance of the minimum death benefit guarantee, allocate their investments more aggressively than they would without that guarantee. If so, the argument goes, the historical risk premium of equities investments (the amount by which equities returns have exceeded returns on more conservative investments to compensate their owners for the additional risk involved) should offer the opportunity both for a greater death benefit—because the guarantee typically is the largest of the account balance at death or other specified amounts—and greater wealth accumulation for the annuity owner during his lifetime.

The authors believe that this argument has merit. However, fairness obliges us to point out that the same objective could perhaps be accomplished with life insurance. If the investor is able to obtain life insurance of a type that is likely to be in force when death occurs, the cost for the coverage could be less than the cost of the guaranteed minimum death benefit. Moreover, the life insurance death proceeds will be payable regardless of how the annuity, or other investment alternative, performs and those proceeds would generally be income tax free, while the death benefit in an annuity is always taxable as ordinary income. If the alternative investment never experiences a decline in value, the combination of a life insurance policy and the investment will pay both the face amount of the insurance plus the (appreciated) value of the investment. The premium for the life insurance will always produce more wealth passing to heirs than would be the case if no insurance were purchased. This is assuming that the insurance death benefit exceeds the total premiums paid into the policy.[7]

By contrast, the annuity death benefit guarantee is not certain to produce more money for the owner's beneficiaries than they would receive without it. If the account balance at death is greater than the other factors taken into account in the guarantee (e.g., the amount contributed to the annuity, that amount compounded at a certain rate of interest, or account balance at some prior policy anniversary), the beneficiaries will receive only the accumulated account balance. The presence of the guaranteed minimum death benefit will produce no additional value, unless the owner happened to achieve a greater return with higher risk (and return) investments because of the presence of the guarantee.

Some critics of variable annuity death benefit guarantees believe that the historical upside bias of equity investments means that if the annuity is held long enough, the probability that the death benefit guarantee will exceed the account balance at death is too small to justify the cost of that guarantee. Over the long haul, it is sometimes said, equity investments have historically returned an average of, say, ten percent per year. Even after reducing that average return by, say, 2.5 percent—to reflect the total expense ratio, including subaccount expenses, of a typical variable annuity—the result is an average return of 7.5 percent. That should, or so the argument goes, produce an account balance at death greater than the original contribution compounded at the five or six percent rate typically used in a Variable Annuity (VA) guaranteed death benefit formula, and far greater than the original contribution. Thus, the argument concludes, the cost of the death benefit guarantee is merely wasted money, nothing more than an annual drag on investment performance.

In the authors' opinion, there are two serious flaws to this argument. First, it amounts to the notion that the market always goes up ...eventually. It is certainly true that the long-term trend of equities markets has generally been upward.[8] However, prolonged bear markets happen, and one cannot be certain that one will not die during, or at the end of, one of them. Second, many death benefit guarantee formulas include as a factor—of which the highest will be paid to beneficiaries—the account balance as of certain prior policy anniversaries. Even the most bullish critic must concede that the upward trend of equities markets is not constant. Corrections happen, and markets often take years to return to a prior high point. A death benefit guarantee that locks in a prior all-time high may be of significant value, especially in a period of high market volatility.

With regard to the cost of the guaranteed death benefit provisions in today's variable annuity contracts, one criticism that is rarely voiced, but which deserves the advisor's serious attention, is how that cost is calculated. Most, but not all, contracts assess the charge for both the standard and enhanced death benefit against the accumulated account balance in the annuity.[9] As of March, 2014 the additional charge for the enhanced death benefit is generally between twenty and thirty-five basis points per year, as a percentage of account balance.[10] As the account balance increases, so does the cost for the guaranteed minimum death benefit. Yet, as the account balance and the amount of gain in the contract increases, the probability that the beneficiary will receive more than that account balance from one of the death benefit guarantees decreases. This occurs because the more that the account balance grows beyond the amount originally invested, the less chance there is that it will fall below that amount. The same is true, though to a lesser degree, of the chance that the account balance will fall below the value of that original investment, accumulated at the rate of return specified in the death benefit guarantee—for death benefits that have this option. To the extent that the annual growth in the annuity exceeds this specified rate, the accumulated value will exceed the death benefit guaranteed using that rate. The greater this excess, the less likelihood that the account balance will later fall below the level of contributions, accumulated at a specified percentage. Thus, in a situation where the annuity performs well, the contract owner will incur an increasing annual cost for a benefit increasingly unlikely to be payable. The cost/benefit ratio actually decreases with the annuity value.

This pattern does not hold true, however, for the account balance at a prior policy anniversary component. If someone believes that the magnitude of a possible market decline, and thus, a decline in the value of the annuity value, increases with the size of the account balance. The higher the market goes, the bigger the correction is likely to be. The reverse may even be true.

When considering the enhanced death benefit as a whole, however, the fact that the cost of the death benefit guarantee is based on the account balance, rather than upon the value guaranteed, appears—to the authors, at least—to be unattractive, from a cost/benefit perspective. A few insurers have recognized this, and now offer guaranteed death benefit provisions where the cost is more directly related to the amount at risk.

Whether the guaranteed death benefit in a variable annuity (either standard or enhanced) is worth its cost is, ultimately, a risk management question. Regrettably, many critics of annuities insist upon treating it as an investment; one where the cost of what is clearly an insurance feature is seen simply as an overhead cost. In the authors' view, this makes sense only if the insurance benefits are dismissed as valueless—or, at the very least, unimportant.

They may, for some investors, be just that. For the client who has no heirs, or who dislikes those he has, a guaranteed minimum death benefit is likely to be of little or no interest, and the cost of that benefit would, indeed, be merely a drag on investment performance. For this individual, a variable annuity—because it charges for insurance he does not want or need—is arguably a poor choice.

The Case for Guaranteed Living Benefits in Variable Annuities

In recent years, the emergence of guaranteed living benefits has made variable annuities increasingly attractive to many investors. As guaranteed death benefits offer beneficiaries the assurance of minimum values, irrespective of the performance of the underlying investment subaccounts, living benefits guarantee minimum values, no matter how the annuity investments perform, to living contract owners. Four basic types are currently available:

1. Guaranteed Minimum Income Benefit (GMIB)

2. Guaranteed Minimum Accumulation Benefit (GMAB)

3. Guaranteed Minimum Withdrawal Benefit (GMWB)

4. Guaranteed Lifetime Withdrawal Benefit (GLWB)

These guaranteed living benefits (described extensively in Chapter 5) assure different things. The first guarantees a minimum income. The second guarantees a minimum future lump sum value. The third guarantees that the contract owner will receive, at a minimum, a benefit base, or the amount invested, or that amount, plus specified interest, in installments, while enjoying the potential figure growth on undistributed amounts. The fourth type guarantees that the contract owner will receive, at a minimum, a specified percentage of that benefit base for life, or for the life of the client and his/her spouse.

While the mechanics and specific guarantees offered by these provisions vary widely from contract to contract, the fundamental issue to be aware of is that they are risk management features, not investment features.

They Are Risk Management Features

Guaranteed living benefits are not designed to maximize the investor's profit; they are risk management features, designed to control loss. In a best-case scenario (e.g., where the investment subaccounts produce double-digit returns in each and every year), living benefits can never be worth their cost, because those benefits will never be triggered. In other scenarios, the costs of the living benefits may increase—because the account balance increases—in all but the final year or two of the contract, but the benefits themselves, when triggered, will be comparatively small. In these scenarios, someone might view these costs, from a purely investment perspective, as excessive, or even wasted money.

In the authors' opinion, such a view is mistaken because it applies a perspective that is inappropriate. A variable annuity, especially one that provides guaranteed living benefits, is not purely an investment and should not be analyzed as if it were. The purpose of guaranteed living benefits is not to maximize wealth, or investment success and future account balance, but to minimize the chance of failure—that the future account balance will be insufficient to meet a client's needs. Electing these benefits is a choice, by the client, to give up some potential excess return as a cost of insurance against the risk that the returns will produce less than the amounts guaranteed. It is a prudent choice for the client who assigns a greater economic value to the risks that are shifted to the insurance company than to the total annual costs for the transfer— including the opportunity cost of those dollars. One might also argue that there is also economic value to peace of mind, quite apart from mathematical probabilities of failure or success.

The Guaranteed Minimum Income Benefit assures a minimum amount of income (for whatever payout period is elected, including lifetime), based on the greater of the actual future account balance or a guaranteed minimum balance. If that guarantee of minimum income is worth the cost,[11] electing it makes sense.

The Guaranteed Minimum Accumulation Benefit assures the contract owner of a minimum future lump sum account balance, even if actual investment performance produces a lower one. If this assurance is worth the cost, electing it makes sense.

The Guaranteed Minimum Withdrawal Benefit assures that the contract owner will be able to recover his investment (by periodic withdrawals), irrespective of adverse investment performance, and be able to participate in investment gains earned by funds not withdrawn. If that guarantee of return of principal is worth the drag on investment performance represented by its cost, electing it makes sense.

The Guaranteed Lifetime Withdrawal Benefit assures the contract owner of at least a certain percentage of the benefit base, as an income that will persist for the client's entire lifetime or the joint lifetime of the client and his/her spouse, regardless of adverse investment performance. If this guarantee of a lifetime income is worth the cost, then including it in the policy benefits makes sense.

Whatever the decision with regard to these options, it must be understood that they are insurance options, not investment ones, and that their costs will necessarily produce a lower future account balance, on average, than would result from the same annuity's performance if these options were not elected, and the costs for them not incurred. This is because the issuing insurance company has expenses associated with its operations, and prices its products to make a profit. For the entire risk pool of contract holders with access to these living benefits, the insurer knows that the premiums paid for them should, over time, be greater than the benefits the insurer will pay out. However, this actuarial certainty has no application to a single individual. For the contract owner concerned about having too small a future account balance, too little income, or losing principal due to investment losses, the experience of his or her account is all that matters. That the cost of these insurance benefits makes the contract offering them less optimal as an investment vehicle may be less worrisome than the prospect of not having those benefits.

The authors suggest that what really matters is not whether the advisor thinks the guarantees represent a good deal, but whether the client, who is assisted by the advisor in making an informed and educated choice, feels that they provide a good value for the client's goals and the desire to ensure those goals are achieved.

Arguments in Favor of Immediate Annuities

An Annuity is the Only Device that Can GUARANTEE a Stated Income for a Stated Period or for Life

An annuity is the only financial instrument that can guarantee a stated level of income for a specific time period or for the life of the recipient. This point was discussed earlier in this chapter.

The Income Produced by an Immediate Annuity is Greater than that Achievable from any Investment Alternative, on a Guaranteed Basis

Because an annuity consists of earnings, the systematic amortization of principal, *and* the contribution of mortality credits, the amount of income produced by an annuity is virtually certain to exceed that of an investment alternative producing an income consisting solely of earnings or interest alone. Conceivably, there may be some device guaranteeing an interest rate high enough that its interest income would exceed an immediate annuity payout over the same guarantee period, but it is exceedingly unlikely, and almost certainly would have different risk characteristics for that level of return.

For example, as of March, 2014, one insurer offers a life annuity with no refund element that will pay a fifty-five-year-old annuitant $486 for life, for a single premium of $100,000. The yield required to produce that income for as long as the recipient lives, if the principal must be preserved, is about 5.8 percent. No investment, that the authors are aware of, can guarantee such a return. Although a rise in future interest rates might allow an interest only investment to produce such higher returns, the available payments that could then be obtained from the above annuity example would almost certainly be more as well, reflecting the same higher interest rate environment.

Of course, principal is not preserved in an immediate annuity payment stream. To equate the income produced by an immediate annuity with that produced solely from earnings is not a valid comparison, unless the only factor of importance is the amount of income. Yet continuing the earlier example, even if the $100,000 principal is amortized over a thirty-year time period (an approximation of life expectancy), an investment portfolio would need to generate a 4.18 percent rate of return to produce $486/month over the time horizon, which is higher than guaranteed (government) bond rates available over a similar time period (and payments would cease after thirty years, whereas they continue to be paid with annuitization!).

As another example, a seventy-one-year-old male, having that same $100,000 to invest, could—using a different company's SPIA, as of March, 2014—receive an income of $600 every month from one insurer's SPIA with a cash refund option, of which approximately seventy-four percent ($446/month) will be excluded from taxable income until he has recovered his entire investment tax-free, which would take nearly nineteen years. That investor might be able to buy an A-rated twenty-year, tax-free bond offering a 3.5 percent yield. That bond would produce less income; $291 per month versus $446, but it would also preserve that investor's principal. The investor could then pass $100,000 to his heirs, assuming that the bond is worth at par at his death. If having as much income as possible on an absolutely certain basis, for as long as he lives is this man's chief concern (he could begin to systematically liquidate the $100,000 to supplement cash flows, but that risks outliving the time period over which he spends down principal!), the huge difference in the income of which he can be certain may be worth the tradeoffs—loss of access to principal and spending the kids' inheritance. In addition, this investor also faces the risk that the tax-free bond may eventually mature, forcing him to reinvest at potentially lower future interest rates; the immediate annuity's guaranteed payment stream does not face any such reinvestment risk.

The Certain Income of an Annuity May Allow a Client to Act Differently with Regard to His Other Assets

One of the curiosities of the Great Debate over annuities is that it often presumes an either-or scenario. Consider, for example, the following two assertions:

- Don't invest your retirement money in an immediate annuity

- An immediate annuity is the ideal retirement investment

The unspoken implication in both statements is that it applies to a person's entire retirement portfolio—that one should either avoid buying an immediate annuity with any of that money or that one should do so with every dollar. Neither scenario necessarily makes good sense.

What often does make sense is the purchase of an immediate annuity with part of a retirement portfolio. There are several benefits to this strategy:

1. The estate owner who wishes to use lifetime gifting may be more willing to do so having the assurance of a certain income for life.

2. A risk averse investor, having invested a portion of his retirement portfolio in an immediate annuity to secure income, may be more comfortable allocating more of the rest of his portfolio to higher return—but higher risk—instruments than he would in the absence of those annuity guarantees.

3. For the client concerned with outliving his retirement portfolio, annuitizing a portion of it may increase the probability that the portfolio as a whole will provide a required income level given the uncertainties of future market performance.

4. The emotional value of a certain income for life is not necessarily limited to that calculable by investment algebra. The confidence that such a client gains from the certainty of his annuity income, like the peace of mind many homeowners gain by paying off the mortgage, may be worth more than a computation of return on investment would indicate.

The utility of annuitization is described more extensively in Chapter 9.

Endnotes

1. Jack Marrion, www.indexannuity.org.

2. I.R.C. § 72(q).

3. Kitces, Michael, "Is Variable Annuity Tax Deferral Worth Paying For Again," http://www.kitces.com/blog/is-variable-annuity-tax-deferral-worth-paying-for-again/ (February 13, 2013).

4. Available at www.navanet.org.

5. A potential exception to these general step-up in basis rules applied for some decedents who passed away in 2010.

6. An itemized income tax deduction for the federal estate tax attributable to this gain is available to the beneficiary, under Code section 691(c).

7. One might argue—and the authors do—that this statement is strictly true only if the insurance proceeds exceed the total premiums paid, accumulated at an appropriate time value of money.

8. It should surprise no one that the argument just presented is offered less often now, after the "black swan" market decline of 2008-2009, than it was previously.

9. The standard death benefit guarantee is usually a part of the standard mortality and expense charge.

10. The more generous the death benefit, the higher the charge.

11. The cost of the Guaranteed Minimum Income Benefit should be considered to include the reduced annuity payout factors that are often applicable to its exercise, as well as any annuitization age setback required. See Chapter 5.

Chapter 14

The Great Debate: Are Annuities Good or Bad? Part Two: Arguments against Annuities

They're Too Expensive

Perhaps the most common argument heard against deferred annuities is that they are too expensive. Usually, this criticism refers to variable contracts, as most fixed annuities assess no front-end or annually recurring charges.[1] We have seen in Chapter 13 how the costs for the insurance offered by the Guaranteed Living Benefits (GLBs) of Variable Annuities (VAs) can be, and often are, seen as excessive, and that this judgment may result from the application of investment analysis methodology to an insurance problem.[2] One example of this misapplication appearing frequently in the financial press is the side-by-side comparison of a VA with a mutual fund, assuming the same gross investment return and liquidation of the investment in a lump sum at the end of a specified period. Even where the analyst attempts to be fair and reasonable with income tax assumptions (e.g., taking into account the turnover rate in the mutual fund portfolio and the fact that not all distributions are taxed at long-term capital gains rates), assuming that both alternatives will earn a specific positive rate of return each year renders the death benefit guarantees of the annuity inoperative. Moreover, the stipulation that the investor will cash out both alternatives in a lump sum obviates the advantages of the taxation of annuitized proceeds and assumes that the annuity payout factors guaranteed in the annuity can never be of any value. The costs for these insurance features are taken into account each year by reducing the gross return assumed on the annuity by the mortality and expense charge, but the potential benefits purchased by those costs are precluded from ever being realized. Such a comparison may be side-by-side, but it is not truly apples to apples.

An even more egregious example of unfairness occurs when the comparison pits a fully commissionable VA against a no-load mutual fund. On the VA side of the ledger, the costs include compensation to the financial advisor, including ongoing renewal commissions. These commissions pay—not simply for the advisor's selling the annuity—but for the financial counsel that the advisor renders to the investor as part of the sale. This includes the initial asset allocation and ongoing servicing, portfolio rebalancing, etc. On the mutual fund side, there are no commission costs—which necessarily imply that the investor is receiving no financial advice. In the authors' opinion, such an analysis is no more fair than a comparison of the bill presented to a client by a competent estate planning attorney with the cost of do-it-yourself legal software such as Quicken Family Lawyer.* The product in both cases may be a valid legal instrument, but the attorney's documents were informed by individual professional counseling and the attorney's client will have recourse for liabilities caused by errors or problems through the attorney's actions or work.

If the investor does not want or need any counsel, he should not be required to pay for it. But where advice is both wanted and needed—where it has clear value—both the benefit of that advice and its cost should be reflected on both sides of the comparison. Thus, if the mutual fund considered, hypothetically, of course, is a no-load product, and where the annuity cost includes compensation to the investment advisor, fairness would require that the mutual fund side of the ledger include a separate cost for advice. That sort of comparison is rarely seen.

With regard to the notion that VAs are too expensive, it should be noted that a few insurers have recently released contracts with very low annual expenses. Some of these contracts offer GLB riders, yet their annual expense ratio is less than the typical VA. Some low-cost annuity providers have deliberately structured contracts to have minimum guarantees (and thus minimum expenses) specifically to serve as more efficient tax-deferred vehicles for nonqualified assets.

They're Too Complicated

The values guaranteed by living benefit provisions in VAs are often the result of formulas and conditions. Rarely can one point to a dollar figure and say "this is the amount guaranteed by this benefit." Perhaps most painfully, the terms under which the guaranteed amounts themselves are payable can be quite complicated. The result is a serious potential for misunderstanding and confusion—both by those purchasing these contracts and by those selling them.

For example, a Guaranteed Lifetime Withdrawal Benefit (GLWB) provision may apply a guaranteed interest rate of six percent to amounts invested, to produce a benefit base from which GLWB payments will be calculated. This does not mean that the contract owner is guaranteed a minimum of a six percent return on his investment, as would be the case if the guaranteed cash value of the contract could never be less than contributions compounded at six percent. Yet the authors have heard this provision explained in just that way on several occasions—not only by policy owners, but also by professional advisors. Clearly, these individuals had no idea how the GLWB provision they were describing actually worked.

In the authors' view, this is potentially a very serious problem, for both advisors and their clients. Any competent decision as to whether a GLB is worth, to a particular client, what the insurer charges for it necessarily requires that all parties to that decision fully understand what they are assessing. Some insurers, recognizing this, have instituted special training programs to ensure that those recommending these complex products understand them. The National Association of Insurance Commissioners (NAIC) has also recognized this problem and included, in its Suitability in Annuity Transactions Model Regulation of 2010 (SATMR), a mandate that agents recommending any annuity complete a four-hour continuing education course specifically devoted to annuities (see the discussion of SATMR in Chapter 15). In the authors' experience, far too many agents selling annuities do not thoroughly understand the complexities of the annuity contracts they are selling, and the SATMR-required training is long overdue. Some, but certainly not all, agents know about the products they offer only by what they read in point-of-sale brochures and hear from product wholesalers. Far too many have never read the annuity contracts. This is especially true of some Index Annuity (IA) contracts. Although some use formulas that are relatively straightforward and easy to understand, others do not.

For the first decade of this century, new product designs, both variable and index, tended to be increasingly complex, as did the living benefit riders in such contracts. Recently, however, there has been a counter-trend toward simplicity, at least in the VA marketplace. This is probably due to several factors. One factor may be insurers' recognition that extremely complex designs were encountering resistance among financial advisors and disapproval among many "consumerists." Another was almost certainly the fact that guaranteed income riders had proven financially troublesome for their issuers—so much so that those insurers had to pare benefits and/or raise costs. Some issuers even stopped issuing these riders. As of March, 2014, there are still many VAs with complex benefit structures and an increasing number of "bare bones" contracts, advertising simplicity and low costs. Whether one trend will overcome the other remains to be seen. The authors suspect that there will remain substantial demand for both types.

On the other hand, it's worth noting that in the IA space, complexity appears to be winning the race. Whether a counter-trend toward simplicity will develop there is not yet clear. One might say that the great shrinkage in the number of interest crediting methods represents such a trend. However, the more recent introduction of GLB riders within indexed annuities has increased the complexity of those products, especially from the perspective of advisors trying to evaluate how those riders impact the policies' interest crediting formulas (and vice versa).

A failure to understand the implications of crediting formulas in all potential return environments—not simply the one illustrated in the marketing materials, which is often not merely an average scenario, but an optimal one—can lead to a mismatch between client expectations and reality.

The authors strenuously recommend to anyone who intends to sell, or offer advice concerning, any type of annuity that he or she study, not merely the marketing material for that product, but the actual contract language. This is especially necessary when the product is complicated and the benefits it provides are subject to complex conditions and/or formulas. We also recommend that any advisor who intends to sell or offer advice concerning these benefits take advantage of special training classes on the subject, even if these classes are not yet mandated in the states in which they work.

GLB riders and IAs, when properly understood, can be of significant value to many clients, but for those clients to recognize that value their advisors must be capable of explaining it in clear, nontechnical language. Product brochures can be very helpful in this respect but they cannot address every question a consumer might raise, nor do they fully illustrate all scenarios a consumer might need to contend with and plan for. It is the job of every advisor to understand the product well enough to be able to explain, in plain English, how it works and its costs and benefits to a consumer wholly unfamiliar with it, and evaluate how it may fit the consumer's goals in a wide range of market scenarios. That takes hard work. It requires comprehension, analysis, and communication skills.

One of the authors, in workshops he conducts for agents, recommends the "spouse test." If after you have presented (as you would to a prospective buyer) an annuity product to your spouse (or "significant other") who has no special insurance or investment expertise, that spouse can explain back to you *accurately* how that product works, what it costs, and how it will benefit the buyer, you have passed the "spouse test." Do not be dismayed if you failed to pass the test the first time; the authors didn't either.

Annuities Should Never Be Used to Fund an IRA or Qualified Plan

A generalization often made about annuities claims that they should never be used to fund an IRA or qualified plan. This sweeping pronouncement has met with surprisingly wide acceptance among financial journalists, attorneys, accountants, and many financial planners. It has become virtually accepted wisdom for many, despite the facts that (a) it ignores the huge differences that exist between immediate and deferred annuities and between the fixed and variable varieties of the latter and (b) the arguments most commonly made in its support are grievously and obviously flawed.

Those who argue that annuities are inappropriate instruments for funding IRAs or qualified plans are almost always referring to deferred annuities and, usually, to variable deferred annuities. The three most common of these arguments are:

1. "You're paying for tax deferral you're not getting." This is simply nonsense. While it is true that an annuity offers no additional tax advantages over any other investment vehicle when used to fund an IRA or qualified plan, no annuity assesses any charge for the benefit of tax deferral. To be sure, variable deferred annuities impose charges that alternatives such as mutual funds do not. Those are, as we have seen, insurance charges. They have absolutely nothing whatsoever to do with the tax treatment enjoyed by the annuity; instead, the reality is that the favorable tax deferral treatment that is

available for annuities is simply an additional benefit granted by Congress under the tax code to encourage consumers to use (and otherwise pay the costs for) an annuity.

While it is true that the tax treatment of an annuity used to fund an IRA or qualified plan is—in all but a few respects—identical to that applicable to any other IRA investment,[3] for better or worse the real decision about holding an annuity in a retirement account is about whether the guarantees that apply to the annuity are desired for those retirement account assets. The tax treatment that would apply to a deferred annuity, if it were not used to fund such a plan, is irrelevant when the annuity is so used based upon that investor's need for the risk management benefits that annuities provide (with retirement assets or otherwise). Conversely, if the insurance benefits are not worth the cost to a particular client, then they should not be paid for, whether the money in question is qualified or not.

2. "The tax deferral of an annuity used to fund an IRA is wasted." This one is doubly flawed. First, because as noted earlier, the tax deferral enjoyed by nonqualified annuities flows from provisions of the Internal Revenue Code that apply only to nonqualified annuities, that deferral cannot be wasted by an IRA annuity because it does not apply to an IRA annuity. Second, the argument rests upon an assumption that the tax treatment that a particular type of investment property would enjoy if it were held in a taxable account is somehow relevant to whether it is an appropriate funding vehicle for an IRA or qualified account. To illustrate the absurdity of this assumption, let us consider the question of whether small cap growth stocks, or a fund investing in these stocks, might be appropriate for an IRA. The investment returns produced by these stocks, or funds, will generally be taxed at Long-Term Capital Gain (LTCG) rates if held for longer than one year. LTCG rates are, of course, significantly lower than the rates for ordinary income (which apply to the withdrawals of growth from retirement accounts). Inasmuch as all nonRoth IRAs and qualified plans, except for basis, are taxed at higher ordinary income rates, it would follow that funding an IRA with small cap growth stocks—or a fund investing in the same—would be a "waste of the capital gains treatment such investments enjoy when they are held in a taxable account." Obviously, the appropriateness of a small cap growth stock for an IRA or qualified plan has nothing to do with how it would be taxed if it were held otherwise; it is a purchase based on investment and risk/return merits. The same holds true for an annuity.

3. "They're Too Expensive." As we have said, if the insurance benefits of the annuity, which are the source of the excessive costs cited by critics, are neither needed nor wanted, they should not be purchased. A deferred annuity, especially a deferred VA with guaranteed death and living benefits, is chiefly a risk management tool. If the risk management features are not desired, an instrument providing and charging for them is, indeed, too expensive. If they are desired, the charges for them must be viewed for what they are—insurance costs.

Annuities Are Sold Mostly because of the High Commissions They Pay

This argument may be accurate to some degree, but it relies upon an assumption: that advisors would recommend other solutions if annuity commissions were lower. It is true that the commissions paid on deferred annuities are often higher than those paid on mutual funds, and common sense suggests that a commissioned advisor, in choosing among alternatives to recommend to a client, may be influenced by the amount of compensation each alternative provides him, and that greater compensation to the advisor represents a greater cost to the client. However, the benefit of any investment to its owner consists in what can be realized from it. The value of that investment must, of course, be reckoned by relating the benefits received to the cost paid. But if a deferred annuity offers benefits not available from alternatives, and its cost to purchase and maintain happens to be higher, the value of that contract still depends upon whether the additional benefits are worth the additional cost; the value is not proven invalid just because there is a higher or different cost in the first place.

For instance, a particular annuity contract that pays 3.5 percent of the investor's contribution to one selling agent, but six percent to another—because those agents have different contracts with their respective broker-dealers—will have the same value to the purchaser, assuming that the advisors are equally competent and diligent. The agents' commissions will be of significance to those agents, and, arguably, may affect their recommendations. But the value of that annuity to its purchaser will be the same, whichever agent makes the sale.

The value of the annuity relative to its costs depends on the features and benefits of the contract and the costs to the client, regardless of where or how those costs may be subsequently allocated. As an extreme and entirely imaginary example, consider an investment that charges the purchaser an overhead cost of five percent per year, but provides a guaranteed return of between fifteen and twenty-five percent. Although the annual cost of the investment is absurdly high, so is the return. This would probably be an extremely good investment, if it existed. Moreover, the decision as to whether this is or is not a good investment depends solely on the costs and benefits of the contract. Whether the issuer uses the five percent per year it collects from the purchaser to compensate a salesman with two, five, ten, or twenty percent of the purchase price has no bearing on the value of the investment to the client.

Some annuities do not pay commissions and generally offer lower charges as a result. These low-load contracts account for only a small fraction of the annuities sold each year. Does this mean that most annuity purchasers are being abused? That conclusion does not follow, for two reasons:

1. The guaranteed death benefits, and especially the GLB offered by low-load, deferred annuity contracts are often less attractive—though, of course, less costly—than those offered by fully loaded annuities. Where these guarantees are important to the client, the lesser benefits offered by low-load contracts may be unattractive, even if the annuity includes a total lower annual cost.[4]

2. Noncommissionable products are sold chiefly by fee-based or fee-only advisors who charge for advisory services. When adding the advisory fee to the annual cost of a low-load annuity, the resulting total annual cost—while it may or may not be less than the annual cost of a fully-commissionable contract—may still be unattractive, as the benefit of that cost will be limited to the generally less attractive guarantees of the low-load annuity.

A Low Percentage of Deferred Annuities Are Ever Annuitized

There are two flaws implicit in this argument. First, the right to annuitize is just that—a right. It is not an obligation. The opportunity to avail oneself of either the payout factors currently available to holders of a deferred annuity, or to elect annuitization using the factors guaranteed in the contract, is just that. It is an opportunity, a choice, and a risk management decision, much more than an investment one. A decision not to exercise an option does not make the option valueless.

An even more serious flaw to this argument is that it is a statistic that is utterly unreliable. Even conceding the accuracy of data on annuitized contracts, the flaw lies in the definition of annuitized. That term means an election, by the owner of a deferred annuity contract, to accept an annuitization option in that contract. In that literal sense, the statistic—of two percent or whatever percentage one happens to use—of contracts that are annuitized may be accurate, but it is entirely meaningless as an indication of how many owners of deferred annuity contracts have chosen to convert their accumulated value to an income stream.

One of the authors has been selling annuities for over forty years and has very rarely recommended that a client exercise any annuity option in his contract. But he has recommended to many clients that they exchange an existing deferred annuity for a single premium immediate annuity from whatever highly rated insurer happened, at the time, to offer the highest annuity payout rate for the option chosen. In the authors' experience, the current annuity payout rates in an existing deferred annuity are almost never as attractive as what is available in the SPIA marketplace, and the *guaranteed* payout rates in that deferred annuity is *never* as attractive.

This procedure (i.e., going shopping for annuity rates on behalf of a client, and recommending a tax-free exchange of that client's existing deferred annuity for an immediate annuity) is a very common practice. It could be argued that the failure to offer this option to a client constitutes a breach of advisor responsibility, since by accepting a payout rate higher than the one guaranteed in his deferred contract, the client cannot fail to benefit so long as the issuer of the immediate annuity is at least as financially strong and viable as the issuer of the deferred contract. These exchanges are done every day both because they are in the client's interest and because the agent selling the immediate annuity earns a commission. They are not reflected in the statistic quoted above. It is certain that the total number of annuity contract holders electing to convert a deferred annuity to an income stream—a number that must include both annuitizations and exchanges of deferred annuities for immediate ones—is far higher than the two percent or so reported. How much higher is anyone's guess.

Arguments against Immediate Annuities

Those who argue against the purchase of immediate annuities usually do so for one or more of the following reasons:

1. *Inflexibility*. Most immediate annuities are inflexible. That is: once begun, the arrangement may not be modified, nor may any remaining payments be commuted to a lump sum. This is certainly a valid concern. The inability of a planning strategy to adapt to changing goals and circumstances is, by definition, a disadvantage. Moreover, an irrevocable annuitization has an emotional component. One loses control over that part of one's wealth that has been annuitized. The feeling of this loss may exact a price not measurable in investment terms. That said, many newer immediate annuity contracts allow for some modification in the payout arrangement, including commutation of remaining payments. There is, of course, a cost to this benefit, usually in the form of a lower initial payout than would be offered without it. Some consumers may find this flexibility worth the price.

   The authors suggest that an alternative might be to consider a conventional immediate annuity—without the flexibility benefits or the cost for same—only for that portion of one's portfolio that one is prepared to lock into an income stream. As noted earlier, the decision whether or not to purchase an immediate annuity need not be all or nothing.

2. *Immediate Annuities Lock In Low Interest Rates*. This argument is usually advanced during periods of low prevailing interest rates, but it has merit at any time. The interest rate used to compute the amount of payments in an immediate annuity contract is always conservative. It has to be because the issuing insurer must make those payments regardless of future changes in the returns the insurer will earn on invested premiums and how long the annuitant lives, in the case of life annuities. When interest rates change, so do annuity payout rates. Although immediate annuities with longer payout periods do not necessarily experience the same level of decline as those with shorter period payouts, a decline in the general interest rate environment will generally reduce the current payout factors of all annuities.

   That said, the argument that the buyer of an immediate annuity is locking in low interest rates for the duration of the annuity period misses the whole point. The point, and the whole purpose of an immediate annuity, is not merely to earn a return on invested principal, but to convert that invested principal into income that is certain as to amount and duration; in the case of life annuities, for as long as the annuitant lives. It is those certainties that constitute the real benefit (along with the mortality credits that are accrued in the case of life-contingent payments), not the rate of return used to compute the payments.

In the end, an immediate annuity is an insurance vehicle that transfers risks from the contract owner to the issuing insurer. The risks transferred are (a) the risk that future changes in the financial markets might cause future income payments to decline and (b) the risk that the annuitant might outlive the income payments. If an investor is willing to assume those risks, other investments offer potentially higher income, from potentially higher interest rates or investment yields, than an immediate annuity, but at the costs of no assurance of either the amount of income or its duration. For someone considering a period certain annuity—for a specified period of years, whether the annuitant outlives that period or not—alternatives may not provide the same initial level of income, but may offer access to principal, and potentially higher returns in later years, due to principal growth. In the end, if the guarantees offered by the annuity produce the actual dollars needed to secure one's goals, the fact that interest rates or investment returns may be higher in the future is not necessarily even relevant to the client.

No Inflation Protection. Most immediate annuities are fixed in amount. Although a few contracts offer the option of either a fixed amount or an annuity increasing at a set percentage each year (usually no more than three to five percent), most do not. For those that do, there is no guarantee that the fixed annual increases will actually keep pace with an uncertain inflationary future.

In addition, a practical challenge of inflation protection (or generally, rising annuity payments) is that the amount of the first year's annuity payment will always be less than that of contracts, offered by the same insurers, without this option. The greater the guaranteed annual increase, the lower the initial payment for any amount invested.

Notwithstanding these concerns, the reality is that a few SPIAs do offer an option that annuity payments will vary directly with the unknown future fluctuations in the rate of inflation, as measured by an index such as the Consumer Price Index (CPI), fully addressing the inflation concern. Why such a contract is not more available, or popular, is bewildering. It may be that insurers are having difficulty determining how to hedge their own exposure to inflation if such a contract is offered, especially given the current (as of the time of this writing) very low real yields on Treasury Inflation-Protected Securities (TIPS). Alternatively, the authors have heard, repeatedly, that there is very little market for this type of product, which seems unpersuasive, given the almost universal recognition of the devastating impact that inflation can have on those living on a fixed income. To be sure, the first year's income from an inflation-adjusted annuity—especially an annuity guaranteed for the life of the annuitant—will be less, or possibly a great deal less, than that guaranteed by an un-indexed fixed/level payment product. It may be that most consumers are simply not willing to accept that trade-off, likley underestimating the damaging long-term effects that inflation can have over the span of a retirement. Nevertheless, in the authors' opinion at least, a contract offering the purchaser a choice between fixed payments and payments that will keep pace with inflation ought to be attractive, and certainly is available from at least a few insurers.

Arguments against GLBs in VAs

The two most commonly advanced criticisms of GLBs are: (a) that they promise benefits that are unlikely to be realized and (b) that they're too expensive. In fact, the two reasons are inseparable. No critic, to the authors' knowledge, asserts that there is no chance of a GLB *ever* producing value. The two criticisms amount, in essence, to a single charge: that the possible benefit derived from a GLB may be too small or too unlikely to be worthwhile relative to the certain cost. See Chapter 5 for a detailed discussion of GLBs and attempts to value them.

Notwithstanding the criticism from some that GLBs are too expensive for the benefits they provide, other critics have charged that insurers issuing these GLBs may not be able to pay them because these insurers either: (1) do not really know how much financial risk they are underwriting, (2) are not charging enough for these benefits, or (3) have not set aside sufficient reserves to pay them. Some critics believe all three conditions are true, implying that insurers should be charging *even more* for the guarantees they offer to ensure that claims can be paid in the face of an uncertain future. In 2007, Moshe Milevsky, a long-time critic of the cost of VA death benefit guarantees, wrote that he believed many of these GLBs to be underpriced, which implied (at the time) a good value for the consumer, as long as the insurance company doesn't lose so much money that it fails to make good on its guarantees.[5] Clearly, he was right, as insurers offering GLBs have in recent years either reduced the benefit levels of these riders, increased their cost, or both. Several major insurers have discontinued issuing GLBs altogether. Indeed, a few insurers have exited the VA marketplace. Ironically, this means that (as long as the insurer doesn't actually default on its annuity guarantees) the GLBs offered in the early years of the past decade may have actually represented a uniquely mispriced guarantee in the favor of consumers who bought them, unlike the ones today that do in fact have higher costs and more limited benefits/guarantees (and/or other restrictions). It's also worth noting that this apparent reality—that many such annuity guarantees may have actually been *underpriced* for years—runs in direct contravention to the objection that annuities are "too expensive" and in fact suggests that at the time the only real fear should have been whether they were "too cheap"!

Although Guaranteed Lifetime Withdrawal Benefits (GLWBs) have generally become more expensive in recent years, it's notable that (as we observed in Chapter 5) this type of GLB has recently become an increasingly popular option available in *IAs*. While the cost of this rider is generally less in IAs than in VAs, the potential benefit is arguably less as well, as the upside potential of market-based growth is reduced in an IA by a participation rate or cap rate. Fairness obliges us to acknowledge that there is considerable debate on this issue of the value of GLWB riders on already-risk-managed IAs.

Whether in the context of IAs, or their more volatile VA cousins, the question of whether the issuer of a GLB can be relied upon to pay the guarantees is a serious issue, and gets directly to the heart of whether such guarantees are too expensive or actually too cheap. Although the separate accounts in a VA are secure from financial failure of the issuing insurance company—because they are, in fact, separate accounts, not subject to creditors of that insurer—the contractual guarantees made in the annuity, including those of guaranteed living and death benefits, are backed only by the financial solvency of the insurance company. If a particular insurer has greatly underpriced its guarantees and/or has not set aside adequate reserves for paying them, the contract holder could, if that insurer fails, find herself with guarantees that are meaningless. In the case of an IA, both the underlying contract value and the GLB features are subject to the credit risk of the insurer.

How can an advisor know if the guarantees he describes are truly safe? In the authors' opinion, there's only one way to be reasonably sure: Do your due diligence! Ask for details of how your company is assessing the risks that it bears under these provisions, how—and if—it hedges those risks, and how it is reserving to pay the benefits associated with them. Don't expect many specifics! Much of this information will be both proprietary and closely guarded, especially hedging strategies. However, a responsible insurer will be willing to address these concerns, at least generally.

The authors also suggest the following guidelines and caveats:

1. The more financially sound the insurer, the better. Check an insurer's ratings from at least three ratings services and stick with a company that holds at least the third-highest rating from at least three services.

2. The less exposure an insurer has to losses from exercise of GLBs, as a percentage of its overall business, the better. If a large chunk of the insurer's book of VA business includes exercisable GLBs, there should be some offsetting factor, such as a large volume of nonvariable annuity business.

3. If an insurer issues both IAs and VAs with GLBs, that's a positive. IAs are call-based instruments, where the derivative providing the nonguaranteed benefit is usually a series of calls on an equity index, typically the S&P 500. By contrast, GLBs are basically put-based instruments, where the insurer's risk increases, not with a rise in the value of the underlying investments, but with a decline. Where an insurer has a sizeable block of business in both product types, the basic risks tend to offset one another. There are numerous academic studies on this subject available on the Internet, and accessible via a browser search on hedging VAs and IAs. Many of these are highly technical and employ mathematical analysis beyond the average person's understanding. However, for the advisor interested in responding to a question such as, "how can I be sure that this insurance company will be able to pay the benefits you just described?" with something more than just "trust me," this is a research project worth undertaking.

At the very least, the authors suggest an advisor pose that "how can I be sure?" question to each insurer whose VA products, with GLBs, he or she intends to recommend. Nonetheless, it's still important to bear in mind that the view that an annuity guarantee is "too expensive" is by definition an assertion that the guarantee is secure (and in fact that the annuity company is collecting *more* in guarantee costs than are necessary); conversely, to be concerned about the solvency of an annuity company due to its guarantees in the first place is a tacit acknowledgement that if anything, the problem is that the guarantee may be too cheap.

The debate over the general question posed at the beginning of this chapter—are annuities good or bad?—will continue. One component of this debate of vital importance to financial advisors is the regulatory responses it provokes. The question of VA suitability has brought forth rulings from the SEC, FINRA, state departments of securities and insurance, and broker-dealers that advisors may ignore only at their peril. The latest of these rulings (as of the publication of this book), FINRA Rule 2330, is included in the appendices to this book.

Endnotes

1. This does not mean, of course, that there are no annual expenses in fixed annuities, but only that those expenses are paid for out of the interest rate spread, rather than by direct charges to the contract owner. See Chapter 4.

2. While a few critics arrive at the conclusion that insurance costs in VAs are too high from a risk management analysis—comparing the death benefit guarantee cost to term life insurance rates, for example—most inappropriately, in the authors' opinion, treat these costs as investment overhead.

3. Annuitized contracts qualify under a special Require Minimum Distribution (RMD) rule, even if the income from them exceeds what would be produced by the "divisor" of the Unified Table. Also, the value of a deferred annuity with a guaranteed minimum death benefit or living benefit rider must include the actuarial value of that death or living benefit for purposes of a Roth conversion or calculating an RMD (subject to certain exceptions). See Chapter 2 for details.

4. It is quite possible that some low-load deferred annuity contracts will begin offering both guaranteed living and guaranteed death benefits comparable to their fully loaded cousins. However, this will increase—substantially—the cost of these contracts. As the chief appeal of low-load annuities appears to be access to the annuity wrapper and the tax treatment that goes with it, at the least annual cost, providers of low-load contracts may be reluctant to increase costs of those contracts—particularly those companies that offer both commissionable and noncommissionable products.

5. Milevsky, Moshe, "Confessions of a VA Critic," *Research* (January, 2007). Availabe at http://www.thinkadvisor.com/2007/01/01/confessions-of-a-va-critic.

Chapter 15

Suitability: The Changing Nature of the Standard of Care

Overview

Annuities are hybrid financial products. They are insurance products, and, as such, are regulated by state insurance departments. Some annuities are also considered to be securities, subject to regulation by federal and state securities agencies. Furthermore, some rules are applied by Federal regulatory bodies, while others are established and administered by states. Thus, the rules governing the sale and marketing of annuities are a matter of jurisdiction, and the rules are not entirely consistent from one jurisdiction to another. This can make compliance with relevant rules complicated and difficult. Adding to the difficulty is the fact that the standard of care required of those who recommend annuities is not uniform.

At the present time, there are actually two standards of care in the financial services industry: *suitability* and the *fiduciary* standard.

Suitability can be defined as "the quality of having the properties that are right for a specific purpose or situation." That is a general definition, but the term suitability has a more specific meaning when applied to recommendations of insurance, investment, and annuity products, a meaning which is evolving constantly. Until recently, there was little, if any, precision as to when the sale or recommendation of an annuity would be considered suitable. Virtually no jurisdictions offered rules with any intentional definitions—that is, specifications of the necessary and sufficient conditions that must apply for the transaction in question to be qualified as suitable—or providing concrete examples. Many state statutes were simply self-recursive; they simply defined a suitable transaction as one that is suitable.

These suitability standards generally apply, at the present time, both to: (a) insurance agents recommending insurance and annuity products that are not securities and to; (b) registered representatives recommending insurance, annuity, and/or investment products that are securities so long as the advice that they render, in the course of making those securities recommendations, is solely incidental to their activities as securities salespersons (in many regulations, the term used is "brokers").

The other standard of care that may apply when an annuity is recommended is the **fiduciary standard**. This is a much higher standard and applies to investment advisers under the Investment Advisers Act of 1940. Section 202(a)(11) of that Act generally defines an investment adviser as any person or firm that: (1) for compensation; (2) is engaged in the business of; (3) providing advice, making recommendations, issuing reports, or furnishing analyses on securities, either directly or through publications. It does not generally apply to registered representatives to whom the broker exclusion of Section 202(a)(11)(C) of the Act applies. That section excludes from the Act's definition of investment advisor registered representatives offering advice in connection with the recommendation of a security provided that two conditions are satisfied:

1. no special compensation is received (for the advice); and

2. the advice is solely incidental to the broker's brokerage activities.

The Standard of Care Debate

There has been, for some time, a strong demand by many consumer advocates, regulators, members of Congress, and financial service professionals for financial services reform, which includes a reworking of the standards of care that should apply to those who provide financial services to consumers. This demand has already produced new regulations at state and federal levels and continues to inspire debate as to whether additional regulations are needed and, if so, what those regulations should require. At the heart of this debate is the issue of financial advice and, on this issue, participants fall generally into one of three broad groups.

The Unified Standard Group holds that the current arrangement, in which some advisors are held to a fiduciary standard while others are subject to a lesser one, is unworkable. Consumers, they insist, cannot reasonably know the nature of the duty owed to them by any particular financial service professional, as some must act as fiduciaries, others need not, and yet others may or may not bear that duty, depending upon the capacity in which they are acting—and even including what type of policy, if insurance, they're recommending or selling. As the fiduciary standard (a) requires that an advisor must act in the consumer's best interest and subordinate his or her own self-interest to that goal, (b) requires that the advisor disclose all conflicts of interest, and (c) is clearly a higher standard than that of suitability, members of this group believe that the uncertainty now faced by consumers should be resolved by holding all advisors to this higher standard.

The "Let the Current Rules Continue" Group believes that such a resolution will create more problems than the resolution is worth. Members of this group point out that not all those who render advice of a financial nature give investment advice, that some financial professionals are legally precluded from doing so, and that many who are not so precluded may offer advice that is merely ancillary to the sale of financial products. They often insist that the adoption of a universal fiduciary standard will create increased costs of doing business and may result in reduced access to financial products and expertise by many consumers—chiefly, those who do not now, and do not wish to, deal with investment advisors.

The "Changes Are Needed, but a Unified Fiduciary Standard Goes Too Far" Group acknowledges that some reform is clearly required, but insists that a single standard is neither needed nor desirable. To understand this position, it is necessary that we clear away the polemic that often clutters the "suitability versus fiduciary" debate. Some who insist upon a unified fiduciary standard, applicable to all those who give any advice regarding financial products maintain that those who resist such a standard are unwilling to "put the client's interest first." This is neither accurate nor fair. It amounts to a declaration that an objection to one element of a standard implies an objection to all elements of that standard.

The *fiduciary standard* prescribes several duties to which all fiduciaries are subject:

1.   putting the client's interest first (Duty of Loyalty);

2.   competence and Prudence (Duty of Care);

3.   confidentiality;

4.   avoidance of conflicts of interest where possible; and

5.   disclosure of unavoidable conflicts of interest (including *all* compensation).

6.   These are generally considered to be the *essential* elements of the fiduciary duty, but there are other elements that some commentators *claim* to be part of the fiduciary standard. These are typically –

     a.   ongoing duty of monitoring and advice; and

     b.   recommending only "the best" solution (product and/or strategy) for the client.

While ethical insurance agents generally acknowledge the first four duties, many object to disclosing commissions. Two common reasons for this objection are (1) the fact that illustrations of product performance (e.g., computerized life insurance or deferred annuity illustrations, mutual fund "hypotheticals," and immediate annuity income quotes) are net of commissions and (2) a disclosure of *agent level* commissions does not disclose the *total* commissions paid on an annuity or life insurance sale. Indeed, insurance agents often do not know the precise value of "overrides" and bonuses that may be paid to the marketing agencies through which they do business.

An ongoing duty of **monitoring** and advice may be inconsistent with the sales activities of some insurance agents or registered representatives. Some agents are engaged by a client solely to recommend a life insurance or annuity product; and an ongoing advisor-client relationship may not be desired. Indeed, some insurance agents cannot perform ongoing product monitoring because they cannot obtain the information necessary to do so. How can this happen? An agent who has sold a *proprietary* product and whose agent's contract with that insurance company has been canceled (perhaps due to insufficient sales volume) will generally be unable to obtain policy information from that insurer or receive annual policy statements.

As to the duty to recommend only the "best" product, it is an impossible task. Not only does such a duty presume that an agent or advisor is aware of every product offered by every product manufacturer but it necessarily implies that a "best" product exists. But how would such an assessment be made? What parameters would be employed? Moreover, the duty of care in the fiduciary standard requires prudence, but does not require perfection (the "best" policy).

> *Example*: Term insurance policy A, with a level death benefit of $500,000 for twenty years, has a guaranteed premium of $1,000 per year. After twenty years, the premium will increase annually. Policy B, for a premium of $2,200 per year, will provide $500,000 of death benefit guaranteed for twenty-five years, but by application of non-guaranteed dividends, will provide both a cash value and a non-guaranteed annual increase in death benefit. Which policy is better? The answer, of course, is "it depends"—not only on the client's facts and circumstances but on the *judgment* of the advisor.

The authors do not suggest that the fiduciary standard is wholly inapplicable to life insurance agents or registered representatives; we do suggest that whatever standard is eventually adopted ought to take into account the kinds of activities engaged in by those who will be subject to that standard. Fundamentally, the fiduciary standard is intended for the delivery of advice, not the sale of products, and there is a place for both salespeople and advisors in providing financial services to consumers.

A thorough discussion of the standard of care debate, and the extent to which it will impact those who recommend annuities, is beyond the scope of this chapter. That said, readers should be aware that there is widespread interest, in the regulatory and consumerist communities, in extending the fiduciary standard of care to those who sell annuities. In the remainder of this chapter, we will focus on the issue of the suitability of annuity transactions using the suitability standard as that is the standard of care currently applicable to most annuity sales.

The Regulatory Players

As noted above, sales of annuities are subject to regulation by both state and Federal agencies. Any annuity sale must meet the requirements of insurance regulations in the state in which the sale is made. Typically, state insurance regulations are consistent with, and often identical to, the Model Regulations adopted by the National Association of Insurance Commissioners (NAIC), the standards-setting and regulatory support organization created and governed by the chief insurance regulators of the fifty states, the District of Columbia, and five U.S. territories.

Variable annuities are regulated as securities, in addition to being regulated as insurance, and, as such, are subject to regulation by the Securities and Exchange Commission (SEC) and the Financial Industry Regulatory Authority (FINRA). FINRA is a private corporation that acts as a self-regulatory authority having oversight over all securities firms that do business with U.S customers. It was created in 2007, in a merger of the National Association of Securities Dealers and New York Stock Exchange (NYSE) Regulation, Inc., the enforcement arm of the NYSE. Many of the rules and regulations of FINRA are adaptations of, or identical to, earlier NASD rules. One of the difficulties financial advisors encounter in attempting to locate and understand the rules to which they are subject is that FINRA often restates earlier NASD rules but with a different numbering. For example, the current FINRA Rule 2330, dealing with the suitability of variable annuity transactions, is a restatement of the earlier NASD rule 2821.

While regulation of insurance and annuity products that are not securities is generally left to the states, the Federal Government is a player, especially since the enactment of the Dodd-Frank Wall Street Reform and Consumer Protection Act of 2010 (Dodd-Frank). As will be discussed later, Section 989J of the Dodd-Frank Act prescribes that recommendations of insurance and annuity products must meet the suitability rules of an NAIC regulation dealing with annuities adopted in 2010.

Suitability Rules Dealing Specifically with Annuities[1]

Suitability rules dealing with annuities can be divided into three groups:

1. rules dealing with annuities that are not deemed securities;

2. rules dealing with annuities that are deemed securities; and

3. rules dealing with annuities that may be securities because the status of those contracts is not yet clear.

Rules Dealing with Annuities that Are Not Securities

Each state insurance department prescribes rules governing the sale of annuities in that state. Annuity contracts must contain certain required language dealing with such things as nonforfeiture provisions, the period of time during which the buyer of an annuity contract may cancel the sale, often termed free look provisions, interest rate guarantees, etc. Annuity sales must be suitable. Often, the state rules are drafted to comport with Model Regulations adopted by the NAIC.

Fixed annuities, with the exception of those few indexed annuities registered as securities, are not securities. However, many agents, when recommending fixed annuities, use "investment language." This can be misleading, causing consumers to view the fixed annuity recommended purely as an "investment," which it is not. Fixed annuities contain *risk transfer* (insurance) features that are best understood using "insurance language." Kim O'Brien, Executive Director of the National Association for Fixed Annuities (NAFA), in her presentation entitled "Why Words Matter," offers six points that agents who sell fixed annuities should keep in mind. The authors heartily agree. They are:

1.   Fixed annuities are *insurance* products, not *investment* products.

2.   Fixed annuities earn *interest*, not *returns* or *gains*.

3.   To avoid misleading the consumer, agents should say that fixed *indexed* annuities "have no investment risk," and *not* say that they "participate in the upside with no downside."

4.   To describe the money used to purchase a fixed annuity, use "premium," not "principal."

5.   Fixed annuities are one of the two types of commercial annuity contracts: (a) fixed and (b) variable

6.   Fixed *indexed annuities* are a *different choice* of *interest crediting*. They are *not* a "hybrid" or third type of annuity (in addition to (a) fixed and (b) variable).

The authors believe that much confusion can be avoided if agents will keep these six points firmly in mind when discussing any fixed annuity with a consumer.

NAIC Model Regulations

NAIC regulations dealing with annuities suitability have evolved over time. The current NAIC Model Regulation is the Suitability in Annuity Transactions Model Regulation #275, which we will refer to as SATMR.

NAIC Suitability in Annuity Transactions Model Regulation #275 of 2010 (SATMR)

As explained in the NAIC's Executive Summary, this Model Regulation was adopted "to set standards and procedures for suitable annuity recommendations and to require insurers to establish a system to supervise recommendations so that the insurance needs and financial objectives of consumers are appropriately addressed." The Executive Summary states:

"Specifically, this Model Regulation was adopted to:

1. Establish a regulatory framework that holds insurers responsible for ensuring that annuity transactions are suitable (based on the criteria in Section 5I [of the Model Regulation], whether or not the insurer contracts with a third-party to supervise or monitor the recommendations made in the marketing and sales of annuities;

2. Require that producers be trained on the provisions of annuities in general, and the specific products they are selling.

3. Where feasible and rational, to make these suitability standards consistent with the suitability standards imposed by the Financial Industry Regulatory Authority (FINRA)."[2]

The Model Regulation requires all producers, or insurance agents selling annuity contracts, to have adequate product specific training, including compliance with the insurer's standards for product training, prior to soliciting the sale of an annuity product. It mandates that such producers complete a one-time, for credit hour, course in general annuity training.

Section 6A, entitled *Duties of Insurer and of Insurance Producers*, provides a general four-part test of suitability, with subparts, and states:

"A. In recommending to a consumer the purchase of an annuity or the exchange of an annuity that results in another insurance transaction or series of insurance transactions, the insurance producer, or the insurer where no producer is involved, shall have reasonable grounds for believing that the recommendation is suitable for the consumer on the basis of facts disclosed by the consumer as to his or her investments and other insurance products and as to his or her financial situation and needs, including the consumer's suitability information, and that there is reasonable basis to believe all of the following:

(1) The consumer has been reasonably informed of various features of the annuity, such as the potential surrender period and surrender charge, potential tax penalty if the consumer sells, exchanges, surrenders or annuitizes the annuity, mortality and expense fees, investment advisory fees, potential charges for and features of riders, limitations on interest returns, insurance and investment components and market risk;

(2) The consumer would benefit from certain features of the annuity, such as tax-deferred growth, annuitization or death or living benefit;

(3) The particular annuity as a whole, the underlying subaccounts to which funds are allocated at the time of purchase or exchange of the annuity, and riders and similar

product enhancements, if any, are suitable (and in the case of an exchange or replacement, the transaction as a whole is suitable) for the particular consumer based on his or her suitability information; and

(4) In the case of an exchange or replacement of an annuity, the exchange or replacement is suitable including taking into consideration whether:

(a) The consumer will incur a surrender charge, be subject to the commencement of a new surrender period, lose existing benefits, such as death, living or other contractual benefits, or be subject to increased fees, investment advisory fees or charges for riders and similar product enhancements;

(b) The consumer would benefit from product enhancements and improvements; and

(c) The consumer has had another annuity exchange or replacement and, in particular, an exchange or replacement within the preceding thirty-six months.[3]

Section 5I of the Model Regulation lists twelve factors that must be considered in any recommendation of an annuity. These factors are:

1. age;

2. annual income;

3. financial situation and need, including the financial resources used for the funding of the annuity;

4. financial experience;

5. financial objectives;

6. intended use of the annuity;

7. financial time horizon;

8. existing assets, including investment and life insurance holdings;

9. liquidity needs;

10. liquid net worth;

11. risk tolerance; and

12. tax status[4]

The recitation of these twelve factors, as elements that must be considered prior to the sale of any annuity product, represents a significant—and, in the authors' opinion, much needed—clarification of suitability rules for annuity transactions. On the other hand, such recitation might be seen as an assumption that the producer does not have discretion in determining the factors that must be considered in any suitability analysis. Nor does SATMR offer a rebuttable presumption of suitability. Interestingly, both discretion about which factors are appropriate for suitability, and a rebuttable presumption of suitability, were included in an earlier NAIC model regulation that was never adopted. That Model Regulation, or NAIC Life Insurance and Annuity Model Regulation of 2002, included the following guidance:

> that "Insurance producers shall have reasonable discretion... To determine what information is relevant or necessary for any specific insurance transaction" [Section 6] and that [Section 7] "a rebuttable presumption that a recommendation was suitable is created if the insurer or insurance producer can demonstrate:
>
> 1. Collection and consideration of relevant information;
>
> 2. Conformance with an insurer's guidelines and procedures, prior to making a recommendation; and
>
> 3. That the insurance transaction assisted the consumer in meeting the consumer's insurable needs or financial objectives."

As of December, 2011, more than twenty states have adopted a form of SATMR, and it is virtually certain that all states will eventually do so, particularly as Section 989J of Dodd-Frank practically compels this. The impact of Dodd-Frank will be discussed later in this chapter.

Rules Dealing with Annuities that Are Securities

Variable annuities, as annuity contracts, are subject to regulation by state insurance departments—and, indirectly, by the NAIC—and, as securities, are subject to regulation by state securities departments and Federal securities regulators. Over the years, rulings by the NASD and FINRA have sought to provide guidance as to when a variable annuity is suitable."

FINRA Rule 2090

The FINRA Rule 2090 Know Your Customer rule, announced in FINRA's Regulatory Notice 11–02 in January, 2011, is modeled after NYSE Rule 405(1). It requires FINRA members to use reasonable diligence and to know the essential facts concerning their customers. The Rule explains that essential facts are: "those required to (a) effectively service the customer's account, (b) act in accordance with any special handling instructions for the account, (c) understand the authority of each person acting on behalf of the customer and (d) comply with applicable laws, regulations, and rules."[5]

The know-your-customer obligation arises at the beginning of the customer-broker relationship and does not depend on whether the broker has made a recommendation.

FINRA Rule 2111

FINRA Rule 2111 is both a "know your customer" and suitability rule. Announced in regulatory notice 11–02, and effective on October 7, 2011, it requires that registered representatives and the firms for which they work have a reasonable basis to believe that a recommended transaction or investment strategy involving a security is suitable for the customer, based upon "the information obtained through the reasonable diligence of the [FINRA] member or associated person to ascertain the customer's investment profile." It is significant that this rule, unlike previous rulings, applies both to recommendations of product and of investment strategy.

The Rule declares that investment profile "includes, but is not limited to, the customer's age, other investments, financial situation and needs, tax status, investment objectives, investment experience, investment time horizon, liquidity needs, risk tolerance, and any other information the customer may disclose to the member or associated person in connection with such recommendation." The factors identified in that list are very similar to those identified in SATMR. This is a common condition in regulatory language. Often, the authors of an NAIC rule will adopt the language of rules previously issued by other regulatory authorities such as FINRA.

FINRA Rule 2330

The current FINRA suitability rule applicable to deferred variable annuities "to recommended purchases and exchanges of deferred variable annuities and recommended initial subaccount allocations," is FINRA Rule 2330, modeled after NASD rule 2821. It provides that:

> "No member or person associated with a member shall recommend to any customer the purchase or exchange of a deferred variable annuity unless such member or person associated with a member has a reasonable basis to believe
>
> > (A) that the transaction is suitable in accordance with Rule 2111 and, in particular, that there is a reasonable basis to believe that
> >
> > > (i)   the customer has been informed, in general terms, of various features of deferred variable annuities, such as the potential surrender period and surrender charge; potential tax penalty if customers sell or redeem deferred variable annuities before reaching the age of fifty-nine-and a half; mortality and expense fees; investment advisory fees; potential charges for and features of riders; the insurance and investment components of deferred variable annuities; and market risk;
> > >
> > > (ii) the customer would benefit from certain features of deferred variable annuities, such as tax-deferred growth, annuitization, or a death or living benefit; and

(iii) the particular deferred variable annuity as a whole, the underlying subaccounts to which funds are allocated at the time of the purchase or exchange of the deferred variable annuity, and riders and similar product enhancements, if any, are suitable (and, in the case of an exchange, the transaction as a whole also is suitable) for the particular customer based on the information required by paragraph (b)(2) of this Rule; and

(B) in the case of an exchange of a deferred variable annuity, the exchange also is consistent with the suitability determination required by paragraph (b)(1)(A) of this Rule, taking into consideration whether

(i) the customer would incur a surrender charge, be subject to commencement of a new surrender period, lose existing benefits (such as death, living, or other contractual benefits), or be subject to increased fees or charges (such as mortality and expense fees, investment advisory fees, or charges for riders and similar product enhancements);

(ii) the customer would benefit from product enhancements and improvements; and

(iii) the customer has had another deferred variable annuity exchange within the preceding thirty-six months.[6]

Like the NAIC's SATMR, FINRA Rule 2330 provides guidance as to the factors that should be considered before the recommendation of an annuity. Indeed, the factors that it cites are virtually identical to those cited in SATMR, which took them from the earlier NASD Rule 2821. Section (b)(2) of Rule 2330 states that:

"Prior to recommending the purchase or exchange of a deferred variable annuity, a member or person associated with a member shall make reasonable efforts to obtain, at a minimum, information concerning the customer's age, annual income, financial situation and needs, investment experience, investment objectives, intended use of the deferred variable annuity, investment time horizon, existing assets (including investment and life insurance holdings), liquidity needs, liquid net worth, risk tolerance, tax status, and such other information used or considered to be reasonable by the member or person associated with the member in making recommendations to customers."

Notwithstanding the similarity of language in FINRA Rule 2330 and SATMR, the regulatory implications are very different. SATMR applies, in those states that have adopted it, to the sale of all annuities, while the FINRA Rule applies only to the sale of variable contracts. As we shall see, however, Section 989J of Dodd-Frank applies the suitability rules of SATMR, including these suitability factors to the sale of all annuity contracts, and, arguably, to the sale of insurance products other than annuities.

The reader will have noted, by this point, that there are many rules, from different agencies, at different jurisdictional levels, governing the sale of an annuity, and he or she might well be asking, "which ones affect me? Do I have to comply with all of them?" The answer is "if you're a registered representative selling a variable annuity, you're subject to all of them." Why? Because, as an insurance agent selling an annuity, you are subject to state rules governing annuity sales, and, as a registered rep selling a registered product, you're subject to FINRA Rules, and any additional rules that may be imposed by your State Department of Securities. A more practical answer might be "observe all the rules, even those that may not apply to you right now, just to be safe."

As the twelve suitability factors cited in SATMR and FINRA Rule 2330 and, as we shall see, incorporated by reference into Section 989J of Dodd-Frank, must be considered by any advisor prior to recommending an annuity, we will now look at each of these factors in more detail.

The 12 Suitability Factors of SATMR/FINRA Rule 2330 in Detail

1. Age. The age of the buyer of an annuity is an extremely important factor in any determination of whether that annuity is suitable. In the case of an immediate annuity payable for life, the age of the annuitant will determine the amount of each annuity payment. If the proposed annuitant is not in good health or if his or her family health history suggests a shorter than average life expectancy, the advisor should question whether a nonunderwritten life annuity is appropriate. For such an applicant, a fully underwritten annuity—where the amount of annuity payments would take into account the annuitant's health status—might offer a substantially greater benefit than a nonunderwritten contract.

If the contract being proposed is a deferred annuity, the age of the prospective owner and of the prospective annuitant, if different, are relevant factors. Many insurers will not issue a deferred annuity contract if the proposed annuitant is older than a certain age, which, in the authors' experience, accounts for many contracts where the annuitant and owner are different individuals. As was noted in Chapter 2, this can create problems.

Even where the prospective owner and annuitant are the same individual, the age of that person is relevant to the suitability of a deferred annuity. The NAIC and insurance regulators of many states have issued consumer alerts, warning seniors of deceptive sales practices, and, in many states, special suitability requirements apply when the applicant of a deferred annuity is a senior citizen. That said, no state regulation of which the authors are aware states that an annuity is inappropriate merely because the prospective buyer has reached a certain age.

Where the proposed deferred annuity includes either a guaranteed minimum death benefit or a living benefit rider, the age of the owner and/or annuitant often determines the availability or the terms of that benefit.

2. Annual Income. The annual income of the buyer of an annuity is relevant to the suitability of that contract for several reasons. If the contract is a flexible premium one, contemplating ongoing contributions, the applicant should be able to make those contributions.

3. Financial Situation and Needs, Including the Financial Resources Used for the Funding of the Annuity. An annuity is a tool designed to meet specific financial needs; therefore, the nature and extent of those needs are relevant to the annuity's suitability to do the job. Moreover, the source of funds is of particular concern when securities are involved. The agent recommending the annuity must be appropriately licensed, not only for the annuity contract being proposed, but also for securities, if the source of funds for the annuity is securities and if he or she is recommending that those securities be sold to fund the annuity.

It is widely believed that if the source of funds includes securities, that anyone recommending an annuity must necessarily be registered to sell the type of securities involved. Sources such as the *Joint Bulletin No. 14-2009* issued by the Arkansas Insurance and Securities departments in September, 2009, are often cited to support this position. However, a close reading of the ruling in question may indicate otherwise. For example, the Arkansas ruling states:

> "The recommendation to replace securities such as mutual funds, stocks, bonds and various other investment vehicles defined as securities under the Arkansas Securities Act is the offering of investment advice. It is unlawful to offer investment advice unless one is registered (licensed) with the Arkansas Securities Department as an investment adviser or investment adviser representative."

This does not say that the proceeds of the sale of securities may never be used to purchase an annuity unless the agent recommending that annuity is securities registered. It says only that the agent may not *recommend* such liquidation without being registered as an investment advisor, or investment advisor representative. Even a Series 6 or Series 7 registration might not suffice in Arkansas because the regulators in that state have defined a recommendation to replace securities as the rendering of investment advice. In another state, that same recommendation might be considered to fall within the solely incidental exception of Section 202(a)(11)(C) of the Investment Advisers Act of 1940. Generally, however, an advisor recommending a nonvariable annuity, to be funded with the proceeds of securities sales, must be registered to sell the type of securities involved, but need not be securities registered if he or she does not actually recommend the sale of securities to purchase the annuity. But this may not be a reliable safe harbor. Can an advisor whose client purchased the annuity he recommended with funds from securities sales rely upon the defense that "I did not know where the money was coming from"? If he or she is obliged to consider "Financial Situation and Needs, Including the Financial Resources Used for the Funding of the Annuity," and SATMR imposes that obligation, the answer would appear to be a flat "no," absent evidence that the client deliberately misled the advisor as to the source of funds.

4. Financial Experience. The financial experience of a consumer is important, especially if the financial product being recommended is complicated or appropriate only for sophisticated buyers. A complaint often made by plaintiffs in annuity-related litigations, is "I did not understand what I was buying." The more complicated the annuity, the more likely this complaint—or, at the least, the more reasonable it may sound to a jury or arbitrator.

5. Financial Objectives. As the authors have noted earlier, an annuity is just a tool. Any assessment of its suitability must necessarily consider the job to be done. It is vital that everyone involved in the sale of an annuity—the applicant, the recommending advisor, and the insurance company issuing the annuity— understand what financial objectives that annuity is being purchased to achieve. In the authors' opinion, it is probably impossible to over-emphasize the importance of this factor or to over-document its consideration. A thorough documentation of why the annuity is, in the opinion of the advisor, the right tool for the job can be invaluable to the defendant in litigation alleging a bad sale. More importantly, it may prevent that litigation by ensuring both that the consumer buys the right product and that he or she understands as much.

6. Intended Use of the Annuity. This is a variation on the theme addressed by factor #5, focusing less on, "is the annuity the right tool for the job?" and more on, "how will that tool be used to do the job?" Consideration of this factor can produce useful, and possibly unexpected, results. For example, if the proposed annuity includes a guaranteed minimum death benefit and the purchaser shows a special interest in this feature, a discussion of life insurance, which is usually a more efficient delivery instrument for death benefits than an annuity, may be in order.

7. Financial Time Horizon. Time horizon can be a confusing term. It can be used to mean the maximum period during which this investment will be held. It can also be used to mean the number of years before which distributions, or income, are expected to be needed. Both are relevant to a proper determination of suitability, and the authors suggest that the advisor and consumer understand how long the annuity will be held, which is particularly important when surrender charges are considered, and over what period of time distributions—whether in the form of withdrawals or regular annuity payments—will be made.

8. Existing Assets, Including Investment and Life Insurance Holdings. Existing assets are important, not only because they are part of that client's financial situation (Factor #3), but because the nature and extent of those assets will help the advisor to determine the extent to which the financial objectives, identified in factor #5, are likely to be met. A review of existing assets can also help the advisor assess the accuracy of the client's responses to the advisor's questions regarding the other suitability factors. For example, a client claiming to have extensive financial experience and sophistication and a great desire for tax-favored treatment of his investments, yet who holds only certificates of deposit, may not understand the extent to which the expressed concerns are inconsistent with his prior financial decisions and current holdings.

9. Liquidity Needs. The liquidity of an asset refers to how quickly and cheaply it can be converted to cash. While a deferred annuity that imposes surrender charges (as most do) can be surrendered for cash relatively quickly, the cash received might, because of those charges, be significantly less than the annuity's value just prior to surrender. In a few indexed annuities, surrender charges never expire, and may even apply to death proceeds taken in a lump sum; those annuities may be considered relatively illiquid. That does not necessarily make them unsuitable, as long as the annuity purchaser is comfortable that the illiquidity is still reasonable, given his or her goals. On the other hand, it's important to note that even those contracts whose charges do expire after a term of years may have a high cost for early liquidity during that surrender charge period, especially in the early years of that period.

10. Liquid Net Worth. After learning the liquid net worth of the annuity applicant, the advisor can compare that figure with the applicant's liquidity needs. If it appears that the liquid net worth is not sufficient to meet the liquidity needs during the surrender charge period, the advisor may wish to recommend that some of the funds being considered for investment in the annuity be placed in a highly liquid account to meet that potential shortfall.

11. Risk Tolerance. Risk tolerance is an essential factor in the determination of the suitability of an annuity because annuities are risk management instruments. Unfortunately, this simple fact is not widely, or well understood by many financial advisors and, sad to say, regulators. Moreover, the very notion of risk is largely misunderstood and, often, misapplied.

What is risk? Textbooks in finance tell us that there are many different kinds of risk, including market risk, interest rate risk, inflation risk, currency risk, credit risk, liquidity risk, etc. Yet many risk tolerance questionnaires used by financial advisors—and often required by insurers and/or broker/dealers to be completed prior to the sale of an annuity, especially a variable annuity—focus only on one of these: market risk, which is commonly defined in either of two very different ways.

One definition says that market risk is the risk that market pressures may cause the value of an investment to fluctuate. In that sense, market risk means volatility. Another definition, also used widely, says that market risk is the possibility that market pressures will cause the value of an investment to decline. In that sense, market risk equals principal risk. Both involve uncertainty—which, the authors believe, is the central element of risk—as to the future value of one's capital.

Certainly, that's an important consideration to any investor; but it's not all-important. The widespread use of risk tolerance assessment tools, such as a questionnaire, that identifies risk only as the possibility of losing one's capital, or principal, focuses attention only on the capital preservation and wealth accumulation potential of the product being considered, concerning which tool is employed.

That can be a problem when one is assessing the suitability of an annuity because the risk that is of greatest concern to a prospective annuity purchaser may not be "that I might lose some principal" but, rather, that "I might run out of income." Moreover, principal risk is never a factor in an immediate annuity, because an immediate annuity is an income stream, and typically has no principal or accessible cash value.[7] It may not be a factor when the product proposed is a fixed deferred annuity, because all fixed deferred annuities guarantee principal, except to the extent that surrender charges or a market value adjustment may erode principal if the contract is surrendered early. Indeed, principal risk may not be a great concern even when the proposed product is a variable deferred annuity if a guaranteed living benefit has been chosen because the income guaranteed with such benefits is often immune to adverse market performance.

The authors do not suggest that market risk should not be a concern in determining the suitability of any proposed investment, including an annuity, but only that many risk tolerance measurement tools focus only on market risk—and, in doing so, marginalize, or ignore completely, the applicant's tolerance for other risks that may be of far greater concern. We believe that any discussion of risk tolerance should be informed by the applicant's responses to the other eleven factors in this list, and by the advisor's understanding of the client's total picture.

12. Tax Status. The tax status of the applicant for an annuity is obviously important because annuities receive special tax treatment. The tax deferral that is enjoyed by a deferred annuity comes with a cost: Namely (a) all ordinary income treatment of all distributions and (b) a ten percent penalty tax on any distribution not qualifying for an exception under Code section 72(q) (2). The benefit of such tax deferral is much greater for applicants in high tax brackets than for applicants in very low brackets, for whom the benefit may be outweighed by its cost.

Some Observations on Liquidity and Deferred Annuity Surrender Charges

Surrender charges should always be considered in any recommendation of a deferred annuity. The ethical advisor will always want to ensure that the client fully understands both the benefits and the costs of what he or she is buying, and surrender charges are part of the cost of the contract. They are also the most commonly cited factor in complaints about allegedly improper annuity sales. Complaints to regulators and lawsuits over annuity sales typically allege that the buyer did not understand either the amount of surrender charges or the conditions under which they would be imposed. Of course, those charges are disclosed in every annuity contract and in most point-of-sale brochures. However, such disclosure is not always in the clearest of language. The conditions under which surrender charges will be waived are not always fully explained in product brochures and, indeed, are sometimes difficult to find in the contracts themselves, even for an expert. How might an advisor improve the chances that a buyer truly understands surrender charges—or that he or she can demonstrate to regulators, arbitrators, or a jury that they were fully explained? The authors suggest a few techniques:

- Where the annuity proposed is a variable contract, the advisor can review the sections in the prospectus detailing surrender charges. Of course, he or she should never underline or highlight the prospectus. For nonvariable contracts, the authors strongly recommend that the advisor obtain a specimen contract, which is sometimes also known as a sample contract, of every product he or she intends to recommend and to review the appropriate specimen contract with every applicant, prior to closing the sale. Sadly, many advisers we have spoken with have never obtained, or even seen, a single specimen contract.

- Many insurers and annuity marketing organizations now require the submission of a risk tolerance questionnaire with every application for an annuity. Often, these documents require that the applicant initial those paragraphs explaining surrender charges and other relevant factors. This is an excellent practice, one that the authors strongly commend. If the insurer offering an annuity or the marketing organization through which that annuity will be submitted does not offer such a document, the advisor may wish to create one and submit it, after completion by the client, along with the annuity application.

- When reviewing point-of-sale material with the client, the advisor may wish to ask the client to initial the paragraphs explaining the various features and costs of the product being recommended, on both the copy being left with the client and the copy to be retained, by the advisor, in the client's file.

- The authors strongly believe that any discussion of annuity surrender charges is incomplete without an explanation of why those charges exist. As explained earlier in this book, surrender charges are not entirely a drawback or disadvantage to the client. Clients who understand why surrender charges are imposed, that they are imposed only on those purchasers who surrender annuities before the issuing insurer has had an opportunity to recover its costs, and that, absent those charges, the benefits offered by the annuity would probably be less, are more likely to be satisfied with their purchase and less likely to complain afterwards.

- The authors believe that many annuity complaints could be avoided if the advisor, prior to closing the sale, tests the willingness of the client to pay surrender charges. This might be accomplished by asking the applicant "is there any chance at all that you'll need access to the funds you're considering putting into this annuity during the next N years (where N = the surrender charge period), given the fact that you have access to the other liquid funds you've told me about? If the answer is "yes," the advisor should not recommend funding the annuity with the amount originally contemplated, but recommend that a portion of that money be allocated to a liquid account (e.g., a money market, checking, or savings account). That done, the process should be repeated— and again, if necessary—until the purchaser's response is "no." At that point, the advisor could ask, "so you're telling me that you're comfortable locking up this amount of money in this annuity for N years in order to obtain the benefits we've discussed?"

Some advisors might object that this technique ignores the fact that most deferred annuities permit penalty-free withdrawals of up to a certain amount or percentage of the annuity value during the surrender charge period and withdrawals in excess of those amounts under certain conditions, such as nursing home confinement). That is true. But how many purchasers, told of a ten-percent free withdrawal privilege, can be sure that they won't need, say, fifteen percent? In the authors' opinion, beginning the discussion of surrender charges by verifying that the purchaser has liquid funds sufficient to pay for emergencies or unexpected expenses during the entire surrender charge period, and then, and only then, reviewing the free withdrawal provisions will go a long way toward ensuring that the annuity is suitable from a liquidity perspective.

Continuing our discussion of FINRA Rule 2330, it should be noted that many annuity contracts, both variable and nonvariable, are sold through broker-dealers, some of which require their registered representatives to submit even nonvariable contracts through them. As the suitability rules for variable annuities are not identical to those imposed by the NAIC and state insurance regulators upon sales of nonvariable annuities, inconsistencies can occur. This issue is addressed in Section 6H of SATMR, the so-called "safe harbor" provision. According to the Executive Summary:

"Sec. 6H (the so-called "safe harbor") is intended to prevent duplicative suitability standards being applied to sales of annuities through FINRA broker-dealers. Sales of insurance products that are securities under federal law, such as variable annuities, are required to meet FINRA suitability rules, and sales in compliance with FINRA rules would comply with NAIC suitability regulation. Broker-Dealers may subject fixed annuity sales to FINRA suitability and supervision rules, and sales made in compliance with such rules would also qualify as complying with the NAIC suitability regulation. However, since FINRA does not have authority to enforce its rules on the sale of fixed annuities, broker-dealers supervising fixed annuity sales may be subject to more intensive insurance examination than for sale of security insurance products. Representatives of a broker-dealer, who are not required by the broker-dealer to comply with the FINRA requirements on the sale of fixed annuities, will have to comply with the insurance suitability regulation adopted by the state. In any case, insurers are responsible for any unsuitable annuity transactions no matter what suitability regulation or rule is applied by a broker-dealer."[8]

Rules Dealing with Annuities that May Be Securities

Variable annuities are securities. Declared rate fixed annuities are not, at least under current rules. The status of indexed annuities is less clear. Despite the fact that indexed annuities share the common defining characteristics of fixed annuities—a guarantee of principal and a minimum rate of interest—the SEC published, in 2008, Rule 151A, which declared these contracts to be securities, subject to its jurisdiction. The rule was successfully challenged and vacated[9] on a technicality; the SEC subsequently withdrew Rule 151A. While many believed, even after those events, that indexed annuities were still, properly speaking, securities, a position still held by many thoughtful observers, the issue was arguably put to rest by Section 989J of Dodd-Frank. It should be noted that the securities regulators in some states continue to assert that indexed annuities are "securities," subject to their jurisdiction. We have addressed this issue at length, including some state regulatory cases on point, in Chapter 16.

Section 989J of Dodd-Frank: The Federal Extension of NAIC Rules for Annuity Transactions to Transactions Involving Annuity and Insurance Products

The language of this section–often known as the Harkin Amendment after the Senator who proposed it—was designed to keep regulation of indexed annuities with the states and not with the SEC. Interestingly, it did so by making such exemption from SEC jurisdiction contingent upon compliance with a new test of suitability.

To qualify for the Section 3(a)(8) exemption of the 1933 Act, any insurance or annuity contract must either:

a. [Sect. 989J(a)(3)(A)] if issued on or after June 16, 2013, be issued in a state, or by an insurer domiciled in a state, that has adopted suitability rules governing sale of such policies that substantially meet or exceed the minimum requirements of the NAIC SATMR and any further successions thereto within five years of the NAIC's adoption of such successors; or

b. be issued by an insurer that has adopted and implemented sales practices on a nation-wide scale that substantially meet or exceed those same minimum requirements, including the successors thereto provision. This condition (Section 989J(a)(3)(B)) does not specify a date by which it must be met, which could mean the only way in which such an insurance or annuity contract issued prior to 6/16/13 can meet the suit-ability requirements of Section 989J would be if the issuing insurer had adopted and implemented sales practices meeting those requirements prior to such issue—even if the state in which the contract is issued had already adopted suitability rules satisfying those same requirements.[10]

There are many uncertainties connected with Section 989J, including:

• Must the insurance comply with SATMR for all its products, or only the products seeking to rely on the safe harbor of Section N989J?

• Must all elements of SATMR be met in all states in which the product is offered, even in those states that have not adopted that Model Regulation?

These questions and others await clarification from the SEC. For the advisor who recommends or gives advice about annuities, however, no clarification is needed; compliance with the suit-ability rules of SATMR is clearly the best course of action for at least two reasons. First, because most states have already adopted rules at least as stringent as those of SATMR and it's a very safe bet that all states will do so within a fairly short time. Second, because it's both ethically and practically the right thing to do.

The Neasham Case

On December 8, 2010, Glenn Neasham, a California insurance agent, was charged with a criminal offense by the prosecuting attorney of Lake County, California. The charge alleged that Neasham had, in selling an indexed annuity to Fran Schuber, an 83-year-old woman, engaged in felony theft from a senior. On October 21, 2011, a jury found Mr. Neasham guilty. Since the announcement of the verdict, the Neasham case has been the subject of daily discussion in the financial services industry. While the authors believe that there is much to criticize in the handling of this affair by the California Department of Insurance and the Lake County California prosecutor's office, we are not attorneys and it is not the business of this book to dissect the court's decision after the fact. That said, we believe that this case presents issues that affect everyone who may become involved in the recommendation of an annuity contract. We will look now at some of those issues.

- The Neasham case involved the sale of a deferred annuity to an aged person who, it was alleged, suffered from cognitive impairment at the time of the sale. The California Department of Insurance determined, in its investigation in 2009–2010, that Ms. Schuber "lacked the mental capacity to enter into this contract and that the terms and conditions of the annuity contract were not in her best financial interest."[11]

- The Lake County prosecutor argued, at Mr. Neasham's trial, that Mr. Neasham should have known of this alleged cognitive impairment at the time he presented the annuity proposal.

That argument, and the fact that it was successful in the Neasham case, should raise concerns for any advisor involved in the sale or recommendation of an annuity. What obligation does an advisor have in this situation? Few, if any, states have enacted statutes that specifically identify an agent's duty to assess the mental competence of a prospective buyer, or how he or she should do so. The charge that a reasonable person, in the agent's position, should have known of an applicant's impaired mental state begs the question of how. Cognitive impairment is not always easy to observe, much less to quantify, especially for someone with no training in this area. That said, the authors suggest that a pro-active approach makes good business sense. The advisor should be especially alert to the possibility of mental confusion when dealing with individuals of an advanced age. It may be good practice to address this issue directly with all applicants over a certain age. For example, the advisor might ask such an applicant if he or she has experienced difficulty in reading financial documents or understanding the costs and benefits of investment or insurance products. One technique that the authors believe ought to be used in all presentations is to ask the buyer who has heard an explanation of the proposed product to explain, in her own words, her understanding of its costs and benefits. This may be especially useful if some time has elapsed since that earlier explanation. Other tools and techniques for ascertaining the cognitive state of an individual are available; tests such as the Blessed Orientation-Memory-Concentration Test.[12]

Agents, of course, are not psychologists, but if advisers, including insurance agents, are to be held accountable for judging whether their prospects and clients are mentally competent or not, they should be provided with the tools necessary to make that judgment.

The authors suggest that issuers of financial products, including annuities, consider providing their sales forces who will be selling to the elderly with both assessment tools (point of sale questionnaires, etc.) and the training to use those tools. Alternatively, insurers may decide that the risks of marketing to the elderly outweigh the benefits. Of course, there is considerable profit in selling annuities to senior citizens and the Neasham case may be simply an anomaly that does not justify so drastic a marketing decision. But if it is not; if advisors and the insurers whose products they recommend are likely to be held accountable in both civil and criminal actions for selling products to elderly consumers whose competence is later questioned, one might well ask if such sales are worth pursuing. In a conversation with one of the authors, Dr. Jack Marrion, whose doctoral work was in cognitive biases in decision-making, addressed this very point when he said:

> "According to research conducted by Plassman and others on the prevalence of dementia, one in four people in their 80s (ages 80-89) have dementia. This raises the question as to whether agents should accept any annuity buyers over age 80. It is unfair to place the burden on determining what is acceptable cognitive ability on an agent. If a carrier decides to accept annuity buyers over age 79 perhaps it should be required to conduct appropriate cognitive testing to determine whether the buyer is acceptable."

Both the California Department of Insurance and the Lake County prosecutor argued that the size and duration of surrender charges of the annuity purchased by Ms. Schuber made that contract unsuitable for her. Yet the annuity in question had been approved by the California Department of Insurance for sale to applicants up to age 85 and Ms. Schuber had signed a disclosure of those surrender charges and had not complained about them—or, indeed, made any complaint regarding the annuity to any authority.

What does this suggest that an advisor must do when presenting a contract, especially to a senior citizen, that includes surrender charges? Are a thorough, and documented, discussion of those charges and a signed disclosure sufficient? The authors believe that, in this climate of increasing litigiousness and regulatory scrutiny, they may well not be. We offer the following as suggested practices:

A.   Before describing the size and duration of surrender charges, the advisor may wish to explain why such charges exist in the first place. One of the authors uses the following method in his practice:

> "Mr. Prospect, you know that insurance companies sell annuities to make a profit. You may not know that any insurer will lose money if the buyer surrenders the annuity before the company has had a chance to recover the costs it incurred in putting

that contract in force. Those costs include commissions, of course, but also the costs of issuing and administering the contract and of setting aside the monies required by law to back the guarantees of that contract. Basically, an insurer can recover such costs in only three ways: first, it could assess a front-end sales charge. That is, it could take a percentage of the buyer's investment immediately, and those dollars would never earn interest or be available to the contract owner. Second, it could reduce the interest it would otherwise be able to pay to the buyer each year or assess an annual recovery charge, which amounts to the same thing. Third, it could recognize that the only annuity buyers who would keep it from recovering its acquisition costs are those buyers who surrender their contracts early and charge only those buyers, by imposing a surrender charge. Which method would you want the insurance company to use for your annuity?"

In decades of selling annuities, one of the authors has never had a prospective buyer answer other than "the third one." Once a prospective buyer understands the reason for surrender charges, a discussion of the size and duration of those charges can proceed.

B.   Merely showing a document describing the surrender charge schedule and asking the applicant to sign it offers, in the authors' opinion, no assurance that the buyer truly understands those charges. We suggest that, following that presentation, the advisor ask the client to state what the charges would be in various surrender years. If an illustration showing projected contract values is used, the client could be handed a calculator and asked to compute the dollar value of the surrender charge in those years. The surrender charge could then be compared with the projected contract gain in those same years.

C.   If the annuity being presented is of the bonus type—that is, it offers an initial interest crediting, over and above the anticipated annual interest—it is, in the authors' opinion, utterly essential that the client understand the conditions under which that bonus interest will be available to the client. Is it available only if the contract is annuitized? Is it subject to a vesting schedule? A thorough discussion of these conditions and documentation of the client's understanding of them may take time, but it is in everyone's interest.

D.   If a bonus annuity is being presented, the authors strongly urge that the advisor also show to the client a nonbonus alternative—a contract having as nearly the same features and benefits as the bonus alternative, including, if possible, current interest crediting and, for indexed annuities, participation rate, cap rate, etc. apart from the surrender charge schedule. A side-by-side comparison should be shown and the client's preference should be documented. We suggest that such a comparison document should include a section with blank lines on which the client should be asked to write, in his or her own words, in his or her own handwriting, the reasons for his/her preference.

The Neasham case involved an elderly client who elected to name, as beneficiary, someone other than a relative. Indeed, this choice of beneficiary was chiefly responsible for the case's being referred to authorities in the first place. The authors suggest that when a client's beneficiary designation is unusual, the prudent advisor will address, with the client, the implications of that designation. This inquiry need not look like an inquisition, nor need the advisor appear to be critical of the client's choice. But some beneficiary designations can present problems. For example, naming a trust as beneficiary may well require a more rapid payout, upon death, than would be required if individuals were named. When a nonfamily member is named, and when the client is elderly, the issue of undue influence may later be raised, as, indeed, it was in the Neasham case.

Suitability is, as we have seen, not a simple matter to determine. Authorities, at various jurisdictional levels, have provided rules and guidelines that the advisor must take into account when making an annuity recommendation. As the Neasham case has demonstrated, adherence to such published rules and guidelines may not be enough. The authors suggest that the prudent advisor will, when making any recommendation for any annuity to any prospective buyer, keep in the back of his or her mind the possibility that his or her words and actions will be later scrutinized in adversarial proceedings.

Update to the Neasham Case

On October 8, 2013, the Court of Appeals of the state of California, in a unanimous 3-0 decision, reversed the conviction of Glenn Neasham.[13]. The court held that the jury instructions given by the trial judge were incorrect, noting that the crime of which Neasham was charged "requires an intent on the part of the perpetrator to steal" but that the jury was "authorized to find the defendant guilty if it agreed with the prosecution that the terms of the annuity had the effect of depriving Schuber of a major portion of the value or enjoyment of her property, even if the defendant had no such intentions."

The Court also noted that Neasham "did not take [Schuber's] funds or convert her property to his own use or the use of any other person" and "did not deprive her of any property but instead placed her funds into an investment instrument of equal value to the monies withdrawn from her certificate of deposit."

In addition, the Court noted that "the prosecution did not allege, and the jury was not instructed to determine, that the defendant made any misrepresentations to Schuber (or to Jochim or anyone else) concerning the terms of the annuity."

The CA Attorney Petitions the CA Supreme Court for a Review

Following the Appellate Court's decision, the California Attorney General's office petitioned the California Supreme Court to review that decision in order to settle, among other things, "the important question whether a non-consensual exchange of property of equivalent value is a taking," a position that the Appellate Court had found non-persuasive. On January 15, 2014, the California Supreme Court denied the petition.[14] In that same week, Glenn Neasham's insurance license was renewed by the California Department of Insurance.

Most commentators, including the authors of this book, considered Glenn Neasham's conviction to be unjust and that, if it were left to stand, would represent a potentially serious threat to any agent selling any annuity to a senior citizen. Whether the sale of that annuity by that agent to that consumer was "suitable" is another question. One of the authors, with Burke Christensen, an attorney and highly respected expert on insurance, dealt with these different issues in an article entitled "The Neasham Case: An Analysis of the Events and Their Implications for Financial Advisors" (*Journal of Financial Service Professionals*, November, 2012).

A Final Note

The issue of suitability, as it applies to the recommendation of annuity products, is a complex one; not only are the rules not entirely consistent from one jurisdiction to another, but the rules of the individual jurisdiction are in almost constant revision, though a few elements will persist.

- The suitability of a particular annuity in a particular situation will always be a matter of facts and circumstances. That said, if the factors cited in SATMR are properly considered by the agent/advisor before recommending an annuity, unsuitability should be minimized, and egregiously unsuitable sales could become a rarity.

- The present suitability standard is almost certain to become more stringent. The current push for harmonization of the two standard of care regimes or for a single fiduciary standard applying to all those who give financial advice will, in the authors' opinion, inevitably produce a standard of care for annuity advisors incorporating elements now confined to the fiduciary standard. Disclosure of commissions will, we believe, probably become obligatory, which should not adversely affect those advisors who are already employing the kind of diligent suitability practices that the regulations we've examined seek to mandate.

- For those advisors who are subject to more than one standard of care (e.g., registered representatives who are also registered investment advisors or advisory associates), it is possible, if not likely, that they will be held to the highest standard that would apply to them, regardless of the type of case. In other words, a broker who, when selling a fixed annuity is currently held only to the standard of suitability may, if he is also an investment advisor, or associate, be held in future to the fiduciary standard applicable when he acts as an investment advisor, even when he is merely selling product. Broker/Dealers are unlikely to be willing to guess, when overseeing the activities of their representatives, which hat those representatives are wearing in any given interaction with consumers.

Education requirements will continue to stiffen. SATMR requires any agent who sells any annuity to complete at least a four-hour course on annuities. Many Broker/Dealers and insurers also require such training. Given the growing complexity of annuity products and a litigious consumer population, increased competency is both ethically laudable and very good business.

One of the authors discusses Standards of Care and the "Source of Funds" issue in an article entitled "Suitability in the Sale of Fixed Insurance Products: A Look at Some of the Murkier Issues" *Journal of Financial Service Professionals* (July, 2013).

Endnotes

1. NAIC Model Reg. 275. http://www.naic.org/store/free/MDL-275.pdf

2. NAIC "Suitability in Annuity Transactions Model Regulation Executive Summary" http://www.naic.org/documents/committees_a_suitability_reg_guidance.pdf:

3. NAIC Mod. Reg. 275.

4. Ibid.

5. FINRA Reg. Not. 11-02. https://www.finra.org/Industry/Regulation/Notices/2011/P122779

6. FINRA Rule 2330. http://www.finra.org/Industry/Issues/Suitability/

7. Newer immediate annuity contracts may offer access to cash in addition to the stated annuity payment.

8. NAIC Mod. Reg. 275 Exec. Sum. p. 4

9. American Equity Investment Life Insurance Co. v. SEC, 2009 WL 2152351 (D.C. Cir. July 21, 2009).

10. Dodd-Frank Wall Street Reform and Consumer Protection Act, Pub. L. No. 111-203, § 989J, 124 Stat. 1376 (2010). The safe harbor language in Section 989J(a)(3)(A)—providing that such a contract will be deemed an exempt security if the issuing state has adopted suitability rules consistent with SATMR (and its successors)—refers only to contracts issued on or after 6/16/13. Arguably, contracts issued earlier cannot claim its protection.

11. CA Dept. of Insurance announcement, quoted in senioradvisor.com, December, 2010.

12. See Katzman R, Brown T, Fuld P, et al. Validation of a short Orientation-Memory-Concentration Test of cognitive impairment. Am. J. Psychiatry 1983;140:734-9. Copyright 1983, American Psychiatric Association.

13. People v. Neasham, 220 Cal. Ct. App. 1st 2013

14. People v. Neasham (2014 Cal. LEXIS 290)

Chapter 16

The "Source of Funds" Issue

One of the most troublesome areas of annuity regulation is the so-called "source of funds" issue. It arises when an insurance agent recommends to a consumer an annuity that is not classed as a security but the money to fund the annuity is currently invested in securities and the agent is not authorized to sell or give advice about securities. Some state insurance regulators view an insurance agent's recommendation to purchase an annuity, even one that is not classed as a security, as a recommendation to sell a financial instrument if the proceeds of the sale of that financial instrument will be used to purchase the annuity. If the instrument to be sold is a security, the agent is thus viewed as "giving personalized advice about securities." This activity would therefore require the agent to be a registered representative, if not an investment advisor.

The securities regulations of many states use the language of Section 202(a)(11) of The Investment Advisor Act of 1940 to define "investment advisor" as "any person who, for compensation, engages in the business of advising others… as to the advisability of investing in, purchasing, or selling securities." By itself, this definition would include the sale by a registered representative of a stock, bond, or mutual fund.

An exception to the above definition is granted by Section 202(a)(11)(C) of the Act, providing that "any broker or dealer whose performance of such services is wholly incidental to the conduct of his business as a broker or dealer and who receives no compensation therefore" is not considered an "investment advisor" and this exception is incorporated in the securities regulations of many states. While this definition may avoid requiring an insurance agent to register as an investment adviser when the source of funds is a security (at least in states where this investment adviser exception applies), it still does not resolve whether the insurance agent must at least become a registered representative when the source of funds were investment securities (even if the annuity being purchased is not classified as a security). In recent years, these rules have been tested in several states with a number of real-world situations.

The Cooper Case

In 2011, Thomas Cooper, a registered investment advisor in the state of Illinois, replaced the variable annuities owned by several clients with new fixed index annuities (the latter were not registered as securities in the state of Illinois). The Department held these sales to be unsuitable and, in addition, declared that "each of the above referenced investment plans is a security."[1] That statement appeared to refer to the fixed annuities sold by Cooper, and the source of the funds was not an issue in this case.

This position, that index annuities are "securities" for purposes of Illinois law drew a great deal of critical response. One issuer of index annuities (Fidelity & Guarantee Life Insurance Company) requested a statement from the Illinois Department of Securities that it would take no enforcement action with respect to sales of index annuities in the state of Illinois by agents of that company. David Finnigan, Senior Enforcement Attorney for the Department, replied in a letter dated January 10, 2013, that the Enforcement Division would not recommend enforcement action against that company's agents in that situation. The letter stated that it "should be treated only as a statement of the staff's enforcement position" and that it was not binding upon the Secretary of State of the State of Illinois.[2] Did this letter suggest that the Illinois Department of Securities no longer considers index annuities to be "securities" under Illinois law? Evidently not, because in March, 2013, that Department adjudicated the Van Dyke case.

The Van Dyke Case

In 2013 the Illinois Depertment of Securities alleged that Dick Van Dyke, an Illinois registered investment advisor, replaced thirty-one index annuities (all but one of which he had sold originally) with new index annuities owned by those same clients, and that as a result of these transactions, those clients paid over $263,000 in surrender charges. The Illinois Department of Securities has filed formal allegations against Mr. Van Dyke on the theory that those replacements were unsuitable for his client. In the Amended Notice of Hearing of this case, the Department noted that "under Illinois law, index annuities are securities under the [Illinois Securities] Act,"[3] though it also noted that if an index annuity meets certain requirements, neither the annuity nor the salesperson needs to be registered. This apparent contradiction was subsequently clarified by the Department's declaration that "although an index annuity may be exempt from registration, *the sale of the product* [authors' emphasis] is still subject to the other provisions of the Act." At the time of print the matter was still pending with the Department and there has been no finding against Mr. Van Dyke, though a final order is expected soon and will be posted on the Illinois Department of Securities website (http://www.ilsos.gov/adminactionssearch/adminactionssearch).

The Illinois Department of Securities is not the only state securities regulatory agency that considers the sale of nonregistered annuities subject to its jurisdiction.

The Kelly Case

In July, 2011, the Missouri Department of Securities issued a Consent Order declaring that William P. Kelly, an "insurance only" agent (holding no securities licenses) had acted as an unregistered investment advisor in selling index annuities to a Missouri consumer.[4] In those sales, the source of funds had been securities accounts.

While the Order did not state specifically that index annuities are "securities" under Missouri law, the Department, in its investigation, requested from the agent "any exemption from registration or exception from the definition of investment advisor upon which the firm relied in offering investment advice in connection with the sale of equity index annuity products in the state." Thus, it was not that the annuities that Kelly sold were "securities," but rather that the source of funds were securities and that Kelly was not licensed to sell securities, that the Department held to be improper. In this case, a securities license alone being held by Kelly would apparently still not have cured the violation because the Department ruled that, in recommending the sale of securities to fund the annuities, Kelly was acting as an unregistered investment advisor notwithstanding the fact that the annuities were fixed contracts that Kelly was licensed to sell.

The Gibson Case

In this case, Bill Gibson, an "insurance only" agent (no securities or advisory registration) sold a fixed annuity to a consumer who paid for it with money from certificates of deposit and his checking account. No securities were involved. But when that consumer complained to the Missouri Department of Securities, that agency investigated the case, asserted jurisdiction, and fined the agent for failing to allocate one of the premiums received to both the fixed and indexed accounts of that fixed index annuity.[5] This occurred even though the state doesn't specifically state that such indexed annuities are securities, nor was the source of funds from securities in this case.

The Utley Case

In July, 2011, Thomas F. Utley sold two fixed annuities to an Illinois resident; the annuities were purchased from the proceeds of the sale of multiple variable annuities. The Illinois Department of Securities investigated, sending a letter to Utley requiring a written response. Utley failed to respond, either to that letter or a follow-up letter from the Department. As a result of this failure, the Department issued an Order of Prohibition and fined Utley $10,000.[6] The Order does not indicate whether Utley held a securities license in Illinois or not, and it may not have mattered because the Order declared that "by recommending and advising [the consumer] to sell her variable annuities in order to purchase the aforesaid fixed indexed annuities, [Utley] was acting as an investment advisor."

This position, that the recommendation to sell securities as part of the purchase of a nonregistered annuity requires, not merely a securities license but registration as an investment advisor, is also held by the regulators in Arkansas.

Arkansas Department of Insurance Bulletin 14-2009

In 2009, the Arkansas Department of Insurance issued Bulletin 14-2009.[7] The bulletin stated that "the insurance commissioner intends to take action against insurance producers who improperly engaged in transactions involving annuities." Specifically, the Bulletin declares that "the recommendation to replace securities such as mutual funds, stocks, bonds and various other investment vehicles classified as securities, is the offering of investment advice." Evidently, such a recommendation to replace securities would be improper even if the agent holds a securities license as "it is unlawful to offer investment advice unless one is registered with the Arkansas Securities Department as an investment advisor or investment advisor representative."

Securities Licensed versus Investment Advisor

These are but a few cases in which state regulators have ruled that an insurance agent who advises a consumer to purchase a fixed annuity and to sell securities to provide the funding is acting as an investment advisor and must be registered as such with the state (and in at least one case, even where the source of funds was not a security.) But it is not clear whether regulators will pursue an agent who did precisely that if he or she holds a securities license.

The authors are unaware of any case in which state securities regulators have held that an agent acted as an unregistered investment advisor (a) if that agent held a license to sell the type of securities involved and (b) if that agent's "investment advice" consisted merely in recommending the securities to be sold. In the cases listed, the agents who held securities licenses were sanctioned not merely for recommending the sale of securities in order to purchase annuities, but for selling those annuities when they were unsuitable. It is not at all clear whether the mere fact that an annuity is purchased with funds from a securities account is, in and of itself, evidence of a securities violation. What if the agent is aware that the annuity will be funded by money from a securities account but makes no recommendation as to which securities should be sold? Is mere awareness that the source of funds is a security sufficient to require a securities license or registration as an investment advisor? At the time of this writing, the answer is unclear. Most commentators on this issue believe that a recommendation to liquidate specific holdings clearly requires security licensure but there is considerable disagreement as to whether investment advisor status is required.

Clear guidance is desperately needed. Agents in most states cannot be sure if they are permitted to sell a fixed annuity where the source of funds is a securities account. Some commentators believe that "insurance only" agents are probably safe if they make no specific sell recommendation. Some suggest that the agent should have the annuity buyer acknowledge same in writing. Others insist that the only safe harbor, as it stands now, is investment advisor status. Some commentators have recommended that every annuity agent become a registered investment advisor (or advisory associate). The authors disagree strongly with this recommendation. While it might be reasonable to require insurance agents who recommend the sale of a security to be registered with a securities license, the job of an investment advisor is very different from that of an insurance agent and involves very different skills and knowledge. If an agent wants to offer investment advice to her clients and possesses, or will acquire, the knowledge to do so competently, becoming an investment advisor makes sense. But acquiring investment advisor status merely to sell fixed annuities "safely," with no intention to behave as an investment advisor and be subject to the fiduciary duty applicable to investment advisors, is not good for any agent—or her clients. Indeed, one agent who did that found himself in trouble.

The Mitchell Case

Tracey Wayne Mitchell, a Missouri insurance agent who specialized in selling index annuities obtained a Series 65 license (permitting him to act as a registered investment advisor). According to his own testimony, Mitchell believed that this would serve as a marketing tool for his business and would "lend credibility" to his annuity recommendations. Missouri securities regulators, responding to a complaint by an attendee of one of Mitchell's annuities seminars, investigated. They determined that while Mitchell held himself out as an investment advisor, he did not act as one and that the only products he promoted were fixed and indexed annuities. The Department concluded that Mitchell had committed multiple violations of prohibited conduct in providing investment advice and had engaged in fraud and deceit and imposed a substantial fine.[8]

Clearly, becoming an investment advisor if one is neither competent nor willing to act as one is no solution to the "source of funds" issue. What, then, is an agent to do if he wishes to sell annuities to consumers who may have to pay for those annuities with securities dollars? What constitutes "advising a consumer to sell securities"? Does the mere awareness on the part of the agent that the proposed annuity will be funded with money from a securities account qualify? What if the agent assists the client in completing the paperwork necessary for a Section 1035 exchange or a trustee-to-trustee transfer (if the annuity is to be held in the client's IRA)? These forms specify the security being liquidated to effect the transfer. Does such specification rise to the level of a "specific recommendation"? Clear guidance from regulators in every state is needed. In 2011, one state attempted to provide this guidance.

Iowa's Bulletin 11-4

On June 24, 2011, the Iowa Commissioner of Insurance issued Insurance Bulletin 11-4, "to provide guidance to insurance producers, investment advisor representatives and securities agents about the permissible and prohibited activities of Insurance-Only Persons and Securities-Only Persons." In this chapter, we will consider only the content of this Bulletin directed to "insurance only" persons because "securities only" persons cannot sell annuities. The guidance provided by this Bulletin is vital to agents who sell annuities, and at least one other state (Tennessee) has adopted this Bulletin almost word for word in its insurance regulations. Other states are, at the time of this writing, considering adopting the Bulletin's language. The entire Bulletin is included in Appendix E, and Sections III ("Permitted Activities for an Insurance-Only Person"), IV ("Prohibited Activity for an Insurance-Only Person"), and VIII ("Insurance Producers Who Are Licensed as Investment Advisers or Investment Adviser Representatives") are below.

Exhibit 16.1

III. Permitted Activities for an Insurance-Only Person.

The following is not intended to be a complete description but rather a description of generally-recognized permissible activities of Insurance-Only Persons.

1. The Insurance-Only Person may discuss with the consumer the consumer's risk tolerance, financial situation, and needs. This may include a discussion of the consumer's:

    - financial experience;

    - financial objectives, including whether the consumer needs to earn a guaranteed rate of interest, needs guaranteed minimum increases in guaranteed values, or wishes to have available a minimum lifetime income stream;

    - risk tolerance, including need for principal protection or protection from market risk;

    - need to balance and diversify risk, including need for product or issuer diversification that may support an insurance position within a consumer's financial plan;

    - tax status, including whether the assets used to purchase the annuity or life insurance are or need to be tax deferred;

    - existing assets, including annuity, investment, and life insurance holdings;

    - financial resources generally available for the funding of the annuity or life insurance;

    - liquidity needs and liquid net worth, including whether there are funds other than those being used to purchase the annuity or life insurance that will be available during the surrender period of the annuity or life insurance for emergency or urgent needs, and where those funds are located;

    - financial time horizon; and

    - intended use of the annuity or life policy.

2. An Insurance-Only Person may discuss with the consumer the stock market in general terms including market risks and recent or historic economic activities that are generally known to the public and regularly discussed in public media.

3. An Insurance-Only Person's general discussion outlined in (1) and (2) should only be to the extent that the discussion is a necessary component of the Insurance-Only Person's insurance services and to the extent that the information is used to give the Insurance-Only Person reasonable grounds for believing that the recommendation to purchase, borrow against, exchange, or replace an annuity or life insurance is suitable for the consumer.

4. In his or her general discussion with the consumer, the Insurance-Only Person may discuss and complete suitability, replacement, and exchange or transfer forms as required by Iowa insurance regulations.

5. In his or her general discussion about the expectations of the funds being considered to purchase the annuity or life insurance, the Insurance-Only Person may discuss: that the funds need protection from market risk; that the tax status of the fund and that tax deferral needs to be utilized or maintained; that the funds may be needed to provide a lifetime income stream; that the funds need to earn a guaranteed interest rate; or that there are other funds available during the surrender period of the annuity or life insurance for emergency or urgent needs and where those funds are located.

6. An Insurance-Only Person may have general discussions about balancing risk, diversification, etc., that support an insurance position within a consumer's financial plan.

7. An Insurance-Only Person may provide advice as part of a financial plan. When doing so, an Insurance-Only Person should clearly identify himself or herself as an individual who holds an Iowa insurance license and explain that such license authorizes the person to discuss how annuities or life insurance products may fit into the consumer's financial plan and that he or she is authorized to sell annuity or life insurance products and not sell, recommend or provide advice about securities.

Exhibit 16.2

IV. Prohibited Activities for an Insurance-Only Person.

The following is not intended to be a complete description but rather a description of generally-recognized activities that are specifically prohibited for an Insurance-Only Person:

1. Discussing risks specific to the consumer's individual securities portfolio.

2. Providing advice regarding the consumer's specific securities or securities investment performance, or comparing the consumer's specific securities or securities investment performance with other financial products, including annuity contracts or life insurance policies.

3.   Recommending the liquidation of specific securities, or identifying specific securities that could be used to fund an annuity or life insurance product.

4.   Recommending specific allocations, in dollars or percentages, between insurance and securities products.

5.   Offering research, analysis or recommendations to a consumer regarding specific securities.

6.   Completing securities forms, except for: 1) providing general information to the consumer related to the consumer's existing or new annuity or life insurance product; 2) assisting with forms that are required by the insurance company to complete an insurance transaction; and 3) assisting with forms that are required by Iowa insurance regulations.

7.   Using the following term or terms: investment adviser, securities agent, or investment adviser representative under Iowa securities laws; and similar titles that tend to indicate to customers that the individual is licensed to provide investment advice, that the individual is licensed to sell securities, or otherwise holding the individual out as providing investment advice to others, when the individual is not so licensed.

Exhibit 16.3

VIII. Insurance Producers Who Are Licensed as Investment Advisers or Investment Adviser Representatives.

Insurance licensed producers who are also licensed as investment advisers or investment adviser representatives as defined in Iowa Code Section 502.102(15) and (16)(2011) may be considered providing investment advice and subjecting themselves to securities rules which require them to adhere to a fiduciary standard and additional disclosure rules. Insurance producers that obtain investment advisers licenses to be able to provide advice to clients concerning the sale of a security, such as a mutual fund, to purchase an insurance product, could be subjecting themselves to the jurisdiction of state and federal securities regulators for violation of securities rules pertaining to fiduciary requirements. Persons who solely provide insurance advice as discussed in Section I of this Bulletin, and who disclose that fact to the consumer, should not be concerned with investment adviser or investment adviser representative requirements.

As this section makes clear, an insurance agent who acquires registered advisory status merely to protect himself when selling fixed annuities to consumers when the source of funds is a security may be making his liability situation worse. As the Mitchell case shows us, regulators expect registered investment advisors to act as such. Registration as an advisor is not a free pass for an agent wishing only to sell fixed insurance products, and in Iowa it is not even necessary as "persons who solely provide insurance advice as discussed in Section I of this Bulletin, and who disclose that fact to the consumer, should not be concerned with investment advisor or investment advisor representative requirements."

The authors strongly urge regulators in every state to adopt clear policies such as those in Iowa's Bulletin 11-4 and to publish clear guidance to agents as to how those policies will be administered. But how can agents protect them selves if they are working in states that have not done so ? The authors suggest the following:

- Make it clear in all of your communications with the public what you do and what you do not do. If you sell fixed insurance and annuity products and do not offer securities or advice involving securities, consider using a title such as "insurance agent." Do not describe yourself as an "advisor" or "consultant." Do not say that you offer "objective advice."

- Avoid using "investment terminology" when you are recommending fixed insurance products. Kim O'Brien, Executive Director of the National Association for Fixed Annuities (NAFA) suggests using "premium" to describe contributions to these products. Explain that fixed annuities earn "interest" and avoid terms like "returns" or "gains." If the sales brochure for an indexed annuity you are recommending refers to the "participation rate" in the chosen equity index, be sure to explain that the consumer will not be participating directly in that index but will receive only interest based on the upward movement of the value of that index.

- Consider using a form, to be signed by the annuity buyer, that acknowledges specifically that you have provided no investment advice or specific suggestions regarding the buyer's existing securities. Some Independent Marketing Organizations (IMOs) require such a form. Others, regrettably, do not. Be certain that you understand the policies of the IMOs and insurers with whom you work, especially as to what point-of-sale documents you are permitted to use.

- Consider having annuity buyers complete any required or permitted Suitability Questionnaires themselves in their own handwriting.

- Whenever you present an insurance or annuity product, consider offering the consumer a choice between two or three alternatives. You may wish to develop a form detailing the costs and benefits of each alternative with a space in which the buyer can state, in his or her own words and handwriting, which alternative has been chosen and why. This is particularly important when you are proposing a "bonus" deferred annuity or "life only" immediate annuity. The authors believe that you should never recommend either of those products without presenting the buyer with alternatives. In the case of a "bonus" deferred annuity, you should show that product together with a "nonbonus" contract with as nearly identical benefits as possible. In the case of a "life only" immediate annuity, you should always show an alternative life annuity with a refund feature.

- After every sale, consider sending the buyer a letter summarizing the sales interview. This letter should state what was said and, perhaps even more importantly, what was not said. Example: "In our discussion, I made no recommendation regarding your existing mutual funds as I am not licensed to do that. You said that you would make the decision as to which of your accounts you will withdraw money to fund the annuity I proposed." If the buyer made that decision and completed any transfer or withdrawal forms during that interview, the letter should reflect that you made no specific recommendation and that the decision was entirely the buyer's.

Endnotes

1. In re: Senior Financial Strategies, Inc., 2011 WL 3295987 (Ill. Dep't Sec. case no. 0800064, May 24, 2011 Order). Available at: http://www.ilsos.gov/adminactionssearch/adminactionssearch.

2. Finnigan, David, Letter re: Sale of Indexed Annuity Contracts (January 10, 2013). Available at: http://nafa.com/wp/wp-content/uploads/2013/01/2013-0110-ADVOCACY-IL-NoActionLetter.pdf

3. In re: Richard Lee Van Dyke, (Ill. Dep't Sec. case no. 1100244, June 13, 2013 Amended Notice of Hearing). Available at: http://www.ilsos.gov/adminactionssearch/adminactionssearch.

4. In re: William P. Kelly, 2011 WL 3098335 (Mo. Div. Sec. case no. AP-11-20, July 14, 2011 Consent Order). Available at: http://www.sos.mo.gov/securities/orders/AP-11-20.asp

5. In re: Bill Paul Gibson 2010 WL 2156876 (Mo. Div. Sec. case no. AP-10-12 May 24, 2010 Consent Order). Available at: http://www.sos.mo.gov/securities/orders/AP-10-12.asp

6. In re: Thomas F. Utley, 2011 WL 5146624 (Ill. Dep't Sec. case no. 0900461, July 29, 2011 Order of Prohibition). Available at: http://www.ilsos.gov/adminactionssearch/adminactionssearch.

7. Bulletin No. 14-2009 (Ark. Ins. Dep't, Sept.18, 2009). Available at: http://www.insurance.arkansas.gov/Legal/Bulletins/14-2009.pdf

8. In re: Tracy Wayne Mitchell, 2010 WL 5558000 (Mo. Div. Sec. case no. AP-10-45, December 30, 2010 Order). Available at: http://www.sos.mo.gov/securities/orders/AP-10-45.asp

Appendix A

Actuarial Tables for Taxing Annuities

As referenced in various places throughout the text of this publication, the tables used for taxing annuities appear on the following pages. Included here are gender-based Tables I, II, IIA, and III and unisex Tables V, VI, VIA, and VII. The gender-based tables are to be used if the investment in the contract does not include a post-June 30, 1986 investment in the contract. The unisex tables are to be used if the investment in the contract does include a post-June 30, 1986 investment in the contract.

However, even if there is no investment in the contract after June 30, 1986, an annuitant receiving annuity payments after June 30, 1986 (regardless of when they first began) may elect to treat his entire investment in the contract as post-June 30, 1986 and apply Tables V-VII. This election may be made for any taxable year in which such amounts are received by the taxpayer; it is irrevocable and applies with respect to all amounts the taxpayer receives as an annuity under the contract in the taxable year for which the election is made or in any subsequent tax year.

If investment in the contract includes both a pre-July 1986 investment and a post-June 1986 investment, an election may be made to make separate computations with respect to each portion of the aggregate investment in the contract using with respect to each portion the tables applicable to it. The amount excludable is the sum of the amounts determined under the separate computations. However, the election is not available (i.e., the entire investment must be treated as post-June 1986 investment) if the annuity starting date is after June 30, 1986 and the contract provides an option, whether or not it is exercised, to receive amounts under the contract other than in the form of a life annuity (Reg. §1.72-6(d)).

Treasury regulations extend some of the tables to higher and lower ages, but the partial tables contained here are adequate for all practical purposes. The multiples in Tables I, II, and IIA or V, VI, and VIA need not be adjusted for monthly payments. For quarterly, semi-annual or annual payments, they must be adjusted according to the Frequency of Payment Adjustment Table, below. Table III and Table VII multiples, giving the percentage value of refund features, are never adjusted.

All tables are entered with the age of the annuitant at his or her birthday nearest the annuity starting date.

Frequency of Payment Adjustment Table												
If the number of whole months from the annuity starting date to the first payment date is	0-1	2	3	4	5	6	7	8	9	10	11	12
And payments under the contract are to be made: Annually	+0.5	+0.4	+0.3	+0.2	+0.1	0	0	−0.1	−0.2	−0.3	−0.4	−0.5
Semiannually	+ .2	+ .1	0	0	− .1	− .2	....	....	....	....	....	....
Quarterly	+ .1	0	− .1	....	....	....	....	....	....	....	....	....

Example. Ed Black bought an annuity contract on January 1 which provides him with an annual payment of $4,000 payable on December 31st of each year. His age on birthday nearest the annuity starting date (January 1) is 66. The multiple from Table V for male age 66, is 19.2. This multiple must be adjusted for annual payment by subtracting .5 (19.2 − .5 = 18.7). Thus, his total expected return is $74,800 (18.7 × $4,000). See Treas. Reg. §1.72-5(a)(2).

Table I – Ordinary Life Annuities – One Life – Expected Return Multiples					
Ages			**Ages**		
Male	*Female*	*Multiples*	*Male*	*Female*	*Multiples*
6	11	65.0	59	64	18.9
7	12	64.1	60	65	18.2
8	13	63.2	61	66	17.5
9	14	62.3	62	67	16.9
10	15	61.4	63	68	16.2
11	16	60.4	64	69	15.6
12	17	59.5	65	70	15.0
13	18	58.6	66	71	14.4
14	19	57.7	67	72	13.8
15	20	56.7	68	73	13.2
16	21	55.8	69	74	12.6
17	22	54.9	70	75	12.1
18	23	53.9	71	76	11.6
19	24	53.0	72	77	11.0
20	25	52.1	73	78	10.5
21	26	51.1	74	79	10.1
22	27	50.2	75	80	9.6
23	28	49.3	76	81	9.1
24	29	48.3	77	82	8.7
25	30	47.4	78	83	8.3
26	31	46.5	79	84	7.8
27	32	45.6	80	85	7.5
28	33	44.6	81	86	7.1
29	34	43.7	82	87	6.7
30	35	42.8	83	88	6.3
31	36	41.9	84	89	6.0
32	37	41.0	85	90	5.7
33	38	40.0	86	91	5.4
34	39	39.1	87	92	5.1
35	40	38.2	88	93	4.8
36	41	37.3	89	94	4.5
37	42	36.5	90	95	4.2
38	43	35.6	91	96	4.0
39	44	34.7	92	97	3.7
40	45	33.8	93	98	3.5
41	46	33.0	94	99	3.3
42	47	32.1	95	100	3.1
43	48	31.2	96	101	2.9
44	49	30.4	97	102	2.7
45	50	29.6	98	103	2.5
46	51	28.7	99	104	2.3
47	52	27.9	100	105	2.1
48	53	27.1	101	106	1.9
49	54	26.3	102	107	1.7
50	55	25.5	103	108	1.5
51	56	24.7	104	109	1.3
52	57	24.0	105	110	1.2
53	58	23.2	106	111	1.0
54	59	22.4	107	112	.8
55	60	21.7	108	113	.7
56	61	21.0	109	114	.6
57	62	20.3	110	115	.5
58	63	19.6	111	116	.0

Table II – Ordinary Joint Life and Last Survivor Annuities – Two Lives – Expected Return Multiples

Ages													
	Male	35	36	37	38	39	40	41	42	43	44	45	46	47
Male	Female	40	41	42	43	44	45	46	47	48	49	50	51	52
35	40	46.2	45.7	45.3	44.8	44.4	44.0	43.6	43.3	43.0	42.6	42.3	42.0	41.8
36	41	...	45.2	44.8	44.3	43.9	43.5	43.1	42.7	42.3	42.0	41.7	41.4	41.1
37	42	...	...	44.3	43.8	43.4	42.9	42.5	42.1	41.8	41.4	41.1	40.7	40.4
38	43	...	...	...	43.3	42.9	42.4	42.0	41.6	41.2	40.8	40.5	40.1	39.8
39	44	...	...	...	...	42.4	41.9	41.5	41.0	40.6	40.2	39.9	39.5	39.2
40	45	...	...	...	...	...	41.4	41.0	40.5	40.1	39.7	39.3	38.9	38.6
41	46	...	...	...	...	...	...	40.5	40.0	39.6	39.2	38.8	38.4	38.0
42	47	...	...	...	...	...	...	...	39.6	39.1	38.7	38.2	37.8	37.5
43	48	...	...	...	...	...	...	...	...	38.6	38.2	37.7	37.3	36.9
44	49	...	...	...	...	...	...	...	...	...	37.7	37.2	36.8	36.4
45	50	...	...	...	...	...	...	...	...	...	...	36.8	36.3	35.9
46	51	...	...	...	...	...	...	...	...	...	...	...	35.9	35.4
47	52	...	...	...	...	...	...	...	...	...	...	...	...	35.0

Ages													
	Male	48	49	50	51	52	53	54	55	56	57	58	59	60
Male	Female	53	54	55	56	57	58	59	60	61	62	63	64	65
35	40	41.5	41.3	41.0	40.8	40.6	40.4	40.3	40.1	40.0	39.8	39.7	39.6	39.5
36	41	40.8	40.6	40.3	40.1	39.9	39.7	39.5	39.3	39.2	39.0	38.9	38.8	38.6
37	42	40.2	39.9	39.6	39.4	39.2	39.0	38.8	38.6	38.4	38.3	38.1	38.0	37.9
38	43	39.5	39.2	39.0	38.7	38.5	38.3	38.1	37.9	37.7	37.5	37.3	37.2	37.1
39	44	38.9	38.6	38.3	38.0	37.8	37.6	37.3	37.1	36.9	36.8	36.6	36.4	36.3
40	45	38.3	38.0	37.7	37.4	37.1	36.9	36.6	36.4	36.2	36.0	35.9	35.7	35.5
41	46	37.7	37.3	37.0	36.7	36.5	36.2	36.0	35.7	35.5	35.3	35.1	35.0	34.8
42	47	37.1	36.8	36.4	36.1	35.8	35.6	35.3	35.1	34.8	34.6	34.4	34.2	34.1
43	48	36.5	36.2	35.8	35.5	35.2	34.9	34.7	34.4	34.2	33.9	33.7	33.5	33.3
44	49	36.0	35.6	35.3	34.9	34.6	34.3	34.0	33.8	33.5	33.3	33.0	32.8	32.6
45	50	35.5	35.1	34.7	34.4	34.0	33.7	33.4	33.1	32.9	32.6	32.4	32.2	31.9
46	51	35.0	34.6	34.2	33.8	33.5	33.1	32.8	32.5	32.2	32.0	31.7	31.5	31.3
47	52	34.5	34.1	33.7	33.3	32.9	32.6	32.2	31.4	31.6	31.9	31.1	30.9	30.6
48	53	34.0	33.6	33.2	32.8	32.4	32.0	31.7	31.4	31.1	30.8	30.5	30.2	30.0
49	54	...	33.1	32.7	32.3	31.9	31.5	31.2	30.8	30.5	30.2	29.9	29.6	29.4
50	55	...	...	32.3	31.8	31.4	31.0	30.6	30.3	29.9	29.6	29.3	29.0	28.8
51	56	...	...	...	31.4	30.9	30.5	30.1	29.8	29.4	29.1	28.8	28.5	28.2
52	57	...	...	...	...	30.5	30.1	29.7	29.3	28.9	28.6	28.2	27.9	27.6
53	58	...	...	...	...	...	29.6	29.2	28.8	28.4	28.1	27.7	27.4	27.1
54	59	...	...	...	...	...	...	28.8	28.3	27.9	27.6	27.2	26.9	26.5
55	60	...	...	...	...	...	...	...	27.9	27.5	27.1	26.7	26.4	26.0
56	61	...	...	...	...	...	...	...	...	27.1	26.7	26.3	25.9	25.5
57	62	...	...	...	...	...	...	...	...	...	26.2	25.8	25.4	25.1
58	63	...	...	...	...	...	...	...	...	...	...	25.4	25.0	24.6
59	64	...	...	...	...	...	...	...	...	...	...	...	24.6	24.2
60	65	...	...	...	...	...	...	...	...	...	...	...	...	23.8

Table II – Ordinary Joint Life and Last Survivor Annuities – Two Lives – Expected Return Multiples – continued

Ages														
	Male	**61**	**62**	**63**	**64**	**65**	**66**	**67**	**68**	**69**	**70**	**71**	**72**	**73**
Male	**Female**	**66**	**67**	**68**	**69**	**70**	**71**	**72**	**73**	**74**	**75**	**76**	**77**	**78**
35	40	39.4	39.3	39.2	39.1	39.0	38.9	38.9	38.8	38.8	38.7	38.7	38.6	38.6
36	41	38.5	38.4	38.3	38.2	38.2	38.1	38.0	38.0	37.9	37.9	37.8	37.8	37.7
37	42	37.7	37.6	37.5	37.4	37.3	37.3	37.2	37.1	37.1	37.0	36.9	36.9	36.9
38	43	36.9	36.8	36.7	36.6	36.5	36.4	36.4	36.3	36.2	36.2	36.1	36.0	36.0
39	44	36.2	36.0	35.9	35.8	35.7	35.6	35.5	35.5	35.4	35.3	35.3	35.2	35.2
40	45	35.4	35.3	35.1	35.0	34.9	34.8	34.7	34.6	34.6	34.5	34.4	34.4	34.3
41	46	34.6	34.5	34.4	34.2	34.1	34.0	33.9	33.8	33.8	33.7	33.6	33.5	33.5
42	47	33.9	33.7	33.6	33.5	33.4	33.2	33.1	33.0	33.0	32.9	32.8	32.7	32.7
43	48	33.2	33.0	32.9	32.7	32.6	32.5	32.4	32.3	32.2	32.1	32.0	31.9	31.9
44	49	32.5	32.3	32.1	32.0	31.8	31.7	31.6	31.5	31.4	31.3	31.2	31.1	31.1
45	50	31.8	31.6	31.4	31.3	31.1	31.0	30.8	30.7	30.6	30.5	30.4	30.4	30.3
46	51	31.1	30.9	30.7	30.5	30.4	30.2	30.1	30.0	29.9	29.8	29.7	29.6	29.5
47	52	30.4	30.2	30.0	29.8	29.7	29.5	29.4	29.3	29.1	29.0	28.9	28.8	28.7
48	53	29.8	29.5	29.3	29.2	29.0	28.8	28.7	28.5	28.4	28.3	28.2	28.1	28.0
49	54	29.1	28.9	28.7	28.5	28.3	28.1	28.0	27.8	27.7	27.6	27.5	27.4	27.3
50	55	28.5	28.3	28.1	27.8	27.6	27.5	27.3	27.1	27.0	26.9	26.7	26.6	26.5
51	56	27.9	27.7	27.4	27.2	27.0	26.8	26.6	26.5	26.3	26.2	26.0	25.9	25.8
52	57	27.3	27.1	26.8	26.6	26.4	26.2	26.0	25.8	25.7	25.5	25.4	25.2	25.1
53	58	26.8	26.5	26.2	26.0	25.8	25.6	25.4	25.2	25.0	24.8	24.7	24.6	24.4
54	59	26.2	25.9	25.7	25.4	25.2	25.0	24.7	24.6	24.4	24.2	24.0	23.9	23.8
55	60	25.7	25.4	25.1	24.9	24.6	24.4	24.1	23.9	23.8	23.6	23.4	23.3	23.1
56	61	25.2	24.9	24.6	24.3	24.1	23.8	23.6	23.4	23.2	23.0	22.8	22.6	22.5
57	62	24.7	24.4	24.1	23.8	23.5	23.3	23.0	22.8	22.6	22.4	22.2	22.0	21.9
58	63	24.3	23.9	23.6	23.3	23.0	22.7	22.5	22.2	22.0	21.8	21.6	21.4	21.3
59	64	23.8	23.5	23.1	22.8	22.5	22.2	21.9	21.7	21.5	21.2	21.0	20.9	20.7
60	65	23.4	23.0	22.7	22.3	22.0	21.7	21.4	21.2	20.9	20.7	20.5	20.3	20.1
61	66	23.0	22.6	22.2	21.9	21.6	21.3	21.0	20.7	20.4	20.2	20.0	19.8	19.6
62	67	…	22.2	21.8	21.5	21.1	20.8	20.5	20.2	19.9	19.7	19.5	19.2	19.0
63	68	…	…	21.4	21.1	20.7	20.4	20.1	19.8	19.5	19.2	19.0	18.7	18.5
64	69	…	…	…	20.7	20.3	20.0	19.6	19.3	19.0	18.7	18.5	18.2	18.0
65	70	…	…	…	…	19.9	19.6	19.2	18.9	18.6	18.3	18.0	17.8	17.5
66	71	…	…	…	…	…	19.2	18.8	18.5	18.2	17.9	17.6	17.3	17.1
67	72	…	…	…	…	…	…	18.5	18.1	17.8	17.5	17.2	16.9	16.7
68	73	…	…	…	…	…	…	…	17.8	17.4	17.1	16.8	16.5	16.2
69	74	…	…	…	…	…	…	…	…	17.1	16.7	16.4	16.1	15.8
70	75	…	…	…	…	…	…	…	…	…	16.4	16.1	15.8	15.5
71	76	…	…	…	…	…	…	…	…	…	…	15.7	15.4	15.1
72	77	…	…	…	…	…	…	…	…	…	…	…	15.1	14.8
73	78	…	…	…	…	…	…	…	…	…	…	…	…	14.4

Table II – Ordinary Joint Life and Last Survivor Annuities – Two Lives – Expected Return Multiples – continued

Ages													
	Male	74	75	76	77	78	79	80	81	82	83	84	85
Male	**Female**	79	80	81	82	83	84	85	86	87	88	89	90
35	40	38.6	38.5	38.5	38.5	38.4	38.4	38.4	38.4	38.4	38.4	38.3	38.3
36	41	37.7	37.6	37.6	37.6	37.6	37.5	37.5	37.5	37.5	37.5	37.5	37.4
37	42	36.8	36.8	36.7	36.7	36.7	36.7	36.6	36.6	36.6	36.6	36.6	36.6
38	43	36.0	35.9	35.9	35.8	35.8	35.8	35.8	35.8	35.7	35.7	35.7	35.7
39	44	35.1	35.1	35.0	35.0	35.0	34.9	34.9	34.9	34.9	34.8	34.8	34.8
40	45	34.3	34.2	34.2	34.1	34.1	34.1	34.1	34.0	34.0	34.0	34.0	34.0
41	46	33.4	33.4	33.3	33.3	33.3	33.2	33.2	33.2	33.2	33.1	33.1	33.1
42	47	32.6	32.6	32.5	32.5	32.4	32.4	32.4	32.3	32.3	32.3	32.3	32.3
43	48	31.8	31.8	31.7	31.7	31.6	31.6	31.5	31.5	31.5	31.5	31.4	31.4
44	49	31.0	30.9	30.9	30.8	30.8	30.8	30.7	30.7	30.7	30.6	30.6	30.6
45	50	30.2	30.1	30.1	30.0	30.0	29.9	29.9	29.9	29.8	29.8	29.8	29.8
46	51	29.4	29.4	29.3	29.2	29.2	29.2	29.1	29.1	29.0	29.0	29.0	28.9
47	52	28.7	28.6	28.5	28.5	28.4	28.4	28.3	28.3	28.2	28.2	28.2	28.1
48	53	27.9	27.8	27.8	27.7	27.6	27.6	27.5	27.5	27.5	27.4	27.4	27.4
49	54	27.2	27.1	27.0	26.9	26.9	26.8	26.8	26.7	26.7	26.6	26.6	26.6
50	55	26.4	26.3	26.3	26.2	26.1	26.1	26.0	26.0	25.9	25.9	25.8	25.8
51	56	25.7	25.6	25.5	25.5	25.4	25.3	25.3	25.2	25.2	25.1	25.1	25.0
52	57	25.0	24.9	24.8	24.7	24.7	24.6	24.5	24.5	24.4	24.4	24.3	24.3
53	58	24.3	24.2	24.1	24.0	23.9	23.9	23.8	23.7	23.7	23.6	23.6	23.5
54	59	23.6	23.5	23.4	23.3	23.2	23.2	23.1	23.0	23.0	22.9	22.9	22.8
55	60	23.0	22.9	22.8	22.7	22.6	22.5	22.4	22.3	22.3	22.2	22.2	22.1
56	61	22.3	22.2	22.1	22.0	21.9	21.8	21.7	21.6	21.6	21.5	21.5	21.4
57	62	21.7	21.6	21.5	21.3	21.2	21.1	21.1	21.0	20.9	20.8	20.8	20.7
58	63	21.1	21.0	20.8	20.7	20.6	20.5	20.4	20.3	20.2	20.2	20.1	20.0
59	64	20.5	20.4	20.2	20.1	20.0	19.9	19.8	19.7	19.6	19.5	19.4	19.4
60	65	19.9	19.8	19.6	19.5	19.4	19.3	19.1	19.0	19.0	18.9	18.8	18.7
61	66	19.4	19.2	19.1	18.9	18.8	18.7	18.5	18.4	18.3	18.3	18.2	18.1
62	67	18.8	18.7	18.5	18.3	18.2	18.1	18.0	17.8	17.7	17.7	17.6	17.5
63	68	18.3	18.1	18.0	17.8	17.6	17.5	17.4	17.3	17.2	17.1	17.0	16.9
64	69	17.8	17.6	17.4	17.3	17.1	17.0	16.8	16.7	16.6	16.5	16.4	16.3
65	70	17.3	17.1	16.9	16.7	16.6	16.4	16.3	16.2	16.0	15.9	15.8	15.8
66	71	16.9	16.6	16.4	16.3	16.1	15.9	15.8	15.6	15.5	15.4	15.3	15.2
67	72	16.4	16.2	16.0	15.8	15.6	15.4	15.3	15.1	15.0	14.9	14.8	14.7
68	73	16.0	15.7	15.5	15.3	15.1	15.0	14.8	14.6	14.5	14.4	14.3	14.2
69	74	15.6	15.3	15.1	14.9	14.7	14.5	14.3	14.2	14.0	13.9	13.8	13.7
70	75	15.2	14.9	14.7	14.5	14.3	14.1	13.9	13.7	13.6	13.4	13.3	13.2
71	76	14.8	14.5	14.3	14.1	13.8	13.6	13.5	13.3	13.1	13.0	12.8	12.7
72	77	14.5	14.2	13.9	13.7	13.5	13.2	13.0	12.9	12.7	12.5	12.4	12.3
73	78	14.1	13.8	13.6	13.3	13.1	12.9	12.7	12.5	12.3	12.1	12.0	11.8
74	79	13.8	13.5	13.2	13.0	12.7	12.5	12.3	12.1	11.9	11.7	11.6	11.4
75	80	...	13.2	12.9	12.6	12.4	12.2	11.9	11.7	11.5	11.4	11.2	11.0
76	81	...	...	12.6	12.3	12.1	11.8	11.6	11.4	11.2	11.0	10.8	10.7
77	82	...	...	...	12.1	11.8	11.5	11.3	11.1	10.8	10.7	10.5	10.3
78	83	...	...	...	...	11.5	11.2	11.0	10.7	10.5	10.3	10.1	10.0
79	84	...	...	...	...	...	11.0	10.7	10.5	10.2	10.0	9.8	9.6
80	85	...	...	...	...	...	...	10.4	10.2	10.0	9.7	9.5	9.3
81	86	...	...	...	...	...	...	...	9.9	9.7	9.5	9.3	9.1
82	87	...	...	...	...	...	...	...	...	9.4	9.2	9.0	8.8
83	88	...	...	...	...	...	...	...	...	...	9.0	8.7	8.5
84	89	...	...	...	...	...	...	...	...	...	...	8.5	8.3
85	90	...	...	...	...	...	...	...	...	...	...	...	8.1

Table IIA–Annuities for Joint Life Only – Two Lives – Expected Return Multiples

Ages Male	Ages Female	35 / 40	36 / 41	37 / 42	38 / 43	39 / 44	40 / 45	41 / 46	42 / 47	43 / 48	44 / 49	45 / 50	46 / 51	47 / 52
35	40	30.3	29.9	29.4	29.0	28.5	28.0	27.5	27.0	26.5	26.0	25.5	24.9	24.4
36	41	...	29.5	29.0	28.6	28.2	27.7	27.2	26.7	26.2	25.7	25.2	24.7	24.2
37	42	...	...	28.6	28.2	27.8	27.3	26.9	26.4	25.9	25.5	25.0	24.4	23.9
38	43	...	...	...	27.8	27.4	27.0	26.5	26.1	25.6	25.2	24.7	24.2	23.7
39	44	...	...	...	...	27.0	26.6	26.2	25.8	25.3	24.8	24.4	23.9	23.4
40	45	...	...	...	...	...	26.2	25.8	25.4	25.0	24.5	24.1	23.6	23.1
41	46	...	...	...	...	...	...	25.4	25.0	24.6	24.2	23.8	23.3	22.9
42	47	...	...	...	...	...	...	...	24.6	24.2	23.8	23.4	23.0	22.6
43	48	...	...	...	...	...	...	...	...	23.9	23.5	23.1	22.7	22.2
44	49	...	...	...	...	...	...	...	...	...	23.1	22.7	22.3	21.9
45	50	...	...	...	...	...	...	...	...	...	...	22.4	22.0	21.6
46	51	...	...	...	...	...	...	...	...	...	...	...	21.6	21.2
47	52	...	...	...	...	...	...	...	...	...	...	...	...	20.9

Ages Male	Ages Female	48 / 53	49 / 54	50 / 55	51 / 56	52 / 57	53 / 58	54 / 59	55 / 60	56 / 61	57 / 62	58 / 63	59 / 64	60 / 65
35	40	23.8	23.3	22.7	22.1	21.6	21.0	20.4	19.8	19.3	18.7	18.1	17.5	17.0
36	41	23.6	23.1	22.5	22.0	21.4	20.8	20.3	19.7	19.1	18.6	18.0	17.4	16.9
37	42	23.4	22.9	22.3	21.8	21.2	20.7	20.1	19.6	19.0	18.4	17.9	17.3	16.8
38	43	23.2	22.6	22.1	21.6	21.1	20.5	20.0	19.4	18.9	18.3	17.8	17.2	16.7
39	44	22.9	22.4	21.9	21.4	20.9	20.3	19.8	19.3	18.7	18.2	17.7	17.1	16.6
40	45	22.7	22.2	21.7	21.2	20.7	20.1	19.6	19.1	18.6	18.0	17.5	17.0	16.5
41	46	22.4	21.9	21.4	20.9	20.4	19.9	19.4	18.9	18.4	17.9	17.4	16.9	16.3
42	47	22.1	21.6	21.2	20.7	20.2	19.7	19.2	18.7	18.2	17.7	17.2	16.7	16.2
43	48	21.8	21.4	20.9	20.5	20.0	19.5	19.0	18.6	18.1	17.6	17.1	16.6	16.1
44	49	21.5	21.1	20.6	20.2	19.8	19.3	18.8	18.4	17.9	17.4	16.9	16.4	15.9
45	50	21.2	20.8	20.4	19.9	19.5	19.1	18.6	18.1	17.7	17.2	16.7	16.3	15.8
46	51	20.9	20.5	20.1	19.7	19.2	18.8	18.4	17.9	17.5	17.0	16.6	16.1	15.6
47	52	20.5	20.1	19.8	19.4	19.0	18.5	18.1	17.7	17.3	16.8	16.4	15.9	15.5
48	53	20.2	19.8	19.4	19.1	18.7	18.3	17.9	17.5	17.0	16.6	16.2	15.7	15.3
49	54	...	19.5	19.1	18.8	18.4	18.0	17.6	17.2	16.8	16.4	16.0	15.5	15.1
50	55	...	...	18.8	18.4	18.1	17.7	17.3	16.9	16.6	16.2	15.8	15.3	14.9
51	56	...	...	...	18.1	17.8	17.4	17.0	16.7	16.3	15.9	15.5	15.1	14.7
52	57	...	...	...	...	17.4	17.1	16.8	16.4	16.0	15.7	15.3	14.9	14.5
53	58	...	...	...	...	...	16.8	16.4	16.1	15.8	15.4	15.1	14.7	14.3
54	59	...	...	...	...	...	...	16.1	15.8	15.5	15.1	14.8	14.4	14.1
55	60	...	...	...	...	...	...	...	15.5	15.2	14.9	14.5	14.2	13.9
56	61	...	...	...	...	...	...	...	...	14.9	14.6	14.3	13.9	13.6
57	62	...	...	...	...	...	...	...	...	...	14.3	14.0	13.7	13.4
58	63	...	...	...	...	...	...	...	...	...	...	13.7	13.4	13.1
59	64	...	...	...	...	...	...	...	...	...	...	...	13.1	12.8
60	65	...	...	...	...	...	...	...	...	...	...	...	...	12.6

Table IIA–Annuities for Joint Life Only – Two Lives – Expected Return Multiples – continued														
Ages														
	Male	**61**	**62**	**63**	**64**	**65**	**66**	**67**	**68**	**69**	**70**	**71**	**72**	**73**
Male	**Female**	**66**	**67**	**68**	**69**	**70**	**71**	**72**	**73**	**74**	**75**	**76**	**77**	**78**
35	40	16.4	15.8	15.3	14.7	14.2	13.7	13.1	12.6	12.1	11.6	11.1	10.7	10.2
36	41	16.3	15.8	15.2	14.7	14.1	13.6	13.1	12.6	12.1	11.6	11.1	10.6	10.2
37	42	16.2	15.7	15.1	14.6	14.1	13.6	13.0	12.5	12.0	11.5	11.1	10.6	10.1
38	43	16.1	15.6	15.1	14.5	14.0	13.5	13.0	12.5	12.0	11.5	11.0	10.6	10.1
39	44	16.0	15.5	15.0	14.5	13.9	13.4	12.9	12.4	11.9	11.5	11.0	10.5	10.1
40	45	15.9	15.4	14.9	14.4	13.9	13.4	12.9	12.4	11.9	11.4	11.0	10.5	10.0
41	46	15.8	15.3	14.8	14.3	13.8	13.3	12.8	12.3	11.8	11.4	10.9	10.5	10.0
42	47	15.7	13.2	14.7	14.2	13.7	13.2	12.7	12.3	11.8	11.3	10.9	10.4	10.0
43	48	15.6	15.1	14.6	14.1	13.6	13.1	12.7	12.2	11.7	11.3	10.8	10.4	9.9
44	49	15.5	15.0	14.5	14.0	13.5	13.1	12.6	12.1	11.7	11.2	10.8	10.3	9.9
45	50	15.3	14.8	14.4	13.9	13.4	13.0	12.5	12.0	11.6	11.1	10.7	10.3	9.8
46	51	15.2	14.7	14.2	13.8	13.3	12.9	12.4	12.0	11.5	11.1	10.6	10.2	9.8
47	52	13.0	14.6	14.1	13.7	13.2	12.8	12.3	11.9	11.4	11.0	10.6	10.1	9.7
48	53	14.9	14.4	14.0	13.5	13.1	12.6	12.2	11.8	11.3	10.9	10.5	10.1	9.7
49	54	14.7	14.3	13.8	13.4	13.0	12.5	12.1	11.7	11.3	10.8	10.4	10.0	9.6
50	55	14.5	14.1	13.7	13.3	12.8	12.4	12.0	11.6	11.2	10.7	10.3	9.9	9.5
51	56	14.3	13.9	13.5	13.1	12.7	12.3	11.9	11.5	11.1	10.7	10.3	9.9	9.5
52	57	14.1	13.7	13.3	12.9	12.3	12.1	11.7	11.3	10.9	10.6	10.2	9.0	9.4
53	58	13.9	13.6	13.2	12.8	12.4	12.0	11.6	11.2	10.0	10.5	10.1	9.7	9.3
54	59	13.7	13.4	13.0	12.6	12.2	11.9	11.5	11.1	10.7	10.3	10.0	9.6	9.2
55	60	13.5	13.2	12.0	12.4	12.1	11.7	11.3	11.0	10.6	10.2	9.9	9.5	9.1
56	61	13.3	12.9	12.6	12.2	11.9	11.5	11.2	10.8	10.3	10.1	9.0	9.4	9.0
57	62	13.0	12.7	12.4	12.1	11.7	11.4	11.0	10.7	10.3	10.0	9.6	9.3	8.9
58	63	12.8	12.5	12.2	11.8	11.5	11.2	10.9	10.3	10.2	9.8	9.5	9.2	8.8
59	64	12.6	12.3	11.9	11.6	11.3	11.0	10.7	10.4	10.0	9.7	9.4	9.1	8.7
60	65	12.3	12.0	11.7	11.4	11.1	10.8	10.3	10.2	9.9	9.6	9.3	8.9	8.6
61	66	12.0	11.8	11.5	11.2	10.9	10.6	10.3	10.0	9.7	9.4	9.1	8.0	8.5
62	67	…	11.5	11.2	11.0	10.7	10.4	10.1	9.8	9.6	9.3	9.0	8.7	8.4
63	68	…	…	11.0	10.7	10.5	10.2	9.9	9.7	9.4	9.1	8.8	0.5	8.2
64	69	…	…	…	10.5	10.2	10.0	9.7	9.0	9.2	0.9	0.7	8.1	8.1
65	70	…	…	…	…	10.0	9.9	9.5	9.3	9.0	8.8	8.5	8.0	8.0
66	71	…	…	…	…	…	9.5	9.3	9.1	8.8	8.6	0.3	8.1	7.8
67	72	…	…	…	…	…	…	9.1	8.9	8.6	8.4	8.1	7.9	7.7
68	73	…	…	…	…	…	…	…	8.6	8.4	8.2	8.0	7.7	7.3
69	74	…	…	…	…	…	…	…	…	8.2	9.0	7.8	7.6	7.3
70	75	…	…	…	…	…	…	…	…	…	7.8	7.6	7.4	7.2
71	76	…	…	…	…	…	…	…	…	…	…	7.4	7.2	7.0
72	77	…	…	…	…	…	…	…	…	…	…	…	7.0	6.8
73	78	…	…	…	…	…	…	…	…	…	…	…	…	6.7

Table IIA–Annuities for Joint Life Only – Two Lives – Expected Return Multiples – continued

Ages														
	Male	74	75	76	77	78	79	80	81	82	83	84	85	86
Male	Female	79	80	81	82	83	84	85	86	87	88	89	90	91
35	40	9.7	9.3	8.9	8.5	8.1	7.7	7.3	6.9	6.6	6.2	5.9	5.6	5.3
36	41	9.7	9.3	8.9	8.4	8.0	7.7	7.3	6.9	6.6	6.2	5.9	5.6	5.3
37	42	9.7	9.3	8.8	8.4	8.0	7.6	7.3	6.9	6.5	6.2	5.9	5.6	5.3
38	43	9.7	9.2	8.8	8.4	8.0	7.6	7.2	6.9	6.5	6.2	5.9	5.6	5.3
39	44	9.6	9.2	8.8	8.4	8.0	7.6	7.2	6.9	6.5	6.2	5.9	5.6	5.3
40	45	9.6	9.2	8.8	8.4	8.0	7.6	7.2	6.9	6.5	6.2	5.9	5.5	5.2
41	46	9.6	9.2	8.7	8.3	7.9	7.6	7.2	6.8	6.5	6.2	5.8	5.5	5.2
42	47	9.5	9.1	8.7	8.3	7.9	7.5	7.2	6.8	6.5	6.2	5.8	5.5	5.2
43	48	9.5	9.1	8.7	8.3	7.9	7.5	7.2	6.8	6.5	6.1	5.8	5.5	5.2
44	49	9.5	9.0	8.6	8.2	7.9	7.5	7.1	6.8	6.4	6.1	5.8	5.5	5.2
45	50	9.4	9.0	8.6	8.2	7.8	7.5	7.1	6.8	6.4	6.1	5.8	5.5	5.2
40	51	9.4	9.0	8.6	8.2	7.8	7.4	7.1	6.7	6.4	6.1	5.8	5.5	5.2
47	52	9.3	8.9	8.5	8.1	7.8	7.4	7.1	6.7	6.4	6.1	5.8	5.5	5.2
48	53	9.3	8.9	8.5	8.1	7.7	7.4	7.0	6.7	6.4	6.0	5.7	5.4	5.1
49	54	9.2	8.8	8.4	8.1	7.7	7.3	7.0	6.7	6.3	6.0	5.7	5.4	5.1
50	55	9.1	8.8	8.4	8.0	7.7	7.3	7.0	6.6	6.3	6.0	5.7	5.4	5.1
51	56	9.1	8.7	8.3	8.0	7.6	7.3	6.9	6.6	6.3	6.0	5.7	5.4	5.1
52	57	9.0	8.6	8.3	7.9	7.6	7.2	6.9	6.6	6.2	5.9	5.6	5.4	5.1
53	58	8.9	8.6	8.2	7.9	7.5	7.2	6.9	6.5	6.2	5.9	5.6	5.3	5.1
54	59	8.9	8.5	8.2	7.8	7.5	7.1	6.8	6.5	6.2	5.9	5.6	5.3	5.0
55	60	8.8	8.4	8.1	7.7	7.4	7.1	6.8	6.4	6.1	5.8	5.6	5.3	5.0
56	61	8.7	8.4	8.0	7.7	7.3	7.0	6.7	6.4	6.1	5.8	5.5	5.3	5.0
57	62	8.6	8.3	7.9	7.6	7.3	7.0	6.7	6.4	6.1	5.8	5.5	5.2	5.0
58	63	8.5	8.2	7.9	7.5	7.2	6.9	6.6	6.3	6.0	5.7	5.5	5.2	4.9
59	64	8.4	8.1	7.8	7.5	7.1	6.8	6.5	6.3	6.0	5.7	5.4	5.2	4.9
60	65	8.3	8.0	7.7	7.4	7.1	6.8	6.5	6.2	5.9	5.6	5.4	5.1	4.9
61	66	8.2	7.9	7.6	7.3	7.0	6.7	6.4	6.1	5.9	5.6	5.3	5.1	4.8
62	67	8.1	7.8	7.5	7.2	6.9	6.6	6.4	6.1	5.8	5.5	5.3	5.0	4.8
63	68	8.0	7.7	7.4	7.1	6.8	6.6	6.3	6.0	5.7	5.5	5.2	5.0	4.7
64	69	7.8	7.6	7.3	7.0	6.7	6.5	6.2	5.9	5.7	5.4	5.2	4.9	4.7
65	70	7.7	7.4	7.2	6.9	6.6	6.4	6.1	5.9	5.6	5.4	5.1	4.9	4.7
66	71	7.6	7.3	7.1	6.8	6.5	6.3	6.0	5.8	5.5	5.3	5.1	4.8	4.6
67	72	7.4	7.2	6.9	6.7	6.4	6.2	6.0	5.7	5.5	5.2	5.0	4.8	4.6
68	73	7.3	7.0	6.8	6.6	6.3	6.1	5.9	5.6	5.4	5.2	4.9	4.7	4.5
69	74	7.1	6.9	6.7	6.4	6.2	6.0	5.8	5.5	5.3	5.1	4.9	4.7	4.5
70	75	7.0	6.8	6.5	6.3	6.1	5.9	5.7	5.4	5.2	5.0	4.8	4.6	4.4
71	76	6.8	6.6	6.4	6.2	6.0	5.8	5.6	5.3	5.1	4.9	4.7	4.5	4.3
72	77	6.6	6.4	6.3	6.1	5.9	5.7	5.5	5.3	5.0	4.9	4.7	4.5	4.3
73	78	6.5	6.3	6.1	5.9	5.7	5.5	5.3	5.1	5.0	4.8	4.6	4.4	4.2
74	79	6.3	6.1	6.0	5.8	5.6	5.4	5.2	5.0	4.9	4.7	4.5	4.3	4.1
75	80	..	6.0	5.8	5.6	5.5	5.3	5.1	4.9	4.8	4.6	4.4	4.2	4.1
76	81	..	..	5.6	5.5	5.3	5.2	5.0	4.8	4.7	4.5	4.3	4.1	4.0
77	82	..	..	..	5.3	5.2	5.0	4.9	4.7	4.5	4.4	4.2	4.1	3.9
78	83	..	..	..	..	5.0	4.9	4.7	4.6	4.4	4.3	4.1	4.0	3.8
79	84	..	..	..	..	..	4.7	4.6	4.5	4.3	4.2	4.0	3.9	3.7
80	85	..	..	..	..	..	..	4.5	4.3	4.2	4.1	3.9	3.8	3.6
81	86	..	..	..	..	..	..	..	4.2	4.1	3.9	3.8	3.7	3.6
82	87		..	..	..	..	..	..	..	4.0	3.8	3.7	3.6	3.5
83	88		..	..	..	..	..	..	..	..	3.7	3.6	3.5	3.4
84	89		..	..	..	..	..	..	..	..	..	3.5	3.4	3.3
85	90		..	..	..	..	..	..	..	..	..	..	3.3	3.2
86	91		..	..	..	..	..	..	..	..	..	..	..	3.1

Table III – Percent Value of Refund Feature

Ages		Duration of guaranteed amount											
		1	2	3	4	5	6	7	8	9	10	11	12
Male	Female	Yr	Yrs	Yrs	Yrs	Yrs	Yrs	Yrs	Yrs	Yrs	Yrs	Yrs	Yrs
		%	%	%	%	%	%	%	%	%	%	%	%
6	11	..	..	..	..	..	..	..	..	1	1	1	1
7	12	..	..	..	..	..	..	..	..	1	1	1	1
8	13	..	..	..	..	..	..	..	1	1	1	1	1
9	14	..	..	..	..	..	..	..	1	1	1	1	1
10	15	..	..	..	..	..	..	..	1	1	1	1	1
11	16	..	..	..	..	..	..	..	1	1	1	1	1
12	17	..	..	..	..	..	..	..	1	1	1	1	1
13	18	..	..	..	..	..	..	..	1	1	1	1	1
14	19	..	..	..	..	..	..	..	1	1	1	1	1
15	20	..	..	..	..	..	..	..	1	1	1	1	1
16	21	..	..	..	..	..	..	..	1	1	1	1	1
17	22	..	..	..	..	..	..	..	1	1	1	1	1
18	23	..	..	..	..	..	..	..	1	1	1	1	1
19	24	..	..	..	..	..	..	..	1	1	1	1	1
20	25	..	..	..	..	..	..	..	1	1	1	1	1
21	26	..	..	..	..	..	..	..	1	1	1	1	1
22	27	..	..	..	..	..	..	1	1	1	1	1	1
23	28	..	..	..	..	..	..	1	1	1	1	1	1
24	29	..	..	..	..	..	..	1	1	1	1	1	1
25	30	..	..	..	..	..	..	1	1	1	1	1	1
26	31	..	..	..	..	..	1	1	1	1	1	1	1
27	32	..	..	..	..	..	1	1	1	1	1	1	1
28	33	..	..	..	..	..	1	1	1	1	1	1	1
29	34	..	..	..	..	..	1	1	1	1	1	1	1
30	35	..	..	..	..	1	1	1	1	1	1	1	2
31	36	..	..	..	..	1	1	1	1	1	1	1	2
32	37	..	..	..	..	1	1	1	1	1	1	2	2
33	38	..	..	..	1	1	1	1	1	1	1	2	2
34	39	..	..	..	1	1	1	1	1	1	2	2	2
35	40	..	..	..	1	1	1	1	1	2	2	2	2
36	41	..	..	..	1	1	1	1	1	2	2	2	2
37	42	..	..	1	1	1	1	1	2	2	2	2	3
38	43	..	..	1	1	1	1	1	2	2	2	2	3
39	44	..	..	1	1	1	1	2	2	2	2	3	3
40	45	..	..	1	1	1	1	2	2	2	3	3	3
41	46	..	..	1	1	1	1	2	2	2	3	3	3
42	47	..	..	1	1	1	2	2	2	3	3	3	4
43	48	..	1	1	1	1	2	2	2	3	3	4	4
44	49	..	1	1	1	1	2	2	3	3	3	4	4
45	50	..	1	1	1	2	2	2	3	3	4	4	5

Table III – Percent Value of Refund Feature – continued

Ages		Duration of guaranteed amount											
Male	Female	1 Yr	2 Yrs	3 Yrs	4 Yrs	5 Yrs	6 Yrs	7 Yrs	8 Yrs	9 Yrs	10 Yrs	11 Yrs	12 Yrs
		%	%	%	%	%	%	%	%	%	%	%	%
46	51	..	1	1	1	2	2	3	3	3	4	4	5
47	52	..	1	1	1	2	2	3	3	4	4	5	5
48	53	..	1	1	2	2	2	3	3	4	5	5	6
49	54	..	1	1	2	2	3	3	4	4	5	5	6
50	55	..	1	1	2	2	3	3	4	5	5	6	7
51	56	..	1	1	2	3	3	4	4	5	6	6	7
52	57	1	1	2	2	3	3	4	5	5	6	7	8
53	58	1	1	2	2	3	4	4	5	6	7	7	8
54	59	1	1	2	2	3	4	5	5	6	7	8	9
53	60	1	1	2	3	3	4	5	6	7	8	8	9
56	61	1	1	2	3	4	4	5	6	7	8	9	10
57	62	1	1	2	3	4	5	6	7	8	9	10	11
58	63	1	2	2	3	4	5	6	7	8	9	10	12
59	64	1	2	3	4	5	6	7	8	9	10	11	12
60	65	1	2	3	4	5	6	7	8	10	11	12	13
61	66	1	2	3	4	5	6	8	9	10	12	13	14
62	67	1	2	3	4	6	7	8	10	11	12	14	15
63	68	1	2	4	5	6	7	9	10	12	13	15	16
64	69	1	3	4	5	7	8	9	11	13	14	16	17
65	70	1	3	4	6	7	9	10	12	13	15	17	19
66	71	1	3	4	6	8	9	11	13	14	16	18	20
67	72	2	3	5	6	8	10	12	14	15	17	19	21
68	73	2	3	5	7	9	11	13	14	16	18	21	23
69	74	2	4	6	7	9	11	13	16	18	20	22	24
70	75	2	4	6	8	10	12	14	17	19	21	23	26
71	76	2	4	6	9	11	13	15	18	20	22	25	27
72	77	2	5	7	9	12	14	16	19	21	24	26	29
73	78	2	5	7	10	12	15	18	20	23	25	28	30
74	79	3	5	8	11	13	16	19	22	24	27	30	32
75	80	3	6	8	11	14	17	20	23	26	29	31	34
76	81	3	6	9	12	15	18	21	24	27	30	33	36
77	82	3	7	10	13	16	20	23	26	29	32	35	38
78	83	4	7	11	14	17	21	24	28	31	34	37	40
79	84	4	8	11	15	19	22	26	29	33	36	39	42
80	85	4	8	12	16	20	24	27	31	34	38	41	44
81	86	4	9	13	17	21	25	29	33	36	40	43	46
82	87	5	9	14	18	23	27	31	35	38	42	45	48
83	88	5	10	15	19	24	28	33	37	40	44	47	50
84	89	5	11	16	21	26	30	34	38	42	46	49	52
85	90	6	11	17	22	27	32	36	41	44	48	51	55

Table III – Percent Value of Refund Feature – continued

Ages		Duration of guaranteed amount											
		13	14	15	16	17	18	19	20	21	22	23	24
Male	Female	Yr	Yrs	Yrs	Yrs	Yrs	Yrs	Yrs	Yrs	Yrs	Yrs	Yrs	Yrs
		%	%	%	%	%	%	%	%	%	%	%	%
6	11	1	1	1	1	1	1	1	1	1	1	1	2
7	12	1	1	1	1	1	1	1	1	1	1	1	2
8	13	1	1	1	1	1	1	1	1	1	1	1	2
9	14	1	1	1	1	1	1	1	1	1	1	1	2
10	15	1	1	1	1	1	1	1	1	1	1	2	2
11	16	1	1	1	1	1	1	1	1	1	1	2	2
12	17	1	1	1	1	1	1	1	1	1	1	2	2
13	18	1	1	1	1	1	1	1	1	1	2	2	2
14	19	1	1	1	1	1	1	1	1	1	2	2	2
15	20	1	1	1	1	1	1	1	1	1	2	2	2
16	21	1	1	1	1	1	1	1	1	2	2	2	2
17	22	1	1	1	1	1	1	1	1	2	2	2	2
18	23	1	1	1	1	1	1	1	2	2	2	2	2
19	24	1	1	1	1	1	1	2	2	2	2	2	2
20	25	1	1	1	1	1	1	2	2	2	2	2	2
21	26	1	1	1	1	1	2	2	2	2	2	2	2
22	27	1	1	1	1	1	2	2	2	2	2	2	3
23	28	1	1	1	1	2	2	2	2	2	2	2	3
24	29	1	1	1	2	2	2	2	2	2	2	3	3
25	30	1	1	1	2	2	2	2	2	2	3	3	3
26	31	1	1	2	2	2	2	2	2	3	3	3	3
27	32	1	2	2	2	2	2	2	3	3	3	3	3
28	33	1	2	2	2	2	2	3	3	3	3	3	4
29	34	2	2	2	2	2	2	3	3	3	3	4	4
30	35	2	2	2	2	2	3	3	3	3	4	4	4
31	36	2	2	2	2	3	3	3	3	4	4	4	5
32	37	2	2	2	3	3	3	3	4	4	4	5	5
33	38	2	2	3	3	3	3	4	4	4	5	5	5
34	39	2	3	3	3	3	4	4	4	5	5	5	6
35	40	2	3	3	3	4	4	4	5	5	5	6	6
36	41	3	3	3	4	4	4	5	5	5	6	6	7
37	42	3	3	3	4	4	4	5	5	6	6	7	7
38	43	3	3	4	4	4	5	5	6	6	7	7	8
39	44	3	4	4	4	5	5	6	6	7	7	8	8
40	45	4	4	4	5	5	6	6	7	7	8	8	9
41	46	4	4	4	5	6	6	7	7	8	8	9	9
42	47	4	5	5	5	6	6	7	8	8	9	9	10
43	48	4	5	5	6	6	7	8	8	9	9	10	11
44	49	5	5	6	6	7	7	8	9	9	10	11	12
45	50	5	6	6	7	7	8	9	9	10	11	12	12

Table III – Percent Value of Refund Feature – continued

Ages		Duration of guaranteed amount											
		13	14	15	16	17	18	19	20	21	22	23	24
Male	Female	Yr	Yrs	Yrs	Yrs	Yrs	Yrs	Yrs	Yrs	Yrs	Yrs	Yrs	Yrs
		%	%	%	%	%	%	%	%	%	%	%	%
46	51	5	6	7	7	8	9	9	10	11	12	12	13
47	52	6	7	7	8	9	9	10	11	12	12	13	14
48	53	6	7	8	8	9	10	11	12	12	13	14	15
49	54	7	8	8	9	10	11	11	12	13	14	15	16
50	55	7	8	9	10	11	11	12	13	14	15	16	17
51	56	8	9	10	10	11	12	13	14	15	16	17	18
52	57	8	9	10	11	12	13	14	15	16	17	18	20
53	58	9	10	11	12	13	14	15	16	17	19	20	21
54	59	10	11	12	13	14	15	16	17	18	20	21	22
55	60	10	11	13	14	15	16	17	18	20	21	22	24
56	61	11	12	13	15	16	17	18	20	21	22	24	25
57	62	12	13	14	16	17	18	20	21	22	24	25	27
58	63	13	14	15	17	18	19	21	22	24	25	27	28
59	64	14	15	16	18	19	21	22	24	25	27	28	30
60	65	15	16	18	19	20	22	24	25	27	28	30	32
61	66	16	17	19	20	22	23	25	27	28	30	32	33
62	67	17	18	20	22	23	25	27	28	30	32	33	35
63	68	18	20	21	23	25	26	28	30	32	33	35	37
64	69	19	21	23	24	26	28	30	32	33	35	37	39
65	70	20	22	24	26	28	30	32	33	35	37	39	41
66	71	22	24	26	28	29	31	33	35	37	39	41	43
67	72	23	25	27	29	31	33	35	37	39	41	43	45
68	73	25	27	29	31	33	35	37	39	41	43	45	47
69	74	26	28	30	33	35	37	39	41	43	45	47	48
70	75	28	30	32	34	37	39	41	43	45	47	49	50
71	76	29	32	34	36	39	41	43	45	47	49	51	52
72	77	31	34	36	38	41	43	45	47	49	51	53	54
73	78	33	35	38	40	43	45	47	49	51	53	55	56
74	79	35	37	40	42	45	47	49	51	53	55	57	58
75	80	37	39	42	44	47	49	51	53	55	57	58	60
76	81	39	41	44	46	49	51	53	55	57	59	60	62
77	82	41	43	46	48	51	53	55	57	59	61	62	64
78	83	43	45	48	50	53	55	57	59	61	62	64	65
79	84	45	48	50	53	55	57	59	61	63	64	66	67
80	85	47	50	52	55	57	59	61	63	64	66	67	69
81	86	49	52	54	57	59	61	63	65	66	68	69	70
82	87	51	54	56	59	61	63	65	66	68	69	71	72
83	88	53	56	58	61	63	65	66	68	70	71	72	73
84	89	55	58	60	63	65	67	68	70	71	73	74	75
85	90	57	60	62	65	67	68	70	71	73	74	75	76

Table III – Percent Value of Refund Feature – continued

Ages		Duration of guaranteed amount										
		25	26	27	28	29	30	31	32	33	34	35
Male	Female	Yr	Yrs	Yrs	Yrs	Yrs	Yrs	Yrs	Yrs	Yrs	Yrs	Yrs
		%	%	%	%	%	%	%	%	%	%	%
6	11	2	2	2	2	2	2	2	2	2	2	2
7	12	2	2	2	2	2	2	2	2	2	2	3
8	13	2	2	2	2	2	2	2	2	2	2	3
9	14	2	2	2	2	2	2	2	2	2	3	3
10	15	2	2	2	2	2	2	2	2	3	3	3
11	16	2	2	2	2	2	2	2	2	3	3	3
12	17	2	2	2	2	2	2	2	3	3	3	3
13	18	2	2	2	2	2	2	2	3	3	3	3
14	19	2	2	2	2	2	2	3	3	3	3	3
15	20	2	2	2	2	2	3	3	3	3	3	3
16	21	2	2	2	2	3	3	3	3	3	3	4
17	22	2	2	2	2	3	3	3	3	3	4	4
18	23	2	2	2	3	3	3	3	3	4	4	4
19	24	2	2	3	3	3	3	3	4	4	4	4
20	23	2	3	3	3	3	3	4	4	4	4	5
21	26	3	3	3	3	3	4	4	4	4	5	5
22	27	3	3	3	3	4	4	4	4	5	5	5
23	28	3	3	3	3	4	4	4	5	5	5	5
24	29	3	3	3	4	4	4	5	5	5	5	6
25	30	3	3	4	4	4	5	5	5	6	6	6
26	31	3	4	4	4	5	5	5	6	6	6	7
27	32	4	4	4	5	5	5	6	6	6	7	7
28	33	4	4	5	5	5	6	6	6	7	7	8
29	34	4	5	5	5	6	6	6	7	7	8	8
30	35	5	5	5	6	6	6	7	7	8	8	9
31	36	5	5	6	6	6	7	7	8	8	9	9
32	37	5	6	6	7	7	7	8	8	9	10	10
33	38	6	6	7	7	7	8	8	9	10	10	11
34	39	6	7	7	8	8	9	9	10	10	11	12
35	40	7	7	8	8	9	9	10	10	11	12	12
36	41	7	8	8	9	9	10	10	11	12	13	13
37	42	8	8	9	9	10	11	11	12	13	13	14
38	43	8	9	9	10	11	11	12	13	13	14	15
39	44	9	9	10	11	11	12	13	14	14	15	16
40	45	9	10	11	11	12	13	14	15	15	16	17
41	46	10	11	11	12	13	14	15	16	16	17	18
42	47	11	12	12	13	14	15	16	17	18	18	19
43	46	12	12	13	14	15	16	17	18	19	20	21
44	49	12	13	14	15	16	17	18	19	20	21	22
45	50	13	14	15	16	17	18	19	20	21	22	23
46	51	14	15	16	17	18	19	20	21	22	24	25

Table III – Percent Value of Refund Feature – continued

Ages		Duration of guaranteed amount										
		25	26	27	28	29	30	31	32	33	34	35
Male	Female	Yr	Yrs	Yrs	Yrs	Yrs	Yrs	Yrs	Yrs	Yrs	Yrs	Yrs
		%	%	%	%	%	%	%	%	%	%	%
47	52	15	16	17	18	19	20	21	23	24	25	26
48	53	16	17	18	19	20	22	23	24	25	26	28
49	54	17	18	19	21	22	23	24	25	27	28	29
50	55	18	20	21	22	23	24	26	27	28	29	31
51	56	20	21	22	23	25	26	27	28	30	31	32
52	57	21	22	23	25	26	27	29	30	31	33	34
53	58	22	24	25	26	28	29	30	32	33	34	36
54	59	24	25	26	28	29	31	32	33	35	36	38
55	60	25	26	28	29	31	32	34	35	36	38	39
56	61	27	28	29	31	32	34	35	37	38	40	41
57	62	28	30	31	33	34	36	37	39	40	41	43
58	63	30	31	33	34	36	37	39	40	42	43	45
59	61	31	33	35	36	38	39	41	42	44	45	47
60	65	33	35	36	38	40	41	43	44	46	47	48
61	66	35	37	38	40	41	43	44	46	47	49	50
62	67	37	38	40	42	43	45	46	48	49	51	52
63	68	39	40	42	44	45	47	48	50	51	52	54
64	69	41	42	44	46	47	49	50	52	53	54	55
65	70	42	44	46	47	49	50	52	53	55	56	57
66	71	44	46	48	49	51	52	54	55	56	58	59
67	72	46	48	50	51	53	54	56	57	58	59	61
68	73	48	50	52	53	55	56	57	59	60	61	62
69	74	50	52	53	55	56	58	59	60	62	63	64
70	75	52	54	55	57	58	60	61	62	63	64	65
71	76	54	56	57	59	60	61	63	64	65	66	67
72	77	56	58	59	60	62	63	64	65	66	67	68
73	78	58	59	61	62	64	65	66	67	68	68	70
74	79	60	61	63	64	65	66	67	68	69	70	71
75	80	62	63	64	66	67	68	69	70	71	72	72
76	81	63	65	66	67	68	69	70	71	72	73	..
77	82	65	66	68	69	70	71	72	73	74	..	..
78	83	67	68	69	70	71	72	73	74	..	..	..
79	84	68	70	71	72	73	74	75	..	..	..	..
80	85	70	71	72	73	74	75	..	..	..	..	..
81	86	72	73	74	75	75	..	..	..	..	..	..
82	87	73	74	75	76	..	..	..	..	..	..	..
83	88	74	75	76	..	..	..	..	..	..	..	..
84	89	76	77	..	..	..	..	..	..	..	..	..
85	90	77	..	..	..	..	..	..	..	..	..	..

Table V – Ordinary Life Annuities – One Life – Expected Return Multiples

Age	Multiple	Age	Multiple	Age	Multiple
5	76.6	42	40.6	79	10.0
6	75.6	43	39.6	80	9.5
7	74.7	44	38.7	81	8.9
8	73.7	45	37.7	82	8.4
9	72.7	46	36.8	63	7.9
10	71.7	47	35.9	84	7.4
11	70.7	48	34.9	85	6.9
12	69.7	49	34.0	86	6.5
13	68.8	50	33.1	87	6.1
14	67.8	51	32.2	88	5.7
15	66.8	52	31.3	89	5.3
16	65.8	53	30.4	90	5.0
17	64.8	54	29.5	91	4.7
18	63.9	55	28.6	92	4.4
19	62.9	56	27.7	93	4.1
20	61.9	57	26.8	94	3.9
21	60.9	58	25.9	95	3.7
22	59.9	59	25.0	96	3.4
23	59.0	60	24.2	97	3.2
24	58.0	61	23.3	98	3.0
25	57.0	62	22.5	99	2.8
26	56.0	63	21.6	100	2.7
27	55.1	64	20.8	101	2.5
28	54.1	65	20.0	102	2.3
29	53.1	66	19.2	103	2.1
30	52.2	67	18.4	104	1.9
31	51.2	68	17.6	105	1.8
32	50.2	69	16.8	106	1.6
33	49.3	70	16.0	107	1.4
34	48.3	71	15.3	108	1.3
35	47.3	72	14.6	109	1.1
36	46.4	73	13.9	110	1.0
37	45.4	74	13.2	111	.9
38	44.4	75	12.5	112	.8
39	43.5	76	11.9	113	.7
40	42.5	77	11.2	114	.6
41	41.5	78	10.6	115	.5

Table VI – Ordinary Joint Life and Last Survivor Annuities – Two Lives – Expected Return Multiples

AGES	35	36	37	38	39	40	41	42	43	44	45	46	47	48	49	50
35	54.0	...	...	...	...	...	...	...	...	...	...	...	...	...	...	...
36	53.5	53.0	...	...	...	...	...	...	...	...	...	...	...	...	...	...
37	53.0	52.5	52.0	...	...	...	...	...	...	...	...	...	...	...	...	...
38	52.6	52.0	51.5	51.0	...	...	...	...	...	...	...	...	...	...	...	...
39	52.2	51.6	51.0	50.5	50.0	...	...	...	...	...	...	...	...	...	...	...
40	51.8	51.2	50.6	50.0	49.5	49.0	...	...	...	...	...	...	...	...	...	...
41	51.4	50.8	50.2	49.6	49.1	48.5	48.0	...	...	...	...	...	...	...	...	...
42	51.1	50.4	49.8	49.2	48.6	48.1	47.5	47.0	...	...	...	...	...	...	...	...
43	50.8	50.1	49.5	48.8	48.2	47.6	47.1	46.6	46.0	...	...	...	...	...	...	...
44	50.5	49.8	49.1	48.5	47.8	47.2	46.7	46.1	45.6	45.1	...	...	...	...	...	...
45	50.2	49.5	48.8	48.1	47.5	46.9	46.3	45.7	45.1	44.6	44.1	...	...	...	...	...
46	50.0	49.2	48.5	47.8	47.2	46.5	45.9	45.3	44.7	44.1	43.6	43.1	...	...	...	...
47	49.7	49.0	48.3	47.5	46.8	46.2	45.5	44.9	44.3	43.7	43.2	42.6	42.1	...	...	...
48	49.5	48.8	48.0	47.3	46.6	45.9	45.2	44.5	43.9	43.3	42.7	42.2	41.7	41.2	...	...
49	49.3	48.5	47.8	47.0	46.3	45.6	44.9	44.2	43.6	42.9	42.3	41.8	41.2	40.7	40.2	...
50	49.2	48.4	47.6	46.8	46.0	45.3	44.6	43.9	43.2	42.6	42.0	41.4	40.8	40.2	39.7	39.2
51	49.0	48.2	47.4	46.6	45.8	45.1	44.3	43.6	42.9	42.2	41.6	41.0	40.4	39.8	39.3	38.7
52	48.8	48.0	47.2	46.4	45.6	44.8	44.1	43.3	42.6	41.9	41.3	40.6	40.0	39.4	38.8	38.3
53	48.7	47.9	47.0	46.2	45.4	44.6	43.9	43.1	42.4	41.7	41.0	40.3	39.7	39.0	38.4	37.9
54	48.6	47.7	46.9	46.0	45.2	44.4	43.6	42.9	42.1	41.4	40.7	40.0	39.3	38.7	38.1	37.5
55	48.5	47.6	46.7	45.9	45.1	44.2	43.4	42.7	41.9	41.2	40.4	39.7	39.0	38.4	37.7	37.1
56	48.3	47.5	46.6	45.8	44.9	44.1	43.3	42.5	41.7	40.9	40.2	39.5	38.7	38.1	37.4	36.8
57	48.3	47.4	46.5	45.6	44.8	43.9	43.1	42.3	41.5	40.7	40.0	39.2	38.5	37.8	37.1	36.4
58	48.2	47.3	46.4	45.5	44.7	43.8	43.0	42.1	41.3	40.5	39.7	39.0	38.2	37.5	36.8	36.1
59	48.1	47.2	46.3	45.4	44.5	43.7	42.8	42.0	41.2	40.4	39.6	38.8	38.0	37.3	36.6	35.9
60	48.0	47.1	46.2	45.3	44.4	43.6	42.7	41.9	41.0	40.2	39.4	38.6	37.8	37.1	36.3	35.6
61	47.9	47.0	46.1	45.2	44.3	43.5	42.6	41.7	40.9	40.0	39.2	38.4	37.6	36.9	36.1	35.4
62	47.9	47.0	46.0	45.1	44.2	43.4	42.5	41.6	40.8	39.9	39.1	38.3	37.5	36.7	35.9	35.1
63	47.8	46.9	46.0	45.1	44.2	43.3	42.4	41.5	40.6	39.8	38.9	38.1	37.3	36.5	35.7	34.9
64	47.8	46.8	45.9	45.0	44.1	43.2	42.3	41.4	40.5	39.7	38.8	38.0	37.2	36.3	35.5	34.8
65	47.7	46.8	45.9	44.9	44.0	43.1	42.2	41.3	40.4	39.6	38.7	37.9	37.0	36.2	35.4	34.6
66	47.7	46.7	45.8	44.9	44.0	43.1	42.2	41.3	40.4	39.5	38.6	37.8	36.9	36.1	35.2	34.4
67	47.6	46.7	45.8	44.8	43.9	43.0	42.1	41.2	40.3	39.4	38.5	37.7	36.8	36.0	35.1	34.3
68	47.6	46.7	45.7	44.8	43.9	42.9	42.0	41.1	40.2	39.3	38.4	37.6	36.7	35.8	35.0	34.2
69	47.6	46.6	45.7	44.8	43.8	42.9	42.0	41.1	40.2	39.3	38.4	37.5	36.6	35.7	34.9	34.1
70	47.5	46.6	45.7	44.7	43.8	42.9	41.9	41.0	40.1	39.2	38.3	37.4	36.5	35.7	34.8	34.0
71	47.5	46.6	45.6	44.7	43.8	42.8	41.9	41.0	40.1	39.1	38.2	37.3	36.5	35.6	34.7	33.9
72	47.5	46.6	45.6	44.7	43.7	42.8	41.9	40.9	40.0	39.1	38.2	37.3	36.4	35.5	34.6	33.8
73	47.5	46.5	45.6	44.7	43.7	42.8	41.8	40.9	40.0	39.0	38.1	37.2	36.3	35.4	34.6	33.7
74	47.5	46.5	45.6	44.7	43.7	42.7	41.8	40.9	39.9	39.0	38.1	37.2	36.3	35.4	34.5	33.6
75	47.4	46.5	45.5	44.7	43.6	42.7	41.8	40.8	39.9	39.0	38.1	37.1	36.2	35.3	34.5	33.6
76	47.4	46.5	45.5	44.7	43.6	42.7	41.7	40.8	39.9	38.9	38.0	37.1	36.2	35.3	34.4	33.5
77	47.4	46.5	45.5	44.7	43.6	42.7	41.7	40.8	39.8	38.9	38.0	37.1	36.2	35.3	34.4	33.5
78	47.4	46.4	45.5	44.5	43.6	42.6	41.7	40.7	39.8	38.9	38.0	37.0	36.1	35.2	34.3	33.4
79	47.4	46.4	45.5	44.5	43.6	42.6	41.7	40.7	39.8	38.9	37.9	37.0	36.1	35.2	34.3	33.4
80	47.4	46.4	45.5	44.5	43.6	42.6	41.7	40.7	39.8	38.8	37.9	37.0	36.1	35.2	34.2	33.4
81	47.4	46.4	45.5	44.5	43.5	42.6	41.6	40.7	39.8	38.8	37.9	37.0	36.0	35.1	34.2	33.3
82	47.4	46.4	45.4	44.5	43.5	42.6	41.6	40.7	39.7	38.8	37.9	36.9	36.0	35.1	34.2	33.3
83	47.4	46.4	45.4	44.5	43.5	42.6	41.6	40.7	39.7	38.8	37.9	36.9	36.0	35.1	34.2	33.3
84	47.4	46.4	45.4	44.5	43.5	42.6	41.6	40.7	39.7	38.8	37.8	36.9	36.0	35.0	34.1	33.2
85	47.4	46.4	45.4	44.5	43.5	42.6	41.6	40.7	39.7	38.8	37.8	36.9	36.0	35.0	34.1	33.2
86	47.3	46.4	45.4	44.5	43.5	42.5	41.6	40.6	39.7	38.8	37.8	36.9	36.0	35.0	34.1	33.2
87	47.3	46.4	45.4	44.5	43.5	42.5	41.6	40.6	39.7	38.7	37.8	36.9	35.9	35.0	34.1	33.2
88	47.3	46.4	45.4	44.5	43.5	42.5	41.6	40.6	39.7	38.7	37.8	36.9	35.9	35.0	34.1	33.2
89	47.3	46.4	45.4	44.4	43.5	42.5	41.6	40.6	39.7	38.7	37.8	36.9	35.9	35.0	34.1	33.2
90	47.3	46.4	45.4	44.4	43.5	42.5	41.6	40.6	39.7	38.7	37.8	36.9	35.9	35.0	34.1	33.2

Table VI – Ordinary Joint Life and Last Survivor Annuities – Two Lives – Expected Return Multiples – continued

AGES	51	52	53	54	55	56	57	58	59	60	61	62	63	64	65	66
51	38.2	...	...	...	...	...	...	...	...	...	...	...	...	...	...	...
52	37.8	37.3	...	...	...	...	...	...	...	...	...	...	...	...	...	...
53	37.3	36.8	36.3	...	...	...	...	...	...	...	...	...	...	...	...	...
54	36.9	36.4	35.8	35.3	...	...	...	...	...	...	...	...	...	...	...	...
55	36.5	55.9	35.4	34.9	34.4	...	...	...	...	...	...	...	...	...	...	...
56	36.1	35.6	35.0	34.4	33.9	33.4	...	...	...	...	...	...	...	...	...	...
57	35.8	35.2	34.6	34.0	33.5	33.0	32.5	...	...	...	...	...	...	...	...	...
58	35.5	34.8	34.2	33.6	33.1	32.5	32.0	31.5	...	...	...	...	...	...	...	...
59	35.2	34.5	33.9	33.3	32.7	32.1	31.6	31.1	30.6	...	...	...	...	...	...	...
60	34.9	34.2	33.6	32.9	32.3	31.7	31.2	30.6	30.1	29.7	...	...	...	...	...	...
61	34.6	33.9	33.3	32.6	32.0	31.4	30.8	30.2	29.7	29.2	28.7	...	...	...	...	...
62	34.4	33.7	33.0	32.3	31.7	31.0	30.4	29.9	29.3	28.8	28.3	27.8	...	...	...	...
63	34.2	33.5	32.7	32.0	31.4	30.7	30.1	29.5	28.9	28.4	27.8	27.3	26.9	...	...	...
64	34.0	33.2	32.5	31.8	31.1	30.4	29.8	29.2	28.6	28.0	27.4	26.9	26.4	25.9	...	...
65	33.8	33.0	32.3	31.6	30.9	30.2	29.5	28.9	28.2	27.6	27.1	26.5	26.0	25.5	25.0	...
66	33.6	32.9	32.1	31.4	30.6	29.9	29.2	28.6	27.9	27.3	26.7	26.1	25.6	25.1	24.6	24.1
67	33.5	32.7	31.9	31.2	30.4	29.7	29.0	28.3	27.6	27.0	26.4	25.8	25.2	24.7	24.2	23.7
68	33.4	32.5	31.8	31.0	30.2	29.5	28.8	28.1	27.4	26.7	26.1	25.5	24.9	24.3	23.8	23.3
69	33.2	32.4	31.6	30.8	30.1	29.3	28.6	27.8	27.1	26.5	25.8	25.2	24.6	24.0	23.4	22.9
70	33.1	32.3	31.5	30.7	29.9	29.1	28.4	27.6	26.9	26.2	25.6	24.9	24.3	23.7	23.1	22.5
71	33.0	32.2	31.4	30.5	29.7	29.0	28.2	27.5	26.7	26.0	25.3	24.7	24.0	23.4	22.8	22.2
72	32.9	32.1	31.2	30.4	29.6	28.8	28.1	27.3	26.5	25.8	25.1	24.4	23.8	23.1	22.5	21.9
73	32.8	32.0	31.1	30.3	29.5	28.7	27.9	27.1	26.4	25.6	24.9	24.2	23.5	22.9	22.2	21.6
74	32.8	31.9	31.1	30.2	29.4	28.6	27.8	27.0	26.2	25.5	24.7	24.0	23.3	22.7	22.0	21.4
75	32.7	31.8	31.0	30.1	29.3	28.5	27.7	26.9	26.1	25.3	24.6	23.8	23.1	22.4	21.8	21.1
76	32.6	31.8	30.9	30.1	29.2	28.4	27.6	26.8	26.0	25.2	24.4	23.7	23.0	22.3	21.6	20.9
77	32.6	31.7	30.8	30.0	29.1	28.3	27.5	26.7	25.9	25.1	24.3	23.6	22.8	22.1	21.4	20.7
78	32.5	31.7	30.8	29.9	29.1	28.2	27.4	26.6	25.8	25.0	24.2	23.4	22.7	21.9	21.2	20.5
79	32.5	31.6	30.7	29.9	29.0	28.2	27.3	26.5	25.7	24.9	24.1	23.3	22.6	21.8	21.1	20.4
80	32.5	31.6	30.7	29.8	29.0	28.1	27.3	26.4	25.6	24.8	24.0	23.2	22.4	21.7	21.0	20.2
81	32.4	31.5	30.7	29.8	28.9	28.1	27.2	26.4	25.5	24.7	23.9	23.1	22.3	21.6	20.8	20.1
82	32.4	31.5	30.6	29.7	28.9	28.0	27.2	26.3	25.5	24.6	23.8	23.0	22.3	21.5	20.7	20.0
83	32.4	31.5	30.6	29.7	28.8	28.0	27.1	26.3	25.4	24.6	23.8	23.0	22.2	21.4	20.6	19.9
84	32.3	31.4	30.6	29.7	28.8	27.9	27.1	26.2	25.4	24.5	23.7	22.9	22.1	21.3	20.5	19.8
85	32.3	31.4	30.5	29.6	28.8	27.9	27.0	26.2	25.3	24.5	23.7	22.8	22.0	21.3	20.5	19.7
86	32.3	31.4	30.5	29.6	28.7	27.9	27.0	26.1	25.3	24.5	23.6	22.8	22.0	21.2	20.4	19.6
87	32.3	31.4	30.5	29.6	28.7	27.8	27.0	26.1	25.3	24.4	23.6	22.8	21.9	21.1	20.4	19.6
88	32.3	31.4	30.5	29.6	28.7	27.8	27.0	26.1	25.2	24.4	23.5	22.7	21.9	21.1	20.3	19.5
89	32.3	31.4	30.5	29.6	28.7	27.8	26.9	26.1	25.2	24.4	23.5	22.7	21.9	21.1	20.3	19.5
90	32.3	31.3	30.5	29.5	28.7	27.8	26.9	26.1	25.2	24.3	23.5	22.7	21.8	21.0	20.2	19.4

Table VI – Ordinary Joint Life and Last Survivor Annuities – Two Lives – Expected Return Multiples – continued

AGES	67	68	69	70	71	72	73	74	75	76	77	78	79	80	81	82
67	23.2	...	...	...	...	...	...	...	...	...	...	...	...	...	...	...
68	22.8	22.3	...	...	...	...	...	...	...	...	...	...	...	...	...	...
69	22.4	21.9	21.5	...	...	...	...	...	...	...	...	...	...	...	...	...
70	22.0	21.5	21.1	20.6	...	...	...	...	...	...	...	...	...	...	...	...
71	21.7	21.2	20.7	20.2	19.8	...	...	...	...	...	...	...	...	...	...	...
72	21.3	20.8	20.3	19.8	19.4	18.9	...	...	...	...	...	...	...	...	...	...
73	21.0	20.5	20.0	19.4	19.0	18.5	18.1	...	...	...	...	...	...	...	...	...
74	20.8	20.2	19.6	19.1	18.6	18.2	17.7	17.3	...	...	...	...	...	...	...	...
75	20.5	19.9	19.3	18.8	18.3	17.8	17.3	16.9	16.5	...	...	...	...	...	...	...
76	20.3	19.7	19.1	18.5	18.0	17.5	17.0	16.5	16.1	15.7	...	...	...	...	...	...
77	20.1	19.4	18.8	18.3	17.7	17.2	16.7	16.2	15.8	15.4	15.0	...	...	...	...	...
78	19.9	19.2	18.6	18.0	17.5	16.9	16.4	15.9	15.4	15.0	14.6	14.2	...	...	...	...
79	19.7	19.0	18.4	17.8	17.2	16.7	16.1	15.6	15.1	14.7	14.3	13.9	13.5	...	...	...
80	19.5	18.9	18.2	17.6	17.0	16.4	15.9	15.4	14.9	14.4	14.0	13.5	13.2	12.8	...	...
81	19.4	18.7	18.1	17.4	16.8	16.2	15.7	15.1	14.6	14.1	13.7	13.2	12.8	12.5	12.1	...
82	19.3	18.6	17.9	17.3	16.6	16.0	15.5	14.9	14.4	13.9	13.4	13.0	12.5	12.2	11.8	11.5
83	19.2	18.5	17.8	17.1	16.5	15.9	15.3	14.7	14.2	13.7	13.2	12.7	12.3	11.9	11.5	11.1
84	19.1	18.4	17.7	17.0	16.3	15.7	15.1	14.5	14.0	13.5	13.0	12.5	12.0	11.6	11.2	10.9
85	19.0	18.3	17.6	16.9	16.2	15.6	15.0	14.4	13.8	13.3	12.8	12.3	11.8	11.4	11.0	10.6
86	18.9	18.2	17.5	16.8	16.1	15.5	14.8	14.2	13.7	13.1	12.6	12.1	11.6	11.2	10.8	10.4
87	18.8	18.1	17.4	16.7	16.0	15.4	14.7	14.1	13.5	13.0	12.4	11.9	11.4	11.0	10.6	10.1
88	18.8	18.0	17.3	16.6	15.9	15.3	14.6	14.0	13.4	12.8	12.3	11.8	11.3	10.8	10.4	10.0
89	18.7	18.0	17.2	16.5	15.8	15.2	14.5	13.9	13.3	12.7	12.2	11.6	11.1	10.7	10.2	9.8
90	18.7	17.9	17.2	16.5	15.8	15.1	14.5	13.8	13.2	12.6	12.1	11.5	11.0	10.5	10.1	9.6

AGES	83	84	85	86	87	88	89	90
83	10.8	...	...	...	...	...	...	...
84	10.5	10.2	...	...	...	...	...	...
85	10.2	9.9	9.6	...	...	...	...	...
86	10.0	9.7	9.3	9.1	...	...	...	...
87	9.8	9.4	9.1	8.8	8.5	...	...	...
88	9.6	9.2	8.9	8.6	8.3	8.0	...	...
89	9.4	9.0	8.7	8.3	8.1	7.8	7.5	...
90	9.2	8.8	8.5	8.2	7.9	7.6	7.3	7.1

Table VIA – Annuities for Joint Life Only – Two Lives – Expected Return Multiples

AGES	35	36	37	38	39	40	41	42	43	44	45	46	47	48	49	50
35	40.7	...	...	...	...	...	...	...	...	...	...	...	...	...	...	...
36	40.2	39.7	...	...	...	...	...	...	...	...	...	...	...	...	...	...
37	39.7	39.3	38.8	...	...	...	...	...	...	...	...	...	...	...	...	...
38	39.2	38.7	38.3	37.9	...	...	...	...	...	...	...	...	...	...	...	...
39	38.6	38.2	37.8	37.4	36.9	...	...	...	...	...	...	...	...	...	...	...
40	38.0	37.7	37.3	36.9	36.4	36.0	...	...	...	...	...	...	...	...	...	...
41	37.4	37.1	36.7	36.3	35.9	35.5	35.1	...	...	...	...	...	...	...	...	...
42	36.8	36.5	36.2	35.8	35.4	35.0	34.6	34.1	...	...	...	...	...	...	...	...
43	36.2	35.9	35.6	35.2	34.9	34.5	34.1	33.7	33.2	...	...	...	...	...	...	...
44	35.5	35.2	34.9	34.6	34.3	34.0	33.6	33.2	32.8	32.3	...	...	...	...	...	...
45	34.8	34.6	34.3	34.0	33.7	33.4	33.0	32.7	32.3	31.8	31.4	...	...	...	...	...
46	34.1	33.9	33.7	33.4	33.1	32.8	32.5	32.1	31.8	31.4	30.9	30.3	...	...	...	...
47	33.4	33.2	33.0	32.8	32.5	32.2	31.9	31.6	31.2	30.8	30.5	30.0	29.6	...	...	...
48	32.7	32.5	32.3	32.1	31.8	31.6	31.3	31.0	30.7	30.3	30.0	29.6	29.2	28.7	...	...
49	32.0	31.8	31.6	31.4	31.2	30.9	30.7	30.4	30.1	29.8	29.4	29.1	28.7	28.3	27.9	...
50	31.3	31.1	30.9	30.7	30.5	30.3	30.0	29.8	29.5	29.2	28.9	28.5	28.2	27.4	27.4	27.0
51	30.5	30.4	30.2	30.0	29.8	29.6	29.4	29.2	28.9	28.6	28.3	28.0	27.7	27.3	26.9	26.5
52	29.7	29.6	29.5	29.3	29.1	28.9	28.7	28.5	28.3	28.0	27.7	27.4	27.1	26.8	26.5	26.1
53	29.0	28.9	28.7	28.6	28.4	28.2	28.1	27.9	27.6	27.4	27.1	26.9	26.6	26.3	25.9	25.6
54	28.2	28.1	28.0	27.8	27.7	27.5	27.4	27.2	27.0	26.8	26.5	26.3	26.0	25.7	25.4	25.1
55	27.4	27.3	27.2	27.1	27.0	26.8	26.7	26.5	26.3	26.1	25.9	25.7	25.4	25.1	24.9	24.6
56	26.7	26.6	26.5	26.3	26.2	26.1	26.0	25.8	25.6	25.4	25.2	25.0	24.8	24.6	24.3	24.0
57	25.9	25.8	25.7	25.6	25.5	25.4	25.2	25.1	24.9	24.8	24.6	24.4	24.2	24.0	23.7	23.5
58	25.1	25.0	24.9	24.8	24.7	24.6	24.5	24.4	24.2	24.1	23.9	23.7	23.5	23.3	23.1	22.9
59	24.3	24.2	24.1	24.1	24.0	23.9	23.8	23.6	23.5	23.4	23.2	23.1	22.9	22.7	22.5	22.3
60	23.5	23.4	23.4	23.3	23.2	23.1	23.0	22.9	22.8	22.7	22.5	22.4	22.2	22.1	21.9	21.7
61	22.7	22.6	22.6	22.5	22.4	22.4	22.3	22.2	22.1	22.0	21.8	21.7	21.6	21.4	21.2	21.1
62	21.9	21.9	21.8	21.7	21.7	21.6	21.5	21.4	21.3	21.2	21.1	21.0	20.9	20.7	20.6	20.4
63	21.1	21.1	21.0	21.0	20.9	20.8	20.8	20.7	20.6	20.5	20.4	20.3	20.2	20.1	19.9	19.8
64	20.3	20.3	20.2	20.2	20.1	20.1	20.0	20.0	19.9	19.8	19.7	19.6	19.5	19.4	19.3	19.1
65	19.6	19.5	19.5	19.4	19.4	19.3	19.3	19.2	19.1	19.1	19.0	18.9	18.8	18.7	18.6	18.5
66	18.8	18.8	18.7	18.7	18.6	18.6	18.5	18.5	18.4	18.4	18.3	18.2	18.1	18.0	17.9	17.8
67	18.0	18.0	18.0	17.9	17.9	17.9	17.8	17.8	17.7	17.6	17.6	17.5	17.4	17.3	17.3	17.2
68	17.3	17.3	17.2	17.2	17.2	17.1	17.1	17.0	17.0	16.9	16.9	16.8	16.7	16.7	16.6	16.5
69	16.5	16.5	16.5	16.5	16.4	16.4	16.4	16.3	16.3	16.2	16.2	16.1	16.1	16.0	15.9	15.8
70	15.8	15.8	15.8	15.7	15.7	15.7	15.6	15.6	15.6	15.5	15.5	15.4	15.4	15.3	15.3	15.2
71	15.1	15.1	15.1	15.0	15.0	15.0	15.0	14.9	14.9	14.9	14.8	14.8	14.7	14.7	14.6	14.5
72	14.4	14.4	14.4	14.3	14.3	14.3	14.3	14.2	14.2	14.2	14.1	14.1	14.1	14.0	14.0	13.9
73	13.7	13.7	13.7	13.7	13.7	13.6	13.6	13.6	13.6	13.5	13.5	13.5	13.4	13.4	13.3	13.3
74	13.1	13.0	13.0	13.0	13.0	13.0	13.0	12.9	12.9	12.9	12.8	12.8	12.8	12.7	12.7	12.7
75	12.4	12.4	12.4	12.4	12.3	12.3	12.3	12.3	12.3	12.2	12.2	12.2	12.2	12.1	12.1	12.1
76	11.8	11.8	11.7	11.7	11.7	11.7	11.7	11.7	11.6	11.6	11.6	11.6	11.6	11.5	11.5	11.5
77	11.1	11.1	11.1	11.1	11.1	11.1	11.1	11.1	11.0	11.0	11.0	11.0	11.0	10.9	10.9	10.9
78	10.5	10.5	10.5	10.5	10.5	10.5	10.5	10.5	10.5	10.4	10.4	10.4	10.4	10.4	10.3	10.3
79	10.0	10.0	9.9	9.9	9.9	9.9	9.9	9.9	9.9	9.9	9.9	9.8	9.8	9.8	9.8	9.8
80	9.4	9.4	9.4	9.4	9.4	9.4	9.4	9.3	9.3	9.3	9.3	9.3	9.3	9.3	9.2	9.2
81	8.9	8.8	8.8	8.8	8.8	8.8	8.8	8.8	8.8	8.8	8.8	8.8	8.7	8.7	8.7	8.7
82	8.3	8.3	8.3	8.3	8.3	8.3	8.3	8.3	8.3	8.3	8.3	8.2	8.2	8.2	8.2	8.2
83	7.8	7.8	7.8	7.8	7.8	7.8	7.8	7.8	7.6	7.8	7.8	7.8	7.7	7.7	7.7	7.7
84	7.3	7.3	7.3	7.3	7.3	7.3	7.3	7.3	7.3	7.3	7.3	7.3	7.3	7.3	7.3	7.2
85	6.9	6.9	6.9	6.9	6.9	6.9	6.9	6.9	6.9	6.9	6.8	6.8	6.8	6.8	6.8	6.8
86	6.5	6.5	6.5	6.5	6.4	6.4	6.4	6.4	6.4	6.4	6.4	6.4	6.4	6.4	6.4	6.4
87	6.1	6.0	6.0	6.0	6.0	6.0	6.0	6.0	6.0	6.0	6.0	6.0	6.0	6.0	6.0	6.0
88	5.7	5.7	5.7	5.7	5.7	5.7	5.7	5.6	5.6	5.6	5.6	5.6	5.6	5.6	5.6	5.6
89	5.3	5.3	5.3	5.3	5.3	5.3	5.3	5.3	5.3	5.3	5.3	5.3	5.3	5.3	5.3	5.3
90	5.0	5.0	5.0	5.0	5.0	5.0	5.0	5.0	5.0	5.0	5.0	4.9	4.9	4.9	4.9	4.9

Table VIA – Annuities for Joint Life Only – Two Lives – Expected Return Multiples – continued

AGES	51	52	53	54	55	56	57	58	59	60	61	62	63	64	65	66
51	26.1	…	…	…	…	…	…	…	…	…	…	…	…	…	…	…
52	25.7	25.3	…	…	…	…	…	…	…	…	…	…	…	…	…	…
53	25.2	24.8	24.4	…	…	…	…	…	…	…	…	…	…	…	…	…
54	24.7	24.4	24.0	23.6	…	…	…	…	…	…	…	…	…	…	…	…
55	24.2	23.9	23.5	23.2	22.7	…	…	…	…	…	…	…	…	…	…	…
56	23.7	23.4	23.1	22.7	22.3	21.9	…	…	…	…	…	…	…	…	…	…
57	23.2	22.9	22.6	22.2	21.9	21.5	21.1	…	…	…	…	…	…	…	…	…
58	22.6	22.4	22.1	21.7	21.4	21.1	20.7	20.3	…	…	…	…	…	…	…	…
59	22.1	21.8	21.5	21.2	20.9	20.6	20.3	19.9	19.5	…	…	…	…	…	…	…
60	21.5	21.2	21.0	20.7	20.4	20.1	19.8	19.5	19.1	18.7	…	…	…	…	…	…
61	20.9	20.6	20.4	20.2	19.9	19.6	19.3	19.0	18.7	18.3	17.9	…	…	…	…	…
62	20.2	20.0	19.8	19.6	19.4	19.1	18.8	18.5	18.2	17.9	17.5	17.1	…	…	…	…
63	19.6	19.4	19.2	19.0	18.8	18.6	18.3	18.0	17.7	17.4	17.1	16.8	16.4	…	…	…
64	19.0	18.8	18.6	18.5	18.3	18.0	17.8	17.5	17.3	17.0	16.7	16.3	16.0	15.6	…	…
65	18.3	18.2	18.0	17.9	17.7	17.5	17.3	17.0	16.8	16.5	16.2	15.9	15.6	15.3	14.9	…
66	17.7	17.6	17.4	17.3	17.1	16.9	16.7	16.5	16.3	16.0	15.8	15.5	15.2	14.9	14.5	14.2
67	17.1	16.9	16.8	16.7	16.5	16.3	16.2	16.0	15.8	15.5	15.3	15.0	14.7	14.5	14.1	13.8
68	16.4	16.3	16.2	16.1	15.9	15.8	15.6	15.4	15.2	15.0	14.8	14.6	14.3	14.0	13.7	13.4
69	15.8	15.7	15.6	15.4	15.3	15.2	15.0	14.9	14.7	14.5	14.3	14.1	13.9	13.6	13.3	13.1
70	15.1	15.0	14.9	14.8	14.7	14.6	14.5	14.3	14.2	14.0	13.8	13.6	13.4	13.2	12.9	12.6
71	14.5	14.4	14.3	14.2	14.1	14.0	13.9	13.8	13.6	13.5	13.3	13.1	12.9	12.7	12.5	12.2
72	13.8	13.8	13.7	13.6	13.5	13.4	13.3	13.2	13.1	12.9	12.8	12.6	12.4	12.3	12.0	11.8
73	13.2	13.2	13.1	13.0	13.0	12.9	12.8	12.7	12.5	12.4	12.3	12.1	12.0	11.8	11.6	11.4
74	12.6	12.6	12.5	12.4	12.4	12.3	12.2	12.1	12.0	11.9	11.8	11.6	11.5	11.3	11.2	11.0
75	12.0	12.0	11.9	11.9	11.8	11.7	11.7	11.6	11.5	11.4	11.3	11.1	11.0	10.9	10.7	10.5
76	11.4	11.4	11.3	11.3	11.2	11.2	11.1	11.0	10.9	10.9	10.8	10.6	10.5	10.4	10.3	10.1
77	10.8	10.8	10.8	10.7	10.7	10.6	10.6	10.5	10.4	10.3	10.3	10.2	10.0	9.9	9.8	9.7
78	10.3	10.2	10.2	10.2	10.1	10.1	10.0	10.0	9.9	9.8	9.8	9.7	9.6	9.5	9.4	9.2
79	9.7	9.7	9.7	9.6	9.6	9.6	9.5	9.5	9.4	9.3	9.3	9.2	9.1	9.0	8.9	8.8
80	9.2	9.2	9.1	9.1	9.1	9.0	9.0	9.0	8.9	8.9	8.8	8.7	8.7	8.6	8.5	8.4
81	8.7	8.7	8.6	8.6	8.6	8.5	8.5	8.5	8.4	8.4	8.3	8.3	8.2	8.1	8.0	8.0
82	8.2	8.2	8.1	8.1	8.1	8.1	8.0	8.0	8.0	7.9	7.9	7.8	7.8	7.7	7.6	7.5
83	7.7	7.7	7.7	7.6	7.6	7.6	7.6	7.5	7.5	7.5	7.4	7.4	7.3	7.3	7.2	7.1
84	7.2	7.2	7.2	7.2	7.2	7.1	7.1	7.1	7.1	7.0	7.0	7.0	6.9	6.9	6.8	6.7
85	6.8	6.8	6.8	6.7	6.7	6.7	6.7	6.7	6.6	6.6	6.6	6.5	6.5	6.5	6.4	6.4
86	6.4	6.4	6.3	6.3	6.3	6.3	6.3	6.3	6.2	6.2	6.2	6.2	6.1	6.1	6.0	6.0
87	6.0	6.0	6.0	5.9	5.9	5.9	5.9	5.9	5.9	5.8	5.8	5.8	5.8	5.7	5.7	5.6
88	5.6	5.6	5.6	5.6	5.6	5.5	5.5	5.5	5.5	5.5	5.5	5.4	5.4	5.4	5.3	5.3
89	5.2	5.2	5.2	5.2	5.2	5.2	5.2	5.2	5.2	5.1	5.1	5.1	5.1	5.1	5.0	5.0
90	4.9	4.9	4.9	4.9	4.9	4.9	4.9	4.9	4.9	4.8	4.8	4.8	4.8	4.8	4.7	4.7

Table VIA – Annuities for Joint Life Only – Two Lives – Expected Return Multiples – continued

AGES	67	68	69	70	71	72	73	74	75	76	77	78	79	80	81	82
67	13.5	...	...	...	...	...	...	...	...	...	...	...	...	...	...	...
68	13.1	12.8	...	...	...	...	...	...	...	...	...	...	...	...	...	...
69	12.8	12.5	12.1	...	...	...	...	...	...	...	...	...	...	...	...	...
70	12.4	12.1	11.8	11.5	...	...	...	...	...	...	...	...	...	...	...	...
71	12.0	11.7	11.4	11.2	10.9	...	...	...	...	...	...	...	...	...	...	...
72	11.6	11.4	11.1	10.8	10.5	10.2	...	...	...	...	...	...	...	...	...	...
73	11.2	11.0	10.7	10.5	10.2	9.9	9.7	...	...	...	...	...	...	...	...	...
74	10.8	10.6	10.4	10.1	9.9	9.6	9.4	9.1	...	...	...	...	...	...	...	...
75	10.4	10.2	10.0	9.8	9.5	9.3	9.1	8.8	8.6	...	...	...	...	...	...	...
76	9.9	9.8	9.6	9.4	9.2	9.0	8.8	8.5	8.3	8.0	...	...	...	...	...	...
77	9.5	9.4	9.2	9.0	8.8	8.6	8.4	8.2	8.0	7.8	7.5	...	...	...	...	...
78	9.1	9.0	8.8	8.7	8.5	8.3	8.1	7.9	7.7	7.5	7.3	7.0	...	...	...	...
79	8.7	8.6	8.4	8.3	8.1	8.0	7.8	7.6	7.4	7.2	7.0	6.8	6.6	...	...	...
80	8.3	8.2	8.0	7.9	7.8	7.6	7.5	7.3	7.1	6.9	6.8	6.6	6.3	6.1	...	...
81	7.9	7.9	7.7	7.5	7.4	7.3	7.1	7.0	6.8	6.7	6.5	6.3	6.1	5.9	5.7	...
82	7.5	7.4	7.3	7.2	7.1	6.9	6.6	6.7	6.5	6.4	6.2	6.0	5.9	5.7	5.5	5.3
83	7.1	7.0	6.9	6.8	6.7	6.6	6.5	6.4	6.2	6.1	5.9	5.8	5.6	5.5	5.3	5.1
84	6.7	6.6	6.5	6.4	6.4	6.3	6.2	6.0	5.9	5.8	5.7	5.5	5.4	5.2	5.1	4.9
85	6.3	6.2	6.2	6.1	6.0	5.9	5.8	5.7	5.6	5.5	5.4	5.3	5.2	5.0	4.9	4.7
86	5.9	5.9	5.8	5.8	5.7	5.6	5.5	5.4	5.4	5.3	5.1	5.0	4.9	4.8	4.7	4.5
87	5.6	5.6	5.5	5.4	5.4	5.3	5.2	5.2	5.1	5.0	4.9	4.8	4.7	4.6	4.4	4.3
88	5.3	5.2	5.2	5.1	5.1	5.0	5.0	4.9	4.8	4.7	4.6	4.5	4.4	4.3	4.2	4.1
89	5.0	4.9	4.9	4.8	4.8	4.7	4.7	4.6	4.5	4.5	4.4	4.3	4.2	4.1	4.0	3.9
90	4.7	4.6	4.6	4.6	4.5	4.5	4.4	4.4	4.3	4.2	4.2	4.1	4.0	3.9	3.8	3.8

AGES	83	84	85	86	87	88	89	90
83	4.9	...	...	...	...	...	...	...
84	4.7	4.6	...	...	...	...	...	...
85	4.6	4.4	4.2	...	...	...	...	...
86	4.4	4.2	4.1	3.9	...	...	...	...
87	4.2	4.1	3.9	3.8	3.6	...	...	...
88	4.0	3.9	3.8	3.6	3.5	3.4	...	...
89	3.8	3.7	3.6	3.5	3.4	3.2	3.1	...
90	3.7	3.5	3.4	3.3	3.2	3.1	3.0	2.9

Table VII – Percent Value of Refund Feature Duration of Guaranteed Amount

Age	1 Yr.	2 Yrs.	3 Yrs.	4 Yrs.	5 Yrs.	6 Yrs.	7 Yrs.	8 Yrs.	9 Yrs.	10 Yrs.	11 Yrs.	12 Yrs.	13 Yrs.	14 Yrs.	15 Yrs.	16 Yrs.	17 Yrs.	18 Yrs.	19 Yrs.	20 Yrs.
19	...	...	...	...	...	...	...	...	...	...	...	...	...	...	...	...	...	...	...	...
20	...	...	...	...	...	...	...	...	...	...	...	...	...	...	...	...	...	...	...	1
21	...	...	...	...	...	...	...	...	...	...	...	...	...	...	...	...	...	...	...	1
22	...	...	...	...	...	...	...	...	...	...	...	...	...	...	...	...	...	...	...	1
23	...	...	...	...	...	...	...	...	...	...	...	...	...	...	...	...	...	1	1	1
24	...	...	...	...	...	...	...	...	...	...	...	...	...	...	...	...	...	1	1	1
25	...	...	...	...	...	...	...	...	...	...	...	...	...	...	...	...	1	1	1	1
26	...	...	...	...	...	...	...	...	...	...	...	...	...	...	...	...	1	1	1	1
27	...	...	...	...	...	...	...	...	...	...	...	...	...	...	...	1	1	1	1	1
28	...	...	...	...	...	...	...	...	...	...	...	...	...	...	1	1	1	1	1	1
29	...	...	...	...	...	...	...	...	...	...	...	...	...	...	1	1	1	1	1	1
30	...	...	...	...	...	...	...	...	...	...	...	...	...	1	1	1	1	1	1	1
31	...	...	...	...	...	...	...	...	...	...	...	...	...	1	1	1	1	1	1	1
32	...	...	...	...	...	...	...	...	...	...	...	...	...	1	1	1	1	1	1	1
33	...	...	...	...	...	...	...	...	...	...	...	...	1	1	1	1	1	1	1	1
34	...	...	...	...	...	...	...	...	...	...	...	1	1	1	1	1	1	1	1	1
35	...	...	...	...	...	...	...	...	...	...	...	1	1	1	1	1	1	1	1	1
36	...	...	...	...	...	...	...	...	...	...	1	1	1	1	1	1	1	1	1	1
37	...	...	...	...	...	...	...	...	...	1	1	1	1	1	1	1	1	1	1	1
38	...	...	...	...	...	...	...	...	...	1	1	1	1	1	1	1	1	1	1	2
39	...	...	...	...	...	...	...	1	1	1	1	1	1	1	1	1	1	1	2	2
40	...	...	...	...	...	...	...	1	1	1	1	1	1	1	1	1	1	2	2	2
41	...	...	...	...	...	...	...	1	1	1	1	1	1	1	1	1	2	2	2	2
42	...	...	...	...	...	...	1	1	1	1	1	1	1	1	1	2	2	2	2	2
43	...	...	...	...	...	...	1	1	1	1	1	1	1	1	2	2	2	2	2	3
44	...	...	...	...	...	1	1	1	1	1	1	1	1	2	2	2	2	2	3	3
45	...	...	...	...	...	1	1	1	1	1	1	1	2	2	2	2	2	3	3	3
46	...	...	...	...	1	1	1	1	1	1	1	2	2	2	2	2	3	3	3	3
47	...	...	...	...	1	1	1	1	1	1	1	2	2	2	2	2	3	3	3	4
48	...	...	...	...	1	1	1	1	1	1	2	2	2	2	2	3	3	3	4	4
49	...	...	...	1	1	1	1	1	1	2	2	2	2	2	3	3	3	4	4	4
50	...	...	...	1	1	1	1	1	1	2	2	2	2	3	3	3	3	4	4	5
51	...	...	...	1	1	1	1	1	2	2	2	2	3	3	3	3	4	4	4	5
52	...	...	...	1	1	1	1	1	2	2	2	2	3	3	3	4	4	5	5	5
53	...	...	1	1	1	1	2	2	2	2	3	3	3	3	4	4	5	5	5	6
54	...	...	1	1	1	1	2	2	2	3	3	3	4	4	4	5	5	5	6	7
55	...	...	1	1	1	1	2	2	2	2	3	3	4	4	4	5	5	6	7	7
56	...	...	1	1	1	1	2	2	2	3	3	3	4	4	5	5	6	7	7	8

Table VII – Percent Value of Refund Feature Duration of Guaranteed Amount – continued

Age	1 Yr.	2 Yrs.	3 Yrs.	4 Yrs.	5 Yrs.	6 Yrs.	7 Yrs.	8 Yrs.	9 Yrs.	10 Yrs.	11 Yrs.	12 Yrs.	13 Yrs.	14 Yrs.	15 Yrs.	16 Yrs.	17 Yrs.	18 Yrs.	19 Yrs.	20 Yrs.
57	...	...	1	1	1	2	2	2	3	3	3	4	4	5	5	6	6	7	8	9
58	...	1	1	1	1	2	2	2	3	3	4	4	5	5	6	6	7	8	9	9
59	...	1	1	1	1	2	2	3	3	4	4	5	5	6	6	7	8	9	9	10
60	...	1	1	1	2	2	2	3	3	4	4	5	6	6	7	8	9	10	10	11
61	...	1	1	1	2	2	3	3	4	4	5	6	6	7	8	9	10	10	11	13
62	...	1	1	2	2	2	3	4	4	5	5	6	7	8	9	10	11	12	13	14
63	...	1	1	2	2	3	3	4	5	5	6	7	8	9	10	11	12	13	14	15
64	...	1	1	2	2	3	4	4	5	6	7	8	8	9	10	12	13	14	15	17
65	...	1	2	2	3	3	4	5	6	6	7	8	9	10	12	13	14	15	17	18
66	1	1	2	2	3	4	5	5	6	7	8	9	10	12	13	14	15	17	18	20
67	1	1	2	3	3	4	5	6	7	8	9	10	11	13	14	15	17	18	20	22
68	1	1	2	3	4	5	6	7	8	9	10	11	13	14	15	17	19	20	22	24
69	1	1	2	3	4	5	6	7	8	10	11	12	14	15	17	19	20	22	24	26
70	1	2	3	4	5	6	7	8	9	11	12	14	15	17	19	20	22	24	26	28
71	1	2	3	4	5	6	8	9	10	12	13	15	17	18	20	22	24	26	28	30
72	1	2	3	4	6	7	8	10	11	13	15	17	18	20	22	24	26	28	30	32
73	1	2	4	5	6	8	9	11	13	14	16	18	20	22	24	26	28	31	33	35
74	1	3	4	5	7	9	10	12	14	16	18	20	22	24	26	28	31	33	35	37
75	1	3	4	6	8	9	11	13	15	17	19	22	24	26	28	31	33	35	38	40
76	2	3	5	7	9	10	12	15	17	19	21	24	26	28	31	33	36	38	40	43
77	2	4	5	7	9	12	14	16	18	21	23	26	28	31	33	36	38	41	43	45
78	2	4	6	8	10	13	15	18	20	23	25	28	31	33	36	38	41	43	46	48
79	2	4	7	9	11	14	17	19	22	25	28	30	33	36	38	41	44	46	48	51
80	2	5	7	10	13	15	18	21	24	27	30	33	36	38	41	44	46	49	51	53
81	3	5	8	11	14	17	20	23	26	29	32	35	38	41	44	47	48	51	54	56
82	3	6	9	12	15	19	22	25	28	32	35	38	41	44	47	49	52	54	56	58
83	3	7	10	13	17	20	24	27	31	34	38	41	44	47	49	52	54	57	59	61
84	4	7	11	15	19	22	26	30	33	37	40	44	47	49	52	55	57	59	61	63
85	4	8	12	16	20	24	28	32	36	40	43	46	49	52	55	57	59	62	63	65
86	4	9	13	18	22	27	31	35	39	42	46	49	52	55	57	60	62	64	66	67
87	5	10	15	20	24	29	33	37	41	45	48	52	55	57	60	62	64	66	68	69
88	5	11	16	21	26	31	36	40	44	48	51	54	57	60	62	64	66	68	70	71
89	6	12	18	23	28	33	38	43	47	50	54	57	60	62	65	67	68	70	72	73
90	7	13	19	25	31	36	41	45	49	53	56	59	62	64	67	69	70	72	74	75

Table VII – Percent Value of Refund Feature Duration of Guaranteed Amount – continued

	21	22	23	24	25	26	27	28	29	30	31	32	33	34	35	36	37	38	39	40
Age	Yr.	Yrs.	Yrs.	Yrs.	Yrs.	Yrs.	Yrs.	Yrs.	Yrs.	Yrs.	Yrs.	Yrs.	Yrs.	Yrs.	Yrs.	Yrs.	Yrs.	Yrs.	Yrs.	Yrs.
5	…	…	…	…	…	…	…	…	…	…	…	1	1	1	1	1	1	1	1	1
6	…	…	…	…	…	…	…	…	…	…	…	1	1	1	1	1	1	1	1	1
7	…	…	…	…	…	…	…	…	…	…	1	1	1	1	1	1	1	1	1	1
8	…	…	…	…	…	…	…	…	…	1	1	1	1	1	1	1	1	1	1	1
9	…	…	…	…	…	…	…	…	1	1	1	1	1	1	1	1	1	1	1	1
10	…	…	…	…	…	…	…	1	1	1	1	1	1	1	1	1	1	1	1	1
11	…	…	…	…	…	…	1	1	1	1	1	1	1	1	1	1	1	1	1	1
12	…	…	…	…	…	…	1	1	1	1	1	1	1	1	1	1	1	1	1	1
13	…	…	…	…	…	1	1	1	1	1	1	1	1	1	1	1	1	1	1	1
14	…	…	…	…	1	1	1	1	1	1	1	1	1	1	1	1	1	1	1	1
15	…	…	…	1	1	1	1	1	1	1	1	1	1	1	1	1	1	1	1	1
16	…	…	1	1	1	1	1	1	1	1	1	1	1	1	1	1	1	1	1	1
17	…	…	1	1	1	1	1	1	1	1	1	1	1	1	1	1	1	1	1	1
18	…	1	1	1	1	1	1	1	1	1	1	1	1	1	1	1	1	1	1	2
19	1	1	1	1	1	1	1	1	1	1	1	1	1	1	1	1	1	2	2	2
20	1	1	1	1	1	1	1	1	1	1	1	1	1	1	1	1	2	2	2	2
21	1	1	1	1	1	1	1	1	1	1	1	1	1	1	1	2	2	2	2	2
22	1	1	1	1	1	1	1	1	1	1	1	1	1	1	2	2	2	2	2	2
23	1	1	1	1	1	1	1	1	1	1	1	1	1	2	2	2	2	2	2	2
24	1	1	1	1	1	1	1	1	1	1	1	1	2	2	2	2	2	2	2	3
25	1	1	1	1	1	1	1	1	1	1	1	2	2	2	2	2	2	2	3	3
26	1	1	1	1	1	1	1	1	1	1	2	2	2	2	2	2	2	3	3	3
27	1	1	1	1	1	1	1	1	1	2	2	2	2	2	2	2	3	3	3	3
28	1	1	1	1	1	1	1	1	2	2	2	2	2	2	2	3	3	3	3	3
29	1	1	1	1	1	1	1	2	2	2	2	2	2	2	3	3	3	3	3	4
30	1	1	1	1	1	1	2	2	2	2	2	2	2	3	3	3	3	3	4	4
31	1	1	1	1	1	2	2	2	2	2	2	2	3	3	3	3	3	4	4	4
32	1	1	1	1	2	2	2	2	2	2	2	3	3	3	3	3	4	4	4	5
33	1	1	1	2	2	2	2	2	2	2	3	3	3	3	3	4	4	4	5	5
34	1	1	2	2	2	2	2	2	2	3	3	3	3	3	4	4	4	5	5	5
35	1	2	2	2	2	2	2	2	3	3	3	3	3	4	4	4	5	5	5	6
36	2	2	2	2	2	2	2	3	3	3	3	4	4	4	4	5	5	5	6	6
37	2	2	2	2	2	2	3	3	3	3	4	4	4	4	5	5	6	6	6	7
38	2	2	2	2	2	3	3	3	3	4	4	5	5	5	6	6	7	7	7	8
39	2	2	2	2	3	3	3	3	4	4	4	5	5	5	6	6	7	7	8	8
40	2	2	3	3	3	3	3	4	4	4	5	5	5	6	6	7	7	8	8	9
41	2	3	3	3	3	3	4	4	4	5	5	5	6	6	7	7	8	9	9	10
42	3	3	3	3	3	4	4	4	5	5	6	6	6	7	7	8	9	9	10	11
43	3	3	3	4	4	4	4	5	5	6	6	7	7	8	8	9	9	10	11	12
44	3	3	4	4	4	4	5	5	6	6	7	7	8	8	9	10	10	11	12	13
45	3	4	4	4	5	5	5	6	6	7	7	8	8	9	10	10	11	12	13	14
46	4	4	4	5	5	5	6	6	7	7	8	9	9	10	11	11	12	13	14	15
47	4	4	5	5	5	6	6	7	7	8	9	9	10	11	12	12	13	14	15	16
48	4	5	5	5	6	6	7	7	8	9	9	10	11	12	13	14	15	16	17	18
49	5	5	5	6	6	7	8	8	9	10	10	11	12	13	14	15	16	17	18	19
50	5	5	6	6	7	8	8	9	10	10	11	12	13	14	15	16	17	18	20	21

Table VII – Percent Value of Refund Feature Duration of Guaranteed Amount – continued

Age	21 Yr.	22 Yrs.	23 Yrs.	24 Yrs.	25 Yrs.	26 Yrs.	27 Yrs.	28 Yrs.	29 Yrs.	30 Yrs.	31 Yrs.	32 Yrs.	33 Yrs.	34 Yrs.	35 Yrs.	36 Yrs.	37 Yrs.	38 Yrs.	39 Yrs.	40 Yrs.
51	5	6	6	7	8	8	9	10	11	11	12	13	14	15	16	17	19	20	21	22
52	6	7	7	8	8	9	10	11	11	12	13	14	15	17	18	19	20	21	23	24
53	7	7	8	8	9	10	11	12	13	14	15	16	17	18	19	20	22	23	24	26
54	7	8	8	9	10	11	12	13	14	15	16	17	18	19	21	22	23	25	26	28
55	8	9	9	10	11	12	13	14	15	16	17	18	20	21	22	24	25	27	28	30
56	9	9	10	11	12	13	14	15	16	18	19	20	21	23	24	26	27	29	30	32
57	9	10	11	12	13	14	15	17	18	19	20	22	23	25	26	28	29	31	32	34
58	10	11	12	13	14	16	17	18	19	21	22	24	25	27	28	30	31	33	34	36
59	11	12	13	15	16	17	18	20	21	22	24	25	27	28	30	32	33	35	36	38
60	12	14	15	16	17	19	20	21	23	24	26	27	29	31	32	34	35	37	38	40
61	14	15	16	17	19	20	22	23	25	26	28	29	31	33	34	36	37	39	40	42
62	15	16	18	19	20	22	23	25	27	28	30	32	33	35	36	38	40	41	42	44
63	16	18	19	21	22	24	25	27	29	30	32	34	35	37	39	40	42	43	45	46
64	18	19	21	23	24	26	28	29	31	33	34	36	38	39	41	42	44	45	47	48
65	20	21	23	25	26	28	30	31	33	35	37	38	40	42	43	45	46	47	49	50
66	21	23	25	27	28	30	32	34	35	37	39	41	42	44	45	47	48	50	51	52
67	23	25	27	29	31	32	34	36	38	40	41	43	45	46	48	49	50	52	53	54
68	25	27	29	31	33	35	37	38	40	42	44	45	47	48	50	51	52	54	55	56
69	28	29	31	33	35	37	39	41	43	44	46	48	49	51	52	53	54	56	57	58
70	30	32	34	36	38	40	42	43	45	47	48	50	51	53	54	55	57	58	59	60
71	32	34	36	38	40	42	44	46	47	49	51	52	54	55	56	57	59	60	61	62
72	35	37	39	41	43	45	46	48	50	51	53	54	56	57	58	59	60	62	62	63
73	37	39	41	43	45	47	49	51	52	54	55	57	58	59	60	61	62	63	64	65
74	40	42	44	46	48	50	51	53	54	56	57	59	60	61	62	63	64	65	66	67
75	42	44	46	48	50	52	54	55	57	58	59	61	62	63	64	65	66	67	68	69
76	45	47	49	51	53	54	56	58	59	60	62	63	64	65	66	67	68	69	69	70
77	47	50	51	53	55	57	58	60	61	62	64	65	66	67	68	69	70	70	71	72
78	50	52	54	56	57	59	61	62	63	64	66	67	68	69	70	70	71	72	73	73
79	53	55	56	58	60	61	63	64	65	66	67	68	69	70	71	72	73	73	74	75
80	55	57	59	60	62	63	65	66	67	68	69	70	71	72	73	74	74	75	76	76
81	58	59	61	63	64	66	67	68	69	70	71	72	73	74	74	75	76	76	77	78
82	60	62	63	65	66	68	69	70	71	72	73	74	74	75	76	77	77	78	78	79
83	62	64	66	67	68	70	71	72	73	74	74	75	7~6	77	77	7~8	79	79	80	80
84	65	66	68	69	70	71	72	73	74	75	76	77	77	78	79	79	80	80	81	81
85	67	68	70	71	72	73	74	75	76	77	78	78	79	79	80	81	81	82	82	83
86	69	70	72	73	74	75	76	77	77	78	79	80	80	81	81	82	82	83	83	84
87	71	72	73	75	76	76	77	78	79	80	80	81	81	82	83	83	83	84	84	85
88	73	74	75	76	77	78	79	80	80	81	82	82	83	83	84	84	85	85	85	86
89	74	76	77	78	79	79	80	81	81	82	83	83	84	84	85	85	85	86	86	87
90	76	77	78	79	80	81	81	82	83	83	84	84	85	85	86	86	86	87	87	87

Appendix B

Examples of Exclusion Ratio Calculations

Single Life Annuity

Example 1. On October 1, 2013, Mr. Smith purchased an immediate non-refund annuity that will pay him $125 a month ($1,500 a year) for life, beginning November 1, 2013. He paid $16,000 for the contract. Mr. Smith's age on his birthday nearest the annuity starting date (October 1st) was sixty-eight. According to Table V, which he uses because his investment in the contract is post-June 1986, his life expectancy is 17.6 years. Consequently, the expected return under the contract is $26,400 (12 × $125 × 17.6). The exclusion percentage for the annuity payments is 60.6 percent ($16,000 ÷ $26,400). Because Mr. Smith received two monthly payments in 2013 (a total of $250), he will exclude $151.50 (60.6 percent of $250) from his gross income for 2013, and he must include $98.50 ($250 − $151.50). Mr. Smith will exclude the amounts so determined for 17.6 years. In 2013, he could exclude $151.50; each year thereafter through 2029, he could exclude $909, for a total exclusion of $15,604.50 ($151.50 excluded in 2013 and $15,453 excluded over the next seventeen years). In 2030, he could exclude only $395.50 ($16,000 − $15,604.50), which is all the investment in the contract he has left. In 2031, he would include in his income $1,104.50 ($1,500 − $395.50). In 2032 and each year thereafter, all cost basis has been recovered, and he would include $1,500 in income each year.

Example 2. If Mr. Smith purchased the contract illustrated above on October 1, 1986, so that it had an annuity starting date before January 1, 1987, he would exclude $151.50 (60.6 percent of $250) from his 1986 gross income and would include $98.50 ($250 − $151.50). For each succeeding tax year in which he receives twelve monthly payments, even if he outlives his life expectancy of 17.6 years, he will exclude $909 (60.6 percent of $1,500), and he will include $591 ($1,500 − $909), even after 17.6 years worth of payments have been made.

Refund or Period Certain Guarantee

Example 1. On January 1, 2013 a husband, age sixty-five, purchased for $21,053 an immediate installment refund annuity that pays $100 a month for life. The contract provides that in the event the husband does not live long enough to recover the full purchase price, payments will be made to his wife until the total payments under the contract equal the purchase price. The investment in the contract is adjusted for the purpose of determining the exclusion ratio as follows:

Unadjusted investment in the contract	$ 21,053
Amount to be received annually	$ 1,200
Duration of guaranteed amount ($21,053 ÷ $1,200)	17.5 yrs.
Rounded to nearest whole number of years	18
Percentage value of guaranteed refund (Table VII for age 65 and 18 years)	15%
Value of refund feature rounded to nearest dollar (15% of $21,053)	$ 3,158
Adjusted investment in the contract ($21,053 – $3,158)	$ 17,895

Example 2. Assume the contract in Example 1 was purchased as a deferred annuity and the pre-July 1986 investment in the contract is $10,000 and the post-June 1986 investment in the contract is $11,053. If the annuitant elects, as explained earlier, to compute a separate exclusion percentage for the pre-July 1986 and the post-June 1986 amounts, separate computations must be performed to determine the adjusted investment in the contract. The pre-July 1986 investment in the contract and the post-June 1986 investment in the contract are adjusted for the purpose of determining the exclusion ratios in the following manner:

Pre-July 1986 adjustment:	
Unadjusted investment in the contract	$10,000
Allocable part of amount to be received annually (($10,000 ÷ $21,053) × $1,200)	$ 570
Duration of guaranteed amount ($10,000 ÷ $570)	17.5 yrs.
Rounded to nearest whole number of years	18
Percentage in Table III for age 65 and 18 years	30%
Present value of refund feature rounded to nearest dollar (30% of $10,000)	$ 3,000
Adjusted pre-July 1986 investment in the contract ($10,000 – $3,000)	$ 7,000
Post-June 1986 adjustment:	
Unadjusted investment in the contract	$11,053

Allocable part of amount to be received annually (($11,053 ÷ $21,053) × $1,200)	$ 630
Duration of guaranteed amount ($11,053 ÷ $630)	17.5 yrs.
Rounded to nearest whole number of years	18
Percentage in Table VII for age 65 and 18 years	15%
Present value of refund feature rounded to nearest dollar) (15% of $11,053)	$ 1,658
Adjusted post-June 1986 investment in the contract ($11,053 – $1,658)	$ 9,395

Once the investment in the contract has been adjusted by subtracting the value of the refund or period certain guarantee, an exclusion ratio is determined in the same way as for a straight life annuity. The expected return is computed, then the adjusted investment in the contract is divided by expected return. Taking the two examples above, the exclusion ratio for each contract is determined as follows:

Example (1) above.

Investment in the contract (adjusted for refund guarantee)	$17,895
One year's guaranteed annuity payments (12 × $100)	$ 1,200
Life expectancy from Table V, age 65	20 yrs.
Expected return (20 × $1,200)	$24,000
Exclusion ratio ($17,895 ÷ $24,000)	74.6%
Amount excludable from gross income each year in which 12 payments are received (74.6% of $1,200)*	$895.20
Amount includable in gross income ($1,200 – $895.20)*	$304.80

*Since the annuity starting date is after December 31, 1986, the total amount excludable is limited to the investment in the contract; after that has been recovered, the remaining amounts received are includable in income. However, if the annuity has a refund or guarantee feature, the value of the refund or guarantee feature is not subtracted when calculating the unrecovered investment.[1]

Example (2) above.

Pre-July 1986 investment in the contract (adjusted for period certain guarantee)	$ 7,000
One year's guaranteed annuity payments (12 × $100)	$ 1,200
Life expectancy from Table I, male age 65	15 yrs.
Expected return (15 × $1,200)	$ 18,000
Exclusion ratio ($7,000 ÷ $18,000)	38.9%

Post-June 1986 investment in the contract (adjusted for period certain guarantee)	$ 9,395
One year's guaranteed annuity payments (12 × $100)	$ 1,200
Life expectancy from Table V, age 65	20 yrs.
Expected return (20 × $1,200)	$ 24,000
Exclusion ratio ($9,395 ÷ $24,000)	39.1%
Sum of pre-July and post-June 1986 ratios	78%
Amount excludable from gross income each year in which twelve payments are received (78% of $1,200)*	$ 936
Amount includable in gross income ($1,200 – 936)*	$ 264

*Since the annuity starting date is after December 31, 1986, the total amount excludable is limited to the investment in the contract; after that has been recovered, the remaining amounts received are includable in income.

Joint and Survivor Annuity (Same Income to Survivor as to Both Annuitants Before Any Death)

Example 1. After June 30, 1986, Mr. and Mrs. Jones purchase an immediate joint and survivor annuity. The annuity will provide payments of $100 a month while both are alive and until the death of the survivor. Mr. Jones' age on his birthday nearest the annuity starting date is sixty-five; Mrs. Jones', sixty-three. The single premium is $22,000.

Investment in the contract	$22,000
One year's annuity payments (12 × $100)	$ 1,200
Joint and survivor life expectancy multiple from Table VI (ages 65, 63)	26
Expected return (26 × $1,200)	$31,200
Exclusion ratio ($22,000 ÷ $31,200)	70.5%
Amount excludable from gross income each year in which 12 payments are received (70.5% of $1,200)*	$ 846
Amount includable in gross income each year ($1,200 – $846)*	$ 354

*If the annuity starting date is after December 31, 1986, the total amount excludable is limited to the investment in the contract; after that has been recovered, the remaining amounts received are includable in income.

Joint and Survivor Annuity (Income to Survivor Differs from Income before First Death)

Example 1. After July 30, 1986, Mr. and Mrs. Smith buy an immediate joint and survivor annuity that will provide monthly payments of $117 ($1,404 a year) for as long as both live, and monthly payments of $78 ($936 a year) to the survivor. As of the annuity starting date he is sixty-five years old; she is sixty-three. The expected return is computed as follows:

Joint and survivor multiple from Table VI (ages 65,63)	26
Portion of expected return (26 × $936)	$24,336.00
Joint life multiple from Table VIA (ages 65, 63)	15.6
Difference between annual annuity payment before the first death and annual annuity payment to the survivor ($1,404 – $936)	$468
Portion of expected return (15.6 × $468)	$ 7,300.80
Expected return	$31,636.80

Assuming that the Smiths paid $22,000 for the contract, the exclusion ratio is 69.5 percent ($22,000 ÷ $31,636.80). During their joint lives the portion of each monthly payment to be excluded from gross income is $81.31 (69.5 percent of $117), or $975.72 a year. The portion to be included is $35.69 ($117 – $81.31), or $428.28 a year. After the first death, the portion of each monthly payment to be excluded from gross income will be $54.21 (69.5 percent of $78), or $650.52 a year. Of that monthly payment, $23.79 ($78 – $54.21), or $285.48 a year, will be included.

If the annuity starting date is after December 31, 1986, the total amount excludable is limited to the investment in the contract. Thus, if Mr. Smith lives for twenty-three years, he may exclude $81.31 from each payment for twenty-two years ((12 × 22) × $81.31 = $21,465.84). In the next year, he may exclude $534.16 ($22,000 – $21,465.84) or $81.31 from each of the first six payments, but only $46.30 from the seventh. The balance is entirely includable in his income, and on his death, his widow must include the full amount of each payment in income.

Example 2. Assume that in the example above, there is a pre-July 1986 investment in the contract of $12,000 and a post-June 1986 investment in the contract of $10,000. Mr. Smith elects to calculate the exclusion percentage for each portion. The pre-July exclusion ratio would be 44.6 percent ($12,000 ÷ $26,910, the expected return on the contract determined by using Tables II and IIA and the age and sex of both annuitants). The post-June 1986 exclusion ratio is $10,000 ÷ $31,636.80 or 31.6 percent. The amount excludable from each monthly payment while both are alive would be $89.15 (44.6 percent of $117 plus 31.6 percent of $117) and the remaining $27.85 would be included in gross income. If the annuity starting date is after December 31, 1986, the total amount excludable is limited to the investment in the contract.

Endnote

1.　I.R.C. §72(b)(4).

Appendix C

Internal Revenue Code Sections

Selected Portions of Internal Revenue Code Section 72

26 USC § 72 - Annuities; certain proceeds of endowment and life insurance contracts

(a) General Rules for Annuities

(1) Income inclusion

Except as otherwise provided in this chapter, gross income includes any amount received as an annuity, whether for a period certain or during one or more lives, under an annuity, endowment, or life insurance contract.

(2) Partial annuitization

If any amount is received as an annuity for a period of 10 years or more or during one or more lives under any portion of an annuity, endowment, or life insurance contract:

    (A) such portion shall be treated as a separate contract for purposes of this section,

    (B) for purposes of applying subsections (b), (c), and (e), the investment in the contract shall be allocated pro rata between each portion of the contract from which amounts are received as an annuity and the portion of the contract from which amounts are not received as an annuity, and

    (C) a separate annuity starting date under subsection (c)(4) shall be determined with respect to each portion of the contract from which amounts are received as an annuity.

(b) Exclusion Ratio

1. In general

Gross income does not include that part of any amount received as an annuity under an annuity, endowment, or life insurance contract which bears the same ratio to such amount as the investment in the contract, as of the annuity starting date, bears to the expected return under the contract, as of such date.

2. Exclusion limited to investment

The portion of any amount received as an annuity which is excluded from gross income under paragraph (1) shall not exceed the unrecovered investment in the contract immediately before the receipt of such amount.

3. Deduction where annuity payments cease before entire investment recovered

(A) In general

If:

> (i)   after the annuity starting date, payments as an annuity under the contract cease by reason of the death of an annuitant, and

> (ii) as of the date of such cessation, there is unrecovered investment in the contract, the amount of such unrecovered investment, in excess of any amount specified in subsection (e)(5) which was not included in gross income, shall be allowed as a deduction to the annuitant for his last taxable year.

(B) Payments to other persons

In the case of any contract which provides for payments meeting the requirements of subparagraphs (B) and (C) of subsection (c)(2), the deduction under subparagraph (A) shall be allowed to the person entitled to such payments for the taxable year in which such payments are received.

(C) Net operating loss deductions provided

For purposes of section 172, a deduction allowed under this paragraph shall be treated as if it were attributable to a trade or business of the taxpayer.

4.   Unrecovered Investment

For purposes of this subsection, the unrecovered investment in the contract as of any date is:

(A)   the investment in the contract, determined without regard to subsection (c)(2), as of the annuity starting date, reduced by

(B)   the aggregate amount received under the contract on or after such annuity starting date and before the date as of which the determination is being made, to the extent such amount was excludable from gross income under this subtitle.

(c) Definitions

(1)   Investment in the contract

For purposes of subsection (b), the investment in the contract as of the annuity starting date is:

(A)   the aggregate amount of premiums or other consideration paid for the contract, minus

(B)   the aggregate amount received under the contract before such date, to the extent that such amount was excludable from gross income under this subtitle or prior income tax laws.

(2)   Adjustment in investment where there is refund feature

If:

(A)   the expected return under the contract depends in whole or in part on the life expectancy of one or more individuals,

(B)   the contract provides for payments to be made to a beneficiary, or to the estate of an annuitant, on or after the death of the annuitant or annuitants, and

(C)   such payments are in the nature of a refund of the consideration paid, then the value, computed without discount for interest, of such payments on the annuity starting date shall be subtracted from the amount determined under paragraph (1). Such value shall be computed in accordance with actuarial tables prescribed by the Secretary. For purposes of this paragraph and of subsection (e)(2)(A), the term "refund of the consideration paid" includes amounts payable after the death of an annuitant by reason of a provision in the contract for a life annuity with minimum period of payments certain, but, if part of the consideration was contributed by an employer, does not include that part of any payment to a beneficiary (or to the estate of the annuitant) which is not attributable to the consideration paid by the employee for the contract as determined under paragraph (1)(A).

(3) Expected Return

For purposes of subsection (b), the expected return under the contract shall be determined as follows:

(A) Life expectancy

If the expected return under the contract, for the period on and after the annuity starting date, depends in whole or in part on the life expectancy of one or more individuals, the expected return shall be computed with reference to actuarial tables prescribed by the Secretary.

(B) Installment payments

If subparagraph (A) does not apply, the expected return is the aggregate of the amounts receivable under the contract as an annuity.

(4) Annuity starting date

For purposes of this section, the annuity starting date in the case of any contract is the first day of the first period for which an amount is received as an annuity under the contract; except that if such date was before January 1, 1954, then the annuity starting date is January 1, 1954.

(d) Special Rules for Qualified Employer Retirement Plans

(1) Simplified method of taxing annuity payments

(A) In general

In the case of any amount received as an annuity under a qualified employer retirement plan:

(i)   subsection (b) shall not apply, and

(ii) the investment in the contract shall be recovered as provided in this paragraph.

(B) Method of recovering investment in contract

(i) In general Gross income shall not include so much of any monthly annuity payment under a qualified employer retirement plan as does not exceed the amount obtained by dividing:

(I) the investment in the contract, as of the annuity starting date, by

(II) the number of anticipated payments determined under the table contained in clause

(III) or, in the case of a contract to which subsection (c)(3)(B) applies, the number of monthly annuity payments under such contract.

(ii) Certain rules made applicable Rules similar to the rules of paragraphs (2) and (3) of subsection (b) shall apply for purposes of this paragraph.

(iii) Number of anticipated payments If the annuity is payable over the life of a single individual, the number of anticipated payments shall be determined as follows:

If the age of the annuitant on the annuity starting date is:	The number of anticipated payments is:
Not more than 55	360
More than 55 but not more than 60	310
More than 60 but not more than 65	260
More than 65 but not more than 70	210
More than 70	160

(iv) Number of anticipated payments where more than one life If the annuity is payable over the lives of more than 1 individual, the number of anticipated payments shall be determined as follows:

If the combined ages of annuitants are:	The number is:
Not more than 110	410
More than 110 but not more than 120	360
More than 120 but not more than 130	310
More than 130 but not more than 140	260
More than 140	210

(C) Adjustment for refund feature not applicable

For purposes of this paragraph, investment in the contract shall be determined under subsection (c)(1) without regard to subsection (c)(2).

(D) Special rule where lump sum paid in connection with commencement of annuity payments

If, in connection with the commencement of annuity payments under any qualified employer retirement plan, the taxpayer receives a lump-sum payment:

    (i)   such payment shall be taxable under subsection (e) as if received before the annuity starting date, and

    (ii) the investment in the contract for purposes of this paragraph shall be determined as if such payment had been so received.

(E) Exception

This paragraph shall not apply in any case where the primary annuitant has attained age 75 on the annuity starting date unless there are fewer than 5 years of guaranteed payments under the annuity.

(F) Adjustment where annuity payments not on monthly basis

In any case where the annuity payments are not made on a monthly basis, appropriate adjustments in the application of this paragraph shall be made to take into account the period on the basis of which such payments are made.

(G) Qualified employer retirement plan

For purposes of this paragraph, the term qualified employer retirement plan means any plan or contract described in paragraph (1), (2), or (3) of section 4974 (c).

(2) Treatment of employee contributions under defined contribution plans

For purposes of this section, employee contributions, and any income allocable thereto, under a defined contribution plan may be treated as a separate contract.

(f) Special Rules for Computing Employees' Contributions

In computing, for purposes of subsection (c)(1)(A), the aggregate amount of premiums or other consideration paid for the contract, and for purposes of subsection (e)(6), the aggregate premiums or other consideration paid, amounts contributed by the employer shall be included, but only to the extent that:

    (1)   such amounts were includible in the gross income of the employee under this subtitle or prior income tax laws; or

    (2)   if such amounts had been paid directly to the employee at the time they were contributed, they would not have been includible in the gross income of the employee under the law applicable at the time of such contribution.

Paragraph (2) shall not apply to amounts which were contributed by the employer after December 31, 1962, and which would not have been includible in the gross income of the employee by reason of the application of section 911 if such amounts had been paid directly to the employee at the time of contribution. The preceding sentence shall not apply to amounts which were contributed by the employer, as determined under regulations prescribed by the Secretary, to provide pension or annuity credits, to the extent such credits are attributable to services performed before January 1, 1963, and are provided pursuant to pension or annuity plan provisions in existence on March 12, 1962, and on that date applicable to such services, or to the extent such credits are attributable to services performed as a foreign missionary, within the meaning of section 403 (b)(2)(D)(iii), as in effect before the enactment of the Economic Growth and Tax Relief Reconciliation Act of 2001.

(g) Rules for Transferee Where Transfer Was for Value

Where any contract, or any interest therein, is transferred, by assignment or otherwise, for a valuable consideration, to the extent that the contract, or interest therein, does not, in the hands of the transferee, have a basis which is determined by reference to the basis in the hands of the transferor, then:

(1) for purposes of this section, only the actual value of such consideration, plus the amount of the premiums and other consideration paid by the transferee after the transfer, shall be taken into account in computing the aggregate amount of the premiums or other consideration paid for the contract;

(2) for purposes of subsection (c)(1)(B), there shall be taken into account only the aggregate amount received under the contract by the transferee before the annuity starting date, to the extent that such amount was excludable from gross income under this subtitle or prior income tax laws; and

(3) the annuity starting date is January 1, 1954, or the first day of the first period for which the transferee received an amount under the contract as an annuity, whichever is the later.

For purposes of this subsection, the term "transferee" includes a beneficiary of, or the estate of, the transferee.

(h) Option to Receive Annuity In Lieu of Lump Sum

If:

(1) a contract provides for payment of a lump sum in full discharge of an obligation under the contract, subject to an option to receive an annuity in lieu of such lump sum;

(2)   the option is exercised within 60 days after the day on which such lump sum first became payable; and

(3)   part or all of such lump sum would, but for this subsection, be includible in gross income by reason of subsection (e)(1),

then, for purposes of this subtitle, no part of such lump sum shall be considered as includible in gross income at the time such lump sum first became payable.

(p) Loans Treated As Distributions

For purposes of this section:

(1)   Treatment as distributions

(A)   Loans

If during any taxable year a participant or beneficiary receives, directly or indirectly, any amount as a loan from a qualified employer plan, such amount shall be treated as having been received by such individual as a distribution under such plan.

(B)   Assignments or pledges

If during any taxable year a participant or beneficiary assigns, or agrees to assign, or pledges, or agrees to pledge, any portion of his interest in a qualified employer plan, such portion shall be treated as having been received by such individual as a loan from such plan.

(2)   Exception for certain loans

(A)   General rule

Paragraph (1) shall not apply to any loan to the extent that such loan—when added to the outstanding balance of all other loans from such plan whether made on, before, or after August 13, 1982—does not exceed the lesser of:

   (i) $50,000, reduced by the excess (if any) of;

      (I) the highest outstanding balance of loans from the plan during the 1-year period ending on the day before the date on which such loan was made; over

      (II) the outstanding balance of loans from the plan on the date on which such loan was made; or

(ii)   the greater of;

> (I) one-half of the present value of the nonforfeitable accrued benefit of the employee under the plan; or

> (II) $10,000.

For purposes of clause (ii), the present value of the nonforfeitable accrued benefit shall be determined without regard to any accumulated deductible employee contributions, as defined in subsection (o)(5)(B).

(B)   Requirement that loan be repayable within 5 years

(i)   In general Subparagraph (A) shall not apply to any loan unless such loan, by its terms, is required to be repaid within 5 years.

(ii)   Exception for home loans Clause (i) shall not apply to any loan used to acquire any dwelling unit which within a reasonable time is to be used—determined at the time the loan is made—as the principal residence of the participant.

(C)   Requirement of level amortization

Except as provided in regulations, this paragraph shall not apply to any loan unless substantially level amortization of such loan—with payments not less frequently than quarterly—is required over the term of the loan.

(D)   Related employers and related plans

For purposes of this paragraph:

(i)   the rules of subsections (b), (c), and (m) of section 414 shall apply, and

(ii)   all plans of an employer—determined after the application of such subsections— shall be treated as 1 plan.

(3)   Denial of interest deductions in certain cases

(A)   In general

No deduction otherwise allowable under this chapter shall be allowed under this chapter for any interest paid or accrued on any loan to which paragraph (1) does not apply by reason of paragraph (2) during the period described in subparagraph (B).

(B) Period to which subparagraph (A) applies

For purposes of subparagraph (A), the period described in this subparagraph is the period:

(i)   on or after the 1st day on which the individual to whom the loan is made is a key employee, as defined in section 416 (i)); or

(ii)   such loan is secured by amounts attributable to elective deferrals described in subparagraph (A) or (C) of section 402 (g)(3).

(4) Qualified employer plan, etc.

For purposes of this subsection:

(A) Qualified employer plan

(i)   In general The term "qualified employer plan" means:

(I) a plan described in section 401 (a) which includes a trust exempt from tax under section 501 (a);

(II) an annuity plan described in section 403 (a); and

(III) a plan under which amounts are contributed by an individual's employer for an annuity contract described in section 403 (b).

(ii)   Special rule The term "qualified employer plan" shall include any plan which was, or was determined to be, a qualified employer plan or a government plan.

(B) Government plan

The term "government plan" means any plan, whether or not qualified, established and maintained for its employees by the United States, by a State or political subdivision thereof, or by an agency or instrumentality of any of the foregoing.

(5) Special rules for loans, etc., from certain contracts

For purposes of this subsection, any amount received as a loan under a contract purchased under a qualified employer plan, and any assignment or pledge with respect to such a contract, shall be treated as a loan under such employer plan.

(q) 10 Percent Penalty for Premature Distributions from Annuity Contracts

(1) Imposition of penalty

If any taxpayer receives any amount under an annuity contract, the taxpayer's tax under this chapter for the taxable year in which such amount is received shall be increased by an amount equal to 10 percent of the portion of such amount which is includible in gross income.

(2) Subsection not to apply to certain distributions

Paragraph 1 shall not apply to any distribution:

(A) made on or after the date on which the taxpayer attains age 59 1/2;

(B) made on or after the death of the holder—or, where the holder is not an individual, the death of the primary annuitant, as defined in subsection (s)(6)(B);

(C) attributable to the taxpayer's becoming disabled within the meaning of subsection (m)(7);

(D) which is a part of a series of substantially equal periodic payments, not less frequently than annually, made for the life, or life expectancy, of the taxpayer or the joint lives, or joint life expectancies, of such taxpayer and his designated beneficiary;

(E) from a plan, contract, account, trust, or annuity described in subsection (e)(5)(D);

(F) allocable to investment in the contract before August 14, 1982; or [2]

(G) under a qualified funding asset, within the meaning of section 130 (d), but without regard to whether there is a qualified assignment;

(H) to which subsection (t) applies, without regard to paragraph (2) thereof;

(I) under an immediate annuity contract (within the meaning of section 72 (u)(4)); or

(J) which is purchased by an employer upon the termination of a plan described in section 401 (a) or 403 (a) and which is held by the employer until such time as the employee separates from service.

(3) Change in substantially equal payments

If:

(A) paragraph (1) does not apply to a distribution by reason of paragraph (2)(D), and

(B)   the series of payments under such paragraph are subsequently modified (other than by reason of death or disability);

    (i)   before the close of the 5-year period beginning on the date of the first payment and after the taxpayer attains age 591/2; or

    (ii) before the taxpayer attains age 591/2;

the taxpayer's tax for the 1st taxable year in which such modification occurs shall be increased by an amount, determined under regulations, equal to the tax which—but for paragraph (2) (D)— would have been imposed, plus interest for the deferral period, within the meaning of subsection (t)(4)(B).

(s) Required Distributions Where Holder Dies before Entire Interest Is Distributed

(1)   In general

A contract shall not be treated as an annuity contract for purposes of this title unless it provides that:

(A)   if any holder of such contract dies on or after the annuity starting date and before the entire interest in such contract has been distributed, the remaining portion of such interest will be distributed at least as rapidly as under the method of distributions being used as of the date of his death, and

(B)   if any holder of such contract dies before the annuity starting date, the entire interest in such contract will be distributed within 5 years after the death of such holder.

(2)   Exception for certain amounts payable over life of beneficiary

If:

(A)   any portion of the holder's interest is payable to, or for the benefit of, a designated beneficiary,

(B)   such portion will be distributed, in accordance with regulations, over the life of such designated beneficiary, or over a period not extending beyond the life expectancy of such beneficiary; and

(C)   such distributions begin not later than 1 year after the date of the holder's death or such later date as the Secretary may by regulations prescribe, then for purposes of paragraph (1), the portion referred to in subparagraph (A) shall be treated as distributed on the day on which such distributions begin.

(3)   Special rule where surviving spouse is beneficiary

If the designated beneficiary referred to in paragraph (2)(A) is the surviving spouse of the holder of the contract, paragraphs (1) and (2) shall be applied by treating such spouse as the holder of such contract.

(4)   Designated beneficiary

For purposes of this subsection, the term "designated beneficiary" means any individual designated a beneficiary by the holder of the contract.

(5)   Exception for certain annuity contracts

This subsection shall not apply to any annuity contract:

(A)   which is provided;

    (i)   under a plan described in section 401 (a) which includes a trust exempt from tax under section 501, or

    (ii)   under a plan described in section 403 (a),

(B)   which is described in section 403 (b),

(C)   which is an individual retirement annuity or provided under an individual retirement account or annuity, or

(D)   which is a qualified funding asset (as defined in section 130 (d), but without regard to whether there is a qualified assignment).

(6)   Special rule where holder is corporation or other nonindividual

(A)   In general

For purposes of this subsection, if the holder of the contract is not an individual, the primary annuitant shall be treated as the holder of the contract.

(B)   Primary annuitant

For purposes of subparagraph (A), the term "primary annuitant" means the individual, the events in the life of whom are of primary importance in affecting the timing or amount of the payout under the contract.

(7)   Treatment of changes in primary annuitant where holder of contract is not an individual

For purposes of this subsection, in the case of a holder of an annuity contract which is not an individual, if there is a change in a primary annuitant, as defined in paragraph (6)(B), such change shall be treated as the death of the holder.

(u) Treatment of Annuity Contracts Not Held by Natural Persons

(1)   In general

If any annuity contract is held by a person who is not a natural person:

> (A)   such contract shall not be treated as an annuity contract for purposes of this subtitle, other than subchapter L, and

> (B)   the income on the contract for any taxable year of the policyholder shall be treated as ordinary income received or accrued by the owner during such taxable year.

For purposes of this paragraph, holding by a trust or other entity as an agent for a natural person shall not be taken into account.

(2)   Income on the contract

(A)   In general

For purposes of paragraph (1), the term "income on the contract" means, with respect to any taxable year of the policyholder, the excess of:

> (i)   the sum of the net surrender value of the contract as of the close of the taxable year plus all distributions under the contract received during the taxable year or any prior taxable year, reduced by;

> (ii)   the sum of the amount of net premiums under the contract for the taxable year and prior taxable years and amounts includible in gross income for prior taxable years with respect to such contract under this subsection.

Where necessary to prevent the avoidance of this subsection, the Secretary may substitute "fair market value of the contract" for "net surrender value of the contract" each place it appears in the preceding sentence.

(B)   Net premiums

For purposes of this paragraph, the term "net premiums" means the amount of premiums paid under the contract reduced by any policyholder dividends.

(3) Exceptions

This subsection shall not apply to any annuity contract which:

(A) is acquired by the estate of a decedent by reason of the death of the decedent,

(B) is held under a plan described in section 401 (a) or 403 (a), under a program described in section 403 (b), or under an individual retirement plan,

(C) is a qualified funding asset, as defined in section 130 (d), but without regard to whether there is a qualified assignment,

(D) is purchased by an employer upon the termination of a plan described in section 401 (a) or 403 (a) and is held by the employer until all amounts under such contract are distributed to the employee for whom such contract was purchased or the employee's beneficiary, or

(E) is an immediate annuity.

(4) Immediate annuity

For purposes of this subsection, the term "immediate annuity" means an annuity:

(A) which is purchased with a single premium or annuity consideration,

(B) the annuity starting date (as defined in subsection (c)(4)) of which commences no later than 1 year from the date of the purchase of the annuity, and

(C) which provides for a series of substantially equal periodic payments (to be made not less frequently than annually) during the annuity period.

(v) 10 Percent Additional Tax for Taxable Distributions
from Modified Endowment Contracts

(1) Imposition of additional tax

If any taxpayer receives any amount under a modified endowment contract, as defined in section 7702A, the taxpayer's tax under this chapter for the taxable year in which such amount is received shall be increased by an amount equal to 10 percent of the portion of such amount which is includible in gross income.

(2) Subsection not to apply to certain distributions

Paragraph (1) shall not apply to any distribution:

(A) made on or after the date on which the taxpayer attains age 591/2,

(B) which is attributable to the taxpayer's becoming disabled, within the meaning of subsection (m)(7), or

(C) which is part of a series of substantially equal periodic payments—not less frequently than annually—made for the life, or life expectancy, of the taxpayer or the joint lives, or joint life expectancies, of such taxpayer and his beneficiary.

Internal Revenue Code Section 1035

26 USC § 1035 – Certain Exchanges of Insurance Policies

Note: Section 1035(a) below applies to exchanges after 2009.

(a) General rules

No gain or loss shall be recognized on the exchange of

(1) a contract of life insurance for another contract of life insurance or for an endowment or annuity contractor for a qualified long-term care insurance contract; or

(2) a contract of endowment insurance (A) for another contract of endowment insurance which provides for regular payments beginning at a date not later than the date payments would have begun under the contract exchanged, or (B) for an annuity contract, or (C) for a qualified long-term care insurance contract;

(3) an annuity contract for an annuity contract or for a qualified long-term care insurance contract; or

(4) a qualified long-term care insurance contract for a qualified long-term care insurance contract.

Note: Section 1035(b) below applies to exchanges after 2009.

(b) Definitions

For the purpose of this section:

(1) Endowment Contract

A contract of endowment insurance is a contract with an insurance company which depends in part on the life expectancy of the insured, but which may be payable in full in a single payment during his life.

(2) Annuity Contract

An annuity contract is a contract to which paragraph (1) applies but which may be payable during the life of the annuitant only in installments. For purposes of the preceding sentence, a contract shall not fail to be treated as an annuity contract solely because a qualified long-term care insurance contract is a part of or a rider on such contract.

(3) Life Insurance Contract

A contract of life insurance is a contract to which paragraph (1) applies but which is not ordinarily payable in full during the life of the insured. For purposes of the preceding sentence, a contract shall not fail to be treated as a life insurance contract solely because a qualified long-term care insurance contract is a part of or a rider on such contract.

(c) Exchanges Involving Foreign Persons

To the extent provided in regulations, subsection (a) shall not apply to any exchange having the effect of transferring property to any person other than a United States person.

(d) Cross References

(1)   For rules relating to recognition of gain or loss where an exchange is not solely in kind, see subsections (b) and (c) of section 1031.

(2)   For rules relating to the basis of property acquired in an exchange described in subsection (a), see subsection (d) of section 1031.

Internal Revenue Code Section 2033

26 USC § 2033. Property In Which The Decedent Had An Interest

The value of the gross estate shall include the value of all property to the extent of the interest therein of the decedent at the time of his death.

Internal Revenue Code Section 2039

26 USC § 2039. Annuities

(a)   General

The gross estate shall include the value of an annuity or other payment receivable by any beneficiary by reason of surviving the decedent under any form of contract or agreement entered into after March 3, 1931—other than as insurance under policies on the life of the decedent—if, under such contract or agreement, an annuity or other payment was payable to the decedent, or the decedent possessed the right to receive such annuity or payment, either alone or in conjunction with another for his life or for any period not ascertainable without reference to his death or for any period which does not in fact end before his death.

(b)   Amount Includible

Subsection (a) shall apply to only such part of the value of the annuity or other payment receivable under such contract or agreement as is proportionate to that part of the purchase price therefor contributed by the decedent. For purposes of this section, any contribution by the decedent's employer or former employer to the purchase price of such contract or agreement— whether or not to an employee's trust or fund forming part of a pension, annuity, retirement, bonus or profit sharing plan—shall be considered to be contributed by the decedent if made by reason of his employment.

Appendix D

FINRA RULE 2330 for Recommended Purchases of Exchanges of Deferred Variable Annuities

FINRA Regulatory Notice 10 05 Deferred Variable Annuities

FINRA Rekminds Firms of Their Responsibilities Under FINRA Rule 2330 for Recommended Purchases or Exchanges of Deferred Variable Annuities

Executive Summary

FINRA reminds firms of their responsibilities under the new consolidated FINRA rule on deferred variable annuities.[1] The implementation date of the FINRA rule—as well as previously approved amendments to parts of the rule covering principal review and supervisory procedures—is February 8, 2010.[2] This Notice also addresses issues raised about a firm's ability to hold Checks made payable to entities other than itself (third parties) pursuant to interpretive relief that FINRA previously issued.[3] For easy reference, the text of new FINRA Rule 2330 is set forth in Attachment A.

Questions regarding this Notice should be directed to:

James S.Wrona, Associate Vice President and Associate General Counsel, Office of General Counsel, at (202) 728-8270; or Lawrence N. Kosciulek, Director, Investment Companies Regulation, at (240) 386-4535.

Background & Discussion

FINRA Rule 2330 (formerly NASD Rule 2821) establishes sales practice standards regarding recommended purchases and exchanges of deferred variable annuities.[4] The rule has the following six main sections:

General considerations, such as the rule's applicability;

Recommendation requirements, including suitability and disclosure obligations;

Principal review and approval obligations;

Requirements for establishing and maintaining supervisory procedures;

Training obligations; and

Supplementary material that addresses a variety of issues ranging from the handling of customer funds and checks to information gathering and sharing.

As noted above, all of the rule's provisions are applicable as of February 8, 2010.

Recently, questions have been raised regarding FINRA's limited interpretive relief from the requirements of FINRA Rule 2150(a) (formerly NASD Rule 2330(a)) and FINRA Rule 2320(d) (formerly NASD Rule 2820(d)).[5] The former rule generally prohibits firms from making improper use of customer funds, and the latter requires firms to transmit promptly to issuers applications and purchase payments for variable contracts. FINRA provided limited interpretive relief from these rules to allow firms to perform comprehensive and rigorous reviews of recommended transactions in deferred variable annuities under FINRA Rule 2330.[6]

FINRA originally stated that "a firm may hold an application for a deferred variable annuity and a customer's non-negotiated check payable to an insurance company for up to seven business days without violating either NASD Rule 2330 or 2820 if the reason for the hold is to allow completion of principal review of the transaction pursuant to NASD Rule 2821."[7] After the SEC approved amendments that changed the starting point for the review period—from the date when the customer signs the application to the date when a firm's office of supervisory jurisdiction (OSJ) receives a complete and correct application package—FINRA explained that its limited interpretive relief "continues to apply even though the triggering event for the principal review period has changed via the recently approved amendments."[8]

Concerns have been expressed, however, regarding the breadth of the interpretive relief and the conditions that must be present for it to apply. FINRA now clarifies that the interpretive relief applies only if the seven conditions delineated below are present.[9]

1. The reason that the firm is holding the application for a deferred variable annuity and/ or a customer's non-negotiated check payable to a third party is to allow completion of principal review of the transaction pursuant to FINRA Rule 2330.

2. The associated person who recommended the purchase or exchange of the deferred variable annuity makes reasonable efforts to safeguard the check and to promptly prepare and forward a complete and correct copy of the application package to an OSJ.

3. The firm has policies and procedures in place that are reasonably designed to ensure that the check is safeguarded and that reasonable efforts are made to promptly prepare and forward a complete and correct copy of the application package to an OSJ.

4. A principal reviews and makes a determination of whether to approve or reject the purchase or exchange of the deferred variable annuity in accordance with the provisions of FINRA Rule 2330.

5. The firm holds the application and/or check no longer than seven business days from the date an OSJ receives a complete and correct copy of the application package.

6. The firm maintains a copy of each such check and creates a record of the date the check was received from the customer and the date the check was transmitted to the insurance company or returned to the customer.

7. The firm creates a record of the date when the OSJ receives a complete and correct copy of the application package.

If these seven conditions are not present, FINRA's interpretive relief will not apply and it will enforce FINRA Rules 2150(a) and 2320(d), as appropriate.

Attachment A

Text of FINRA Rule 2330

2000. Duties and Conflicts

2300. Special Products

2330. Members' Responsibilities Regarding Deferred Variable Annuities

(a) General Considerations

(1) Application. This Rule applies to recommended purchases and exchanges of deferred variable annuities and recommended initial subaccount allocations. This Rule does not apply to reallocations among subaccounts made or to funds paid after the initial purchase or exchange of a deferred variable annuity. This Rule also does not apply to deferred variable annuity transactions made in connection with any tax-qualified, employer-sponsored retirement or benefit plan that either is defined as a "qualified plan" under Section 3(a)(12)(C) of the Exchange Act or meets the requirements of Internal Revenue Code Sections 403(b), 457(b), or 457(f), unless, in the case of any such plan, a member or person associated with a member makes recommendations to an individual plan participant regarding a deferred variable annuity, in which case the Rule would apply as to the individual plan participant to whom the member or person associated with the member makes such recommendations.

(2) Creation, Storage, and Transmission of Documents. For purposes of this Rule, documents may be created, stored, and transmitted in electronic or paper form, and signatures may be evidenced in electronic or other written form.

(3) Definitions. For purposes of this Rule, the term "registered principal" shall mean a person registered as a General Securities Sales Supervisor (Series 9/10), a General Securities Principal (Series 24) or an Investment Company Products/Variable Contracts Principal (Series 26), as applicable.

(b) Recommendation Requirements

(1) No member or person associated with a member shall recommend to any customer the purchase or exchange of a deferred variable annuity unless such member or person associated with a member has a reasonable basis to believe

(A) that the transaction is suitable in accordance with NASD Rule 2310 and, in particular, that there is a reasonable basis to believe that

(i) the customer has been informed, in general terms, of various features of deferred variable annuities, such as the potential surrender period and surrender charge; potential tax penalty if customers sell or redeem deferred variable annuities before reaching the age of 59½; mortality and expense fees; investment advisory fees; potential charges for and features of riders; the insurance and investment components of deferred variable annuities; and market risk;

(ii) the customer would benefit from certain features of deferred variable annuities, such as tax-deferred growth, annuitization, or a death or living benefit; and

(iii) the particular deferred variable annuity as a whole, the underlying subaccounts to which funds are allocated at the time of the purchase or exchange of the deferred variable annuity, and riders and similar product enhancements, if any, are suitable (and, in the case of an exchange, the transaction as a whole also is suitable) for the particular customer based on the information required by paragraph (b)(2) of this Rule; and

(B) in the case of an exchange of a deferred variable annuity, the exchange also is consistent with the suitability determination required by paragraph (b)(1)(A) of this Rule, taking into consideration whether

(i) the customer would incur a surrender charge, be subject to the commencement of a new surrender period, lose existing benefits (such as death, living, or other contractual benefits), or be subject to increased fees or charges (such as mortality and expense fees, investment advisory fees, or charges for riders and similar product enhancements);

(ii) the customer would benefit from product enhancements and improvements; and

(iii) the customer has had another deferred variable annuity exchange within the preceding 36 months.

The determinations required by this paragraph shall be documented and signed by the associated person recommending the transaction.

(2) Prior to recommending the purchase or exchange of a deferred variable annuity, a member or person associated with a member shall make reasonable efforts to obtain, at a minimum, information concerning the customer's age, annual income, financial situation and needs, investment experience, investment objectives, intended use of the deferred variable annuity, investment time horizon, existing assets (including investment and life insurance holdings), liquidity needs, liquid net worth, risk tolerance, tax status, and such other information used or considered to be reasonable by the member or person associated with the member in making recommendations to customers.

(3) Promptly after receiving information necessary to prepare a complete and correct application package for a deferred variable annuity, a person associated with a member who recommends the deferred variable annuity shall transmit the complete and correct application package to an office of supervisory jurisdiction of the member.

(c) Principal Review and Approval

Prior to transmitting a customer's application for a deferred variable annuity

To the issuing insurance company for processing, but no later than seven business days after an office of supervisory jurisdiction of the member receives a complete and correct application package, a registered principal shall review and determine whether he or she approves of the recommended purchase or exchange of the deferred variable annuity.

A registered principal shall approve the recommended transaction only if he or she has determined that there is a reasonable basis to believe that the transaction would be suitable based on the factors delineated in paragraph (b) of this Rule.

The determinations required by this paragraph shall be documented and signed by the registered principal who reviewed and then approved or rejected the transaction.

(d) Supervisory Procedures

In addition to the general supervisory and recordkeeping requirements of NASD Rules 3010, 3012, and 3110, and Rule 3130, a member must establish and maintain specific written supervisory procedures reasonably designed to achieve compliance with the standards set forth in this Rule. The member also must (1) implement surveillance procedures to determine if any of the member's associated persons have rates of effecting deferred variable annuity exchanges that raise for review whether such rates of exchanges evidence conduct inconsistent with the applicable provisions of this Rule, other applicable FINRA rules, or the federal securities laws ("inappropriate exchanges") and (2) have policies and procedures reasonably designed to implement corrective measures to address inappropriate exchanges and the conduct of associated persons who engage in inappropriate exchanges.

(e) Training

Members shall develop and document specific training policies or programs reasonably designed to ensure that associated persons who effect and registered principals who review transactions in deferred variable annuities comply with the requirements of this Rule and that they understand the material features of deferred variable annuities, including those described in paragraph (b)(1)(A)(i) of this Rule.

Supplementary Material

.01 Depositing of Funds by Members Prior to Principal Approval. Under Rule 2330, a member that is permitted to maintain customer funds under SEA Rules 15c3-1 and 15c3-3may, prior to the member's principal approval of the deferred variable annuity, deposit and maintain customer funds for a deferred variable annuity in an account that meets the requirements of SEA Rule 15c3-3.

.02. Treatment of Lump-Sum Payment for Purchases of Different Products. If a customer provides a member that is permitted to hold customer funds with a lump sum or single check made payable to the member (as opposed to being made payable to the insurance company) and requests that a portion of the funds be applied to the purchase of a deferred variable annuity and the rest of the funds be applied to other types of products, Rule 2330 would not prohibit the member from promptly applying those portions designated for purchasing products other than a deferred variable annuity to such use. A member that is not permitted to hold customer funds can comply with such requests only through its clearing firm that will maintain customer funds for the intended deferred variable annuity purchase in an account that meets the requirements of SEA Rule 15c3-3. In such circumstances, the checks would need to be made payable to the clearing firm.

.03 Forwarding of Checks/Funds to Insurer Prior to Principal Approval. Rule 2330 does not prohibit a member from forwarding a check made payable to the insurance company or, if the member is fully subject to SEA Rule 15c3-3, transferring funds for the purchase of a deferred variable annuity to the insurance company prior to the member's principal approval of the deferred variable annuity, as long as the member fulfills the following requirements: (a) the member must disclose to the customer the proposed transfer or series of transfers of the funds and (b) the member must enter into a written agreement with the insurance company under which the insurance company agrees that, until such time as it is notified of the member's principal approval and is provided with the application or is notified of the member's principal rejection, it will (1) segregate the member's customers' funds in a bank in an account equivalent to the deposit of those funds by a member into a "Special Account for the Exclusive Benefit of Customers" (set up as described in SEA Rules 15c3-3(k)(2)(i) and 15c3-3(f)) to ensure that the customers' funds will not be subject to any right, charge, security interest, lien, or claim of any kind in favor of the member, insurance company, or bank where the insurance company deposits such funds or any creditor thereof or person claiming through them and hold those funds either as cash or any instrument that a broker or dealer may deposit in its Special Reserve Account for the Exclusive Benefit of Customers, (2) not issue the variable annuity contract prior to the member's principal approval, and (3) promptly return the funds to each customer at the customer's request prior to the member's principal approval or upon the member's rejection of the application.

.04 Forwarding of Checks/Funds to IRA Custodian Prior to Principal Approval. A member is not prohibited from forwarding a check provided by the customer for the purpose of purchasing a deferred variable annuity and made payable to an IRA custodian for the benefit of the customer (or, if the member is fully subject to SEA Rule 15c3-3, funds) to the IRA custodian prior to the member's principal approval of the deferred variable annuity transaction, as long as the member enters into a written agreement with the IRA custodian under which the IRA custodian agrees (a) to forward the funds to the insurance company to complete the purchase of the deferred variable annuity contract only after it has been informed that the member's principal has approved the transaction and (b), if the principal rejects the transaction, to inform the customer, seek immediate instructions from the customer regarding alternative disposition of the funds (e.g., asking whether the customer wants to transfer the funds to another IRA custodian, purchase a different investment, or provide other instructions), and promptly implement the customer's instructions.

.05 Gathering of Information Regarding Customer Exchanges. Rule 2330 requires that the member or person associated with a member consider whether the customer has had another deferred variable annuity exchange within the preceding 36 months. Under this provision, a member or person associated with a member must determine whether the customer has had such an exchange at the member and must make reasonable efforts to ascertain whether the customer has had an exchange at any other broker-dealer within the preceding 36 months. An inquiry to the customer as to whether the customer has had an exchange at another broker-dealer within 36 months would constitute a "reasonable effort" in this context. Members shall document in writing both the nature of the inquiry and the response from the customer.

.06 Sharing of Office Space and/or Employees. Rule 2330 requires principal review and approval "[p]rior to transmitting a customer's application for a deferred variable annuity to the issuing insurance company for processing..." In circumstances where an insurance company and its affiliated broker-dealer share office space and/or employees who carry out both the principal review and the issuance process, FINRA will consider the application "transmitted" to the insurance company only when the broker-dealer's principal, acting as such, has approved the transaction, provided that the affiliated broker-dealer and the insurance company have agreed that the insurance company will not issue the contract prior to principal approval by the broker-dealer.

.07 Sharing of Information. Rule 2330 does not prohibit using the information required for principal review and approval in the issuance process, provided that the broker dealer and the insurance company have agreed that the insurance company will not issue the contract prior to principal approval by the broker-dealer. For instance, the rule does not prohibit a broker-dealer from inputting information used as part of its suitability review into a shared database (irrespective of the media used for that database, i.e., paper or electronic) that the insurance company uses for the issuance process, provided that the broker-dealer and the insurance company have agreed that the insurance company will not issue the contract prior to principal approval by the broker-dealer.

FINRA Regulatory Notice 11 02

Know Your Customer and Suitability

SEC Approves Consolidated FINRA Rules Governing Know-Your-Customer and Suitability Obligations

Effective Date: October 7, 2011

Executive Summary

The SEC approved FINRA's proposal to adopt rules governing know-your-customer and suitability obligations[10] for the consolidated FINRA rulebook.[11] The new rules are based in part on and replace provisions in the NASD and NYSE rules.

The text of the new rules is set forth in Attachment A. The rules take effect on October 7, 2011.

Questions regarding this *Notice* should be directed to James S. Wrona, Associate Vice President and Associate General Counsel, Office of General Counsel, at (202) 728-8270.

Discussion

The know-your-customer and suitability obligations are critical to ensuring investor protection and promoting fair dealing with customers and ethical sales practices. As part of the process of developing the consolidated FINRA rulebook, FINRA proposed and the SEC approved FINRA Rule 2090 (Know Your Customer) and FINRA Rule 2111 (Suitability). The new rules retain the core features of these important obligations and at the same time strengthen, streamline and clarify them.[12] The new rules are discussed separately below.

Know Your Customer

In general, new FINRA Rule 2090 (Know Your Customer) is modeled after former NYSE Rule 405(1) and requires firms to use "reasonable diligence,"[13] in regard to the opening and maintenance[14] of every account, to know the "essential facts" concerning every customer.[15] The rule explains that "essential facts" are "those required to (a) effectively service the customer's account, (b) act in accordance with any special handling instructions for the account, (c) understand the authority of each person acting on behalf of the customer, and (d) comply with applicable laws, regulations, and rules."[16] The know-your-customer obligation arises at the beginning of the customer-broker relationship and does not depend on whether the broker has made a recommendation. Unlike former NYSE Rule 405, the new rule does not specifically address orders, supervision or account opening—areas that are explicitly covered by other rules.

Suitability

New FINRA Rule 2111 generally is modeled after former NASD Rule 2310 (Suitability) and requires that a firm or associated person "have a reasonable basis to believe that a recommended transaction or investment strategy involving a security or securities is suitable for the customer, based on the information obtained through the reasonable diligence of the member or associated person to ascertain the customer's investment profile."[17] The rule further explains that a "customer's investment profile includes, but is not limited to, the customer's age, other investments, financial situation and needs, tax status, investment objectives, investment experience, investment time horizon, liquidity needs, risk tolerance, and any other information the customer may disclose to the member or associated person in connection with such recommendation."[18]

The new rule continues to use a broker's "recommendation" as the triggering event for application of the rule and continues to apply a flexible "facts and circumstances" approach to determining what communications constitute such a recommendation. The new rule also applies to recommended investment strategies, clarifies the types of information that brokers must attempt to obtain and analyze, and discusses the three main suitability obligations. Finally, the new rule modifies the institutional-investor exemption in a number of important ways.

Recommendations

The determination of the existence of a recommendation has always been based on the facts and circumstances of the particular case.[19] That remains true under the new rule. FINRA reiterates, however, that several guiding principles are relevant to determining whether a particular communication could be viewed as a recommendation for purposes of the suitability rule.

For instance, a communication's content, context and presentation are important aspects of the inquiry. The determination of whether a "recommendation" has been made, moreover, is an objective rather than subjective inquiry.[20] An important factor in this regard is whether—given its content, context and manner of presentation—a particular communication from a firm or associated person to a customer reasonably would be viewed as a suggestion that the customer take action or refrain from taking action regarding a security or investment strategy. In addition, the more individually tailored the communication is to a particular customer or customers about a specific security or investment strategy, the more likely the communication will be viewed as a recommendation. Furthermore, a series of actions that may not constitute recommendations when viewed individually may amount to a recommendation when considered in the aggregate. It also makes no difference whether the communication was initiated by a person or a computer software program. These guiding principles, together with numerous litigated decisions and the facts and circumstances of any particular case, inform the determination of whether the communication is a recommendation for purposes of FINRA's suitability rule.

Strategies

The new rule explicitly applies to recommended investment strategies involving a security or securities.[21] The rule emphasizes that the term "strategy" should be interpreted broadly.[22] The rule is triggered when a firm or associated person recommends a security or strategy regardless of whether the recommendation results in a transaction. Among other things, the term "strategy" would capture a broker's *explicit* recommendation to hold a security or securities.[23] The rule recognizes that customers may rely on firms' and associated persons' investment expertise and knowledge, and it is thus appropriate to hold firms and associated persons responsible for the recommendations that they make to customers, regardless of whether those recommendations result in transactions or generate transaction-based compensation.

FINRA, however, exempted from the new rule's coverage certain categories of educational material—which the strategy language otherwise would cover—as long as such material does not include (standing alone or in combination with other communications) a recommendation of a particular security or securities.[24] FINRA believes that it is important to encourage firms and associated persons to freely provide educational material and services to customers.

Customer's Investment Profile

The new rule includes an expanded list of explicit types of information that firms and associated persons must attempt to gather and analyze as part of a suitability analysis. The new rule essentially adds age, investment experience, time horizon, liquidity needs and risk tolerance[25] to the existing list (other holdings, financial situation and needs, tax status and investment objectives).[26] Recognizing that not every factor regarding a "customer's investment profile" will be relevant to every recommendation, the rule provides flexibility concerning the type of information that firms must seek to obtain and analyze.[27] However, because the listed factors generally are relevant (and often crucial) to a suitability analysis, the rule requires firms and associated persons to document with specificity their reasonable basis for believing that a factor is not relevant in order to be relieved of the obligation to seek to obtain information about that factor.[28]

Main Suitability Obligations

The new suitability rule lists in one place the three main suitability obligations: reasonable-basis, customer-specific and quantitative suitability.[29]

Reasonable-basis suitability requires a broker to have a reasonable basis to believe, based on reasonable diligence, that the recommendation is suitable for at least some investors. In general, what constitutes reasonable diligence will vary depending on, among other things, the complexity of and risks associated with the security or investment strategy and the firm's or associated person's familiarity with the security or investment strategy. A firm's or associated person's reasonable diligence must provide the firm or associated person with an understanding of the potential risks and rewards associated with the recommended security or strategy.

Customer-specific suitability requires that a broker have a reasonable basis to believe that the recommendation is suitable for a particular customer based on that customer's investment profile. As noted above, the new rule requires a broker to attempt to obtain and analyze a broad array of customer-specific factors.

Quantitative suitability requires a broker who has actual or de facto control over a customer account to have a reasonable basis for believing that a series of recommended transactions, even if suitable when viewed in isolation, are not excessive and unsuitable for the customer when taken together in light of the customer's investment profile. Factors such as turnover rate, cost-equity ratio and use of in-and-out trading in a customer's account may provide a basis for finding that the activity at issue was excessive.

The new rule makes clear that a broker must have a firm understanding of both the product and the customer.[30] It also makes clear that the lack of such an understanding itself violates the suitability rule.[31]

Institutional-Investor Exemption

FINRA Rule 2111(b) provides an exemption to customer-specific suitability for recommendations to institutional customers under certain circumstances. The new exemption harmonizes the definition of institutional customer in the suitability rule with the more common definition of "institutional account" in NASD Rule 3110(c)(4).[32] Beyond the definitional requirements, the exemption's main focus is whether the broker has a reasonable basis to believe the customer is capable of evaluating investment risks independently, both in general and with regard to particular transactions and investment strategies,[33] and whether the institutional customer affirmatively acknowledges that it is exercising independent judgment.[34]

In regard to an institutional investor, a firm that satisfies the conditions of the exemption fulfils its customer-specific obligation,[35] but not its reasonable-basis and quantitative obligations under the suitability rule. FINRA believes that, even when institutional customers are involved, it is crucial that brokers understand the securities they recommend and that those securities are appropriate for at least some investors. FINRA also believes that it is important that a firm not recommend an unsuitable number of transactions in those circumstances where it has control over the account. FINRA emphasizes, however, that quantitative suitability generally would apply only with regard to that portion of an institutional customer's portfolio that the firm controls and only with regard to the firm's recommended transactions.[36]

Attachment

New FINRA rules.

2000. DUTIES AND CONFLICTS

2090. Know Your Customer

Every member shall use reasonable diligence, in regard to the opening and maintenance of every account, to know (and retain) the essential facts concerning every customer and concerning the authority of each person acting on behalf of such customer.

Supplementary Material

.01 Essential Facts. For purposes of this Rule, facts "essential" to "knowing the customer" are those required to (a) effectively service the customer's account, (b) act in accordance with any special handling instructions for the account, (c) understand the authority of each person acting on behalf of the customer, and (d) comply with applicable laws, regulations, and rules.

2100. TRANSACTIONS WITH CUSTOMERS

2110. Recommendations

2111. Suitability

(a) A member or an associated person must have a reasonable basis to believe that a recommended transaction or investment strategy involving a security or securities is suitable for the customer, based on the information obtained through the reasonable diligence of the member or associated person to ascertain the customer's investment profile. A customer's investment profile includes, but is not limited to, the customer's age, other investments, financial situation and needs, tax status, investment objectives, investment experience, investment time horizon, liquidity needs, risk tolerance, and any other information the customer may disclose to the member or associated person in connection with such recommendation.

(b) A member or associated person fulfills the customer-specific suitability obligation for an institutional account, as defined in NASD Rule 3110(c)(4), if (1) the member or associated person has a reasonable basis to believe that the institutional customer is capable of evaluating investment risks independently, both in general and with regard to particular transactions and investment strategies involving a security or securities and (2) the institutional customer affirmatively indicates that it is exercising independent judgment in evaluating the member's or associated person's recommendations. Where an institutional customer has delegated decision making authority to an agent, such as an investment adviser or a bank trust department, these factors shall be applied to the agent.

Supplementary Material

.01 General Principles. Implicit in all member and associated person relationships with customers and others is the fundamental responsibility for fair dealing. Sales efforts must therefore be undertaken only on a basis that can be judged as being within the ethical standards of FINRA's rules, with particular emphasis on the requirement to deal fairly with the public. The suitability rule is fundamental to fair dealing and is intended to promote ethical sales practices and high standards of professional conduct.

.02 Disclaimers. A member or associated person cannot disclaim any responsibilities under the suitability rule.

.03 Recommended Strategies. The phrase "investment strategy involving a security or securities" used in this Rule is to be interpreted broadly and would include, among other things, an explicit recommendation to hold a security or securities. However, the following communications are excluded from the coverage of Rule 2111 as long as they do not include (standing alone or in combination with other communications) a recommendation of a particular security or securities:

(a)   General financial and investment information, including (i) basic investment concepts, such as risk and return, diversification, dollar cost averaging, compounded return, and tax deferred investment, (ii) historic differences in the return of asset classes (e.g., equities, bonds, or cash) based on standard market indices, (iii) effects of inflation, (iv) estimates of future retirement income needs, and (v) assessment of a customer's investment profile;

(b)   Descriptive information about an employer-sponsored retirement or benefit plan, participation in the plan, the benefits of plan participation, and the investment options available under the plan;

(c)   Asset allocation models that are (i) based on generally accepted investment theory, (ii) accompanied by disclosures of all material facts and assumptions that may affect a reasonable investor's assessment of the asset allocation model or any report generated by such model, and (iii) in compliance with NASD IM-2210-6 (Requirements for the Use of Investment Analysis Tools) if the asset allocation model is an "investment analysis tool" covered by NASD IM-2210-6; and

(d)   Interactive investment materials that incorporate the above.

.04 Customer's Investment Profile. A member or associated person shall make a recommendation covered by this Rule only if, among other things, the member or associated person has sufficient information about the customer to have a reasonable basis to believe that the recommendation is suitable for that customer. The factors delineated in Rule 2111(a) regarding a customer's investment profile generally are relevant to a determination regarding whether a recommendation is suitable for a particular customer, although the level of importance of each factor may vary depending on the facts and circumstances of the particular case. A member or associated person shall use reasonable diligence to obtain and analyze all of the factors delineated in Rule 2111(a) unless the member or associated person has a reasonable basis to believe, documented with specificity, that one or more of the factors are not relevant components of a customer's investment profile in light of the facts and circumstances of the particular case.

.05 Components of Suitability Obligations. Rule 2111 is composed of three main obligations: reasonable-basis suitability, customer-specific suitability, and quantitative suitability.

(a)   The reasonable-basis obligation requires a member or associated person to have a reasonable basis to believe, based on reasonable diligence, that the recommendation is suitable for at least some investors. In general, what constitutes reasonable diligence will vary depending on, among other things, the complexity of and risks associated with the security or investment strategy and the member's or associated person's familiarity with the security or investment strategy. A member's or associated person's reasonable diligence must provide the member or associated person with an understanding of the potential risks and rewards associated with the recommended security or strategy. The lack of such an understanding when recommending a security or strategy violates the suitability rule.

(b)   The customer-specific obligation requires that a member or associated person have a reasonable basis to believe that the recommendation is suitable for a particular customer based on that customer's investment profile, as delineated in Rule 2111(a).

(c)   Quantitative suitability requires a member or associated person who has actual or de facto control over a customer account to have a reasonable basis for believing that a series of recommended transactions, even if suitable when viewed in isolation, are not excessive and unsuitable for the customer when taken together in light of the customer's investment profile, as delineated in Rule 2111(a). No single test defines excessive activity, but factors such as the turnover rate, the cost-equity ratio, and the use of in-and-out trading in a customer's account may provide a basis for a finding that a member or associated person has violated the quantitative suitability obligation.

.06 Customer's Financial Ability. Rule 2111 prohibits a member or associated person from recommending a transaction or investment strategy involving a security or securities or the continuing purchase of a security or securities or use of an investment strategy involving a security or securities unless the member or associated person has a reasonable basis to believe that the customer has the financial ability to meet such a commitment.

.07 Institutional Investor Exemption. Rule 2111(b) provides an exemption to customer-specific suitability regarding institutional investors if the conditions delineated in that paragraph are satisfied. With respect to having to indicate affirmatively that it is exercising independent judgment in evaluating the member's or associated person's recommendations, an institutional customer may indicate that it is exercising independent judgment on a trade-by-trade basis, on an asset-class-by-asset-class basis, or in terms of all potential transactions for its account.

Endnotes

1.   On November 20, 2009, the Financial Industry Regulatory Authority, Inc. (FINRA) filed with the Securities and Exchange Commission (SEC or Commission) a proposed rule change, for immediate effectiveness, to transfer NASD Rule 2821 into the Consolidated FINRA Rulebook, as FINRA Rule 2330, without any substantive changes. See Exchange Act Release No. 61122 (December 7, 2009), 74 FR 65816 (December 11, 2009) (File No. SR-FINRA-2009-083); Regulatory Notice 09-72 (December 2009) (discussing adoption of consolidated FINRA rules, including FINRA Rule 2330 covering deferred variable annuities). The current FINRA rulebook consists of (1) FINRA Rules; (2) NASD Rules; and (3) rules incorporated from NYSE (Incorporated NYSE Rules) (together, the NASD Rules and Incorporated NYSE Rules are referred to as the Transitional Rulebook).While the NASD Rules generally apply to all FINRA members, the Incorporated NYSE Rules apply only to those members of FINRA that are also members of the NYSE (Dual Members). The FINRA Rules apply to all FINRA members, unless such rules have a more limited application by their terms. For more information about the rulebook consolidation process, see Information Notice, 3/12/08 (Rulebook Consolidation Process).

2. See *Exchange Act Release No. 61122* (December 7, 2009), 74 FR 65816 (December 11, 2009) (File No. SR-FINRA-2009-083); *Regulatory Notice 09-72* (December 2009) (discussing adoption of consolidated FINRA rules and an operative date for FINRA Rule 2330 of February 8, 2010); *Exchange Act Release No. 59772* (April 15, 2009), 74 FR 18419 (April 22, 2009) (Order Approving File No. SR-FINRA-2008-019); *Regulatory Notice 09-32* (June 2009) (announcing SEC approval of amendments to NASD Rule 2821 governing purchases and exchanges of deferred variable annuities and an effective date for those amendments of February 8, 2010). FINRA notes that paragraphs (a) (General Considerations), (b) (Recommendation Requirements), and (e) (Training) of NASD Rule 2821 became effective on May 5, 2008.

3. See Regulatory Notice 07-53 (November 2007). 3 See *Regulatory Notice 07-53* (November 2007); see also *Regulatory Notice 09-32* (June 2009).

4. In general, a variable annuity is a contract between an investor and an insurance company, whereby the insurance company promises to make periodic payments to the contract owner or beneficiary, starting immediately (an immediate variable annuity) or at some future time (a deferred variable annuity). *See* Joint SEC and NASD Staff Report on Broker-Dealer Sales of Variable Insurance Products (June 2004), available at: *www.sec.gov/news/studies/secnasdvip.pdf.*

5. See *Regulatory Notice 07-53 (November 2007)*; see also *Regulatory Notice 09-32 (June 2009).*

6. See *Regulatory Notice 07-53 (November 2007)*: see also *Regulatory Notice 09-32 (June 2009).* The SEC previously has noted that "many broker-dealers are subject to lower net capital requirements under SEA Rule 15c3-1 and are exempt from the requirement to establish and fund a customer reserve account under SEA Rule 15c3-3 because they do not carry customer funds or securities." See *Exchange Act Release No. 56376 (Sept. 7, 2007)*, 72 FR 52400 (Sept. 13, 2007) (Order Granting Exemption to Broker-Dealers from Requirements in SEA Rules 15c3-1 and 15c3-3 to Promptly Transmit Customer Checks). Although some of these firms receive checks from customers made payable to third parties, the SEC does not deem a firm to be carrying customer funds if it "promptly transmits" the checks to third parties. The SEC has interpreted "promptly transmits" to mean that "such transmission or delivery is made no later than noon of the next business day after receipt of such funds or securities." *Id.* at 52400. The SEC provided a conditional exemption for broker-dealers from any additional requirements of Rules 15c3-1 and 15c3-3 due solely to a failure to promptly transmit a check made payable to an insurance company for the purchase of a deferred variable annuity product by noon of the business day following the date the broker-dealer receives the check from the customer, provided (i) the transaction is subject to the principal review requirements of NASD Rule 2821 and a registered principal has reviewed and determined whether he or she approves of the purchase or exchange of the deferred variable annuity within seven business days in accordance with that rule; (ii) the broker-dealer promptly transmits the check no later than noon of the business day following the date a registered principal reviews and determines whether he or she approves of the purchase or exchange of the deferred variable annuity; and (iii) the broker dealer maintains a copy of each such check and creates a record of the date the check was received from the customer and the date the check was transmitted to the insurance company if approved, or returned to the customer if rejected. *Id.* at 52400. In its order approving recent amendments, the SEC explained that the exemption order continues to apply, notwithstanding the new starting point for the principal review period under NASD Rule 2821. *See* Exchange Act Release No. 59772 (April 15, 2009), 74 FR 18419, at 18422 n.37 (April 22, 2009) (Order Approving File No. SR-FINRA-2008-019).

7. Regulatory Notice 07-53 (November 2007).

8. Regulatory Notice 09-32 (June 2009).

9. FINRA emphasizes that firms are not required to collect and hold checks or funds prior to principal review and approval. A firm may elect to wait until after a principal approves the transaction to collect the check or funds for a deferred variable annuity. Moreover, in accordance with Supplementary Material .03 under FINRA Rule 2330, a firm can forward a check made payable to the insurance company or, if the firm is fully subject to SEA Rule 15c3-3, transfer "funds for the purchase of a deferred variable annuity to the insurance company prior to the member's principal approval of the deferred variable annuity, as long as the member fulfills the following requirements: (a) the member must disclose to the customer the proposed transfer or series of transfers of the funds and (b) the member must enter into a written agreement with the insurance company under which the insurance company agrees that, until such time as it is notified of the member's principal approval and is provided with the application or is notified of the member's principal rejection, it will (1) segregate the member's customers' funds in a 'Special Account for the Exclusive Benefit of Customers' (set up as described in SEA Rules 15c3-3(k)(2)(i) and 15c3-3(f)) to ensure that the customers' funds will not be subject to any right, charge, security interest, lien, or claim of any kind in favor of the member, insurance company, or bank where the insurance company deposits such funds or any creditor thereof or person claiming through the man hold those funds either as cash or any instrument that a broker or dealer may deposit in its Special Reserve Account for the Exclusive Benefit of Customers, (2) not issue the variable annuity contract prior to the member's principal approval, and (3) promptly return the funds to each customer at the customer's request prior to the member's principal approval or upon the member's rejection of the application."

10. See *Securities Exchange Act Release No. 63325* (November 17, 2010), *75 FR 71479* (November 23, 2010) (Order Approving Proposed Rule Change; File No. SR-FINRA-2010-039).

11. The current FINRA rulebook consists of (1) FINRA rules; (2) NASD rules; and (3) rules incorporated from NYSE (NYSE rules). While the NASD rules generally apply to all FINRA member firms, the NYSE rules apply only to those members of FINRA that are also members of the NYSE. The FINRA rules apply to all FINRA member firms, unless such rules have a more limited application by their terms. For more information about the rulebook consolidation process, see Information Notice, 3/12/08 (Rulebook Consolidation Process).

12. To the extent that past *Notices to Members, Regulatory Notices*, case law, etc., do not conflict with new rule requirements or interpretations thereof, they remain potentially applicable, depending on the facts and circumstances of the particular case.

13. FINRA notes that it replaced the term "due diligence" used in former NYSE Rule 405(1) with the term "reasonable diligence" in new FINRA Rule 2090 for consistency with the language used in new FINRA Rule 2111. FINRA did not intend by such action to impair or adversely affect established case law and other interpretations discussing the diligence that is required to comply with know-your-customer or suitability obligations.

14. A broker-dealer must know its customers not only at account opening but also throughout the life of its relationship with customers in order to, among other things, effectively service and supervise the customers' accounts. Since a broker-dealer's relationship with its customers is dynamic, FINRA does not believe that it can prescribe a period within which broker-dealers must attempt to update this information. As with a customer's investment profile under the suitability rule, a firm should verify the "essential facts" about a customer under the know-your-customer rule at intervals reasonably calculated to prevent and detect any mishandling of a customer's account that might result from the customer's change in circumstances. The reasonableness of a broker-dealer's efforts in this regard will depend on the facts and circumstances of the particular case. Firms should note, however, that SEA Rule 17a-3 requires broker-dealers to, among other things, attempt to update certain account information every 36 months regarding accounts for which the broker-dealers were required to make suitability determinations.

15. FINRA Rule 2090.

16. FINRA Rule 2090.01.

17. FINRA Rule 2111(a). Former NASD Rule 2310 contained interpretive material (IMs) discussing a variety of types of misconduct. Although FINRA eliminated those IMs, most of the types of misconduct that the IMs discussed were either explicitly covered by other rules or incorporated in some form into the new suitability rule. The exception was unauthorized trading, which had been discussed in IM-2310- 2. However, it is well-settled that unauthorized trading violates just and equitable principles of trade under FINRA Rule 2010 (previously NASD Rule 2110). *See, e.g., Robert L. Gardner*, 52 S.E.C. 343, 344 n.1 (1995), *aff'd*, 89 F.3d 845 (9th Cir. 1996) (table format); *Keith L. DeSanto*, 52 S.E.C. 316, 317 n.1 (1995), *aff'd*, 101 F.3d 108 (2d Cir. 1996) (table format); *Jonathan G. Ornstein*, 51 S.E.C. 135, 137 (1992); *Dep't of Enforcement v. Griffith*, No. C01040025, 2006 NASD Discip. LEXIS 30, at *11-12 (NAC December 29, 2006); *Dep't of Enforcement v. Puma*, No. C10000122, 2003 NASD Discip. LEXIS 22, at *12 n.6 (NAC August 11, 2003). The new suitability rule does not alter that conclusion. Unauthorized trading continues to be serious misconduct that violates FINRA Rule 2010.

18. FINRA Rule 2111(a).

19. See *Michael Frederick Siegel*, Securities Exchange Act Release No. 58737, 2008 SEC LEXIS 2459, at *21 (October 6, 2008) (explaining that whether a communication "constitutes a recommendation is a 'facts and circumstances inquiry to be conducted on a case-by-case basis"), *aff'd in relevant part*, 592 F.3d 147 (D.C. Cir. 2010), *cert. denied*, 2010 U.S. LEXIS 4340 (May 24, 2010). FINRA has stated that "defining the term 'recommendation' is unnecessary and would raise many complex issues in the absence of specific facts of a particular case." Securities Exchange Act Release No. 37588, 1996 SEC LEXIS 2285, at *29 (August 20, 1996), 61 FR 44100, 44107 (August 27, 1996) (Notice of Filing and Order Granting Accelerated Approval of NASD's Interpretation of Its Suitability Rule).

20. FINRA has repeatedly explained that a broker cannot avoid suitability obligations through a disclaimer where—given its content, context and presentation—the particular communication reasonably would be viewed as a recommendation. *See Notice to Members 01-23* (April 2001). FINRA Rule 2111.02, moreover, explicitly states that a firm or associated person "cannot disclaim any responsibilities under the suitability rule." In the same vein, it is well-settled that a "broker's recommendations must be consistent with his customer's best interests" and are "not suitable merely because the customer acquiesces in [them]." *Dane S. Faber*, Securities Exchange Act Release No. 49216, 2004 SEC LEXIS 277, at *23-24 (February 10, 2004); *see also Dep't of Enforcement v. Bendetsen*, No. C01020025, 2004 NASD Discip. LEXIS 13, at *12 (NAC August 9, 2004) ("[A] broker's recommendations must serve his client's best interests and the test for whether a broker's recommendations are suitable is not whether the client acquiesced in them, but whether the broker's recommendations were consistent with the client's financial situation and needs").

21. See FINRA Rules 2111(a) and 2111.03.

22. Id.

23. *Id.* The new rule does not, however, broaden the scope of implicit recommendations. In limited circumstances, FINRA and the SEC have recognized that implicit recommendations can trigger suitability obligations. For example, FINRA and the SEC have held that associated persons who effect transactions on a customer's behalf without informing the customer have implicitly recommended those transactions, thereby triggering application of the suitability rule. See, *e.g., Rafael Pinchas,* 54 S.E.C. 331, 341 n.22 (1999) ("Transactions that were not specifically authorized by a client but were executed on the client's behalf are considered to have been implicitly recommended within the meaning of the NASD rules."); *Paul C. Kettler,* 51 S.E.C. 30, 32 n.11 (1992) (stating that transactions a broker effects for a discretionary account are recommended). Although such holdings continue to act as precedent regarding those issues, FINRA notes that nothing in the new rule is intended to change the longstanding application of the suitability rule on a recommendation-by-recommendation basis. The new rule would not apply, for instance, to *implicit* recommendations to hold securities that are transferred into an account.

24. See FINRA Rule 2111.03.

25. During the rulemaking process, some commenters argued that factors such as a customer's investment experience, time horizon and risk tolerance are ones to be considered when reviewing a customer's portfolio as a whole, not the individual trades. According to those commenters, requiring consideration of such factors on a trade-by-trade basis would prevent customers from creating a diverse portfolio made up of securities with different levels of liquidity, risk and time horizons. FINRA reiterates that a recommendation-by-recommendation analysis and consideration of a customer's investment portfolio are not mutually exclusive concepts. Although suitability is a recommendation-by-recommendation analysis, FINRA Rule 2111 explicitly permits the suitability analysis to be performed within the context of the customer's other investments. In fact, the rule requires (as did the previous suitability rule) firms and associated persons to make reasonable efforts to gather and analyze information about a customer's other investments as part of the suitability review. Moreover, the new rule explicitly covers recommended investment strategies.

26. See FINRA Rule 2111(a).

27. See FINRA Rule 2111.04.

28. Id.

29. See FINRA Rule 2111.05.

30. See FINRA Rule 2111(a); FINRA Rule 2111.04; FINRA Rule 2111.05(a).

31. See FINRA Rules 2111.04 and 2111.05(a).

32. See FINRA Rule 2111(b). FINRA is proposing to adopt NASD Rule 3110(c)(4) as FINRA Rule 4512(c), without material change. *See* Securities Exchange Act Release No. 63181 (October 26, 2010), 75 FR 67155 (November 1, 2010) (Notice of Filing Proposed Rule Change; File No. SR-FINRA-2010-052).

33. See FINRA Rule 2111(b). FINRA reiterates that, in some cases, the broker may conclude that the customer is not capable of making independent investment decisions in general. In other cases, the institutional customer may have general capability, but may not be able to understand a particular type of instrument or its risk. If a customer is either generally not capable of evaluating investment risk or lacks sufficient capability to evaluate the particular product, the scope of a broker's customer-specific obligations under the suitability rule would not be diminished by the fact that the broker was dealing with an institutional customer. However, the fact that a customer initially needed help understanding a potential investment need not necessarily imply that the customer did not ultimately develop an understanding and make an independent decision.

34. FINRA Rule 2111(b).

35. FINRA emphasizes that the institutional-customer exemption applies only if all of the conditions in Rule 2111(b) are satisfied. It is not sufficient, for example, that an institutional customer affirmatively indicates that it is exercising independent judgment in evaluating recommendations. The institutional customer also must meet the definitional criteria and the broker must have a reasonable basis to believe that the institutional customer is capable of evaluating investment risks independently, both in general and with regard to particular transactions and investment strategies.

36. It is axiomatic that the suitability rule applies only to recommended transactions. See, *e.g., Dep't of Enforcement v. Medeck,* No. E9B2003033701, 2009 FINRA Discip. LEXIS 7, at *46 (July 30, 2009) (explaining that transactions that were not recommended could not be used to inflate the cost-to-equity ratio and the turnover rate). Case law also has long established that quantitative suitability "occurs when a registered representative has control over trading in an account and the level of activity in that account is inconsistent with the customer's objectives and financial situation." *Harry Gliksman,*

54 S.E.C. 471, 475 (1999), *aff'd*, 24 F. App'x 702 (9th Cir. 2001); *see also Pinchas*, 54 S.E.C. at 337 (same). In general, the control element "is satisfied if the broker has either discretionary authority or de facto control over the account. De facto control is established when the client routinely follows the broker's advice 'because the customer is unable to evaluate the broker's recommendations and to exercise independent judgment.'" *Medeck*, 2009 FINRA Discip. LEXIS 7, at *34 (citations omitted). In *Pryor, McClendon, Counts & Co.*, Securities Exchange Act Release No. 45402, 2002 SEC LEXIS 284 (February 6, 2002), the SEC analyzed allegations of churning by focusing on that portion of the city of Atlanta's portfolio that the broker-dealer respondent controlled and those transactions that the respondent recommended. *Id*. at *4, *15-16, *20-23. The SEC also held that, for purposes of churning, the respondent controlled the portion of Atlanta's portfolio at issue because the respondent engaged in a scheme to defraud Atlanta with the city's investment officer, who had authority to trade Atlanta's securities portfolio. *Id*. at *20-21 & n.10 (citing *Smith v. Petrou*, 705 F. Supp. 183, 187 (S.D.N.Y. 1989)).

Appendix E

Iowa Insurance Bulletin 11-4[1]

Fields of Opportunities

STATE OF IOWA

TERRY E. BRANSTAD   SUSAN E. VOSS

GOVERNOR   COMMISSIONER OF INSURANCE

KIM REYNOLDS

LT. GOVERNOR

INSURANCE BULLETIN 11-4

To: Persons Licensed in Iowa to Sell Insurance and/or Securities

From: Susan E. Voss, Insurance Commissioner

Re: Licensing Requirements and Permitted Activities

Date: June 24, 2011

I.   Introduction

Since Iowa adopted a rule (191 Iowa Administrative Code rules 15.68-15.73) substantially similar to the April 2010 Suitability in Annuity Transactions Model Regulation of the National Association of Insurance Commissioners ("NAIC"), questions have arisen as to where the line is drawn between providing insurance advice and securities advice. The answers to these questions have become increasingly important because suitability laws at the state and federal level have evolved to the point where any recommendation to a consumer of either an insurance product or a securities product requires an extensive financial analysis of the consumer's financial affairs and a discussion of broad financial trends. How information received from the consumer is applied will be different depending on whether it is an insurance transaction or a securities transaction because of the differing requirements of insurance and securities laws.

References to insurance in this Bulletin include both life insurance and annuities.

Under Iowa law, variable annuities remain an insurance product while under federal law they are securities. Thus, for a sale of variable annuities, dual licensing is required and not covered by this Bulletin except for Section VI.

For purposes of this Bulletin, "Insurance-Only Person" means an individual who holds an Iowa insurance license that authorizes the sale of annuities or life insurance products and who is not Iowa-licensed as an investment adviser, securities agent or investment adviser representative under Iowa securities law.

For purposes of this Bulletin, "Securities-Only Person" means an individual who is licensed as an investment adviser, securities agent or investment adviser representative under Iowa securities law, and who is not Iowa-licensed as an insurance producer under Iowa insurance law.

Any specific waiver request of 191 Iowa Administrative Code rules 15.68-15.73 must be filed in accordance with 191 Iowa Administrative Code rules 4.21-4.36.

Should you have any questions concerning this notice or the rules, please contact Jim Mumford at the Insurance Division. He may be reached at jim.mumford@iid.iowa.gov.

II.   Purpose

This Bulletin is based on current Iowa insurance and securities laws and designed primarily to provide guidance to insurance producers, investment adviser representatives and securities agents about:

- **The permissible and prohibited activities of "Insurance-Only Persons"** under insurance and securities laws and regulations with respect to a recommendation to purchase an annuity contract or life insurance policy (hereafter referred to as annuity or life insurance) made to a consumer who may choose to liquidate a security in connection with such purchase. The guidance in this draft is being provided so that Insurance-Only Persons may have a better understanding of the types of activities and conduct that are within the scope of permissible activities and the types of activities and conduct that are beyond the scope of permissible activities.

- **The permissible and prohibited activities of "Securities-Only Persons"** under insurance and securities laws and regulations with respect to a recommendation to purchase a security made to a consumer who may choose to surrender part or all of the proceeds from an insurance product in connection with such purchase. The guidance in this Bulletin is being provided so a Securities-Only Person may have a better understanding of the types of activities and conduct that are within the scope of permissible activities and the types of activities and conduct that are beyond the scope of permissible activities.

III.   Permitted Activities for an Insurance-Only Person.

The following is not intended to be a complete description but rather a description of generally-recognized permissible activities of Insurance-Only Persons.

1.   The Insurance-Only Person may discuss with the consumer the consumer's risk tolerance, financial situation, and needs. This may include a discussion of the consumer's:

- financial experience;

- financial objectives, including whether the consumer needs to earn a guaranteed rate of interest, needs guaranteed minimum increases in guaranteed values, or wishes to have available a minimum lifetime income stream;

2

- risk tolerance, including need for principal protection or protection from market risk;

- need to balance and diversify risk, including need for product or issuer diversification that may support an insurance position within a consumer's financial plan;

- tax status, including whether the assets used to purchase the annuity or life insurance are or need to be tax deferred;

- existing assets, including annuity, investment, and life insurance holdings;

- financial resources generally available for the funding of the annuity or life insurance;

- liquidity needs and liquid net worth, including whether there are funds other than those being used to purchase the annuity or life insurance that will be available during the surrender period of the annuity or life insurance for emergency or urgent needs, and where those funds are located;

- financial time horizon; and

- intended use of the annuity or life policy.

2. An Insurance-Only Person may discuss with the consumer the stock market in general terms including market risks and recent or historic economic activities that are generally known to the public and regularly discussed in public media.

3. An Insurance-Only Person's general discussion outlined in (1) and (2) should only be to the extent that the discussion is a necessary component of the Insurance-Only Person's insurance services and to the extent that the information is used to give the Insurance-Only Person reasonable grounds for believing that the recommendation to purchase, borrow against, exchange, or replace an annuity or life insurance is suitable for the consumer.

4. In his or her general discussion with the consumer, the Insurance-Only Person may discuss and complete suitability, replacement, and exchange or transfer forms as required by Iowa insurance regulations.

5. In his or her general discussion about the expectations of the funds being considered to purchase the annuity or life insurance, the Insurance-Only Person may discuss: that the funds need protection from market risk; that the tax status of the funds and that tax deferral needs to be utilized or maintained; that the funds may be needed to provide a lifetime income stream; that the funds need to earn a guaranteed interest rate; or that there are other funds available during the surrender period of the annuity or life insurance for emergency or urgent needs and where those funds are located.

6.   An Insurance-Only Person may have-general discussions about balancing risk, diversification, etc., that support an insurance position within a consumer's financial plan.

7.   An Insurance-Only Person may provide advice as part of a financial plan. When doing so, an Insurance-Only Person should clearly identify himself or herself as an individual who holds an Iowa insurance license and explain that such license authorizes the person to discuss how annuities or life insurance products may fit into the consumer's financial plan and that he or she is authorized to sell annuity or life insurance products and not sell, recommend or provide advice about securities.

IV.   **Prohibited Activities for an Insurance-Only Person.**

The following is not intended to be a complete description but rather a description of generally-recognized activities that are specifically prohibited for an Insurance-Only Person:

1.   Discussing risks specific to the consumer's individual securities portfolio.

2.   Providing advice regarding the consumer's specific securities or securities investment performance, or comparing the consumer's specific securities or securities investment performance with other financial products, including annuity contracts or life insurance policies.

3.   Recommending the liquidation of specific securities, or identifying specific securities that could be used to fund an annuity or life insurance product.

4.   Recommending specific allocations, in dollars or percentages, between insurance and securities products.

5.   Offering research, analysis or recommendations to a consumer regarding specific securities.

6.   Completing securities forms, except for: 1) providing general information to the consumer related to the consumer's existing or new annuity or life insurance product; 2) assisting with forms that are required by the insurance company to complete an insurance transaction; and 3) assisting with forms that are required by Iowa insurance regulations.

7.   Using the following term or terms: investment adviser, securities agent, or investment adviser representative under Iowa securities laws; and similar titles that tend to indicate to customers that the individual is licensed to provide investment advice, that the individual is licensed to sell securities, or otherwise holding the individual out as providing investment advice to others, when the individual is not so licensed.

4

V.   Permitted Insurance-Related Activities for a Securities-Only Person.

The following is not intended to be a complete description but rather a description of generally-recognized permissible insurance-related activities of Securities-Only Persons:

1.   The Securities-Only Person may generally discuss the consumer's:

- risk-tolerance;

- financial situation and needs;

- financial experience;

- financial objectives;

- financial time horizon;

- existing assets, including investment and insurance holdings;

- liquidity needs;

- liquid net worth; and

- tax status.

2.   The Securities-Only Person may discuss insurance with the consumer in general terms in the context of managing risks and recent or historic insurance activities that are generally known to the public and regularly discussed in public media.

3.   A Securities-Only Person's general discussion outlined in (1) and (2) should only be to the extent that the discussion is a necessary component of the Securities-Only Person's securities services and to the extent that the information is used to give the Securities-Only Person reasonable grounds for believing that the recommendation to purchase, sell, hold or exchange a security is suitable for the investor.

4.   A Securities-Only Person may discuss diversifying assets and financial objectives using insurance that is solely incidental to the Securities-Only Person's securities services and the recommendation to purchase, sell, hold, exchange, or replace a security product when the Securities-Only Person provides advice as part of a financial plan.

5.   In his or her general discussion about the expectations of the funds being considered to purchase securities or investments, a Securities-Only person may discuss: that the funds could be used for wealth accumulation strategies; the current tax status of the funds and change in tax status; general discussion of "risk versus reward;" or that there are other funds available during the time period used to meet the financial objective of the securities or investments for emergency or urgent needs and where those funds are located.

6.   A Securities-Only Person may have a general discussion about balancing risk, diversification, etc., that support an insurance position within a consumer's financial plan.

7.   A Securities-Only Person may provide advice as part of a financial plan. When doing so, a Securities-Only Person should clearly identify himself or herself as an individual who is licensed as an investment adviser, securities agent or investment adviser representative under Iowa securities law, and who does not hold an insurance license.

VI.   Prohibited Activities for a Securities-Only Person.

The following is not intended to be a complete description but rather a description of generally-recognized activities that are specifically prohibited for Securities-Only Persons:

1.   Discussing the benefits or negatives of insurance, its cost versus benefits, in specific terms relating to the consumer's individual or group insurance policies.

2.   Providing advice regarding the consumer's specific insurance policy performance, or comparing the consumer's specific insurance policy performance with securities.

3.   Recommending the liquidation of an insurance policy, the lapsing of an insurance policy, the taking of policy loans, withdrawals, or surrenders, or otherwise providing any insurance advice or recommendations related to the purchase of a security.

4.   Recommending specific allocation, in dollars or percentages, between securities and insurance products.

5.   Offering research, analysis or recommendations to a prospective consumer regarding specific insurance products or policies.

6.   Completing insurance forms, except for: 1) providing general information to the consumer related to the consumer's existing or new securities product; 2) assisting with forms that are required by the insurance company to complete a securities transaction; and 3) assisting with forms that are required by Iowa securities regulations.

7.   Using the terms insurance professional, agent, producer or similar titles that tend to indicate to customers that an individual is licensed to provide insurance advice, or otherwise holding the individual out as providing insurance advice to others when the individual is not so licensed.

VII. **Certain Unlicensed Persons and Entities Who are Permitted to Give Limited Insurance-Only Advice.**

1. In certain instances, persons who are not insurance licensed are permitted to provide insurance-only advice. This includes individuals:

    a. Who do not receive compensation, directly or indirectly, for the insurance products purchased including the payment of commissions or other remunerations based on transactions in insurance; and

    b. Whose insurance-only advice is incidental to the services they provide.

2. These individuals may include, but are not limited to the following:

    a. An employee of a business whose job includes the explanation of insurance plans or options available during or following employment;

    b. A lawyer, accountant, engineer, or teacher whose providing of insurance advice is solely incidental to the practice of the person's profession;

    c. A publisher, employee, or columnist of a newspaper, news magazine, or business or financial publication, or an owner, operator, producer, or employee of a cable, radio, or television network, station, or production facility, if the financial or business news published or disseminated is made available to the general public and the content does not consist of rendering advice on the basis of the specific insurance situation of a particular customer or audience member; and

    d. A bank or savings institution or its employees whose providing of insurance advice is solely incidental to the conduct of other banking or savings business.

VIII. **Insurance Producers Who Are Licensed as Investment Advisers or Investment Adviser Representatives.**

Insurance licensed producers who are also licensed as investment advisers or investment adviser representatives as defined in Iowa Code Section 502.102(15) and (16)(2011) may be considered providing investment advice and subjecting themselves to securities rules which require them to adhere to a fiduciary standard and additional disclosure rules. Insurance producers that obtain investment advisers licenses to be able to provide advice to clients concerning the sale of a security, such as a mutual fund, to purchase an insurance product, could be subjecting themselves to the jurisdiction of state and federal securities regulators for violation of securities rules pertaining to fiduciary requirements. Persons who solely provide insurance advice as discussed in Section I of this Bulletin, and who disclose that fact to the consumer, should not be concerned with investment adviser or investment adviser representative requirements.

Endnote

1. Available at: http://www.iid.state.ia.us/sites/default/files/commissioners_bulletins/2011/06/24/bulletin_11_4_re_insurance_licensed_persons_june_2_62714.pdf

Index